Exit-Voice Dynamics and the Collapse of East Germany

Exit-Voice Dynamics

and the Collapse of East Germany

THE CRISIS OF LENINISM AND THE REVOLUTION OF 1989

Steven Pfaff

Duke University Press
Durham and London 2006

© 2006 Duke University Press

All rights reserved

Printed in the United States of America on acid-free paper ∞

Designed by Heather Hensley

Typeset in Minion by Keystone Typesetting, Inc.

Library of Congress Cataloging-in-Publication Data appear
on the last printed page of this book.

For Karen

Contents

Illustrations

Tables

Preface and Acknowledgments

In his *Recollections* Alexis de Tocqueville reflected on the genesis of France's February revolution of 1848. The July Monarchy—brought to power by the insurrection of 1830—had fallen "without a struggle, not under the victor's blows, but before they were struck; and the victors were as astonished at their success as the losers at their defeat" (1987: 62). In contemplating how this unplanned and yet so decisive rebellion had been ignited, Tocqueville asserted that chance, or rather the simultaneous incidence of several contingent factors, played a clear role. Yet, even as he noted that unfortunate events and blundering leaders can do a regime great harm, he concluded that factors such as the "senile imbecility" of a Louis-Philippe are only "accidents that render the disease fatal." Neither chance nor personality alone could explain a revolution.

Tocqueville worried that revolutions are born of manifold contingencies and thus nearly impossible to predict, a view endorsed by many contemporary social scientists.[1] Yet leaving chance and personality aside, it is clear that revolutions occur only under particular conditions. Tocqueville posited that a sudden rebellion might take place if an authoritarian regime had grown insensitive to public grievances and accustomed to compliance, thus mistaking coercion for consent. Rebellion might become revolution if repression is "excessive at first, then abandoned," or if demoralization "paralyzes the resistance even of those most interested in maintaining the power being overthrown" (1987: 64). Above all, Tocqueville's memoir urges comparative and historical researchers to go beyond narrative to understand the "antecedent facts, the nature of institutions, turn of mind and the state of mores [that] are the materials from which chance composes those impromptu events that surprise and terrify us" (1987: 62).

Yet how should we integrate history with a sociological analysis of all of those "antecedent facts"? In his magisterial *The Old Regime and the French Revolution*, Tocqueville (1955) advises us that if we wish to understand how a new society is born we should visit the old one in its grave. In considering 1789 Tocqueville wondered why the Bourbon regime was so detested by reformists, why the reformists spawned an unwanted revolution, and why the radicals could neither consolidate their position nor achieve their aims. In state archives—a "mine of information which was not available to contemporaries" (1955: ix)—Tocqueville found documents that were a "living memorial to the spirit of the old regime" and shed new light on the reaction to political centralization that he believed had ignited the revolution.

In researching this project I embarked on a Tocquevillean journey. Having started out as a historian and become a sociologist, I wished to explain one of the great historical surprises of the late twentieth century that so impressed me and my contemporaries: the swift collapse of Communism and the reunification of the two German states. Although fine histories of the German Democratic Republic (Deutsche Demokratische Republik [GDR]) have been written, and the recollections and autobiographies of many of the most famous participants have appeared, social scientists are only beginning to exploit the "mine of information" buried in the archives.[2] While still a history graduate student, I was convinced that the opening up of archival and other documentary sources in the former GDR presented an almost unparalleled opportunity to engage in historical detective work, or what social scientists call "process tracing"—the decomposition of historical narrative into stages and episodes analyzed with the help of sociological theory—in a specific instance of state breakdown and collapse.[3]

In fact, the archives of the former GDR preserved a vast wealth of information for sociological analysis, some of which was complete enough to permit coding for standard statistical evaluation. Subordinating all of society to its control, the Leninist regime in the GDR built an enormous apparatus devoted to gathering and evaluating information not only on its critics and opponents but also over its own functionaries and supporters. These records afforded an invaluable window into what James Scott (1990) calls the "hidden transcripts" of a regime, the behind-the-scenes operation of institutions and the often publicly falsified motivations of rulers and subjects. In the German national archives (Bundesarchiv), in the Saxon state archives (Sächsiches Staatsarchiv), and in the holdings of Leipzig's municipal archives (Stadtarchiv), I examined state and party records, police reports, samiszdat newsletters, Church documents, sermons, and dissident manifestos to explore the origins of opposition, the mobilization of contention, and the regime's collapse. I supplemented archival materials with contemporary newspapers, published documents, census data, and oral histories. By combining varied sources of qualitative evidence to construct a narrative, as well as assembling quantitative data on protest and emigration during 1989–90, I have been able to bring together in-depth analysis of the genesis of protest in a particular city with analysis of the structure of protest across the GDR.

The in-depth study focuses on the industrial region of Saxony, especially on the city of Leipzig.[4] In that "cradle of the revolution," democratic activists did much to spur the popular rebellion against Communism, and it was there that the failure of the state's repressive strategy first became stunningly apparent. In order to avoid generalizing from the specific case of Leipzig, I have compared the city with other regions of the GDR. And for more robust comparative purposes I paid particular attention to the evolution of protest in two other large cities, Dresden and East Berlin. Unlike Leipzig, Dresden did not develop a local opposition organization that achieved public visibility before the autumn of 1989. But, in Dresden and its environs, intensive anti-regime rioting occurred at the peak of the exiting crisis in early October. As in Leipzig, local party and state elites withdrew from confrontation with protesters and defied the will of the regime in East Berlin. While the Saxon cities were the birthplace of the popular rebellion against Communism, East Berlin was the cradle of New Forum and the center of the reformist East German civic movement.

In order to analyze the East German upheaval, I assembled protest event data that were more comprehensive than any previously employed. These data offer particular advantages over those used in past studies of East Germany in 1989, most of which are based on the analysis of protest in a single large city, generally Leipzig (Braun 1994, 1995; Lohmann 1994; Oberschall 1996; Opp, Voss, and Gern 1995; Pfaff 1996), cover a small number of cities based on Western newspaper reports (Mueller 1999), or rely on retrospective surveys (Kluegel and Mason 1999; Opp, Voss, and Gern 1995). The protest event data proved invaluable in describing the distribution of protest activity across the GDR and for testing the explanatory mechanisms proposed.

Before turning to the substance of the study, I have to acknowledge the generous support of teachers, friends, and organizations. Early on, Professor Craig Calhoun nurtured my interest in historical social science at the University of North Carolina at Chapel Hill. Professor Konrad H. Jarausch supervised a master's thesis on postwar East German history and encouraged me to get into the archives. Professors Peter Bearman and Anthony Oberschall introduced me to the study of collective action. A dissertation improvement grant from the Friedrich Ebert Foundation funded my data collection in Germany in 1998. During that time, I enjoyed the hospitality of the Institute for Sociology at the University of Leipzig, where I was sponsored by Professors Georg Vobruba and Karl-Dieter Opp. In studying the Leipzig dissidents I was assisted by archivists Hans-Ulrich Langner and Christina Pürschel at the Leipzig's Civic Movement Archive. Several former Church-based activists in Leipzig consented to informative interviews. Thanks to the hospitality provided by Professor Heiner Ganssmann and Ursula Ganssmann, I was able to conduct research at the Federal Archive in Berlin.

The completion of the dissertation was supported by a Dean's Dissertation Fellowship at New York University, where I worked closely with Craig Calhoun and Professor Jeff Goodwin. The long transformation of the dissertation into a book took place at the University of Washington. My completion of the project was supported by a grant from the American Sociological Association–National Science Foundation Fund for the Advancement of the Discipline and by a University of Washington Royalty Research Fund Fellowship. These grants allowed me to return to Germany to collect detailed information on New Forum membership, to complete the construction of the quantitative data set, and to devote time to writing. My data collection was immeasurably assisted by Professor Siegfried Grundmann, who shared East German demographic data that made possible a precise estimate of out-migration at the county level. Julia Adams, Miriam Angress, and Pam Morrison at Duke University Press provided crucial support in developing the manuscript. Paul Betz was a very able copy editor.

I owe a great deal to my colleagues at the University of Washington. Professors Dan Chirot, Stew Tolnay, Kate Stovel, Debra Minkoff, and James Kitts all commented on drafts of various chapters and provided useful comments and criticism. In my evolution as a historical social scientist, Professors Edgar Kiser and Michael Hechter played a particularly great part. Political scientists, including Steve Hanson, Anthony Gill, Marc M. Howard, Jason Wittenberg, and Jeff Kopstein, lent perspective from the study of comparative politics. Of inestimable importance was my collaboration with Professor Hyojoung Kim. Working with Hyojoung proved vital to my thinking through the central problems associated with exit-voice dynamics and in developing the statistical analysis demonstrating the curvilinear relationship between emigration and protest. Those results first appeared in our coauthored paper "Exit-Voice Dynamics in Collective Action: An Analysis of Emigration and Protest in the East German Revolution," published in September 2003 in the *American Journal of Sociology* (109/2); a revised version of that article appears as chapter 6 with the kind permission of the University of Chicago Press.

Many other friends deserve recognition for their part in encouraging and sustaining me, but I would like to mention in particular Paul Froese, Richard E. Frankel, Matthew Titolo, and Barry Jackisch. Boundless thanks are offered to my parents, Barbara and Edward Pfaff for their love, confidence, and support. I owe the most to my wife, Karen Snedker, for her faith, encouragement, and unfailing love. Without her, this book would never have been completed, and the accomplishment would scarcely be worthwhile.

Introduction

Protest exploded across the socialist world in 1989. Some of these regimes survived; others moved swiftly toward reform; and some collapsed. Fifteen years later, social scientists still wonder what propelled this epochal movement. In studies of many socialist countries in the 1980s, one finds evidence of economic stagnation, declining confidence in Marxist-Leninist ideology, resentment of ruling elites, and recognition that the system was failing to keep up with the West. Dissent and even popular opposition to Communist rule appeared in many societies. Nevertheless, the "crisis of Leninism" (Chirot 1991) had remarkably different origins and trajectories in places as different as Beijing and Berlin.

In some Communist societies, popular unrest in 1989 cemented a transition that had already been in the making. In Poland, seeking a political pact that might lead the way out of the country's political stalemate, a broad coalition of anti-regime forces born in the Solidarity movement of 1979–1980 negotiated with party pragmatists desperate to stabilize the economy. In Hungary, reform Communists initiated political transition, promoting opposition forces and nascent business interests in liberalizing the country. As the former Hungarian party boss Karoly Grosz conceded, "The party was shattered not by its opponents but—paradoxically—by the leadership" (Przeworski 1991: 56). In both Poland and Hungary in 1989, pragmatic elements of the ruling elite worked with moderate dissidents to *instigate* liberal reforms and conceded to demands for free elections.

In many cases, however, a negotiated transition of this kind did not occur. Mass protests unseated party hard-liners in Czechoslovakia's "velvet revolution" only after events in East German cities demonstrated that it was possible to topple the ossified Stalinist elite. But then dissidents formed a civic opposition that staged a general strike, took power from the demoralized Communists, and presided over the institution of a parliamentary regime. Yet not all the rebellions against Communism were so peaceful or had such tidy conclusions. Nicolai Ceausescu's personalist dictatorship in Romania remained intransigent until shaken by a popular rebellion also apparently influenced by previous events in nearby countries. In Romania, however, the triumph of "people power" was not so clear; the regime fell after a mutiny within the ranks of the army and a split within the party apparatus crippled it. The resulting transition appears to have been as much a coup d'état as a popular upsurge as rival factions struggled for dominance. In the People's Republic of China, despite mass support for the student movement, hard-liners ultimately prevailed in the party leadership, suppressed the mass democracy movement through the use of force, and pressed ahead with their state-led program of economic reform. In China's rebellion, unlike those in East Germany, Czechoslovakia, or Romania, which were influenced by an eroding Soviet bloc, the trigger for popular mobilization seems to have been internal. In China, domestic market reforms had divided the party-state apparatus and provided new spaces for dissent, thereby creating conditions for mobilization that did not obtain in orthodox Leninist regimes (Walder 1994; Calhoun 1994; Zhao 2001).

Hence, as inevitable as the rapid, peaceful end of Soviet socialism in Eastern Europe might now appear, things could have gone differently. As the first regime to suffer outright collapse in the fall of 1989, the German Democratic Republic (GDR) demonstrated the unexpected brittleness of Leninist regimes and signaled the possibility of peaceful change to the citizens of other countries. Moreover, events in East Germany showed that the Soviet Union was willing to let a satellite regime be overturned by popular demand. Without the GDR's exit-driven spontaneous rebellion and the unique process of peaceful regime collapse that it caused, it is possible that the exit from Communism might not have been as swift or as bloodless across the region.[1]

Explaining Rebellion and Revolution in 1989

As Timur Kuran (1991: 13) aptly observes of 1989, "Seemingly unshakable regimes saw public sentiment turn against them with astonishing rapidity as tiny oppositions mushroomed into crushing majorities." Indeed, the rebellion in the GDR stands out as being so swift and unusual that it is widely cited as an example of the failure of both area specialists and general social scientists to predict instability, much less the fatal vulnerability, of a hardline Leninist regime to popular revolt (Baylis 1999; Goldstone 1994a; Kuran 1995; Hall 1998; Lipset and Bence 1994). Although we usually expect revolutions to usher in a radical regime through violent means, in the GDR mass demonstrations forced the old regime from power almost entirely without violence; and the state was neither politically recast nor radically reformed but, rather, abolished through German unification.

In terms of regime collapse, by which I mean the inability of the governing system of the state to continue to exercise its functions, East Germany can be thought of as the "first domino" in the fall of Soviet-type socialism that unfolded during 1989–91 (Przeworski 1991).[2] And while the situation of the GDR in 1989 was not entirely unique among hard-line Leninist regimes, only the East Germans had to contend with the threat of mass migration to the West. The entirely unforeseen collapse of the GDR was an instance of insurgent transition in which fight (anti-regime protest) and flight (escape from the GDR) propelled regime change without foreign intervention, a previous period of liberalization, or the political brokerage among elites and challengers that represent the more typical scenarios in the comparative study of politics.[3]

In their comparative study of democratic transitions, Juan Linz and Alfred Stepan (1996: 356) reported that researchers have generally assumed as preconditions an organized set of challengers capable of pressing for change but moderate enough to compromise and some reformist element within a regime willing to compromise with challengers. Strategic players with stable political preferences are implied in the underlying game-theoretic logic of transition studies, particularly as elegantly operationalized by Przeworski (1991). Usually the transition players are taken to be pragmatic elements of the established elite, rival counter-elites, or a coalition representing both elements (see, e.g., Munck and Leff 1999). Other models of transition emphasize the process of "brokering," that is, "coalition formation between segments of ruling classes and constituted political actors that are currently excluded from power" (Tilly 2001: 34). These models imply a stepwise democratization process: Given the expanding power of counter-elites and growing cooperation with regime moderates, liberalization advances to the democratization phase. The new elite, typically drawn from progressive elements of the old regime and opposition forces, takes power. Finally, there is consolidation, in which a leadership is elected and the new regime institutionalized.

In 1989 scholarly observers saw both popular mobilization and elite surrender as unlikely prospects in a country like the GDR. In Poland, generally treated as the paradigmatic case of post-Communist transition, civil opposition to Communism had been built up out of decades of mobilization and compromise with rulers (Ekiert and Kubik 1999; Osa 2003). When the regime saw no other way out from economic stagnation and popular disengagement, reformists turned to the opposition to negotiate a way forward. But in East Germany there were neither elite-led openings nor reformist factions that could move the reform cause forward until the popular revolution was already well under way. Throughout the revolution, the opposition remained marginal, weak, and divided. The dissidents did not manage to channel popular protest behind their own project of reformed, humane socialism. Even after the fall of Honecker, they limited themselves to moral objections to parliamentary-style politics and a reunification that they deemed "colonization" of the GDR. Dissident organizations, which arose among Church-based activists and pastors driven by varying brands of socialist idealism, were dismissed as "unrealistic dreamers" and as "pastors' parties" (*Pfaffenparteien*) by their critics (Neubert 1998: 828).

Political scientist John A. Hall notes that in some societies transition models are unpersuasive because "the absence of partners in society made an orderly decompression impossible" (1998: 527). Clearly, the concept of negotiated transition prevalent in the literature does not seem to capture the central dynamic that drove East German events. Indeed, given the broad variation in processes and outcomes across the region in spite of common institutional and geopolitical variables, Charles Tilly (2000) is right to suggest that transition research has made a largely typological and descriptive contribution. One might liken much of the transition literature to what has been described as the "natural history" school in the study of revolutions, that is, the "gathering of specimens, detailing their major parts and pro-cesses, and seeking common patterns" (Goldstone 2001: 55). While this ap-proach is useful, it does not provide a convincing account of the underlying dynamics that propelled regime change.

Another line of argument in comparative politics focuses on shifting geo-political relations that put dictatorial regimes at a fatal disadvantage. The undeniable importance of exogenous factors—especially the curious posi-tion taken on Eastern European affairs by the region's superpower—led some to explain regime collapse in terms of a general system-level crisis of state socialism (Przeworski 1991; Chirot 1991). Clearly, change in the USSR was a factor accelerating events in the various states of the region (Collins 1995; Elster 1998). But the timing and conditions of the GDR's popular upheaval seem somewhat more complicated than this macro-level explana-tion would suggest. Mikhail Gorbachev came to power in 1985, but the East German rulers did not initiate reforms or suffer the unrest seen in neigh-boring countries. And although the center of the Soviet imperium was in flux, it was more events in the periphery than politics at the center that propelled the collapse of socialism. Erich Honecker's regime fell in the autumn of 1989, and Gorbachev's in the summer of 1991. Soviet reforms and the transformation of the bloc clearly undermined all orthodox regimes, yet focusing only on geopolitics misses the interplay between exogenous (e.g., changes in Soviet policy) and endogenous (e.g., political mobilization) processes and makes no linkage between macro and micro causal mecha-nisms. Valerie Bunce's (1999: 156) call for the study of the internal dynam-ics that led to the collapse of socialism—"Although international factors were important, they influenced, rather than caused, what happened"—is convincing.

The state-centered sociology of revolutions offers an appealing alterna-tive to transitology. The basic conditions for a revolutionary situation that it identifies—a crisis of state authority in which rulers are generally perceived as ineffective and unjust, a counter-elite to rival a divided ruling class, and perceived threats to popular welfare (Goldstone 2003: 81; see also Skocpol 1979; Goodwin 1997)—capture part of what weakened the GDR. However, the GDR's system of coercive surveillance ensured that there were no inter-nal forces capable of mobilizing a serious challenge against the regime. Although there is evidence of popular disaffection reaching well into the ranks of the party apparatus, in the rebellion that toppled Honecker there is no evidence of elite defection, a key variable in state-centered theory. Nor was there significant defection by the intelligentsia; most intellectuals distanced themselves from the tiny Church-based opposition. Mass mobilization into anti-regime demonstrations occurred without the support of elite factions or political parties, which has usually been associated with state-centered theories of popular insurgency.

Another set of explanations of popular rebellion draws on social movement theories that identify "mobilizing structures" such as communities, voluntary associations, interest groups, and political parties, on the one hand, and, on the other, a broad set of constraints and opportunities called "political opportunities" (Tilly 1978; McAdam 1982; McAdam, McCarthy, and Zald 1996; Tarrow 1994).[4] Yet consolidated Leninist regimes like the GDR pose nearly insurmountable obstacles to social movement organization (Johnston and Mueller 2001; Lichbach 1994). Indeed, given the centralization of power and resources by the party apparatus, opposition would be most plausibly initiated or tolerated by factions within the ruling party itself, as transition theory posits (Przeworski 1991). It was in view of such realities that, long before 1989, Anthony Oberschall (1973: 128) reasonably concluded: "In a totalitarian society, opposition movements can occur only when mobilization is initiated by dissidents from within the party who gain temporary control of some organizations and associations normally under party control and use this base for further mobilization."

In fact, opportunities for movement mobilization in Eastern Europe in 1989 did often spring from the de facto toleration of dissident voices and heretical views in divided party elites (Kornai 1992; Ekiert 1996; Linz and Stepan 1996). In some parts of Eastern Europe, such as Hungary and Poland, long periods of elite conflict and state-led reform campaigns provided opponents with the chance to organize. Gorbachev's reforms gave birth to new social movements in the Soviet Union (Zdravomyslova 1996). But where hard-line regimes continued to be unified, "civil society" and political opposition could only remain embryonic. Although Gorbachev's reforms seemed to legitimize heterodox views on the future of socialism, in the GDR the party remained firmly under the control of orthodox elites, and, other than a narrow refuge within the Church, there was no emerging civil society that dissidents could exploit.

It is also not clear that oft-cited political opportunity variables explain the timing or nature of the peaceful rebellion in the GDR. Grzegorz Ekiert (1996) elaborates how the politically integrated states of Eastern Europe suffered repeated "spillover" effects from policy changes elsewhere. In 1989 events in neighboring countries seem to have encouraged popular unrest in many instances. However, although a changing international environment was signaled by the "Gorbachev factor" and Soviet-bloc reforms, during the critical breakthrough phase of the revolution in the GDR when the masses took to the streets (September–October 1989) a regime credibly preparing a "Chinese solution" remained in place and, at least initially, employed its security forces to seal the borders and disperse demonstrations against its rule. The first hint of divisions within the elite emerged after mass protest on October 9, and Honecker's fall from power occurred on October 18. In fact, during the first week of October protest exploded—the police reported thirty-five demonstrations between October 2 and October 10 in the GDR— but so did efforts to repress the growing unrest, with riot policemen injuring scores of demonstrators and arresting more than three thousand protesters.[5] Until the local breakthroughs in Leipzig and Dresden, where midlevel officials defied East Berlin, citizens may not have perceived that the door to greater political freedom had swung open, and it was not obvious at that point that authorities were backing away from their policy of repression. In other words, it appears that popular mobilization, rather than organizations exploiting political opportunities, pressured authorities to tolerate dissent (see also Opp, Voss, and Gern 1995).

Students of the general phenomena of social movements and collective action sometimes analyze a case in detail in order to advance substantive knowledge of important events. East Germany in 1989 is one of those events. As Hall (1998) observes, "No greater challenge to social theory has been presented by history at the end of the twentieth century than the collapse of the socialist project in Eastern Europe"; within that great transformation, East Germany stands out as a unique case: an instance of a political order collapsing under the weight of popular pressure without large-scale violence of any kind—indeed, without a single reported fatality. Detailed information on the East German case allows for the evaluation of theoretical accounts and the specification of action-generating and suppressing mechanisms. Such an evaluation opens up the "black box" of historical causality in political change (Elster 1989; Hedström and Swedberg 1998).

A second reason for examining a case in detail is to advance explanatory theory. Narrative evidence helps us to move beyond the description of social movements and the stylized dilemmas of collective action theory. Case studies provide the richness of data that permits evaluation of hypothesized causes and can be opportunities to evaluate, revise, and amend our theories about causal processes. The detail they provide is often essential to identifying and testing the scope conditions of different mechanisms (Mahoney and Rueschemeyer 2003; Kiser and Hechter 1991, 1998; King, Keohane, and Verba 1994).

In view of anomalies like the GDR, current thinking on social movements rightly emphasizes uncovering and explicating their mechanisms and dynamics. Proponents of political process theory have recently refocused their efforts on dynamic processes of political mobilization and claims making in episodes of political conflict (McAdam, Tarrow, and Tilly 2001; Tarrow 1998). These approaches represent an important shift from static, variable-oriented explanations to dynamic, process-oriented ones. In many instances, however, specifying and demonstrating the effects of hypothesized causal mechanisms remains difficult, and few works have actually focused on analytic mechanisms.[6] The present book takes this further step by identifying the central mechanisms propelling the East German revolution.

Emigration, Protest, and the Collapse of the GDR

For scholars who study revolutions and comparative politics, the GDR's startling trajectory from revolution to reunification raises three principal questions: Why, before 1989, did the GDR have one of the most stable, orthodox Leninist regimes in the socialist world, troubled neither by political factionalism nor by citizen social movements? Why did the East German masses suddenly rise in crushing displays of popular opposition in the fall of 1989? And why did the regime lack resilience, resulting in a peaceful and nearly unprecedented political collapse and eventual German reunification?

To answer these questions, I develop a theory of exit-voice dynamics applied to these linked episodes of collective action. My approach unites two factors generally missing from studies of revolutionary social movements: the implications of no-exit situations for collective action and how introducing an exit option redefines the collective action problems confronted by nascent oppositions and faltering states alike. In theorizing the implications of exit and voice for protest movements and revolutionary episodes, I build on basic insights of collective action theory. Actors are assumed to be self-interested, acting intentionally to realize their interests, which may be material, social, or ideal, at the minimum cost. However, they are constrained by the rules imposed by institutions, by the cost of action, and by the opportunity costs of foregoing one course of action by choosing another. Often they are also constrained by inadequate information to assess the likely costs and benefits of pursuing their preferred course of action. In such circumstances, they will tend to remain inactive until new information on which to act becomes available.

The analysis also assumes that even if there are common interests in a social group, political action to realize them does not necessarily result. When mobilization does occur, members of a group will be tempted to free ride on the efforts of others. Few potential beneficiaries will voluntarily pay costs or hazard risks to advance the cause. Even those that willingly participate in a movement are expected to be opportunistic, seeking advantages that benefit them individually even when personal gains lead away from collective action necessary for the provision of widely desired public goods (Lichbach 1994; Olson 1965; Hardin 1982; Coleman 1990).[7]

Besides the simplicity of these assumptions, the advantage of adopting them is that they bring particular issues into focus. When we consider the many obstacles to political organizing even in a pluralist democracy, it is clear that in an authoritarian context—even when a "state crisis" becomes evident—one cannot take dissident collective action for granted. Early work on collective action showed that because the risks individuals face in joining a revolutionary movement will almost always be greater than an individual's expected contribution to its political success, most rational individuals avoid radical protest (Olson 1965; Tullock 1971). Put another way, in September 1989 opponents of the East German regime faced what Mark Lichbach (1994) calls the "Rebel's Dilemma": dissidents seeking to overthrow a regime or to compel it to redress their grievances must overcome the natural reluctance of potential supporters to join any costly or dangerous venture.

In practice, sometimes citizens do act together to achieve a common good. Yet if state repression manages to deter supporters of collective action and no effective dissident organization takes shape, if they lack the information needed to shape their actions, if actors cannot persuade themselves that it is worth paying the costs of contributing to the cause, or if there is a cheaper alternative to protest that benefits individuals, no protest movement need arise. For their part, the rulers of states try to raise barriers to mobilization such that "the fundamental competition between the regime and the dissidents is over solutions to the Rebel's Dilemma" (Lichbach 1994: 26). The conflict is all the more acute when a highly repressive regime monopolizes the resources of collective action and does employ political repression. Given the conditions under which dissidents operated in the GDR, one might not expect an opposition movement to emerge at all, particularly if lower cost options (such as passivity or emigration) are available.

If mobilization into social movements presents considerable puzzles, this is also true of regime collapse. A state crisis gives way to revolution only if a regime fails to overcome its own obstacles to collective action, as students of revolution as diverse as Tocqueville and Trotsky have observed. Max Weber (1968) noted long ago that, in view of its organizational advantages, military resources, and capacity to reward compliance, the state nearly always has the upper hand against popular challengers. Nevertheless, the ultimate failure of security forces to contain opposition and the failure of the party to counter-mobilize against the rebellion in 1989 are major components of the East German story. Indeed, regime collapse should be considered in light of a "State's Dilemma"; as Mancur Olson observed, "The logic of collective action applies to one side [the regime] as much as to the other [the rebels]" (quoted in Lichbach 1994: 257). Indeed, the "state crisis" variable referred to in transition studies and state-centered theories of revolution is only consequential if it indicates problems of confidence, coordination, and compliance among a regime's supporters and empowered agents.

This study explains why the same process that triggered voice in sufficient volume to make the Honecker regime vulnerable also undermined mobilization to reform the GDR. East Germany's mono-organizational dictatorship suppressed not only political opposition but also effective pressure for reform within the ruling party itself. Blocking exit and voice demobilized the regime's agents, undermined the performance of the socialist system, and provided no opportunity for a negotiated political transition. However, in the summer of 1989 the decay of the Soviet bloc created new opportunities for people to flee the country, triggering a popular rebellion when those left behind recognized the extent of their country's crisis and had to decide whether to flee, fight, or remain silent.

Because of the underlying competition between exit and voice, one would expect that where emigration achieved mass proportion, it should have weakened mobilization. In fact, this assertion is supported both by the narrative, qualitative evidence provided in the chapters of this book and by the statistical analysis of emigration and protest in the GDR. Reinforcing my interpretation of the historical evidence, statistical analysis demonstrates that emigration and protest were positively related in the counties where emigration occurred below a distinct threshold; but the relationship became negative where emigration occurred above it. These dynamics also doomed the reformist movement in the GDR. In early 1990, uniting the aspirations of individual exit and anti-regime voice, East German voters exited the old GDR in toto by supporting unification with the Federal Republic of Germany.

In short, the ambition of this book is to understand the mechanisms that spurred mass demonstrations, led to a peaceful surrender of power by the orthodox Leninist elite, and hastened German reunification. It explains the erosion and demobilization of party and state institutions, the waves of emigration that destabilized the regime, and the ongoing popular protest that helped to propel revolutionary events in East Germany. And it explains the failure of regime elites to mobilize supporters into a repressive campaign and of dissident leaders to sustain loyalist mobilization behind the civic movement, leading East Germany on a swift road from revolution to reunification.

Overview of the Book

Chapter 1 reformulates Hirschman's famed exit-voice-loyalty thesis into a model of exit-voice dynamics, specifying the social mechanisms suggested by the model and developing propositions concerning the implications of exit, voice, and loyalty for collective action in repressive regimes like the Leninist GDR. Chapter 2 uses the model of exit-voice dynamics outlined in the introduction to explain the progressive neutralization of the Communist regime under Erich Honecker, focusing on the causes of demobilization within the ruling party in the late 1980s. Chapter 3 explores why the regime's system of coercive surveillance generated subaltern resistance and how the structure of GDR society provided spaces for submerged opposition. The regime's policy of systematically blocking any exercise of either voice or

exit enhanced its vulnerability by promoting crippling opportunism, ineffi-
ciency, dissimulation, and public withdrawal. The first part of the book thus
identifies the informal social resources on which popular opposition was
based and why, when mass protest appeared, a seemingly immovable regime
was vulnerable to collapse.

Chapter 4 addresses a variant of the Rebel's Dilemma in examining organized dissent in the GDR. Political repression and incentives for opportunistic compliance meant that most disaffected East German citizens registered their opposition only indirectly through private withdrawal ("exit to a
niche"). But the system reached its limits as some dissenting citizens exploited gaps in the system of coercive surveillance to nurture dissident political identities and form loose networks under the umbrella of Church involvement. Despite repressive pressures in Leipzig, dissidents operating out
of a local Lutheran church managed to establish the Monday Peace Prayers
as a political ritual of dissent. The unforeseen result was that this ritual
provided a focal point around which mass protest as an unlikely—and
provisional—alliance of dissidents and would-be exiters crystallized in the
early autumn of 1989.

Chapter 5 explains the emergence of rebellious collective action across the
GDR in the autumn of 1989. The dramatic events of the "exiting crisis"
illustrate how exit triggered voice and why protest spurred by the exiting
wave undermined the regime's stability. Unlike the typical perspective in the
literature on collective action, the genesis of popular protest analyzed here
does not support a one-sided view of the exit-voice nexus. Building on the
exit-voice model, the chapter shows why exit—in the form of an emigration
crisis—can trigger spontaneous collective action. Drawing on quantitative
analysis of emigration and protest at the county level for the entire GDR,
chapter 6 tests the basic social mechanisms of communication (signaling)
and coordination (informal groups and their erosion) identified in the theory of exit-voice dynamics against other potential causal factors. The statistical analysis of protest across GDR counties in 1989–90 indicates why exit
served both to propel and in some instances blunt the development of a
largely unstructured, spontaneous protest movement.

Chapter 7 explores the inability of the Honecker regime to make good on
its threatened "Chinese solution" to political turmoil. It examines why the
regime failed to overcome problems of compliance among its own agents in

its efforts to contain protest and prevent the emergence of an organized opposition movement. The failure of local elites to carry out Berlin's orders to crush the movement points to a central feature of every regime collapse, namely, the incapacity of rulers to overcome demoralization and counter-mobilize their agents to crush challengers.

In the final chapters the book analyzes the dilemmas of loyalist voice and the reform cause. Chapter 8 explains why reformist voice was initially successful but swiftly faltered in its efforts to democratize the GDR. This chapter points to a different interpretation of voice from that usually encountered in the social movement literature, arguing that when studying protest movements one must distinguish between anti-regime protest (insurgency) motivated by fundamental opposition from reformist voice inspired by critical loyalty. The failure of the nascent opposition movement to exploit opportunities and regime concessions points to one of the great paradoxes of the East German case: the activists who led the opposition movement preferred a reform of socialism to political revolution and thus split from the mass of protesters. While the signaling mechanism that triggered reformist mobilization was the same as with insurgent voice, it was unaffected by the erosion of social capital that undercut protest at the highest magnitudes. Finally, Chapter 9 analyzes the dynamics driving the "national turn" in the revolution. It shows why the regime's desperate concession propelled the widening rebellion, why the civic movement could not adapt to radically altered political opportunities, and why the popular embrace of nationalism was determined, in large measure, by the appeal of exit.

The conclusion returns to the original theoretical premises of the book in light of its findings and considers the implications of exit-voice dynamics for comparative research on rebellions, revolts, and revolutions—those "impromptu events that surprise and terrify us"—to suggest how introducing an exit option into studies of movements might help us better understand the structure and dynamics of real world collective action.

CHAPTER 1

Exit-Voice Dynamics and Collective Action

> When I do an analysis myself I never think of economics as a whole and of
> sociology as a whole and how the two can meet; where are the interfaces;
> and so on. I do it in connection with specific phenomena. And almost
> inevitably I find ways in which it is the intermingling that explains.
>
> —ALBERT O. HIRSCHMAN, QTD. IN R. SWEDBERG, ECONOMICS
> AND SOCIOLOGY

The events of 1989–90 in East Germany reveal a remarkable coincidence of emigration and protest. The archives of the GDR Interior Ministry indicate that more than fifteen hundred public protest events occurred between September 1989, when the crisis began, and March 1990, when parliamentary elections voted in a pro-unification government. Demographic reports show that in the period between the first anti-regime protests and the parliamentary elections that voted for German unity more than four hundred thousand GDR citizens (nearly 3 percent of the population) abandoned the country and fled to West Germany. (See figure 1.)

All accounts are united in seeing emigration as playing an important part in the East German revolution (see Pollack 1994; Offe 1994, 1997; Zapf 1993; Naimark 1992; Mueller 1999). The apparent correlation between exit (emigration) and voice (protest) has been widely noted, with many scholars drawing on the insights of economist Albert O. Hirschman's pioneering essay *Exit, Voice, and Loyalty* (1970) to explain it. Indeed, Hirschman's thinking profoundly influenced our understanding of 1989, as reflected in a number of scholarly treatments of the subject applying his theory, not least his own conceptual essay (Hirschman 1993; see also Brubaker 1990; Pollack 1990; Goldstone 1994b; Lohmann 1994; Mueller 1999). Yet these studies have generally only considered one side of the relationship between exit and voice, such as how emigration to West Germany before 1989 stunted the development of an opposition movement in comparison with developments in Poland or Czechoslovakia (Torpey 1995; Joppke 1995; also see Huntington 1968: 310–11) or provided "exit repertoires" that were an alternative to social movements (Mueller 1999).

In fact, nearly all perspectives in the collective action literature concur that an exit option should suppress voice by providing the rational actor with a typically low-cost alternative to protest that avoids collective action problems (MacDonald 1963; Barry 1974; Adas 1986; Blair and Jost 2003). This interpretation is reinforced by previous studies of the GDR. As John Torpey (1995: 9) says with regard to the East German intellectuals, "For their part, those who chose to leave the GDR rather than suffer the travails of the struggle for a better society naturally reduced the direct pressures on the regime to change and, perhaps equally significantly, demoralized those who wished to stay and fight the battle." In his study of the dissident movement, Christian Joppke (1995: 29) argues that "in East Germany, the equivalent to the dissident quest for the open society was exit to West Germany, where everyone who managed to cross the Wall could pick up automatic citizenship. The exit option, which could be taken only individually, neutralized the appearance of antipolitical dissidence as political claim."

The implication is evident: as the availability of exit increases, collective action should decrease. In this scenario, mass emigration would prevent a revolution. On the other hand, if the costs of collective action fall, emigration should decrease as the balance of incentives shifts from exit to voice as a means of redressing grievances. In this scenario, revolution prevents emigration (Lichbach 1994: 106). Although both of these theoretical scenarios are plausible, neither seems to capture the dynamic driving the East German revolution. Lichbach's (1994: 105) discussion of the implications of exit for the Rebel's Dilemma suggests an ambiguous role for emigration: "Without the safety valve of exit, voice is the only resort left for changing one's situation. Voice will thus be wielded by those with literally no place else to go. Moreover, as the possibility of exit increases, the best and brightest (i.e., the most motivated and best able) leave, taking the clearest voices out of the

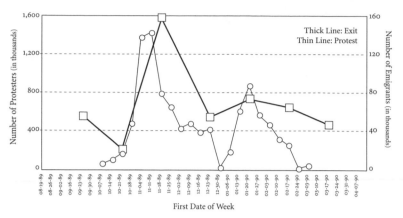

FIGURE 1. Trends in the Number of GDR Protesters and Emigrants, 1989–1990

Sources: GDR Interior Ministry and Zentrales Einwohnerregister (ZER) data reported in Grundmann 1998.
Note: The number of emigrants at the middle point of a month refers to the total number of persons who emigrated during the corresponding month.

picture." When the exit option presents itself in the study of collective action, it appears as safety valve, as a factor depleting social capital, and as a last resort. But are there other possibilities?

However important emigration was for its ultimate political fate, emigration alone was unlikely to have led to the capitulation of an intransigent, orthodox Leninist regime like the GDR. During the period that emigration shook the GDR, mass mobilization went on concurrently. The historical evidence shows that, despite the importance of the emigration crisis in triggering protest and weakening the regime's grip, the East German state collapsed because of the direct pressure of the people in the streets. The great breakthroughs in the democratic revolution—the fall of Honecker in mid-October, the fall of the Berlin Wall in early November, the January 1990 announcement that free parliamentary elections would be held in March—came after massive, intensifying protests convinced regime elites that they had to change course or hasten the pace of change. And yet exit was never displaced by voice, and reformists found that efforts to restabilize the GDR were repeatedly undermined by waves of emigration. Voice vied with exit in the political arena.

What has been missing so far in the embrace of the exit-voice-loyalty thesis is a reformulation of Hirschman's concepts with clear implications for the study of social movements and collective action. Despite the widespread use of exit-voice-loyalty as a heuristic device, its application has been hampered both by conceptual imprecision and by the lack of empirical data on these separate phenomena in the same episode of collective action (see Dowding et al. 2000). As Hirschman does not clearly propose the constituent mechanisms in the relationships he describes, it is necessary to specify them.[1] In particular, it is necessary to discern under what circumstances mass exit acts as a trigger to collective action rather than as a safety valve. When does flight spur fight and when is it only a substitute?

Specifying Exit-Voice Dynamics

Exit, Voice, and Loyalty offers a simple theory of how actors register disapproval with the unsatisfactory provision of goods and what the implications for the fate of organizations then are. Hirschman's theory combines typically "economic" action (exit) and typically "political" action (voice) with the "sociological" factor of loyalty (that is, sentiments born of identity and interests) in order to understand how actors respond to organizational decline. Hirschman's intent was to explore how market and nonmarket forces impact behavior. He argued that consumers have two basic options: they can demand a better product, or they can turn to competing firms. Exit and voice thus constitute the two alternative means of expressing grievances. In ordinary market situations, voice will generally only occur when the exit alternative is unavailable or unattractive, either because of a lack of alternatives (e.g., the firm is a monopoly) or because material investment or subjective feelings of attachment impose high costs on individual exit. In other words, redress of grievances is achieved not only by "exiting" to a more efficient provider, as is typical in open-market situations, but also through influence, complaint, and even protest, especially where material, ideal, or social investments make exit unappealing.

Clearly, different conditions shape exit and voice in politics as opposed to markets. Where exit means leaving one's homeland, it tends to be much costlier than simply changing jobs or finding a rival supplier. And the home or the destination state often removes this option by forbidding free migration. However, if they are abused, and exit is viable, highly aggrieved citizens will likely go over to a competing state (either as immigrants or as refugees).

In an authoritarian state, voice would mean the expression of grievances through petition or protest. Unlike democracies that institutionalize voice (through voting, lobbying, and interest group formation), authoritarian states usually limit or ban the expression of grievances. Here, Hirschman's insight was that exit and voice are implicitly linked so that elimination of one option has implications for the other. If exit is eliminated, voice is the only way to improve one's circumstances. However, an exit option is usually the prerequisite for asserting influence: "The effectiveness of the voice mechanism is strengthened by the *possibility* of exit" (Hirschman 1970: 83, emphasis added). In historical practice, rulers tend to grant more concessions to those citizens with opportunities for mobility than to those that have none (North 1981). Thus whether exit or voice predominates can be explained largely by the institutional conditions that limit one or both of these options.

In an effort to adequately develop the connection between exit and voice, I offer the following basic definitions of terms: *exit* refers to an actor's decision to leave an organization or a state because of his or her dissatisfaction with its performance in favor of an alternative supplier; and *voice* refers to an actor's decision to petition or protest an organization or a state in order to replace it or to improve its performance. As noted by previous scholars, the logic of Hirschman's model suggested that the availability of an exit option would not so much spur demands for redress (voice) as it would undermine it. His fundamental insight was that exit and voice are contrasting responses to grievances that may fail to advance the same end. For one thing, when exit is easily available, it may tend to siphon off those alert and resourceful individuals who are the most ambitious and most discontented, subtracting from the reservoir of creativity and social capital remaining in the collectivity. Thus voice—"various types of actions and protests, including those meant to mobilize public opinion" (1970: 30)—is the "residual of exit" (33), that is, what is available to discontented individuals who find the exit option overly costly.

In contemplating the East German case, Hirschman (1993) refined his arguments. He explained: "Exit (out-migration) and voice (protest demonstrations against the regime) worked in tandem and reinforced each other, achieving jointly the collapse of the regime" (1993: 177). However, this revolution begotten of "exit" but driven by "voice" raises important theoretical questions that make straightforward application of the model difficult. Previously, Hirschman had argued, "In the case of any one particular firm or organization and its deterioration, either exit or voice will ordinarily have the role of the dominant reaction mode. The subsidiary mode is then likely to show up in such a limited volume that it will never become destructive. . . . The job of destruction is accomplished single-handedly by the dominant mode" (1970: 33). How then did the two contrasting behaviors act "in tandem"?

Critics have long noted that Hirschman's theory does not contend with the implications of social dilemmas for voice (Barry 1974).[2] Clearly, exit and voice are alternative responses to discontent. While the relative cost of exit and voice may vary across settings, it is generally true that under highly repressive and mono-organizational regimes exit is often a lower cost option than voice that relies on collective action. And once an individual has exited, particularly from a state, he or she is no longer available for voice. So, as a rule, easily available, low-cost exit that offers immediate improvement in one's circumstances should tend to undercut the capacity for collective action, no matter how necessary it may be from the vantage of the collectivity. Voice may arise even with an exit option present, but only if individuals are sufficiently convinced that it will be effective. Thus "voice will depend also on the willingness to take the chances of the voice option as against the certainty of the exit option and on the probability with which a consumer expects improvements to occur as a result of actions" (Hirschman 1970: 39). The implication should be fairly clear and allows us to state *Proposition 1: All things being equal, the lower their cost of an exit option relative to voice options, the more actors will choose exit over voice.*

Hirschman identifies *loyalty* as a factor that stimulates voice. It implies an ideological, material, or emotional commitment to an organization that sometimes overrides the maximization of individual interest in favor of the collectivity (see also North 1981: 45–58). Hirschman predicts that when performance is declining and there are no effective constraints on exiting, individuals without a high degree of loyalty to the organization will be motivated to leave. If loyalty is high, or incentives to remain in place are offered, individuals may be less likely to exit even when exit is a readily available option. Hirschman observed, "A member with a considerable attachment to . . . [an] organization will often search for ways to make himself influential, especially when the organization moves in what he believes is the wrong direction" (1970: 77–78). Hirschman proposed that "the likelihood of voice increases with the degree of loyalty" (1970: 78). Hence, all other things being equal, individual loyalty should deter exit and spur voice.

However suggestive the concept of loyalty may be, it remains largely ambiguous in Hirschman's treatment.[3] In the present study, loyalty is not treated as a course of action but as the dispositions and preferences that determine an actor's relative costs and benefits for voice and exit behaviors. Even if we restrict our definition, though, it is difficult to employ the concept because we often lack adequate measures of such complex sentiments or cannot be assured of its sincere expression. For example, in a repressive society such as the GDR, opinion data, voluntarism, contributions, and so on are scarce, compulsory, or prone to falsification (Kuran 1995).

Even with these qualifications in mind, we would expect that individual loyalty is most stable where it has an institutional and relational foundation in an organization that rewards compliance (Olson's "selective" incentives; see Olson 1965). Loyalty is especially likely to be robust where members are dependent on a collectivity for scarce or highly desired goods (Hechter 1987; Coleman 1990). Yet material interests alone do not determine loyalty. It is also plausible that the social incentives of community membership would motivate loyalty and, because ideologies are jointly produced goods that individuals cannot develop nor enjoy on their own (think of political philosophies, religions, and the like), ideal incentives for loyalty could also attach to groups dedicated to producing and consuming these kinds of public goods (Hirschman 1978). Accordingly, in this study *loyalty* refers to an actor's subjective attachment to an organization or state because of his or her material, ideal, or social investment in its success.

Hirschman recognized the importance of "alert loyalists" for reform causes. Without committed members willing to engage in public-spirited collective action for the benefit of the organization, the organization will tend either to stagnate or collapse. In other words, contrary to the way it is often treated, loyalty need not imply unreasoning emotion, unlimited contribution to the common good, reactionary hostility to change, or mute toleration of substandard performance. Loyalty is rather a set of dispositions that influences exit and voice behaviors. Because loyalists are committed, they constitute a crucial constituency or force for reform, and yet they remain capable of "reasoned calculation" (79) in their fulfillment of goals.

What Hirschman failed to consider, however, is that just such reasonable calculation can lead loyalists into social dilemmas that undercut the likelihood of concerted voice to achieve public goods. The typical loyalist will not pay unlimited costs on behalf of the cause and may abandon collective action that becomes difficult or ineffective. Indeed, Hirschman (1970: 78) acknowledges that "in the face of discontent with the way things are going in an organization, an individual member can remain loyal without being influential himself, but hardly without the expectation that *someone* or *something* will happen to improve matters." In this observation, despite his general dismissal of Olson's (1965) free-rider problem, Hirschman identifies precisely the attitude that can generate it. It is not when loyal individuals trust others to reform the organization that loyalty is politically consequential, but rather when loyalty inspires the "If I don't do it nobody else will" conviction that sustains public-spirited action even during the political doldrums or when costs are high (Oliver 1984; but see also Hirschman 1982).

In considering the implications of loyalty for the exit-voice dynamic in collective action, we suppose that loyalty should lead people to postpone exit, perhaps indefinitely, and inspire voice in favor of improvement or reform if individuals are convinced that their action will be influential. The implications of loyalty for exit can be clearly stated. *Proposition 2: All things being equal, the greater an individual's subjective loyalty to an organization or a state, the less likely he or she should be to exit it.*

Activism spurred by loyalty to an organization or state, however, will not tend to be revolutionary. In most circumstances, loyalty gives birth to reformism, not radicalism. In order to make clear what is meant by this distinction, *reformist voice* refers to political action intended to improve the performance or responsiveness of an organization or state, and *insurgent voice* refers to political action designed to rebel against an organization or state and thereby replace it or compel it to change its policies.

With regard to either type of voice, Hirschman's theory underestimates the difficulties associated with collective action even for alert and well-informed citizens or the most committed loyalists. The turn to voice may risk sanctions, raise coordination and free-riding problems, and rely on a higher degree of creativity and initiative than individual exiting. In fact, East

Germans were facing considerable obstacles to mobilization. Even if over-throwing the socialist regime was a widely shared collective good, there were significant obstacles to effective collective action, not least the high costs that individuals risked by standing up to a repressive state, the small likelihood that anyone's individual voice would achieve the desired end, and the obsta-cles to communication and coordination that citizens faced.

Although it is not impossible to imagine "an optimally effective mix of exit and voice" (Hirschman 1970: 125), such that the threat and/or practice of exit makes authorities vulnerable and increases the chance of success through voice, the conditions for so favorable a mix are rare, as Hirschman concedes. Thus, in his configuration, exit and voice ultimately occupy a seesaw relationship: where one is predominant we expect a decline in the other. Voice is fed by loyalty, by the likely efficacy of voice, and, more important, by lack of opportunities for exit. The central message is clear: "The exit alternative can therefore tend to *atrophy the development of the art of voice*" (43, emphasis in original) "by depriving it of its principal agents" (51). Thus, as we noted earlier, voice—"various types of actions and protests, including those meant to mobilize public opinion" (1970: 30)—is often the "residual of exit" (33).

To illustrate this distinction, in the East German case one can draw a contrast between street protests and the mobilization into the reformist civic movement. Street protests developed spontaneously and made use of ele-mentary mobilizing structures to expand rapidly. These protests grew into a decisively anti-Communist populist movement. This sort of popular insur-gency had as its object the removal of Honecker and the toppling of the socialist state. The civic movement, including New Forum and other groups, grew out of dissident circles and made its stated object the reform of social-ism and the preservation of the state. It too employed protest as a way of compelling regime elites to democratize politics, but the point of this protest was never to put the survival of the state in jeopardy. It relied on the activa-tion of loyalty to reverse deteriorating circumstances.

The implications of loyalty for voice are captured in *Proposition 3: If loyalists are dissatisfied, they will be more likely than others to engage in reformist voice rather than in insurgent voice.*

Most of Hirschman's thinking on the exit-voice dynamic contradicts the notion that an effective balance between exit and voice could be reached and does not provide a mechanism to explain how a balance might be achieved. In order to apply the theory to the GDR, one must consider the impact of political institutions on exit and voice and explore why voice—be it insurgent or reformist—can get started at all if it has to compete with exit.

Exit, Voice, and Loyalty in Mono-organizational Regimes

As Hirschman understood, the possibility of exit is often essential to voice. Investors can threaten a state with a withdrawal of capital if their policy preferences are not met. An unhappy spouse can threaten to leave unless concessions are made. Workers can threaten a walkout unless pay and conditions improve. Research suggests that in everyday life the threat of exit commonly provides contending parties with leverage in their interactions, functioning as an effective sanction against mistreatment (Rusbult and Zembrodt 1983; Schuessler 1989). Yet in many repressive societies, as was the case in East Germany, the cost of exit is prohibitively high, and this has substantial implications for voice.

Because they do not offer market-like conditions, regimes of the Leninist type complicate Hirschman's schema (see Jowitt 1992; Solnick 1998; Bunce 1999). Exit is difficult in Leninist societies primarily because of the political and economic monopoly enjoyed by the ruling party. Citizens are denied substantive political rights, and all formal organizations are under the direct or indirect control of the Communist Party, meaning that the choice of mobility is limited and citizens have no alternative supplier to which they can exit. Infamously, the GDR went so far as to build a physical wall between the two Germanys in order to make unauthorized exit from the country nearly impossible. And within those walls the regime created a system in which the party was the only distributor of power and privilege (Bunce 1999; Lenski 1978), leaving few resources outside its control.

Emigration from the GDR was nearly impossible, and exit from the organizations of the state-party apparatus was also extremely costly. Leaving the ruling party entailed a grueling investigation by party control committees, demotion or dismissal from one's occupation, the sacrifice of privileges, and the effective surrender of political influence. Those who risked exiting the ruling party or its affiliated organizations were treated as traitors, apostates, and deviants. Leninist regimes like the GDR, with their combination of mono-organizational control and political dictatorship, are thus no-exit situations in which there is no alternative supplier and in which the costs of defection are prohibitively high.

Hirschman thought that in no-exit situations voice was still possible: "The role of voice would increase as the opportunities for exit decline, up to the point where, with exit wholly unavailable, voice must carry the entire burden of alerting management to its failings" (1970: 34). Following Hirschman, we would expect that such voice would be most common among loyalists. It is reasonable to assume, for example, that those people who had benefited most from Communist rule and whose cultural capital was invested in socialist ideology—such as party members and the intelligentsia (see Fuller 1999)—would be most likely to remain loyal to the socialist state and initiate its reform.

However, the institutional design of Leninist regimes goes a step beyond traditional authoritarianism in limiting the exercise of voice. Leninist ruling parties enforce strict cadre principles, selecting officials who are both highly committed and highly dependent on the party (Šik 1981; Jowitt 1992; Kornai 1992). With relative standing in the party or state apparatus the only avenue to career success and material privilege in Leninism (Djilas 1957; Kuvacic 1993; Atkinson and Mickelwright 1992), a system of what Andrew Walder (1994) has called "organized dependence" is instituted by which the most ambitious people are bound to the regime and subject to extraordinary control. State and party functionaries are chosen, as the Marxist dissident Ota Šik (1981: 97) observed, on the basis of demonstrated "obedience, conformism and deference." In a state like the GDR, the power this apparatus wielded over individuals was uniquely suited to silencing independent voice. "With all key positions filled by a monopolistic party apparatus that also had the power of dismissing officials, a dependency on this apparatus was to develop that is not conceivable under democratic conditions" (23).

In fact, in the selection, deployment, and control of its agents, the Leninist party became the "archetypal" monitoring agency (Solnick 1998: 27). In strict bureaucratic-military fashion, it deterred and detected conduct not in accord with the instrumental or ideological goals of the party. It became the fundamental institution of socialist society, exclusive and ubiquitous provider of the rules that governed public life, and the chief source of both private and public goods (Kornai 1992). Even among the relatively politically privileged ranks of the party cadres, Leninist norms forbade questioning the decisions reached by the party leadership and mandated revolutionary zeal. Dissent of any kind was condemned as "deviationism," "factionalism," or "anti-socialist ideology" (Šik 1981).

Above all, in a Leninist regime the political monopoly of the party is enforced by a surveillance and policing apparatus that raises the costs of voice and exit and reduces their expected efficacy in achieving political ends. The GDR was infamous for its state security service, or Stasi, which cast an almost universal net of coercive surveillance over its citizens. In a setting like this, exit and voice are almost completely blocked, and so the chances that ordinary citizens and party members alike will voice opposition should decline to practically nil. As Brian Barry (1974: 92) noted of contexts far less severe than these, "In the absence of exit, silence will often be more rational than voice. . . . Although voice may be 'needed' socially in such cases, the logic of collective action suggests that it will not be forthcoming on the basis of any calculations of rational self-interest and that the quality-conscious consumer, denied exit, will simply suffer in silence."

Based on these considerations, one can define the situation in the GDR in terms of mono-organizational dictatorship, a monopoly regime in which the exercise of both exit and voice is prohibitively costly. In fact, because both exiting from official organizations and publicly criticizing the party-state were uncertain and costly prospects, risking not only repression but also loss of economic benefits, social status, and influence, one would expect that even loyalists became averse to risking criticism that might lead to punishment or expulsion. Even if deterioration has become obvious, loyal-ists may prefer silence to gambling on the unlikely prospect that voice will improve things. The situation in a mono-organizational dictatorship should conform to *Proposition 4: In a consolidated mono-organizational dictatorship, a repressive equilibrium can be instituted such that political voice (insurgent and reformist) will be too costly for most citizens no matter how dissatisfied.*

Under the resulting repressive equilibrium, we would expect nearly every individual to comply nearly all of the time even if he or she detests the regime. In this situation loyalty loses its meaning as opportunistic com-pliance, and political dissimulation becomes commonplace even among the regime's putative beneficiaries (Jowitt 1992). Since expressions of political loyalty are unreliable, the party elite has no way of knowing whether the party is held together by genuine loyalty or merely by force and fraud. Hirschman (1970: 97) rightly foresaw the perverse effects, noting that organizations that repress exit and voice "largely deprive themselves of both recuperation mechanisms." In practice, social psychology has found that with exit and voice blocked, dissatisfied actors resort to inactivity and neglect (Rusbult, Zembrodt, and Gunn 1982; Rusbult and Zembrodt 1983). Without risking open rebellion, such neglect allows continued decay to the point where the damage becomes irreparable, the institution collapses, and dissolution must occur.

Thus a repressive equilibrium creates a false sense of security for rulers. In East Germany, where both exit and voice options were long blocked by a consolidated, hard-line regime, no widespread exercise of voice could be expected. But neutralization might have posed a threat. Poorly performing organizations are generally corrected only when exit or voice demonstrates the need for reform and empowers actors to make necessary changes.

Exit-Voice Dynamics and Revolutionary Mobilization

Under what conditions can the repressive equilibrium established in a dictatorial mono-organizational regime be disturbed? Recall that Hirschman posits that competition from an alternative supplier will ordinarily tend to motivate actors to exit rather than to protest. Actors without loyalty to an organization should be more motivated to leave than loyalists. In the case of a state, however, exit means flight from one's homeland, which is usually not as easy as from an organization. So how would the sudden availability of exit in the spring of 1989 have destabilized the GDR, and what were the effects of exit on voice? The answer lies in understanding the social mechanisms implied by exit and voice.

Exit expresses dissatisfaction and offers a lower cost alternative to protest as a means of addressing individual grievances. This tendency should be even more pronounced in dictatorial or repressive regimes in which public-spirited collective action is systematically blocked or discouraged. Secondly, widespread exit signals to those remaining behind that the organization may be in decline. Exit is the primary form of expressing dissatisfaction when it is readily available; unless actors have a strong preference for remaining in an organization (that is, loyalty) or a lack of opportunity, they will prefer to exit rather than try to remain and change the organization (see Proposition 3).

Voice risks sanctions, involves the coordination of diverse actors, and relies on a higher degree of creativity than exiting. Where exit is cheaper and more accessible than voice, it should predominate. However, in considering the East German case, Hirschman (1993) argued that under certain conditions exit may actually be the ally of voice, especially when authorities make an effort to block defection or when increasing numbers of exiters impose costs on those who remain behind. Yet it follows from the attractiveness of exit options that if the risks associated with exit and voice decrease, more people should exit rather than remain behind to engage in the costly business of arranging a movement for change. The "optimally effective mix of exit and voice" is an unlikely outcome if individual exit is more efficacious and less costly than voice. If the volume of exit is too great, voice movements may never get started, or they may falter as the social fabric of mobilization frays.

There is another way in which exit may stifle voice. It is also plausible that large-scale emigration could mollify grievances and reinforce political control. Exit could even boost popular satisfaction by offering remaining citizens new advantages and removing dissenting voices. Discontented citizens and social deviants might be the first to flee. Large-scale flight could create opportunities for those remaining behind and scarce goods—such as housing space, consumer goods, and attractive jobs—may become easier to obtain. Queues at shops, clinics, and other service providers may become shorter. Historical evidence suggests that opportunities for migration reduced the threat of agrarian radicalism in developing countries (Huntington 1968; MacDonald 1963), stabilized the Castro regime in the 1980s (Eckstein 1989), improved social conditions in the GDR in the 1950s (Ross 2002), and compelled local elites to temper racial violence in some counties in the American South (Tolnay and Beck 1992).

So why did increasing exit appear to stimulate both additional exit and, at the same time, increase voice in the GDR? The original exit-voice formulation maintained that "the chances for voice to function effectively . . . are appreciably strengthened if voice is backed up by the threat of exit, whether it is made openly or whether the possibility of exit is merely well understood to be an element in the situation in question" (Hirschman 1970: 82). Hence ordinary people may have been convinced by large-scale exit that the situation in the GDR was dire enough for them to demand action and improved their bargaining position vis-à-vis the regime. In larger volumes exit might only portend worsening economic conditions for those left behind. Citizens might well prefer engaging in collective action over inaction that would only allow ongoing erosion of their security or access to collective goods (Lindenburg 1991). They may even become more willing to engage in voice since there is nothing to be gained through free-riding if the protest movement is inadequate to dislodge the regime. Karl-Dieter Opp found that mass flight in 1989 stimulated high-risk protest by awakening moral incentives, by magnifying grievances, and by boosting perceptions of protest's efficacy (Opp, Voss, and Gern 1995: 83–84, 193).

Yet even if citizens were willing to protest, they still lacked organization and leadership. Without those elements, how was coordination possible? Theories of collective action suggest that commonly understood signals of regime vulnerability, such as mass flight, might raise expectations that others will protest (Schelling 1960, 1978; Granovetter 1978; Chwe 1999). An exiting crisis could become a focal point that rallies dispersed actors who had previously been deprived of coordination. If citizens think other citizens will protest as a result of the crisis, the likelihood of collective action should increase as the prospect of individual danger recedes and the expected efficacy of voice increases.

But these protest-inducing effects may be in competition with the social erosion that large-scale exit implies. Exit may deprive a locality of the social capital it needs to organize and sustain voice by removing alert and interested citizens. Large-scale exit would tend to drain away precisely the sort of people—young, educated, urban residents—who are generally understood to be the most prone to participate in protest movements (McAdam 1986). So, in the GDR, even if those left behind felt aggrieved and were convinced that a voice movement had to be organized, exit may have drained off vital social capital. Similarly, if alert and resourceful citizens had already exited, others remaining behind may have been less likely to risk voice or been unable to sustain it. This modification of Hirschman's model is well supported by social-psychological research that finds that actors prefer exit to cooperation when exit costs are low (Yamagishi 1988) and where monitoring the behavior of others is difficult (Van Lange 1994). Highly identified group members (i.e., those who are "loyal") widely resort to exit if voice is difficult to coordinate (Blair and Jost 2003). In short, even if they would prefer cooperation to achieve public goods jointly, prudent actors tend to exit unfavorable situations if a viable option is available and collective action seems too costly (Vanberg and Congleton 1992).

Although we would expect that the relative cost of exit and voice would vary across settings, in a repressive mono-organizational regime like East Germany exit is often easier to employ than voice and is relatively unaffected by impoverished conditions for collective action. And once an individual has exited, particularly from a state, he or she is no longer available for voice. So, as a rule, easily available, low-cost exit would tend to undercut the capacity for collective action.

The exit-voice dynamics outlined here do not suggest a simple positive or negative linear relationship between exit and voice. Voice is fed by loyalty, by the likely efficacy of voice, and, more important, by lack of opportunities for exit. If a valued organization is threatened, prudent loyalists should favor reform (voice) to inaction. Should the perceived costs or benefits of either exit or voice change, however, there may be a rapid upsurge of protest.

The positive effect of exit on voice is as a trigger for collective action. Exit signifies regime vulnerability, makes popular grievances manifest, and activates pressure for reform. Certain conditions do have to obtain in order for exit to trigger voice. There has to be an exit destination that can provide rival resources and opportunities, thus changing the balance of incentives that produced inactivity. In order for voice to emerge in a mono-organizational setting, citizens have to be widely dissatisfied with the performance of the state and share many common grievances. Disaffection cannot be limited to the most alert and resourceful citizens.

If the magnitude of exit surpasses a certain level, exit runs the risk of stifling voice by draining away its proponents and eroding support for movements. In particular, it may remove actors from the social networks that initiate and sustain collective action. Hence, should emigration occur en masse, the positive signaling effect of exit will decrease with the degree of social erosion that exit causes. These contending social mechanisms lead to *Proposition 5: Exit can trigger voice, but during an episode of political contention propelled by exit, beyond a certain point the occurrence of exit depresses the occurrence of voice.*

An exiting crisis may thus spark a general rebellion in which a diversity of actors pursue both insurgent and reformist voice. Even if unconcerted, their activities pose a direct threat to a dictatorship that must crush the rebellion or give way. However, because of the double-sided nature of exit-voice dynamics, a high magnitude of exit may doom any reform movement. If voice does not supplant exit as the dominant mode of opposition and loyalists cannot swiftly achieve results, then any project of reform is likely to be doomed so long as exit remains an option.

The following chapters will now evaluate the empirical implications of the propositions developed here in light of narrative and quantitative evidence. Our hope is to explain East Germany's surprising course from repression to rebellion to reunification.

CHAPTER 2

Blocked Voice, Demobilization, and the Crisis of East German Communism

The Party in the last analysis is always right, because the Party is the single historic instrument given to the proletariat for the solution of its fundamental problems. I have already said that in front of one's own Party nothing could be easier than to acknowledge a mistake, nothing easier to say: All my criticisms, my statements, my warnings, my protests—the whole thing was a mere mistake. I, comrades, cannot say that because I cannot think it. I know that one cannot be right against the Party. One can be right only with the Party, for history has created no other road for the realization of what is right.

—LEON TROTSKY, ADDRESS TO THE THIRTEENTH PARTY CONGRESS

With the benefit of hindsight, it is easy to regard East Germany's failure as inevitable. We should pause, however, when we remember that, even in the West, in the 1970s and 1980s the GDR was generally regarded as a socialist success story. Despite reporting exaggerated gross domestic product (GDP) figures, compared with other socialist states and even some developed capitalist states, the "other" Germany reached enviable levels of industrial and scientific achievement. Its social system provided extensive health and social security benefits. It was a leading manufacturing center in the Soviet bloc, even exporting to Western markets. The rulers of the GDR seemed to secure their rule through both "guns" and "butter"; they maintained an intimidating police state buttressed by a first-rate welfare system.

For political sociologists, the swift and unexpected collapse of Communism in East Germany poses a basic question: why, in the end, was the once nearly unassailable Communist system so brittle? The GDR, like other regimes in the region, had proven capable of crushing popular unrest and restoring stability before 1989 (see Ekiert 1996). As Jeff Goodwin (2001) observes in his study of twentieth-century revolutions, the Leninist regimes of the Soviet bloc, including the GDR, were what political sociologists call "strong states"; they had considerable administrative capacities, provided a diversity of public goods, and enjoyed an absolute monopoly over the means of violence. In short, they were not states of the sort generally found to be vulnerable to popular upheavals, much less sudden collapse.

Students of revolution have long observed that no matter how unloved a tyrant or how great the popular discontent may be, an authoritarian regime is only really vulnerable if the governing elite is unable or unwilling to preserve its rule by force. It is in this sense that the GDR regime proved extraordinarily brittle when it had to face down an unarmed popular rebellion in October 1989. In attempting to explain this paradox, some scholars have argued for a crippling loss of confidence in Marxist-Leninist ideology among the elite that robbed socialist regimes of their potency (Chirot 1991; Meuschel 1992; Friedheim 1997; Hollander 1999). Others have claimed that the collapse resulted from nearly universal popular disaffection, pointing to the failure of political socialization (Shlapentohk 1989; Lemke 1991; Kopstein 1997; Kharkhordin 1997; Garcelon 1997b). These explanations fail to take into account two questions. First, how much willing consent or ideological legitimacy is required for an authoritarian regime to maintain itself? And, second, how would we identify ideological decay other than by arguing backward from its purported effects? After all, detestable, poorly performing authoritarian states are commonplace; it is revolutions that are unusual.

Ordinarily in a Leninist regime accurate evidence of both loyalty and opposition is unavailable. Political preferences are falsified; loyalty is tainted by opportunism; and disaffection is generally expressed only in the most discreet settings (Scott 1990; Jowitt 1992; Kuran 1995). But in the case of the GDR we are fortunate. The state and party archives of the departed regime are available to researchers, and they reveal evidence of how state and party organizations functioned at the grassroots level, the depth of dissatisfaction among both ordinary citizens and party members, and the factors that constrained the exercise of reform-minded voice within the ruling Socialist Unity Party (Sozialistsche Einheitspartei Deutschlands, SED).

That party was the heart and brain of the system. It was a sprawling apparatus; more than two million people, about a fifth of the adult population, were party members in 1988. Party structures reached into every enterprise, school, hospital, newspaper, administrative bureau, club, and association (the *Grundparteiorganisationen*), ascending to county-level organizations (*Kreise*), district-level organizations (*Bezirke*), and finally the Central Committee (ZK) in Berlin, which selected the ruling Politburo. Günter Schabowski, the former Berlin party chief, recalled that "the party apparatus was like a kind of second skin over all public affairs" (Kuhrt 1996: 33). Of particular interest in understanding the inner life of this organization are the records of the Party Control Commissions (PKKs), the monitoring and sanctioning arm of the party. In accord with Lenin's principles, these commissions maintained party discipline, upheld official ideology, and monitored professional competence and workplace performance. The Politburo charged them with a broad mandate, calling on them to suppress "hostile agents . . . manifestations of corruption, misuse of party and state offices, careerism, and the spread of hostile rumors" (quoted in Otto 1995: 1444).

The view that PKK archives provide behind the outward mask of compliance indicates that growing dissent and demobilization were occurring within the ranks of the party-state apparatus as internal and external challenges to ideological orthodoxy became apparent and the rewards that sustained loyalty diminished. At the grassroots the result was a silent break with the party leadership that progressively neutralized the regime's control apparatus.

The Politics of Economic Decline in the GDR

In the late 1980s it was becoming clear that East Germany was suffering a reversal of economic fortune. In the 1960s and early 1970s, under the rubric of a planned "technological-scientific revolution," the state had ruthlessly centralized production and planning, creating large-scale industrial conglomerates (*Kombinate*). For a time, it seemed the regime had achieved a socialist *Wirtschaftswunder* that would make it a "world-class" economic power. The GDR's level of industrialization and standards of living com-

TABLE 1. Selected Indicators of Development in Socialist and Nonsocialist States

Country	Per capita GNP in US$, 1987	Energy use per capita in kg of coal (equiv.), 1987	Telephone sets per 100 pop., 1987	Television sets in use per 1,000 pop., 1987	Infant mortality per 1,000 live births, 1989	Life expectancy at birth, 1989
Socialist states						
GDR	11,860	7,276	23	754	10	72.8
ČSSR	9,709	6,364	24.6	285	13	71.7
Hungary	8,260	3,819	15.2	402	20	69.1
Poland	6,879	4,935	12.2	263	21	70.2
USSR	8,662	5,549	11.3	314	25	69.2
China (PRC)	340	776	0.9	2.4	32	NA
Nonsocialist states						
FRG	18,450	5,264	65	385	5	75.9
USA	18,570	9,542	76	811	11	75.4

Source: United Nations, *Comparative International Statistics*, 1989.

pared quite favorably with those of other socialist countries and, at least in terms of social indicators, placed the country just behind much wealthier capitalist states. (See table 1.) However, even as the GDR made strides toward emulating the information revolution and developing new microelectronic technologies, it was fast becoming the buckle of what Daniel Chirot (1991) has called a "socialist rust belt" of highly polluting industries, wasteful energy policies, and inadequate capital investment.

The economic fate of the GDR was largely tied to the fortunes of the Soviet bloc. Closely emulating the Soviet model, the GDR stressed bureaucratic planning, heavy industry, intensive exploitation of natural resources, and mass distribution of basic consumer goods (Kuhrt et al. 1996; Dennis 1993; Kornai 1991; Brus 1986; Kaser 1986). Early on, these policies seemed to bear fruit. Through about 1970, the growth rate in per capita national income in the GDR kept pace with West Germany's (SB 1988; SJDDR 1988). Yet by the late 1980s stagnation became evident. Heavy industries were well suited to Soviet-style planning and control mechanisms, less so the new flexible and service-intensive industries. As Charles Maier (1997) has pointedly observed, the GDR was perfecting its version of mass production just as the highly industrialized capitalist economies were developing "post-Fordist" models. The lack of incentives for innovation, as well as deficiencies in communication between innovators and producers, undermined the GDR's efforts to keep up with rapidly evolving forms of production in the West (Caldwell 2003; Stiglitz 1994). One indicator of the growing gap is that in the 1960s the GDR was an exporter of machine tools and equipment to Western markets; by the 1980s it was heavily reliant on Western imports.

The GDR did manage to double its output of microcomputers and electronics during the 1980s. But the growing technology sector did not reflect a system committed to innovation. During the same decade that the government spent large sums to build a microelectronics industry, the overall share of GDP invested in the productive sector steadily shrank (*SJDDR* 1990; Petschow, Meyerhoff, and Thomasberger 1990). In 1989 GDR economists estimated that over half of all industrial plants were outdated and nearly a fifth beyond repair. Subsidies expended on failing industries cost billions of marks that might have been spent on technical modernization. In 1987 planning authorities reported that a third of production targets were not achieved. Despite costly efforts to subsidize consumption through foreign loans and imports, the supply of consumer goods actually fell by more than 5 percent over the previous year (Gutmann 1999: 52–57). In the late 1980s the Central Committee was receiving reports of widespread popular dissatisfaction with shortages of spare parts, household articles, and the "thousand little things" of everyday life. In some districts, particularly in the industrial south, there were even shortages of many foodstuffs.[1]

A serious structural hurdle in the way of restructuring the GDR economy was its dependence on favorable terms of Soviet bloc trade. The principal market for East Germany's manufactured goods was the Comecon (CMEA) states. While this arrangement guaranteed market access, it discouraged innovation. With fully 70 percent of GDR technology exports remaining in the Soviet bloc, there was little compelling pressure to innovate. And just as the economy was beginning to stagnate, the rising cost of imported raw materials became a dire threat to prosperity. Although its per capita economic activity was a third smaller than West Germany's, the GDR's per capita energy consumption was nearly 30 percent higher than the West German level.

This wasteful imbalance had long been encouraged by Soviet subsidies. The SED's Tenth Party Congress in 1980 had put cheap Soviet energy imports at the center of its planning, proclaiming "price fixing principles employed by the CMEA" are "very advantageous for the GDR" and "will continue to be lower than on the capitalist world market in the years ahead."[2] In fact, nearly 70 percent of imports from the USSR were in the form of raw materials, principally hydrocarbons. But Soviet largesse had its limits; in the decade after 1980, the Soviets nearly doubled the price it charged its allies for hydrocarbons (Ruben 1998). According to Wolfgang Schürer (1999), head of the GDR's state planning commission, the unanticipated rise in energy costs triggered a serious economic shock. Costlier inputs left little room for technological innovation at exactly the moment that inadequate capital investment burdened the system.

In meeting its enormous energy demand, the GDR tried to compensate by exploiting its own lignite (brown coal) deposits. But lignite made the country's power plants and factories among Europe's greatest producers of sulfur dioxide (responsible for "acid rain") and airborne soot. Forty percent of East Germans lived in areas with airborne emissions four times greater than the official state-imposed limit. Heavily tied to the lignite industry, the Leipzig-Halle region became one of the most heavily polluted in Europe. Although evidence of a looming environment catastrophe mounted, discussion of ecological problems was strictly taboo.[3]

The chemical industry, in particular, was emblematic of the several difficulties facing the GDR. It produced more than 10 percent of the gross national product in 1988 and was the most valuable source of export earnings. Yet, because it relied on the import of cheap Soviet hydrocarbons that were reprocessed and sold on the Western market, by the late 1980s the industry was in crisis. An Institute for Economic Research study of the petrochemical industry reported, "The technical level of the facilities is deplorable and they function unprofitably, unreliably, and with ecological damage" (Petschow, Meyerhoff, and Thomasberger 1990: 42). The 1989 report concluded, "Its reconstruction or general improvement can no longer be accomplished through socialist economics" (42).

Local officials and enterprise managers coped with the crisis by conspiring to hoard resources and obstruct central monitoring of their performance. As political reports from the provinces to the Central Committee make evident, the top party leadership often had an exaggerated impression of economic achievements. Senior economic officials even intervened in the collection and tabulation of statistical materials so that "contradictions" of official economic policy could be ignored or denied (Lippe 1999: 5). Managers and officials at the local and regional level were aware of the fiction of official views, yet had little incentive to take the risk of challenging them. Indeed, although the damning reports that the Ministry for State Security provided on the economy were often accurate (Mitter and Wolle 1990), Honecker's Politburo generally discounted such unflattering news (McAdam 1993: 196). The Leipzig district archives reveal in many instances that the locally produced reports were "sanitized" before being sent to the Central Committee or to state planning agencies.

Official deception could not entirely hide the reality of economic difficulties from the public. Economic crisis helped to decertify an official ideology that promised, according to an SED party handbook, "maximum satisfaction of continually rising material and cultural needs," "unbroken growth and continual improvement of socialist production," and the "most highly developed technology" (Gutmann 1999: 27). Part of the problem was simply that socialist productivity failed to keep pace with continually rising social expenditures and consumer demands. East Germans' average labor productivity in 1988 was just over half of West German levels (ECE 1990). Thanks to the nearly universal availability of West German television, as well as the millions of cross-border visits that had by this time become a routine part of East-West détente, East Germans could compare the performance of the GDR economy with that of the Federal Republic. In countering a growing sense of relative deprivation vis-à-vis its capitalist neighbor, the regime's domestic media monopoly provided only a partial defense. Government slogans promising "security and welfare" lost their attraction when austerity at home was compared with the sense of a continually improving quality of life on West German television.

The regime was well aware of the burden of expectations it bore and tried to meet them. Even as the rate of economic growth slowed, total social spending more than tripled between 1970 and 1989 (SJDDR 1989: 350). As Jeffrey Kopstein (1997) has shown, investment in the productive sector was one of the chief victims of this effort to purchase consent, falling by a third during the 1980s. Wolfgang Bermann, director of the high-tech firm Carl-

Zeiss-Jena, estimated that 75 billion marks per year were extracted from productive industries to subsidize basic consumption and welfare (Schluchter 1996: 32). Attempting to meet popular expectations meant mounting foreign debt. In 1989 the state owed more than $26 billion in convertible currencies and faced an annual debt-servicing burden of $4.5 billion, a sum representing over 60 percent of annual export earnings (Hertle and Stephan 1997: 63; Gutmann 1999: 53–54). In June 1989 the Politburo reluctantly resolved to introduce an austerity program that would decrease total domestic investment by more than 6 percent in 1990 and impose cuts on consumer energy use, housing construction, and basic consumption.[4] Such a course would be politically damaging: reports already described deep popular resentment at declining living standards.[5]

Instead of politically dangerous reforms, the regime promised a technological solution to the crisis. Rejecting Gorbachev's calls for "perestroika" (economic restructuring), the SED instead endorsed "intensification" of socialist production and management (Dennis 1993). The Five-Year Plan covering the years 1986–90 emphasized automation, computer-assisted development, and robotics. In 1987 Honecker assured a conference of leading party functionaries that reform experiments were unnecessary: "By 1990 there will be the necessary prerequisites for the massive deployment of computer technology and computer-supported technologies to achieve a considerable growth in production in all economic areas." He even boasted that the GDR would catch up with the West through "highly productive, flexible automation" resulting in nothing less than a "revolution in work and living conditions."[6] A leader of the party's scientific bureau exhorted researchers at Karl Marx University in March 1989 to embrace the possibilities of the information age (or else): "We have placed certain key technologies, especially microelectronics to improve productivity, at the center of our development plans. Without microelectronics the future of the GDR is unimaginable, and they are the decisive basis for a complete structural transformation of our economy."[7]

In fact, in the late 1980s the GDR was manufacturing tens of thousands of computers, producing about 80 percent of the microcomputer chips that it required for domestic use and exporting thirty thousand microcomputers annually, mostly to the Soviet bloc. However, enormous investments in microcomputing failed to yield a product with comparative advantage. In the West the time required between the development of a prototype and production was roughly two years; it took nearly five years in the GDR. And, despite the GDR's advantage in cheap technical labor, East German microprocessors actually cost more than Western models.[8] Despite the public face leaders put on the issue, state economists reported to the Politburo in July 1989 that uncompetitive costs, the sluggish pace of innovation, and the limited export potential of the GDR's computer industry made it an unsuitable basis for sustained economic development (Gutmann 1999: 52–53).[9]

State economic advisers made efforts to convince political leaders of the need for decisive reforms but found themselves blocked by influential conservatives in the Politburo (Schürer 1999). Even so, an inflexible ideology and statistical falsification could only hide the truth for so long, and East German consumers knew what to conclude from mounting shortages. In September 1988 economics chief Günter Mittag conceded to the Politburo, "We are at a point at which things could just fall over" (Hertle and Stephan 1997: 37). Meanwhile, leaders continued to insist that the GDR's advanced technology, sophistication in planning, and productivity would make market reforms in the Chinese mode unnecessary.[10] Meanwhile, a report prepared for the Central Committee after the June 1989 CMEA conference explained that the GDR would have to begin purchasing Soviet commodities at world market prices. The USSR and Hungary had announced plans to join the General Agreement on Tariffs and Trade and submit to International Monetary Fund and World Bank oversight. Such steps threatened not only diplomatic isolation but also the collapse of East German import markets.[11]

As the situation grew bleaker, a sense of defeat reportedly haunted party leaders and top economic planners (Weber 2000; Hollander 1999; Gedmin 1993). Yet none took the risk of openly criticizing socialism, calling for a change of course, or denouncing the top party leadership. Despite the magnitude of the economic crisis in the GDR, no reformist faction threatened Honecker's grip. The threat to the party organization became manifest at the fraying periphery, in the industrial provinces of the GDR.

Disaffection in the Industrial Province of the GDR

Economic stagnation and diminished expectations haunted East Germans at the close of the 1980s. But the pain was not shared equally. Politically advantaged regions benefited from state investment in new industries, while the old industrial heartland of the GDR lost ground. The region of Saxony in the south of the country had been a wealthy, highly industrialized area with a distinct regional cultural and political identity. But in order to break up vestiges of regional autonomy, the provinces disappeared in the GDR's 1952 administrative reorganization. Saxony was divided into districts organized around its three principal cities of Leipzig, Dresden, and Karl-Marx-Stadt (Chemnitz). The following decades resulted in the relative stagnation of the region relative to progress made by northern districts and the administrative, economic, and scientific center in the East Berlin district (Kopstein 1999; Grundmann 1998; Friedheim 1997).

Between 1970 and 1987 gross industrial output in the districts of Dresden, Leipzig, and Karl-Marx-Stadt failed to keep up with the national average, with Leipzig having the smallest gains of any GDR district. Although the Saxon districts accounted for more than 40 percent of the GDR's gross industrial output, they were largely passed over for new investments in favor of the greater Berlin region or the high-tech belt in neighboring Thuringia (*SJDDR* 1989). Saxons also had reason to complain about their share of public goods. In the provision of health and social welfare benefits, the Saxon districts were generally at or near the GDR average. But in the crucial area of child care for working mothers, a hallmark of GDR social policy, the Saxon districts were all below the GDR average. The age and quality of housing in the south were also considerably below the national standard.

As the GDR economy attempted to modernize, Saxony fell behind in its proportion of tertiary-sector employment (38 percent of the labor force versus the GDR average of 43 percent). The gap can be seen as most pronounced when Saxon districts are compared with East Berlin, where about two-thirds of employees worked in tertiary sector (SB 1994/14: 32). In a socialist economy where the ownership of capital bestows few advantages, high household savings rates can be taken as an indicator of unmet consumer demand and thus of endemic shortages (Kornai 1992). Again, in the industrial south we find the highest levels of personal savings in the late 1980s. In Saxony, where, party sources make clear, citizens routinely and most loudly objected to shortages, residents of the Karl-Marx-Stadt district, for example, had per capita savings in 1988 nearly 20 percent greater than the GDR average, while Dresden districts residents had savings about 14 percent

FIGURE 2. Map of the Principal Cities and Regional Administrative Districts (*Bezirke*) of the GDR

1 INCH = 125 KM

TABLE 2. Economic and Social Indicators in the Saxon Districts, East Berlin, and the GDR on Average, 1988

District	Labor tertiary sector (%)	Index of gross industrial output in 1988 (1970 = 100)	Pop. growth 1980–88 (%)	Per capita savings (000s marks)
Leipzig	31.1	189	−2.9	9.6
Dresden	29.6	227	−2.2	10.5
Karl-Marx-Stadt	26.9	216	−3.1	10.9
Berlin (East)	47.1	235	+9.5	8.3
GDR average	31.7	228	−0.2	9.2

greater than average. By contrast, residents of East Berlin, with their better opportunities for consumption, had per capita savings 10 percent lower than the GDR average (*SJDDR* 1989). (See table 2.)

Although the reliable opinion data that would allow us to assess relative deprivation in Saxony is unavailable, population trends can be strong indicators of responses to perceived regional inequalities (Richter 1991; Grundmann, Müller-Hartmann, and Schmidt 1992). In the GDR patterns of internal migration reinforce the impression of a flourishing center and a declining industrial periphery. Although there was a slight decline of population in the GDR taken as a whole (−0.2 percent) during the 1980s, the decline in the three Saxon districts was considerably greater (−2.2 percent in Dresden, −2.9 percent in Leipzig, and −3.1 percent in Karl-Marx-Stadt). Indeed, since 1946 the population of the Saxon region had fallen by nearly 10 percent.

In 1988 80 percent of internal migration had East Berlin as its destination. East German demographers noted that "Berlin-centrism was a noticeable feature of the economic and social policy of the SED following the Eighth Party Congress [1974]. In order to realize the special plan for the development of the capital, a large portion of the economic resources of the GDR were concentrated in and around Berlin in order to make it the 'showplace of socialism'" (Grundmann, Müller-Hartmann, and Schmidt 1992: 1583).

Hospital beds per 1,000 pop.	Infant care spaces per 1,000 pop.	Housing with inside toilet in 1989 (%)	Housing new or modernized since 1971 (%)
11.8	2.0	69	9.6
9.6	1.76	73	9.8
9.3	1.76	54	6.5
11.6	2.58	95	25.3
10	2.18	76	13.5

Sources: *SJDDR* 1989, 1990; Kuhrt 1996: 33.

By way of contrast, demographers found in the south the "desolate and permanently worsening condition of the infrastructure," housing shortages, and a scarcity of attractive jobs that apparently sent migrants northward (1514).

Finally, the risky and difficult process of petitioning the state for permission to emigrate to the West is one of the best indicators of discontent with prevailing conditions in the GDR. Saxony, with less than a third of the GDR population, accounted for more than half of all applications for exit visas.[12] In the Dresden district the proportion of citizens willing to file applications for exit was nearly three times the GDR average. Although there were also many exit applicants in Berlin, the northern districts of Neubrandenburg, Rostock, Schwerin, and Frankfurt an der Oder, which were beneficiaries of GDR development strategies, had a demand for exit about half that of the GDR average. (See figure 3.) And when the Iron Curtain began to give way in the spring of 1989, about half of the nearly forty thousand citizens who risked illegal exit were from Saxon districts (Mitter and Wolle 1991: 82–92).

Saxons tended to blame the party leadership at the center for their deteriorating position. As a Leipzig white-collar worker explained, "Berlin was not the GDR. The GDR was in the provinces."[13] Saxon party officials were annoyed that profits generated by local industries were diverted to the "showplace" capital and felt snubbed by the decision to build newer,

FIGURE 3. Exit Applicants per 10,000 Population in GDR Districts, 1988

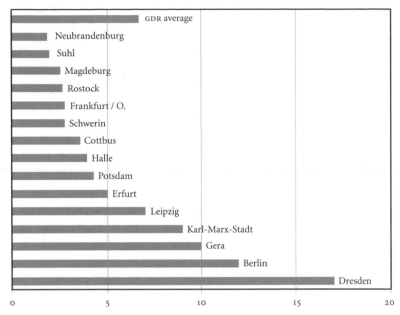

Source: Stiftung Archiv Parteien und Massenorganisationen der Deutschen Demokratischen Republik im Bundesarchiv DY 30/IV/2/2.039/308, p. 115.

more innovative industries elsewhere (Koch and Matthes 1993: 144; Friedheim 1997: 161–63). Moreover, the political impotence of the region was obvious during Honecker's tenure as chairman of the SED: no sitting member or candidate for the Politburo (twenty-five members) was drawn from the regional leadership of either Leipzig or Dresden (Koch and Matthes 1993: 145).

Although there was no open rupture with the party center, the archives of the Leipzig municipal and regional party organizations are replete with references to economic decline and its effect on local party coherence. Between 1987 and 1989 a range of enterprises reported an inability to meet planned production targets. Living standards and wages had actually begun to decline, and shortages of consumer goods became common. Capital investment was in short supply; factories deteriorated; and shortages of material and spare parts were constant problems. Leipzig, once a showplace of Saxon prosperity, provided dramatic visual evidence of sustained decline, neglect, and even rot. While the old town fell into decay, huge concrete housing estates went up on the outskirts of the city (the largest had more than thirty-five thousand units). Even so, in the decades since the Second World War, Leipzig's population declined by 12 percent.

Local officials bemoaned their inability to offer any concrete incentives to address production problems, the poor state of housing, and failing work discipline.[14] In the district less than 10 percent of housing units were new or had been modernized since 1971, and less than 70 percent were furnished with a bathroom. And a study of Leipzig's construction conglomerate in February 1989 uncovered "inadequate use of labor time, shortages, production delays, and poor organization."[15] Letters of complaint (*Eingaben*) also make clear that local officials knew how deeply angered citizens were by shortages of consumer goods. In 1988 the editors of the daily newspaper the *Leipziger Volkszeitung* reported to district leaders that fully half of all letters to the editor complained about poor or unavailable goods and services and long queues at state shops.[16]

In July 1988 municipal officials drafted a report depicting a restive population suffering from shortages, decaying housing, a dismal natural environment, and degraded infrastructure.[17] Officials and plant managers failed to enforce work rules, overlooking drunkenness and sloth on the job. Increasingly, rank-and-file party members openly lacked ideological commitment and were "seduced by the image of the West."[18] In one case from the summer of 1989, thirty-two employees of an engineering firm collectively resigned their party memberships on the grounds that they had lost faith in the party leadership. In statements explaining their action to the PKK, most cited support for Gorbachev's perestroika, gross economic mismanagement, and political errors by the ruling elite as grounds for their career-threatening resignations. One engineer realized during a visit to Japan as part of a technical delegation that "what I saw there we could never realize." Unwilling to "wait vainly for the bright economy of the future," he protested that "one should expect more than this after forty years of socialism."[19]

District officials also bemoaned the economic crisis. At a March 1989 party assembly, Leipzig's district party chairman, Horst Schumann, complained that Leipzig had the oldest housing stock in the GDR, the highest population density of any city, the greatest concentration of polluting industry, and the worst residential infrastructure in the country. Moreover, his district also had the fewest kindergartens, day-care centers, and schools relative to its population of any district. And yet, after bemoaning all this, the comrades had no choice but to follow the course being steered by East Berlin.[20]

Cadre Politics and the Erosion of Party Loyalty

Although the monitoring and sanctioning capacities of a regime are its front line of defense, the effectiveness of political control is rooted in the material and ideological rewards that can be offered by the authorities to their agents (Kiser 1999; see also North 1981: chap. 5). In short, loyalty is not merely a matter of idealism. It is also nourished by the material rewards that attend to faithful service. Without an expanding resource base, it becomes harder for a regime to retain the loyalty of existing agents and to attract new recruits.

Because it undercut its stated goals, economic decline tugged at the fabric of party rule in the GDR. It was the promise of social mobility and material prosperity even for people of humble origins that provided one of the great appeals of socialism. Without economic expansion, it was hard to sustain opportunities for social mobility or continually improving lifestyles. In the GDR of the 1980s, opportunities for upward mobility through the party cadres were vanishing, and the SED was becoming a "worker's party" in name only. Like other Marxist-Leninist ruling parties, the SED was increasingly dominated by administrative and professional occupations (Djilas 1953; Walder 1995; Szelenyi 1978; Szelenyi 1987). Between 1966 and 1986 the share of the party membership composed of highly educated cadres more than doubled. In 1986 nearly 40 percent of the cadres had completed higher education compared with less than 10 percent of the GDR labor force (Weber 1999: 334). As a new socialist middle class solidified its hold on the party, the proportion of production workers fell sharply, from nearly 60 percent in 1975 to less than 40 percent in 1988 (Ammer 1989: 4). In 1988 white-collar workers (7 percent), the intelligentsia (22 percent), and full-time state, party, and economic functionaries (23 percent) held a majority of party cards (Ammer 1989: 4; Weber 2000: 102).[21]

Party status promised privileges, including preferential opportunities for education, employment, and occupational advancement. It was a route into the socialist middle class for workers and peasants and their children. Yet in 1988 nearly 80 percent of the GDR's university students were the children of that middle class while only 10 percent were of working-class origin (Jessen 1999: 347; Solga 1994). Party members in good standing could enjoy access denied ordinary citizens, including not only scarce goods but also even travel in the "non-socialist world." By the 1980s, however, opportunities to join the party were also increasingly limited to those with educational credentials or social status, substantially limiting opportunities for upward mobility (Huinink and Solga 1994). The social closure that monopolized advantages for educated cadres began to immobilize the social system. In a 1986 survey conducted by the Central Institute for Youth Research (ZIJ), 65 percent of apprentice workers (ages 16–24) reported that they had no chance of entering party ranks (Friedrich, Förster, and Starke 1999: 142).

The evolution of the party cadre into a privileged caste was clearly reflected in a growing generational divide in the GDR. By the late 1980s more than a third of party members were over fifty years of age, with an average of forty-five years.[22] The leadership of the party was aging even more rapidly: the average age of the twenty-six members and candidates for the Politburo of the SED in 1989 was sixty-six. And the top of the pyramid had become a gerontocracy. Honecker and his inner circle had been members of the Communist Party since the 1920s. Nearly every Leipzig PKK study of party organizations noted poor relations with young workers. Local officials had so little to offer in the way of career advancement, recreational opportunities, or foreign travel that, in the words of one exasperated Leipzig official, "The youth are just not interested."[23] The "founding generation" of the 1950s could take pride in how people of working-class and peasant origins had attained professional and technical occupations as a result of the "antifascist-democratic" revolution and the mass exodus of the old middle class. Oral histories report that this era of social mobility created a strong sense of attachment to the socialist system (Plato 1993: 39–40; see also Niethammer 1991) and an instinctive loyalty to the party, especially among the intelligentsia (see, e.g., Schürer 1999).

For younger East Germans the old sources of loyalty apparently did not obtain, or they did not obtain as forcefully. The high rates of social mobility typical of the first decades of socialist rule could not be sustained once emigration tapered off after 1961 (Solga 1995; Huinink and Solga 1994; Jessen 1999). Elite social closure and economic stagnation further reduced opportunities for blue-collar workers and their children. Accordingly, from the mid-1980s on there was a well-documented decline in identification with the regime reported by the Institute for Youth Research. In 1975 nearly half of youth enrolled in training for blue-collar jobs reported strong identification with Marxism-Leninism, a support that fell to less than 10 percent in May 1989 (Friedrich, Förster, and Starke 1999: 146). During the same period the share of tenth-grade pupils that failed to identify with the GDR rose tenfold (4 percent to 43 percent).

The SED continued to enjoy success in winning support from those citizens whose life chances were deeply invested in party rule. For intellectuals who were in the shadow of the Third Reich and fearful of a revival of popular nationalism, the official ideology of antifascism and anti-imperialism was a source of attachment (Torpey 1995; Joppke 1995; Jarausch 1991). Surveys carried out by the Institute for Youth Research found a drastic decline in young peoples' identification with Marxism-Leninism, although students remained far more ideologically affiliated than their blue-collar counterparts. (See figure 4.) Despite generally gloomy reports concerning recruitment, Leipzig district party officials could point to successful recruitment in higher education and few on-campus expressions of political heterodoxy.[24]

The challenge to the loyalty that the privileged ranks of GDR citizens had to their system only became prominent with the rise of Gorbachev's reform agenda in the Soviet Union. PKK files drawn from two municipal districts in Leipzig with a total membership of about twenty thousand reveal that between January and September 1989 ninety-nine members illegally defected and more than two hundred were charged with political deviance. This is more than twice as many for these districts in 1988 and triple as many as in 1987.[25] The most common political offense by party members was the filing of exit petitions, which accounted for more than 60 percent of the actionable violations. Only 10 percent of the cases involved participation in a collective protest. Similar trends are evident across the country. In the months between January and August 1989, about thirty-six thousand members and member candidates of the SED were expelled for violations of party norms (Otto 1995: 1491).

Defection from the GDR while traveling abroad and the filing of legal petitions for exit visas among party members were the most common offenses resulting in expulsion.[26] But instances of collective defiance also began to appear in the late 1980s. In one episode from early September 1989 at a

FIGURE 4. Percentage of GDR Youth (16–24) Strongly Identifying with Marxism-Leninism, by Social Category, 1975–1988

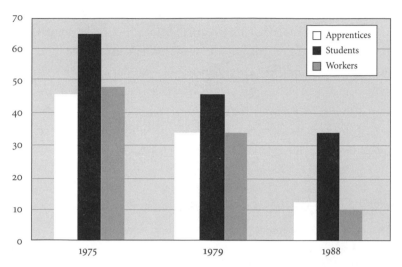

Source: Zentralinstitut für Jugendforschung data reported in Friedrich, Förster, and Starke 1999: 145–46.

Leipzig engineering firm, thirty-three longtime party members (almost 10 percent of the local party organization) collectively resigned their party cards.[27] The group consisted of twenty-nine men and four women, who on average were forty-three years old and had eighteen years of tenure in the party. A third of them were engineers and administrators. In the twenty-eight surviving letters of resignation, sixty-seven concrete reasons for resignation were given, nearly half of which (thirty-one) were political disagreements with the policies of the SED and its leaders, about a third (twenty-four) were economic complaints, and an eighth (eight) made reference to workplace grievances. Only four letters listed personal convictions—religious, environmental, political—that were at odds with socialism.[28] Ideological "deviants" of this kind were a dangerous manifestation for the regime. They were not the "naïve" young people, "seduced by Western capitalism," nor the "reactionaries" and "antisocial elements" that state propaganda routinely blamed for spreading dissent, but rather disappointed loyalists who had reason to expect better performance from the system.

Before October 1989, when the regime began its swift collapse, such incidents of critical voice were rare. Although disaffection was becoming evident within the ranks, PKK files make clear that dissenting voices were usually silenced. Despite warnings from the secret police to the contrary, the party leadership under Honecker misinterpreted the apparent lack of dissent as pointing to the strength of their regime. In its remoteness from the leadership, however, the party apparatus was substantially decayed. A Leipzig PKK report described the party membership as "impatient and wanting rapid change" and increasingly prepared to resign when corrected or threatened with party sanctions.[29] The first public indication of this in the form of critical voice from within the ranks came only when Gorbachev's reforms ran up directly against Marxist-Leninist orthodoxy.

The Sputnik *Affair*

Throughout the Soviet bloc in the 1980s, reform movements made the most progress when they arose from within the party itself or when a significant number of party members shifted their loyalty to the opposition. Yet in the GDR the party had no reform wing and offered no openings to dissidents or party reformists (Klein 1997; Fricke 1984; Weber 2001). Just two orthodox leaders, Walter Ulbricht (1949–71) and Erich Honecker (1971–89), dominated the party from its founding until the verge of its collapse. Both insisted on narrow interpretations of Marxism-Leninism and enforced strict norms of party discipline. The SED proudly distinguished itself as an implacable foe of liberalism and deviation from the Leninist model.

Under these conditions socialist intellectuals had little choice but to endure the degeneration of Marxism into what Ota Šik describes as "sacrosanct 'Marxist-Leninist' doctrine, the pseudoscholastic confrontation of current ideas and theories with these axiomatic dogmas" (1981: 24). Nevertheless, because of the disasters of German history the GDR's official antifascism remained appealing for many. The regime trumpeted its moral superiority to West Germany, proclaiming that its antifascist policies and loyalty to the USSR made it Europe's "pillar of peace and socialism" (Honecker 1979). But as space for political dialogue expanded elsewhere in the region, and with fresh winds blowing in from Moscow, many East German intellectuals began to experience alienation from a regime they had once accepted as a historical necessity. Some reported feeling trapped in an "Ice Age" of political and ideological immobility (Philipsen 1993: 86). Still, few dared criticize the course of the party leadership. Silenced by their encapsulation in party-controlled institutions, even self-proclaimed reformers like philosopher Michael Brie were prepared to do no more than hope for "gradual self-transformation of the society" and to exercise oblique criticism "from on bended knee."[30]

In view of Honecker's intransigence and his Politburo's full control over the party's mechanisms of surveillance and cadre selection, only externally initiated challenges to the prevailing orthodoxy were possible. On assuming power, Gorbachev used a policy of "glasnost"—that is, openness and debate—as a weapon to attack conservative opposition to his reform program, even encouraging "self-criticism" within the Soviet party (Nove 1989; Hansen 1991; Kotkin 2001). In addition to reform initiatives at home, Gorbachev pursued détente with the West and approved of innovation in the socialist camp. In 1986 he directly chided his East German comrades for their failure to reexamine their course. However, at the Eleventh Party Congress that year Honecker indignantly refused to follow Moscow's lead. In place of reform, the GDR resolved to pursue a policy of "renewal through continuity" (Kuhrt 1996).

Honecker's abrupt turn from the GDR's accustomed subservience to the USSR proved a cognitive blow to the system. Party ideologues began to invoke the early (and previously denounced) idea of "national roads to socialism," seeking new legitimacy in classical German culture and newly defined "progressive" figures of German history like Bismarck and Luther (Meuschel 1992: 287–88). The old slogan "Learning from the Soviet Union means learning to win!" was replaced with "GDR, socialist fatherland" and "Socialism in the colors of the GDR." The party's leading ideologist went so far as to dismiss the idea of reform by explaining that the GDR need not change its own wallpaper just because the USSR wanted to do some remodeling.[31]

For its part, the ruling elite of the GDR rightly regarded Gorbachev with deep suspicion. He regarded them as "little Brezhnevs" out of step with new realities. His calls for democratization made little sense to the GDR elite; unlike Gorbachev, Honecker and his clique faced no threat from powerful regional party bosses against whom glasnost could be a weapon. Furthermore, Honecker and his close associates were justifiably fearful of the political consequences of reform. The East German elite saw perestroika as leading to the "restoration of the market economy" and feared glasnost would create "free space for demagogues and backward forces" through naïve endorsement of human rights (Eberlein 2000: 449). Additionally, the past prosperity of the GDR provided a false sense of insulation. Even with mounting evidence of stagnation, Economics Minister Günter Mittag quipped that Russians could have "full shops or perestroika" because one could not have both (Schabowski 1991: 183). Indeed, so complete was the rejection of Gorbachev that discussion of reform became taboo even within the Politburo.[32] As the two "brother" states grew apart, the personal animosity between Honecker and Gorbachev also grew increasingly apparent. In 1988 the Soviet premier learned that his counterpart was failing to disclose the details of their meetings to members of his government (Adomeit 1998: 238–39). Yet as there was no routine mechanism to facilitate a change of leadership, without a palace coup the anti-reformers would remain in power no matter how much East Germans craved change. Gorbachev made gestures indicating that his comrades in East Berlin were out of step, but he did not play a role in changing the SED leadership until weeks after the fall of Honecker (Bunce 1999: 59–63; Kotkin 2001).

Regardless of what the party elite did to suppress reformism, Gorbachev's endorsement of reform and greater freedom quickened hopes for change and could not be blamed on "bourgeois human rights demagoguery," as would have been done in the past. According to Stasi reports, a substantial majority of SED members apparently favored Gorbachev's reforms over Honecker's policies, and violations of Leninist norms were mushrooming (Kuhrt 1996: 249–52; Otto 1995: 1487–88). And the limited public opinion data that we have from Leipzig's Institute for Youth Research makes the trend of mounting disaffection obvious, with trust in the party falling sharply among both students (−21 percent) and SED members (−33 percent) between 1986 and 1989. In 1988 the institute found that 83 percent of East German young people were sympathetic to Gorbachev, rising to 90 percent or more for students and party members (Friedrich, Förster, and Starke 1999: 152). For them, Gorbachev was a bright symbol of hope for change. By the spring of 1989 fewer than half of party members under age twenty-five were confident in the leadership of the SED.[33] (See figure 5.)

With reformism spreading across the Soviet bloc, Polish, Hungarian, and even Soviet books, films, and publications became gradually unavailable in

FIGURE 5. Percentage of GDR Youth (16–24) Reporting "Full Trust" in SED Leadership, by Social Category, 1970–1989

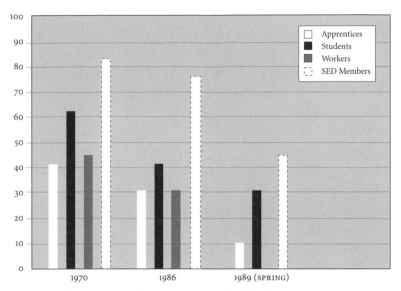

Source: Zentralinstitut für Jugendforschung data reported in Friedrich, Förster, and Starke 1999: 141–42.

the GDR, and in 1988 a host of critical Soviet films were banned.[34] Honecker made clear that Gorbachev's liberalism had no place in the GDR. In a speech delivered in Leipzig in 1987, he was defiant in his defense of censorship: "Communists are duty-bound to take a position against attacks on the policies of the party, on the socialist state of workers and peasants, and against any displacement and falsification of Marxist-Leninist theory, *no matter where it comes from*" (emphasis added).[35]

In this context the sudden ban imposed on the German-language edition of the Soviet press digest *Sputnik* in November 1988 provoked the first public opposition to his conservative course from within the ranks of the party.[36] *Sputnik*'s circulation had increased markedly since Gorbachev announced perestroika, reaching nearly two hundred thousand subscribers in 1988.[37] An East Berlin worker explained, "Prior to Gorbachev, nobody ever looked at a Soviet newspaper, but since then the papers sold out quickly; we passed them around, talked about them. We had an incredible desire for freedom of the press" (Philipsen 1993: 130–31). An astute observer in the Politburo interpreted this growing interest as a "signal of general discontent" because there had been so little popular interest in Soviet affairs in the past (Eberlein 2000: 459). Worried that the Soviet press was becoming unacceptably liberal in spirit, the regime let the October 1988 issue of *Sputnik* go undelivered. In response to subscriber outcry, on November 19, 1988, a small notice appeared in the party organ *Neues Deutschland* announcing that the Ministry for Post and Communications had canceled the magazine because it was a threat to "German-Soviet friendship" and contained "distorting contributions to history."[38]

Almost at once a flood of protest letters and petitions began to reach state media and party organizations. A Stasi report on November 20 warned party leaders that they were being almost universally condemned and had "unleashed a massive wave of very critical opinion" (Kuhrt 1996: 249–51). Radio Moscow promptly described the SED's step as the result of a "misunderstanding" and expressed hope "that this troubling incident will be corrected with time." *Neues Deutschland* countered on November 25 that *Sputnik* was neither a theoretical organ of the Communist Party of the USSR nor a reflection of its official positions. The magazine was guilty of "distorted depictions of the social achievements of the Soviet people," which were "unacceptable to those who want friendship with the Soviet Union."[39]

But this time a stern rebuke failed to silence the criticism. From November 19, 1988, through January 1, 1989, the SED received eight hundred petitions and protest letters from the Leipzig district alone, about half written by party members. The Leipzig district PKK reported "aggressive," "closed-minded," and "threatening" reactions to the ban in the party rank and file. In the Dresden district, party leaders reported more than a thousand letters protesting the ban. Both Stasi and PKK sources further reported that universities, technical schools, local branches of the Free German Youth (Freie Deutsche Jugend, FDJ), locals, and local branches of the League for Soviet-German Friendship (Gesellschaft für Deutsch-Sowjetische Freundschaft, DSF) produced an inordinate share of complaints. An analysis of more than four hundred letters to the editor of the party organ *Neues Deutschland* in the month following the *Sputnik* ban reveals that nearly 90 percent directly condemned the party or its press policy. Prior to the ban only about a quarter of letters dared to criticize the party (Koch and Matthes 1993: 139).

As it progressed, the *Sputnik* affair made the greatest impression on two groups essential to the regime's stability: lower-echelon functionaries and the socialist intelligentsia. Close examination of the records of petitions for redress (*Eingaben*) and PKK interrogations show that most petitions had been written by comrades "who for the first time turned against the party with their provocative questions." A longtime party member protested to the Central Committee on November 20, "Here in the rank and file there are ever louder calls for 'more information' and complaints against the rosy reports [*Schönfärberei*] in the press, radio, and television. In my opinion, these attitudes are the result of the changes in the Soviet Union. And now this ban on *Sputnik?* It only throws oil on the fire."[40] Similarly, in a detailed, three-page letter denouncing the government's "shameful" actions (complete with footnotes!), two Leipzig academics reproached the government for failing to accept "glasnost and democratization" and condemned the "Honecker circle" for "fear of change."[41]

PKK files suggest that in response to the outcry party discipline was most effective on those whose careers directly depended on good standing with the party. When the PKK interrogated subjects whose position was not tied to a party function, it found that some refused to withdraw their complaints or further protested the party's "administrative arrogance."[42] A Leipzig Church member who had written a protest letter to the Central Committee told his interrogators, "You cannot simply ban things. I am a free man, and I have the right to read and know everything. I have a feeling that our information is unsatisfactory.... We finally have to publicize our errors and mistakes and admit them like the party of the USSR.... The GDR can't go on this way; the economy is collapsing."[43]

The *Sputnik* ban also stirred collective protest. Workers staged slow-downs; students in Jena and publishers in Berlin drafted protest tracts; collective petitions flooded party offices; and democracy activists released scores of balloons reading "SPUTNIK" into the audience at the international documentary film festival in Leipzig. Dissidents drew the attention of the international press on East Berlin's Alexanderplatz with a banner proclaiming "Freedom for *Sputnik*—For a Free Press."[44] At Weimar's College for Architecture, angry students distributed leaflets calling for press freedoms and walked out of their mandatory seminar on Marxism-Leninism. When authorities tried to restore order, defiant student leaders were applauded for demanding "renewal in the sense of perestroika and glasnost." In the effort to restore order, seventeen students were expelled from the party and five from the college.[45]

Criticism blossomed in unexpected corners. An official in the Society for German-Soviet Friendship reported about its members: "They ask why the ban was imposed rather than opening up an active public debate in our own media and letting the contentious questions be asked. Doesn't the party trust educated citizens of the GDR to separate the wheat from the chaff, even in the case of *Sputnik*?" Party officials worried the ban was simply counterproductive: "Because of the non-distribution of *Sputnik* many more people are interested in it, including those who would have never read it before."[46] In an internal report of the Free German Youth, functionaries warned that the ban produced a "spontaneous reaction" and "unleashed critical discussions."[47]

The *Sputnik* affair proved a particular shock to intellectuals. The philosopher André Brie drafted a collective petition denouncing the ban. Under pressure, including threats that he would be denied academic promotion or be dismissed from the university, Brie withdrew in humiliation (Philipsen 1993: 179). Others, however, made a lasting break with the party leadership as a consequence of the affair. A Leipzig historian, Werner Bramke, explained, "We did not suppress this eruption of outrage by the students, but rather encouraged it. . . . The comrades in Berlin got so nervous because the most severe protests emanated from the very department in which Marxism-Leninism was taught" (Philipsen 1993: 105–6). In Neubrandenburg physicians and hospital staff denounced Leninism and distributed a letter calling for glasnost and the toleration of dissent.[48] At a mandatory assembly at Leipzig's Karl-Marx-University in March 1989, the university's leading party secretary noted with alarm: "We believed that we understood the political situation well and were surprised, therefore, by the lack of class consciousness in a few party and FDJ collectives and in a few instructors, especially in the social sciences, in connection with the *Sputnik* discussion. Clearly apparent in this discussion were underground opinions, insecurities, and, in part, doubts and questions that rejected basic political principles."[49] As the party secretary of the university's commercial school admitted, "Our political situation was also somewhat shaky in the fall of 1988 because so few instructors were clearly loyal to the party in their responses . . . both within and outside the classroom."[50]

Lasting effects of the ban could be felt in work collectives and party organizations throughout the GDR (Deese 1997: 216). In the wake of the controversy, a local party secretary confessed, "I have no credibility with people anymore; they simply make fun of me, ridicule me now" (Philipsen 1993: 130–31). An older worker in a machine-tool factory explained that he was "no longer a true comrade who can actually represent the party," while another admitted to the PKK that "he had carried around the idea [of resigning] for a long time because it was really self-deception for him to work in the party any longer. . . . He does not want to be a member anymore. He has no trust left in the party."[51] Jan J., an FDJ functionary, was accused of making subversive remarks in front of young people. When called before the PKK, he professed loyalty to Gorbachev over the "senile" leadership of the party because "they could not get used to the new style of leadership." One Paul F. stood up at his Monday party assembly and announced that "inner party democracy has ended" and called for the ouster of corrupt party leaders.[52] Local FDJ functionaries justified public dissent in Gorbachev's name.[53]

PKK investigators uncovered shocking statements openly made by party members. Party leaders were criticized openly as "dogmatic, conservative, and incapable of change." In public forums people insisted that "perestroika would also be good for the GDR" and demanded more freedom and democracy.[54] Although economic problems and "diminished faith in GDR socialism" were found to be factors in the upsurge of "doubting our policies, discontent, grumbling, and inactivity among party members," the archival evidence reveals that many wayward comrades objected not to socialism as such but rather to the regime and its policies (Kuhrt 1996: 249–52). For them, the *Sputnik* ban was a sign that there could be no renaissance of socialism under Honecker.

The *Sputnik* ban seems to have functioned as the kind of public shock that sometimes breaks through prevailing conventions of preference falsification and public dissimulation (Kuran 1998). The incident revealed, in hundreds of petty protests, a clear preference among a substantial portion of party members for reform and liberalization. Once the first sincere expressions of support for Gorbachev were made, a cascade of complaints followed. In January 1989 the PKK reported to the Central Committee in Berlin: "There are a growing number of party members and candidate members that must be excluded from the party because they have stood against the general line of the party, negated the successes of the socialist state, and damage the party or betray the GDR through their continual grumbling and complaint."[55]

In its resolution, however, the *Sputnik* affair points to the obstacles to reformist voice in an orthodox Leninist regime. The records of the Leipzig PKK make clear that the apparatus of control still functioned: nearly 80 percent of party members called before a disciplinary committee to "clarify" their objections to the ban withdrew their criticism as a result of interrogation.[56] Incidents like *Sputnik* did not lead to party collapse or mass defection: the regime's control over the Leninist disciplinary apparatus and the mechanisms of cadre selection blocked reformists from mobilizing support or articulating a clear ideological alternative to current policies. Nevertheless, the affair was evidently damaging. The largely spontaneous manifestation of voice evident in the *Sputnik* affair revealed to individual party members that their private disdain for the regime was more widely shared than they might have imagined. In this sense, the coherence of the party had been compromised.

Leninism and the Perversion of Voice

In an 1842 essay Karl Marx observed, "Censorship makes every banned text, bad or good, into an extraordinary text" (1972: 60). SED conservatives rightly feared satisfying demands for political liberalization as a threat to political control, but in 1988 Honecker's censorship of a Soviet *Reader's Digest* provoked an extraordinary show of defiance. The *Sputnik* affair was a symptom of a system confronting institutional blockage of what were widely perceived as necessary reforms. Although it revealed widely held preferences for reform within the ranks of the SED, in the end the *Sputnik* affair pointed to the ineffectiveness of dissent in an orthodox Leninist party. So long as hardliners retained control over cadre selection and the apparatus of surveillance, there could be no grassroots reform movement. As Rosa Luxemburg's (1919) critique of Leninism foresaw, silencing critical voice secured Communist power at a terrible and ultimately disabling cost to the party of Lenin.

In a very general sense, the decay of the GDR shows that it was not immune to the institutional pathologies of the Leninist system, such as falsified performance data, soft budgets, and the politics of dissimulation (Kornai 1992; Jowitt 1991; Kuran 1995; Solnick 1998). The Czech socialist Ota Šik observed: "Whatever the functionaries have not reported does not exist. But since information from the base is filtered on its way up and, by generalizing, is made to conform to regulations . . . the final result will be mis-information" (1981: 61). The GDR's state and party archives reveal abundant evidence of these pathologies in the everyday life of the regime.

Yet, as the *Sputnik* affair indicates, even a sick mono-organizational re-gime need not die from its institutional afflictions; some change in the repressive equilibrium must occur either to affect a cure or to render the disease fatal. Janos Kornai argues: "Stalinist classical socialism is repressive and inefficient, but it constitutes a coherent system. When it starts reforming itself, that coherence slackens and its internal contradictions strengthen. . . . Reform is doomed to fail: the socialist system is unable to renew itself so as to prove viable in the long run" (1992: xxv). Similarly, Andrew Walder (1994) contends, "Just as departures from Leninist party principles—in the form of organized opposition within the party and without—would lead to exten-sive political changes in these regimes, so would departures from central planning, by weakening the party's control over property and opportunity" (1994: 299).[57]

Market reforms and political liberalization allowed social movements, small entrepreneurs, and political reformists to act as "seeds of pluralism" (Kornai 1992: 418). In the Soviet Union Gorbachev's reforms provided sub-ordinates with opportunities to seize administrative means for their own ends, thereby facilitating the "disintegration of structural controls" (Solnick 1998: 3).[58] The unintended result was a "bank run" by officials eager to seize "their" share of collapsing enterprises as agents began "preparing for a life after Communism" (Solnick 1998: 245; see also Bunce 1999). Something like this appears to have happened in China and in large parts of Eastern Europe in the late 1980s, but not in the GDR.

If it was not reform that undermined the SED, then the demobilization of the Communist state has to be explained, according to many researchers, by reference to an ideological crisis of socialism. For a Leninist regime, or any other type, it is not enough for the citizens to obey simply out of fear or out of their narrow material interest; to be effective, there must be at least some identification between rulers and their agents (Kiser 1999). North observes that "the costs of maintenance of an existing order are inversely related to the perceived legitimacy of the existing system. To the extent that the partici-pants believe the system is fair, the costs of enforcing the rules are enor-mously reduced" (1981: 53–54). But Ken Jowitt (1991) maintains that vital

Leninist regimes are based on a staff of "true believers" for whom revolutionary idealism is the prime motivation and whose ruthlessness and selflessness animates the system.

Like any faith, however, this one can subside. Changing conditions that reduce tension with the outside world or undermine the "purported certainty and purported effectiveness" (Goldfarb 1991) of Marxism-Leninism—such as Gorbachev's call for liberalization and reform—create terrible dilemmas for ideological "true believers." Ideological loyalists unhappy with the performance of the regime either must exit the party and abandon all institutional influence or remain within its structure and express the required fealty to the party leadership. Indeed, because of the peculiar characteristics of the Leninist system, true believers are not always the last to leave the party, as we would otherwise expect. In the comparative history of Communism, we see over and over again that a handful of zealous true believers (generally intellectuals) openly break with the party out of a sense of frustrated idealism. Inevitably forced out of the party, they are confined to the dissident camp, where they fight for the "true" ideals of socialism.[59]

Let us examine again Hirschman's model. If the returns to loyalty are decreasing, we would expect a stepwise neutralization of the organization that reduces its effectiveness. This neutralization would be born of a passivity that mimics loyalty but in practice destroys initiative and eschews sacrifice. Because this process is silent, it helps to unravel Tocqueville's puzzle of the intransigent regime that suddenly collapses. Prior to an opportunity for exit or voice, creeping demobilization could hobble the basic organs of even a well-consolidated regime. As Timur Kuran (1995) has shown, the withdrawal of active support would remain largely opaque to leaders because their agents have been given such clear incentives to dissimulate.

In this scenario, reformist voice would only emerge once a profound crisis has become so obvious that the system begins to disintegrate and elites begin to factionalize. But by this point the cause of reform is severely, if not fatally, compromised.[60] In the case of the GDR, it is clear that the Honecker regime remained in control in the wake of the *Sputnik* episode, but it is also evident that it failed to provide compelling incentives—material or ideal—to sustain its agents' zeal. There was neither a cadre of committed officials prepared to risk everything to save the dictatorship nor a set of credible reformers in the SED ready to take up the reigns of power when conditions reached the crisis point in the fall of 1989.

CHAPTER 3

No Exit: The Niche Society and the Limits of Coercive Surveillance

The government hears only its own voice. It knows that it hears only its own voice and yet deceives itself that it hears the people's voice and demands of the people that it is also deceived. For its part, the populace sinks partly into dissent, partly into skepticism, and turns entirely away from public life.

—KARL MARX, "DEBATTEN ÜBER DIE PRESSFREIHEIT"

The unexpected turn of events in East Germany in 1989 leaves us trying to explain the apparent failure of mechanisms of social control despite abundant evidence of their prior success. Even if Eastern European regimes were illegitimate in the eyes of their citizens, this need not have led to their collapse. The popular illegitimacy of an authoritarian regime may prove little since it may have been "illegitimate" at birth.[1] Moreover, it risks tautology to take the rise of social movements against Communism as the evidence of its preceding illegitimacy (Przeworski 1991).

As we saw in the preceding chapter, there is substantial evidence that the advent of the Gorbachev era decertified the East German regime's orthodox Marxism-Leninism. But what of the bulk of the population outside the party apparatus, which presumably cared far less for ideological debates than for practical affairs and immediate interests? For Christiane Lemke (1991) and Sabrina Ramet (1995), the failure of political socialization produced an emergent "civil society" of autonomous values and lifestyles that undermined the regime. This argument, however, hinges on a thin conception of civil society. A civil society worthy of the name must possess communicative structures and generate new ideas, networks, and public associations and make reference to a public sphere not entirely subsumed by the state. In contrast to the oppositional civil society that grew out of the Solidarity movement in Poland (Osa 2003; Goldfarb 1991; Ost 1991), East Germany of the late 1980s was not so much a nascent civil society as a fragmented "niche society" of insulated, relatively isolated social networks (Völker and Flap 2001). It is not even clear that the GDR failed to socialize its citizens politically; at the very least it instilled distinctively socialist values among its youth (Friedrich, Förster, and Starke 1999). Long after 1989, egalitarian, collectivist political values and hostility to religion remained strong among East Germans (Kluegel, Mason, and Wegener 1995; Weil, Huffman, and Gautier 1993; Froese and Pfaff 2001). It appears that the GDR did succeed, at least to some extent, in inculcating socialist attitudes and values.

Other explanations of the failure of socialism focus not on popular values but on how everyday forms of resistance slowly undermined the authority of the state. Jeffrey Kopstein (1996) argues that small-scale acts of everyday resistance "chipped away" at the regime such that "long-term creeping immobilization of [the] regime" caused by workers "w[ore] down a despotic state" (393) by raising the costs of securing their compliance. The problem with that argument is, however, that such diffuse pressure is a far cry from political voice. Ordinary East Germans had neither the means nor the opportunity to wear down the state through collective action. Despite abundant evidence of tensions between workers and the party in the workplace, there is no clear evidence of a "culture of rebellion" (Wickham-Crowley 1991) in the GDR. After 1953 the population of the GDR was largely subdued; rebelliousness was more characteristic of neighboring Poland, where mass protest repeatedly shook the state (Fulbrook 1995; on Poland, see Ekiert 1997 and Osa 2003). Regardless of what popular resentment or everyday resistance could achieve, ordinary citizens posed no challenge to party control. Foot-dragging and sloth weakened economic performance, but, in comparison with other countries in the region, the GDR was relatively orderly and productive. And despite growing interest in "everyday" forms of resistance among subaltern groups, despotic regimes usually remain in place in spite of such diffuse opposition (see, e.g., Scott 1990; Wedeen 1999).

Rather than focusing on the penetration of official ideology or on subaltern resistance, we might instead consider the basic political economy underlying the struggle to maintain political order. The GDR regime offered an implicit bargain: political compliance in exchange for social security and material welfare. This bargain provided incentives for most citizens to go along with the regime, given that the status quo was enforced and exit was unavailable. So long as a regime enforces an absolute political monopoly, the majority of people would prefer to improve their own lot through opportunistic compliance than assume the costs of collective action aimed at challenging the state. As Mancur Olson frankly observes, "Regimes can often survive when they are unpopular because they have the selective incentives arising from their guns, tax receipts, their monopoly of the printing press, and so on" (quoted in Lichbach 1994: 259).

Before 1989 the GDR experienced little of the turbulence that affected neighboring socialist states, in part because of material security and levels of social welfare that were envied throughout the world and in part because the police apparatus was so intrusive. The population apparently adapted to the socialist system, and voice was silenced. Nevertheless, mass rebellion suddenly occurred. In order to understand why, we have to explore the twin effects of state repression and state-provided welfare.

Blocked Exit and Social Control in the GDR

The coercive restraint on individual mobility is a hallmark of Leninist states. The USSR forbade emigration and even imposed internal passport controls. With the expansion of Soviet socialism into East Central Europe after World War II, socialist states fenced themselves off from the West. Churchill's metaphor of the "Iron Curtain" that had descended across Europe "from Stettin to Trieste" hinted at the extensive efforts made to deny millions of people an exit option from the expanding Soviet system. For the GDR, exit always posed a special threat. Born of the Soviet occupation, it contained within its territory the old Reich capital of Berlin, now divided among the Four Powers. When the East German state was established in 1949, East Berlin was declared the "capital of the GDR," but the western zones of the city remained a refuge. For its part, the Federal Republic facilitated exit not only by offering safe haven to East German refugees but also by guaranteeing them full citizenship rights. Even when Chancellor Willy Brandt's *Ostpolitik* of the early 1970s sought an accommodation with the GDR that recognized its legitimate statehood, the government of the FRG insisted that Germans made up one nation and that its emigration policy was consistent with the ideal of national self-determination (Stokes 1991: 158).

West Germany and especially its outpost in Berlin thus posed an enduring threat to the GDR so long as the socialist system failed to guarantee its citizens public goods, economic opportunities, and civil liberties comparable to those of its neighbor (Hardin 1974). But the availability of exit varied with its costs. Prior to the crisis of 1989–90, the GDR experienced two distinctive phases of exit as a political phenomenon.

As figure 6 indicates, the emigration phenomenon can be roughly divided into two phases. The first phase (1949–61) was one of mass emigration in reaction to the establishment of the socialist regime in 1949 and the consolidation of Communist power. An abrupt change in 1961 marks the second phase (1962–88), characterized by a policy of selective emigration.

During the first phase about 2.7 million East Germans "voted with their feet" by fleeing westward, chiefly across Berlin's zonal boundaries.[2] The political implications were enormous. As early as 1953 leading Soviet officials observed that mass migration suggested that "huge dissatisfaction" prevailed in the GDR and concluded that armed force was necessary to preserve the stability of the regime (Adomeit 1998: 93; see also Ostermann 2001). The extent of that discontent was made manifest in a single, shattering instance of popular rebellion: in June 1953 the Ulbricht regime faced a massive popular uprising that began with a construction workers' strike. Order was restored when Soviet troops and tanks retook the streets, but the flight of citizens from an unloved regime continued.

Mass flight had crippling economic effects and undermined effective political control (Klessmann 1988; Weber 1999; Ross 2001). Technocrats complained that the exit problem imperiled the state's industrial development plan.[3] An employee of the optical firm Carl-Zeiss-Jena recalled of that time, "There was always somebody else missing."[4] Despairing of its powers of persuasion, the GDR made planning or conducting "flight from the republic" (*Republikflucht*) a state crime (Ross 2001). Nevertheless, between 1957 and 1961 more than one million people fled, including tens of thousands of physicians, scientists, teachers, and engineers (*BfG* 1961). And these exiters

FIGURE 6. Emigration from the GDR, 1949–1990

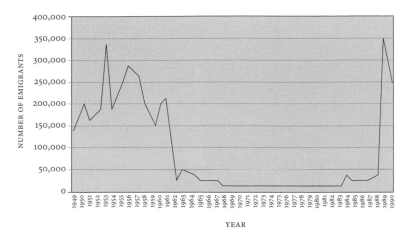

Source: Bundesministerium für Gesamtdeutschenfragen, 1990.

could no longer be written off as "fascist remnants" without whom the GDR could still thrive: 65 percent of the educated cadres that exited in 1960 had attended secondary school or obtained higher education after 1945 and over four thousand were members of the ruling party.[5] In fact, more than half of the refugees to the FRG between 1952 and 1960 were twenty-five years old or younger.

In the first half of 1961, two hundred thousand East Germans fled. In March 1961 Khrushchev and Ulbricht agreed to address the profound "vulnerability" of the GDR (Weber 1999: 221). Rumors of a crackdown were rife, and nearly fifty thousand people fled across the boundaries during the first two weeks of August. And then during the night of August 13, 1961, the security forces backed by party militia closed all crossing points between East and West Berlin along the forty-five-kilometer border. The Council of Ministers defended the extraordinary measure by declaring it necessary to reduce superpower tensions, prevent the intrusion of Western spies, and deter West German "imperialists" and "revanchists" from provoking war. But even the official press conceded that attractive job opportunities in the West had led to intolerable migration.[6]

After August 1961, some citizens continued to attempt exit from the GDR, but few succeeded. Elaborate border fortifications that came to include double cement walls, a "death zone" of minefields, booby traps, and alarm devices, watchtowers, and special units of border troops made flight a deadly gamble. In all, nearly one thousand people lost their lives in accidents or to mines and gunfire in attempting to cross the Berlin Wall or other frontiers right up until November 1989. Less than 5 percent of the thousand or so attempted illegal border crossings each year were successful.[7] Thousands of citizens were also arrested for violating the borders of other socialist countries in hopes of reaching the West.

Only a trickle of emigrants made it out. Between 1962 and 1988 an average of about twenty-five thousand GDR citizens relocated to the FRG annually. The vast majority of these exits were permitted by the government under a policy intended to allow the exit (or expulsion) of citizens considered troublesome, inessential, or prone to disloyalty. The policy was formalized in the revised citizenship law of 1967, which provided guidelines for the "Application for Removal of GDR Citizenship." Citizens found guilty of actions against the interests of the state or prone to "especially serious antisocial behavior" could be expelled by the Interior Ministry. The law also permitted certain citizens to petition for exit visas, especially pension-age people or members of divided families who were deemed "genuinely humane cases."[8] But government policy made it difficult for educated and working-age citizens to exit, with the Interior Ministry setting a guideline that no more than three thousand legal exits of citizens below retirement age should be allowed in a given year.[9] In 1975 half of exit visa applications were granted but only a small fraction of them (6 percent) had attained higher education.[10]

The selective emigration policy was an effective mechanism of social control. In 1976 the Interior Minister decreed, "In order to minimize the political damage to the GDR persons with a hostile, negative attitude as well as criminal and asocial elements that persistently pursue emigration . . . should be allowed to emigrate."[11] In the 1970s more than 60 percent of working-age adults who were permitted to leave had been previously convicted of political offenses or were deemed incorrigibly "oppositional" in attitude. Probably the most effective, inexpensive, and even profitable form of repression at the SED's disposal was the ransoming (*Freiverkauf*) of more than one thousand dissidents and other nonconformists each year to West Germany. These "ransomed" citizens were expelled on such grounds as "ideological disagreement" with the party, public agitation for civil rights, conscientious objection to compulsory military service, and "inappropriate expressions" of religious faith.[12]

Applying for an exit visa came at a high cost. Since it was regarded as de facto sedition, an exit application resulted in expulsion from the party, dismissal from one's job, and a prohibition from pursuing a professional career or occupying a state office (*Berufsverbot*). Upon exit one was forced to surrender all assets to the state. Since it was by no means assured that an application would be granted or that even if it eventually were how long one would have to wait, these were indeed severe sanctions. And applicants forfeited all privileges and benefits the system had to offer. Educated professionals who dared to apply for exit found themselves unemployed or reduced to the lowest sort of manual labor for years at a time. So long as exit came at so high a price and carried such risks, even highly dissatisfied citizens had little choice but to accommodate themselves to the security and welfare arrangements developed by the Honecker regime.

Security and Welfare

The construction of the Wall allowed party leaders to stabilize the economy and look for new ways to buttress social control. Under Honecker (1971–89) the GDR experienced a shift toward a new model of "developed socialist society" in which violence, terror, and ideological mobilization could give way to more subtle forms of control. This was not "liberalization": Honecker's GDR remained a one-party Leninist state; dissent was criminalized; and citizens remained highly dependent on the ruling apparatus for opportunities and privileges. But the government pursued a new strategy of seeking popular consent through improved living standards, on the one hand, and enhanced surveillance and subversion, on the other.[13]

A new, more flexible approach was also evident in foreign policy. The regime responded to West German chancellor Willy Brandt's Ostpolitik of mutual recognition and cooperation. In 1972 the two German states signed a treaty of mutual recognition; the status of Berlin as a divided city was normalized; and new travel regulations and transit routes were established to link West Berlin to the FRG. In exchange for substantial economic access to the West, the government of the GDR agreed to participate in the Conference on Security and Cooperation in Europe (CSCE) and endorsed the 1975 Helsinki treaty that formally pledged it to respect human rights. Thanks to these initiatives, GDR citizens became less isolated from the nonsocialist world; one indication is that the number of visitors from

TABLE 3. Security and Welfare Expenditures by Category
in the GDR State Budget, 1989

State Spending by Category	Billions of GDR Marks
Defense	12.9
Border Security	6.0
Internal Security	8.2
Education	21.9
Social Security and Pensions	44.9

Source: *SB* 1994, Heft 12.

nonsocialist countries (chiefly the FRG) nearly tripled from 1970 to 1988 (*SJDDR* 1989).

Historians have shown how Honecker's "welfare dictatorship" tried to realize the egalitarian aspirations of socialism in a repressive one-party system (Jarausch 1999; Ross 2001). Its "Unity of Social and Economic Policy" linked economic modernization to the expansion of the welfare state and the improvement of consumer supplies (Kuhrt, Buck, and Holzweissig 1999; Maier 1996; Weber 1999, 2000; Staritz 1985). In many ways, the results were impressive: Average household income increased about 70 percent between 1970 and 1985 (*SJDDR* 1986). Ownership of televisions, washing machines, and refrigerators became nearly universal, and by 1988 about half of all households owned an automobile (*SJDDR* 1989). And spending on health care, child care, and price subsidies mushroomed. By 1988 the GDR was spending about forty-five billion marks annually on social welfare, an increase of about 300 percent over 1970—a rate three times greater than the growth of national income (*SB* 1984/12). Yet during the same period that the welfare system expanded, the internal security apparatuses also continued to expand. Expenditures on border defense and internal security reached fourteen billion marks by 1989, a third of the amount allocated to total welfare spending. (See table 3.)

Having produced more guns and more butter, the regime claimed that it had instituted a consensual, egalitarian society of full employment and abundance. This society was one in which the traditional social milieus and classes were eliminated in favor of the "political and moral unity of the people" (see, e.g., Honecker 1979; Grundmann, Lötsch, and Weidig 1976).

With employment in state-controlled sectors nearly complete (97 percent), the government kept wage differentials low (Atkinson and Micklewright 1992), and nearly 90 percent of the population belonged to the state-controlled trade union federation (Woderich 1992; Fuller 1999; Parmalee 1994). With standards of living fairly uniform, the meaningful cleavage in GDR society was less along the lines of traditional social classes than politically defined social status: society against state, people against party, "us" against "them."

The Stasi and the System of Coercive Surveillance

The dissident Reinhard Henkys (1982: 16) observed of his experiences: "Self-organization in the GDR was understood as opposition. Opposition was alien to the system, and, as a result, self-organization had the odium of treason and was explicitly combated." The judiciary and the police remained extensions of the will of the party, blurring the lines between criminal and political policing (Fricke 1984, 1993). Organized political opposition was infiltrated, disrupted, and punished, and the hallmark of the system was to make ordinary citizens agents of the regime. The chief instrument in effecting these policies was the Ministry for State Security, an apparatus popularly known as the Stasi.

The Stasi was the self-proclaimed "sword and shield" of the party (Siebenmorgen 1993). Minister for State Security Erich Mielke defined its mission simply: "The Ministry for State Security is entrusted with the task of preventing or throttling at the earliest stages—using whatever means and methods may be necessary—all attempts to delay or hinder the victory of socialism" (Fulbrook 1995: 47).[14] Mielke was not only a general in the armed forces of the state but also a state minister and from 1971 a member of the Politburo. Under his direction the Stasi evolved from an intelligence agency entrusted with counterespionage and counterinsurgency to an enormous domestic surveillance operation. Mielke's ambition was to modernize secret policing as completely as possible. With the regime secured, the Stasi largely refrained from such classic totalitarian measures as collective detention, murder of dissidents, arbitrary arrests, and the like (see, e.g., Bramstedt 1945). Mielke's technocrats preferred to refine techniques of surveillance and control.

A clear indication of this change in priorities is that although about two hundred thousand people were convicted of political offenses in the GDR (Mueller 1997), the rate of the convictions fell sharply after the 1950s, and all manner of executions ceased by the 1980s (Fricke 1993). From 1950 to 1955 there were on average about fourteen thousand sentences for political offenses each year in the GDR; the annual rate dropped to fewer than four thousand between 1985 and 1988 (Raschka 1997: 201–4). Yet the annual number of Stasi investigations of suspect individuals increased by an average of 50 percent (205).[15]

One of the leading figures in the development of the Stasi, the "spymaster" Markus Wolf, later explained that his generation of secret policemen came to view the old Stalinist methods as "primitive and unproductive solutions" to problems of political control (Hollander 1999: 269). In 1957, the year that Mielke assumed the post of minister, the Stasi employed about fifteen thousand full-time agents. Over the following decades the organization ballooned, increasing its full-time personnel nearly sevenfold. By 1988 the ministry commanded an annual budget of four billion marks (greater than the Interior Ministry's), contained twenty-seven separate divisions entrusted with matters ranging from party loyalty to economic surveillance, and oversaw all foreign and domestic intelligence operations. Among its nearly ninety thousand paid employees (*hauptamtliche Mitarbeiter*), operatives were assigned to open the mail and monitor telephone calls of a random selection of ordinary citizens. With all organized opposition to the regime long since crushed and techniques of surveillance and infiltration in the process of being perfected, an SED handbook confidently proclaimed that "in the socialist state there does not exist any objective political or social basis for an opposition against the ruling social and political relations" (Stoever 1997: 43).

The Stasi's jurisdiction was no less vast than its apparatus. Official ideology intentionally blurred the distinction between domestic policing and counterespionage, treating all categories of crime as "alien factors" (Wolfe 1992). Any action, expression, or opinion that threatened the state or the leadership of the party, which was guaranteed under Article 1 of the constitution, was treated as a political crime under this rubric. An East German criminology textbook explained,

> Crimes against the GDR are crimes of a counter-revolutionary nature. These crimes have no social basis in our Republic, either objectively or subjectively. They are therefore possible only, as a matter of principle,

as crimes carried into the GDR from without. . . . Crimes against the GDR do not spring from the GDR's own social structure. They are aspects of class struggle waged by imperialism against socialism and are directly aimed at the GDR itself. . . . The successful and implacable prosecution and liquidation of that kind of criminality . . . is a decisive contribution by the working class in power and by its allies to the strengthening of the socialist world system and to the protection and consolidation of peace (Buchholz et al. 1974: 12–13).

It has been estimated that in an effort to root out "alien" sentiments and conspiracies, at least one hundred thousand informants were deployed in 1989 (Fricke 1991; Müller-Engbergs 1996; Siebenmorgen 1993; Joppke 1995). The agency kept records on around six million internal and foreign subjects and approximately two hundred thousand active dossiers on GDR citizens whom the Stasi considered threatening or suspicious (Wolfe 1992; Fulbrook 1995).

Stasi doctrine held that the organization should isolate "anti-socialist elements," suppress "anti-state agitation," and reform good socialists "led astray" by deviant ideas (Maier 1997: 47–9; Fulbrook 1995: 1300; Wolfe 1992: 9). Wherever possible, "hostile" and "oppositional" citizens were to be identified and neutralized through coercive surveillance and "systematic discrediting" rather than through imprisonment. A directive of 1976 provided agents with some guidelines for this kind of subversion:

> Systematic discrediting of public reputations, appearance and prestige on the basis of combining true, verifiable discrediting facts with false, but believable and unverifiable discrediting claims; systematic orchestration of career and social failures in order to undermine the self-confidence of individual persons; . . . the instigation of mistrust and mutual suspicion within groups, personal circles and organizations; instigation, exploitation and intensification of rivalries within personal circles, groups and organizations through the use of personal weaknesses among individual members; occupying groups, circles and organizations with their own internal problems while limiting their negative-hostile actions.[16]

And, for the most part, the Stasi succeeded. The historian Charles Maier remarks, "The regime entrapped even its adversaries in a web of pervasive informing" (1997: 151). Neither the Church nor the various opposition groups and dissident circles were immune; it was revealed after 1989 that key leadership figures in a number of opposition groups had been informants at one time or another (Torpey 1995). A Leipzig pastor, Klaus Kaden, described the chilling effect of this intrusive apparatus of surveillance: "This was an ever present fear somehow; it permeated all walks of life; this haunting fear that you could be arrested anytime, right off the street. The Stasi heard everything, knew everything, were everywhere, and everybody knew that" (Philipsen 1993: 158). Indeed, East Germans reportedly assumed that every official organization had at least one informant (Völker and Flap 2001: 39; Niethammer 1995). Stasi infiltration of the intelligentsia was especially deep, reaching an estimated 10 percent of university-educated citizens who provided information (Maier 1997: 47). Hoping to protect themselves, most citizens simply withdrew from public life or else avoided expressing any critical sentiments.

In the 1980s the GDR had the highest per capita military expenditure and one of the highest concentrations of men under arms in Eastern Europe.[17] While this was related to the country's status as a frontline Cold War state, the GDR's armed forces, particularly its military police and border troops, were also intended for civilian functions. Even as state investment in productive enterprises was shrinking during the late 1980s, the GDR was spending ever more on maintaining control. Expenditures on border defense and internal security exceeded the military defense budget. Despite its success in enforcing compliance, the security and welfare system ultimately proved too costly, playing its role in bankrupting the regime and deepening popular disaffection.

Niches and the Informal Organization of Society

In situations in which there is a deep disparity between those in power and the subordinated, a considerable gap may grow between private beliefs and public statements (Scott 1990). At the individual level, people generally falsify in public the preferences they hold in private (Kuran 1995). Although public expressions of affection and loyalty are often insincere, it is critical to the system that everyone goes on acting "as if" it were all genuine (Havel 1985). With the legitimacy of the regime unknowable, the key to the regime's power resides in its ability to cajole and threaten members of society into conforming to this culture of dissimulation (Wedeen 1998). The common knowledge that facilitates collective action disappears. Since no one knows for sure whether or not one's neighbor is a genuine Communist, it is better not to risk honest expression in front of him. To protect oneself, one joins in the same public expressions of loyalty voiced by everyone else, thereby misleading one's neighbor in turn. In Leninist regimes ordinary people see dissidents who insist on speaking out as foolish or crazy, not because they themselves prefer the official reality, but rather "because it [is] apparent that no other public representation of reality within the official sphere [can] occur" (Yurchak 1997: 166).

In his analysis of Leninist political culture, Jowitt (1992) has shown how dissimulation structures relationships between rulers and ruled in Communist society. Ethnographies of Leninist societies reveal widespread cynicism, the abandonment of official life (Burawoy and Lukács 1992), and the development of a "second society" (Shlapentokh 1989; Yurchak 1997) of private nonconformism as an unintended consequence of repression and surveillance. In these deteriorating Leninist societies, ordinary citizens rely on friendship networks for access to scarce goods, for political information, and for sustaining values at odds with official ideology. The "spontaneity, anonymity and lack of formal organization" (Scott 1990) that often marks such circles distinguishes them from staid Leninist public culture.

The society of passive withdrawal that took root in the GDR was famously described by Günter Gauss (1983) as a "niche society," in which citizens retreated into pockets of private life that could provide relief from surveillance and pressure for conformity. Finding niches of like-minded friends and withdrawing into alternative cultural milieus, East Germans quietly exited GDR socialism. Networks of friends and close colleagues provided a venue for political discussions, jokes, and complaints beyond official scrutiny (Deess 1997a; Völker and Flap 2001; Flam 1998).

The niche society was promoted, paradoxically, by features of the "Unity of Economic and Social Policy" that allowed for an "internal exile." As a consequence of the socialist welfare of the 1970s, opportunities for private recreation significantly expanded. Informal sociability thrived as GDR citizens disappeared on weekends and evenings into a "Bermuda triangle" of home, car, and allotment garden.[18] Nearly 15 percent of GDR households owned their own vacation dacha (Grundmann 2001: 145), and in Leipzig alone there were over thirty thousand garden plots, where individuals could grow fruit and vegetables and, even more important, drink, converse, and relax.[19] Above all, the nearly universal form of private escape was through West German television. By the late 1980s GDR citizens owned nearly as many televisions as their American counterparts, with nearly eight hundred televisions per thousand residents. Nocturnal migration via the airwaves was a cherished window into the "nonsocialist world." The opportunity to compare East German media with independent sources and compare what one saw on television with the reality of life in the GDR was also a crucial resource for popular communication and grievance formation.[20] In 1988 a survey of East German youth found that about 90 percent reported tuning into Western television and radio broadcasts and that most were familiar with West German news outlets (Friedrich, Förster, and Starke 1999: 132). By this point the regime's campaigns against "degenerate" Western culture were largely over. Rock-and-roll was tolerated, with some bands even enjoying sponsorship by the Free German Youth (FDJ). In reaction, newer, more rebellious musical forms such as punk rock, "heavy metal," and "skinhead" music attracted adherents. Clashes between fans and the police occurred at banned concerts in Leipzig, East Berlin, and other cities (Ramet 1995: 41–2).

In addition to its purely informal dimensions, the niche society also had an unintended institutional foundation. Organized into work "brigades" and collectives, East German workers spent much of their working time in small- and medium-sized groups under the supervision of state-controlled labor unions and party collectives (Deess 1997b; Müller 1995; Fuller 1999). Many social benefits, vacation packages, and leisure time events were linked to the workplace and organized on this basis. Mandatory workplace collectives were state-sponsored organizations of usually two dozen people operating in workplaces, schools, and state administration. Local party organizations, also organized on the same basis, met every Monday in mandatory assemblies, as did the various "mass organizations" (labor unions, youth leagues, women's associations, and the like). Although they were not tolerated if they became engaged in public attacks, small-scale work assemblies were permitted to have frank discussions, thus enabling them to become sites for veiled expressions of grievances (Fuller 1999; Deess 1997a).

And at work an informally organized world of social networks and friendship circles developed, which provided sociability, workplace solidarity, and mutual assistance in a shortage economy (Schlegelmilch 1995a; Nissen 1992). Leipzig party officials complained that informal organization led to bargaining between industrial managers and employees. As a result, they found themselves unable to improve labor productivity or enforce political and social norms within the enterprises. Problems of excessive alcohol consumption on the job, absenteeism, unscheduled vacations, and other forms of time-wasting and undisciplined behavior became intractable problems. Despite strenuous efforts to enforce discipline and restore the "moral and political leadership of the party," networks of workplace support helped workers evade sanctions and treated deviance as justified.[21]

The political implications of the niche society should not be overstated: so long as it did not escape its limits, this kind of nonconformity was tolerable. An East German woman explained, "We had a little dacha, and this is where we talked and complained and got angry. And this is exactly how every other GDR citizen did it as well. Everybody had a niche in which he sat and quietly complained" (Philipsen 1993: 117). The same logic applied to the world of work. An East Berlin factory worker described how he and his comrades created their own spaces within the factory in which they could socialize, share meals, and avoid onerous tasks. Although the work itself was unrewarding, the niche had its comforts: "It was really a great bunch of people. . . . The niches that were found here and that made life agreeable, they were also at work, they were not only in our free time. And they were to some extent pleasant niches, I must say" (Müller 1995: 260). Regardless of the regime's expectation of involving citizens in "building socialism," in practice most East Germans found niches into which they could quietly retreat.

While the system of coercive surveillance that enveloped the worker-consumer provided individual incentives for compliance, the niche society provided social incentives for deviance. In their niches East Germans expected each other to evade the rules, criticize the party bosses, indulge in forbidden entertainments, and shirk workplace responsibilities. When disciplinary agencies penetrated the opaque world of the niche society they were often surprised to discover the degree of social support that deviants enjoyed. Representatives of local party organizations and plant directors accommodated informal groups, shielded critical voices from scrutiny, and defended lax political enforcement. Policing the niches was simply too costly; officials had little incentive to provoke conflicts with their subordinates or bring local sources of deviance to the attention of their superiors. In one Leipzig factory a former SED member, expelled for previous criticism of the regime, had become an "anti-socialist demagogue." To audiences composed of his workmates he praised Gorbachev, criticized party leaders, and spoke of the necessity of a mixed market economy. To the investigating party commissioner's surprise, "a whole range of comrades did not immediately recognize the politically hostile character" of these heretical positions and, worse still, "provided examples from the factory and from everyday life to support his anti-party formulations." When confronted with their failure to halt this criticism or break up his informal political assemblies, local party officials defended the purged worker "not as a heretic but as a critical intellectual who occasionally went too far."[22]

The Leipzig archives suggest that most often violations of party norms or political offenses at the workplace were ignored, with only the most aggressive or obvious cases reported to PKKs or Stasi officials. Workplace niches reflected an implicit bargain between state officials and workers that traded off productivity and efficiency for compliance and stability (see Kopstein 1997). The bargain was based on a set of conditions such that living standards remained acceptable, emigration was impossible, and the workers were not challenged to be more productive or adaptive. This arrangement is not unusual; in a number of repressive societies, informal groups provide the only avenue for participation in public life and opportunities to pursue interests and needs otherwise "prohibited or ignored by the regime" (Denouex 1993: 16).

In short, in a state that eliminates the public sphere and organizations independent of regime control, local networks nurture collective identities and solidarity, provide informal organization and contacts, and offer information otherwise unavailable to individuals. These networks take on particular importance in Communism because of a political economy shaped by privilege and perpetual economic shortage that makes informal exchange of vital importance (Kornai 1992). Data on the social structure of the GDR reflects the patterns of niche attachments. East German social networks were characterized by a predominance of strong ties and dense local networks (Völker and Flap 2001). Citizens invested in intimate social bonds and tried to limit or exclude weaker ties to acquaintances whose reliability could not be assured. These tightly knit informal groups were coalitions of necessity in a context of weak resources and opportunities (Boissevain 1971). Again, we should not see the niche itself as a form of dissident voice; by and large, it represented the escape from politics, as Vaclav Havel (1985) and other dissidents who tried to mobilize voice realized. Indeed, East German niches were a fundamental element of the "political culture of an apolitical society" (Glaessner 1996).

Even as rebellion against the state loomed in the fall of 1989, the Stasi still believed that it could isolate the threat because it knew that the infant formal opposition was divided and poorly organized (Mitter and Wolle 1990). But it could do little to counter the threat that took root in the recesses of the niche society. Although niches helped to defuse tension by mitigating everyday grievances and keeping dissent confined to private circles, they had considerable potential as vehicles of micro-mobilization because of the local, tightly knit communities they nourished. Yet, unable to act or communicate extralocally, such niches required a common signal to act if anything more than micro-rebellion were to be mobilized.

"Noisy" Exiters and the Corrosion of Conformity

The GDR, born of a "revolution from above" arranged under Soviet auspices, started with a profound legitimacy deficit. Yet every successful authoritarian system has a balancing factor—material incentives, idealism, faith in a grand endeavor—that offsets coercion. Despite the GDR's enormous investments in social welfare, its history suggests that the state did not manage to secure the popular assent or win the spontaneous compliance that Max Weber (1978) saw as so essential to effective authority. Indeed, its system of coercive surveillance was the antithesis of a social order able to regulate itself through common norms, shared goals, and voluntary compliance.

In the GDR most people simply withdrew from public affairs and cooperation was grudgingly rendered. In their groups of intimate friends, relatives, and co-workers, East Germans made expression of disloyalty, especially in their petty acts of defiance, a self-enforcing norm. The perverse effects of coercive surveillance that we find in the case of the GDR have parallels to the limits on social control found in classical penology (Sykes 1958; Goffman 1961; Wilson 1983) and in the sociology of the state (Levi

1997). The sociology of punishment consistently reinforces the insight that systems of social control are always partial and most robust when they balance punitive deterrence with considerable incentives to comply with the rules. Citizens, too, comply most readily with a regime that treats them fairly. A tyranny is most unassailable not when enforced by an external apparatus, however elaborate, but when sanctioning is exercised at the level of the primary group, that is, by one's own intimates and immediate peers (Heckathorn 1988, 1990).

Despite the pervasiveness of informing, the GDR lacked this secondary enforcement of norms that would have made its control apparatus more effective. On the other hand, the niche society it created was so compartmentalized, opaque, and isolated it could not foster general rebellion on its own. So long as the social networks isolated in niches remain apart, a communicative dilemma results such that citizens tend to overestimate the overall level of support for the regime (Noelle-Neumann 1984). This overestimation of regime support, in turn, cripples the capacity for effective collective action. The result is what Kuran (1995) calls "collective conservatism," whereby individuals conform not because they favor the social order but because they think that others support it. In order to dispel such misinformation, something has to activate voice from this submerged opposition. After 1961 the GDR regime achieved a repressive equilibrium that blocked both exit and voice. Eventually, however, the GDR system of control created a paradox: it achieved public conformity to its dictates but unintentionally fostered withdrawal into intimate circles of privatized dissent.

Even though popular dissatisfaction with the regime usually remained confined to the private sphere, a new challenge to political conformity did become increasingly prevalent in the GDR during the late 1980s. The politics of coexistence and détente had unforeseen consequences. Citizens felt encouraged by the GDR's participation in the Conference on Security and Cooperation in Europe (CSCE), which resulted in the Helsinki declaration of 1975. Its basic endorsement of human rights, including the right to individual mobility, persuaded many that it was now a favorable time to apply for emigration. Although the party leadership made clear that it did not recognize a "general right to emigrate" and would reject any application inconsistent with "the social interests of the GDR," some East Germans began to make "noisy" demands for exit. Citizens started to petition GDR authorities for the right to emigrate to the FRG. Some even began to coordinate their efforts and demonstrate in public places for the right to exit.

This new tactic reflected a hybrid form of political action: voice for exit. By 1988 there were more than a hundred thousand standing applications for exit visas, concentrated in the urban districts of the GDR, especially Dresden, East Berlin, Karl-Marx-Stadt and Leipzig (see chapter 2). The trend was also fueled by exposure to West German television, which provided ample information about conditions in the East and the West. Trade and economic relations between the two Germanys were also extensive. Tourism, family reunions, and business travel resulted in nearly thirty million border crossings between the two Germanys in 1988.[23]

Although the extent of the phenomenon was not public knowledge, the regime could not provide an airtight seal around the GDR. The party's security bureau reported: "Despite increasing the number of permitted emigrations and great exertion to undermine and drive down would-be exiters, the number of applications has not been reduced. . . . Moreover, permissions granted as exceptions to the legal regulations are having the opposite of the intended effect on other citizens, and this is leading to new applicants. Every permitted exit generates, as a rule, one or two new applicants."[24] Once some would-be exiters learned that applicants deemed "antisocialist" had a better chance of being granted a visa, they reasoned that if they made enough noise they too might be deemed "hostile and negative elements" that the regime would prefer to expel or ransom. In short, the policy of selective emigration had created a greater demand for exit than the regime was willing or able to accommodate safely. In the 1980s applicants were overwhelmingly the younger, working-age citizens the GDR could least afford to lose. When their applications were rejected, these savvy would-be exiters developed support networks among themselves, often supported by the churches. A report to the Central Committee found that "it can be clearly established that various exit applicants advise each other and exchange information concerning the methods of achieving emigration."[25]

A basic rendering of Hirschman's schema would imply that exit and voice are the only alternatives facing discontented citizens of mono-organizational dictatorships. However, the picture of GDR society presented in this chapter and the one preceding indicates that portraying political behavior in terms of the binary choice of exit or voice overlooks a wide range of alternative behaviors, such as quiet disengagement from public affairs, veiled criticism from within approved organizations, efforts to petition for the right of exit, and so on. When one compares the diffuse forms of opposition that characterized GDR society in the late 1980s along the axis of silence and voice, on the one hand, and exiting and remaining, on the other, one can distinguish between dissent (stationary voice) and false compliance (stationary silence) and between "noisy exit" and "silent exit." "Noisy exiters" attempted to use petition or protest to achieve legal permission or expulsion by the authorities. "Silent exiters," in contrast, engaged in secretive or conspiratorial efforts to escape the state without trying to have a public impact.

The repressive equilibrium of the Wall discouraged political voice in that it successfully blocked the exit option that commonly provides leverage to weaker parties in their conflicts with the powerful. However, the blockage of exit meant that the highly discontented had no choice but to silently endure conditions or raise a voice against them. Opening the door, even a little, threatened the system. Some East German citizens now had an incentive to express voice against the regime. Would-be emigrants began to make common cause with dissidents proclaiming democratization and the human rights of GDR citizens. In the streets of Leipzig, the combination of "noisy exiters" and vocal dissidents provided the rebellion against Communism with its first fuel.

Dona Nobis Pacem: *Political Subcultures, the Church, and the Birth of Dissident Voice*

> *Freedom only for the supporters of the government, only for the members of one party—however numerous they may be—is no freedom at all. Freedom is always and exclusively freedom for the one who thinks differently.... The public life of countries with limited freedom is so poverty-stricken, so miserable, so rigid, so unfruitful, precisely because, through exclusion of democracy, it cuts off the living sources of progress.*
>
> —ROSA LUXEMBURG, *THE RUSSIAN REVOLUTION*

Among the obstacles in the way of social movements in a Leninist regime is the problem that even if citizens want to risk change, they have no way of knowing how widely fellow citizens share this desire. If they rebel, and a sufficient number of others fail to join them, they will be crushed. Dissident leaders therefore have to devise strategies that overcome what social psychologists call "pluralistic ignorance" (Allport 1924; O'Gorman 1986)—the situation in which deficient communication leads to mistaken beliefs about the beliefs of others—on which repressive stability relies. If somehow a sufficiently large number of citizens begin to voice grievances against the government, the reluctance of others might be overcome. Once others join in, confidence may grow, and the result can be a sudden upswing of protest as citizens join the protest bandwagon. But there are several problems standing in the way of the dissident efforts to get the wagon rolling. First, how can dissidents obtain the resources that enable them to organize a coherent group capable of organizing protest? Second, lacking means of coordination and communication with ordinary citizens, how can dispersed and intimidated actors overcome the barriers to collective action that the state puts in their way? Third, how can they possibly convince fellow citizens that if they take a risk, they have a chance of success?

Previous studies of mobilization in the GDR have revealed how Leipzig's Monday evening Peace Prayers served as a rallying point for diverse groups of disgruntled citizens (Lohmann 1994; Opp, Voss, and Gern 1995; Oberschall 1996; Pfaff 1996). In these accounts, the key issue is the interpretation of opportunities that made cascades of leaderless collective action possible. Questions remain, however. How did the requisite common knowledge that would make this scenario possible become widely established across the city's population? And why did cooperation emerge out of a diverse collection of citizens?

These questions direct us toward a prior set of problems surrounding the conditions for protest in the GDR and the role of dissident activism in creating the "common knowledge" that made popular mobilization possible.[1] Theories of collective action suggest that the disadvantage that challengers face in an authoritarian regime can be overcome, in part, if they are able to generate the common knowledge that makes tacit coordination possible (Chwe 1999, 2001). Thomas Schelling (1960) observed that "focal points" that draw dispersed actors to the same space or direct their attention to the same problem help to solve one of the basic problems facing dissenters: "Potential members have to know not only where and when to meet but just when to act in concert. . . . [The] problem is to act in unison without overt leadership, to find some signal that makes everyone confident that, if he acts on it, he will not be acting alone." In the collective action literature, focal points are usually taken as given, either as structural features of the social environment or through some form of mass media. However, particularly in mono-organizational dictatorial regimes in which collective action is an exceptional occurrence, the factors that generate common knowledge in other settings (see, e.g., Chwe 2001) are absent. In a Leninist regime "common" knowledge is not a preexisting resource of collective action but must be created through collective action.

The Infrastructure of Dissent in East Germany

We have seen how, in comparison with some other Eastern European regimes, the GDR was an example of what Linz and Stepan (1996) call a "frozen" post-totalitarian state, one in which hard-line Leninists retain full control of the party and obstruct any move toward political liberalization or economic reform.[2] In this setting, dissent could only take root in gaps in the system of social control that dissidents could exploit. In the GDR this principally meant the churches. As in the first decade or so of Communist control across Eastern Europe (Froese 2003; Ramet 1998), religious organizations and confessional associations were either banned or suppressed in the GDR. In East Germany thousands of clergymen and members of religious organizations were harassed, imprisoned, or forced into exile. Adding to the weight of repression, anticlerical and atheist propaganda, the suppression of the Church-based youth movement, and the forced introduction of a socialist coming-of-age ceremony (*Jugendweihe*) all helped depress identification with the churches. After the late 1950s persecution became largely episodic, but church members continued to suffer social, educational, and career disadvantages, and many occupations were barred to them. Official policy promoted "scientific" atheism, and the State Office for Church Affairs regulated religion in the interests of the state (Pollack 1994; Maser 1999; Goeckel 1990).

The largest religious organization in the GDR and the one that ultimately offered the most significant refuge for dissidents was the Union of Evangelical-Lutheran Churches (BEK).[3] Official doctrine accepted freedom of conscience, but it also expected remaining religious convictions to wither away slowly. Although the regime remained hostile to religion, declining popular religiosity, the resignation of the churches to Communist power, and the welfare services that churches were able to provide seem to have promoted limited toleration of the churches. In 1978 a "Church in Socialism" agreement between the government and the BEK normalized church-state relations on the basis of the "primacy of state interests." The Protestant Church surrendered political voice, assuring the state it would not become "a site of opposition" or a "disguised opposition party" (Neubert 1998: 355). In exchange, it was granted toleration in its own delimited sphere. The Saxon bishop Johannes Hempel later commented on the arrangement: "State representatives at various levels have often said to us over the years: 'The question of power has been decided here—the socialist state has taken power.' We in the Church answered, 'So it is, and we don't want any part of it.' "[4]

Under the Church in Socialism arrangement, East German religious organizations were able to preserve a modest role in society, reinforced by links with West German religious communities that provided vital external sources of funding. The Lutheran Church received a total of about two billion West German marks from 1963 through 1989 (Maser 1995: 318–19, 578). These funds supported the salaries of clergymen, a religious press, the upkeep of churches, and a host of cultural and social welfare institutions under religious administration. The BEK employed about four thousand clergymen and about fifteen thousand administrators, teachers, and social workers. And Church ties offered a coveted window into the non-Communist world. Pastor Rainer Eppelmann recalled, "With the construction of the Wall, I know directly that the Lutheran Church established a regular network of contacts between Eastern and Western congregations. . . . There were a few cases of congregations in which that was constant, where such contact was active for the whole period from 1961 to 1989."[5]

East Germany was nevertheless a highly secularized society. The proportion of the population identified with a religious confession steadily declined: in 1950 more than 90 percent of East Germans belonged to a religious organization; by 1986, the proportion had fallen to less than 40 percent (SJDDR 1990). Religious participation was also shrinking: Baptism was nearly universal in 1950, but by 1989 only about 15 percent of East German children were baptized (Hartmann and Pollack 1998: 332). In Leipzig only a quarter of the residents were formally Protestant Church members, and only 5 percent regularly attended religious services. In surveys conducted by the Central Institute for Youth Research, only about a tenth of East German youth reported active religious belief (Friedrich, Förster, and Starke 1999). Yet as disappointment with the regime grew in the 1980s, surveys conducted by the institute revealed a modest increase in the proportion willing to identify as religious believers. (See figure 7.) Renewed interest in religion was especially evident among working-class youth, whose religious identification increased from 5 percent in 1970 to 16 percent in 1988. Because their worldviews were so at odds with Marxism-Leninism, the religious minority was especially productive of dissenting attitudes. As the New Forum activist Jens

FIGURE 7. Religious Identification of GDR Youth, 1969–1988

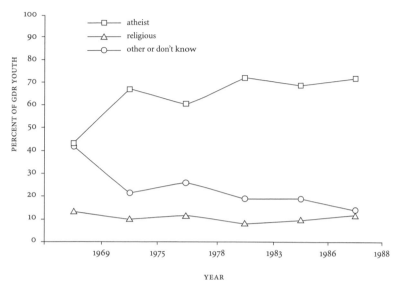

Source: Zentralinstitut für Jugendforschung data reported in Friedrich, Förster, and Starke 1999.

Reich (2002: 5) recalled of his Christian household in the 1950s, "We learned, in accordance with Matthew 22:21, to give to Ulbricht what was Ulbricht's and to give to God what belonged to God." Indeed, youth researchers found religious believers far less loyal to the GDR and more skeptical about official ideology than their secular counterparts. (See table 4.)

Religious communities were often a reservoir of opposition and a pole of attraction for the disaffected. Activist clergymen tried to exploit this by reaching out to discontented youth. As the Leipzig pastor Christoph Wonneberger (1994: 193) explained, "For me engagement was always about giving people voice. And not only in the Church but everywhere. . . . I ever more hated adjusting to the ruling lies and having to live that way. . . . I always tried to help young people along in their first steps towards becoming vocal."[6] Led by liberal clergymen in the 1970s and 1980s, the Church became a haven for "political-religious activists" (Hartmann and Pollack 1998: 177). Under the rubric of Christian engagement, groups embraced a loose mixture of issues including, as one dissident put it, "demilitarization, democratization, decentralization and self-determination" (Gerd Poppe, quoted in Dietrich 1994: 42). The activist Cornelia Matzke conceded: "You see, the Church was

TABLE 4. Political Orientation of Youth (16–24) in the GDR by Religious Worldview in 1975

Agree with the Statement:	Atheist (%)	Religious (%)	Other/Undecided (%)
"Proud to be a GDR citizen"	65	35	49
"Socialism will triumph worldwide"	66	42	49
"Gladly take part in communist youth (FDJ) events"	58	39	47
"Readily lay down my life to protect the GDR"	56	27	41
"The Soviet Union is the nation's best friend"	66	44	57

Source: Zentralinstitut für Jugendforschung (ZIJ) data reported in Friedrich, Förster, and Starke 1999: 191.
Note: N = 11,800, of which 10% were religious.

the only possible alternative for any kind of political activism. There was absolutely nothing else" (Philipsen 1993: 69). A former Rostock pastor, Joachim Gauck, acknowledged: "Religious things could not be forbidden. Protest meetings would have been forbidden and so everything had a religious character."[7] But the association was not entirely opportunistic. Another Leipzig pastor, Klaus Kaden, maintained that the Gospel "represented an immense life support" for dissenting people (Philipsen 1993: 145). And in spite of its tradition of subordination to the state, German Lutheranism also provided symbols of moral resistance stretching from Luther at the Diet of Worms to the confessing clergy's defiance of Hitler (Gritzsch 2002). Indeed, directly echoing Luther, Pastor Wonneberger (1994: 196–97) declared, "For me, what I did was not only contradiction or protest, rather, it was of course always resistance . . . 'Here I stand and I will not yield'; resistance, in this sense."

Some congregations and seminaries allowed dissidents to use scarce resources, such as their telephones, typewriters, copying machines, and meeting rooms. And dissidents dismissed from state employment or prohibited from university careers sometimes pursued careers as clergymen and Church officials or found work in charitable institutions. Yet as the opposition groups became more confrontational in 1988–89, conflicts between dissidents and the Church leadership and between the Church and the state became evident. The activist Ludwig Melhorn observed of this strained relationship: "Most of our energy was spent just trying to create a bit of free space. . . . Yes, even within the Church" (Philipsen 1993: 82). In fact, the Lutheran Church was always an uncertain refuge; in Leipzig, well known for its Church-based opposition in the late 1980s, less than 10 percent of clergymen provided shelter or assistance to political groups. About the same percentage apparently served as informants (Findeis, Pollack, and Schilling 1994: 254).

The political subcultures that took refuge in the Church involved only a tiny proportion of the population, drawn largely from pastors and their families, draft resisters, or people who grew up in religious households. Only a small number from the embattled Christian minority defied the state openly. In the case of the Jugendweihe, the mandatory coming-of-age ceremony, the rate of noncompliance was less than 5 percent in the mid-1980s, meaning that a sizable number of Christians took part in it even though it had been denounced as a violation of the first commandment (Smith 1985; Goeckel 1990). Failure to serve in regular divisions of the National People's Army was also treated as a black mark on a young person's record. By the late 1970s there were a few thousand current and former objectors who composed another reservoir of support for dissenting groups. With their pacifist sympathies the churches became important refuges for conscientious objectors in the GDR. Under the aegis of the churches, the objectors created support networks and played a large role in organizing peace seminars that criticized GDR militarism.

A final group of outsiders—the "would-be exiters"—were also attracted to the free spaces within the Church in the late 1980s. East Germans applying for exit visas faced discrimination and official harassment and could find their applications refused or delayed indefinitely. Some sought refuge in the churches where a loosely organized "exiting movement" (*Ausreiserbewegung*) began to take shape. Exit applicants met in church facilities and were supported by sympathetic pastors. They cultivated solidarity in small acts of defiance, such as tying white ribbons to their auto antennae or painting over the "DR" of their "DDR" auto identification stickers (leaving only the "D" for "Deutschland"). The state denounced Church officials for allowing congregations to be exploited as "political clubs" and "emigration offices" by disloyal citizens and heavily sanctioned activists.[8] But these citizen-outsiders composed a distinctive milieu that had already paid, often early in their lives, some of the penalties the regime reserved for noncompliance. One interview respondent, for example, explained that once he had resisted the Jugendweihe he knew he would be excluded from the university, so why not also avoid military service? And once he had been punished for draft avoidance, why not get involved with a dissident group?[9]

Although there were networks within the Church (for example, Arbeitskreis Solidarische Kirche) that were pressing for greater autonomy from episcopal oversight and for greater confrontation with the state, for the most part the dissident presence in the Church was informally organized. Intimate relationships forged the bonds of dissident groups more than did organizational ties. The Leipzig democracy activist Jochen Lässig recalled: "A portion of the group . . . became practically a commune. . . . There they had lots of parties, sang together and performed street-music. It was a community . . . without them the whole thing wouldn't have gone on. Action sprang from the community" (Pollack, Findeis, and Schilling 1994: 241). The human rights activist Gerd Poppe later reflected: "To live as a minority in a society and to endure repression . . . requires that one has basic support from a group. . . . [Otherwise] the individual would really go under" (Dietrich 1994: 243). Another Leipzig activist, Matthias Kittlitz, explained: "The group helped me and others quite a lot. And out of participation in this group, the desire arose to give more people a chance to emancipate themselves, to make opportunities to identify themselves, and to put fear aside for the first time (Lindner and Grüneberger 1992: 64). Reinhard Richter, a lay Christian activist, said of his participation, "The feeling of not being alone was a very important part of it . . . the feeling of powerlessness could be better endured" (Lindner and Grüneberger 1992: 292–93). The East Berlin artist Bärbel Bohley referred to her dissident circle as "a kind of family" because "if you were going to do political work, then one had to have trust" (Findeis, Pollack, and Schilling 1994: 241–42). Opportunities for socializing with like-minded people, romance, and a sense of adventure drew in participants and sustained involvement. The Leipzig environmentalist Ralf Elsässer noted, "In every case, I believe, the groups would not have survived so long had they only concerned themselves with serious affairs" (Findeis, Pollack, and Schilling 1994: 243).

Although interpersonal networks and affective ties account for the attraction and resilience of political subcultures in the GDR, the same factors may also explain some of their limitations. The intimacy of the groups and the narrowness of the activist milieu made it difficult to reach the broader society or relate to popular grievances. As the filmmaker Konrad Weiss (1990: 3) remarked of his fellow dissidents: "They were, in a certain sense, outsiders who lived alternative lifestyles or were isolated from the people through intellectual careers. Their dissatisfaction was not the dissatisfaction of the people . . . whose grievances were directed at everyday things." The lack of formal organization made it hard for larger groups to operate and for activists to work outside their locality, and it complicated the resolution of disputes and schisms. The activist Martin Schramm reports that the groups worked best "when we had eight to ten people and about as many temporary helpers" (Findeis, Pollack, and Schilling 1994: 249).

Despite their diffuse and marginal presence in GDR life, these critical voices drew attention. Gerd Poppe observed: "In a closed society such as the GDR, it was, comparatively speaking, easy for a handful of people to have a political impact. And that was our self-understanding, proceeding from a minority position . . . to draw attention to social problems" (Findeis, Pollack, and Schilling 1994: 244). The effort to bring young people to the Church and the modest degree of political influence its political subcultures exercised explains why cautious Church officials tolerated the dissidents beneath their roof. Despite the limited reach of the Church in East German society, by the mid-1980s dissident voices and the growing sympathy of many clergymen for activist causes had increased its influence. As Politburo member Günter Schabowski (1991) recalled, "The surprising growth of its cultural impact made the Church an inner-political rival to the party, competing with it for ideological adherence."

The Alternative Public Sphere

In the 1980s modern communications technology and East-West trade and travel began to dissipate the political isolation of intellectuals in the socialist world (Coser 1990; Collins 1995). Dissidents in the GDR were inspired by encouraging developments elsewhere, first in Poland and Czechoslovakia and later in Gorbachev's Soviet Union. In those countries critical intellectuals called for the self-organization of society as the necessary precondition for reform of the state (Glenn 2003; Ost 1990). At the same time, the rise of "new social movements" in Western Europe, particularly the emergence of the West German Greens (Knabe 1988; Markovits and Gorski 1993), provided East Germans with an appealing model of how to fight for democratization.

An additional resource in trying to reach a broader public was the GDR's endorsement of the Helsinki human rights accords in 1975, which obliged signatories to recognize the United Nations' Universal Declaration of Human Rights (Stokes 1991: 161–62). Citing Jan Urban of the Czech Charter 77, Sidney Tarrow (1991: 16) explains that even if it was only meant as a formal gesture, the endorsement of the Helsinki accords provided a common metric with which Soviet bloc dissidents could evaluate government actions and frame their opposition in language that would gain foreign sympathy for their struggles. In the late 1980s East German dissidents found that human rights messages resonated with Western journalists and humanitarian organizations, whose attention afforded some protection. And with so many East German households watching West German television, coverage of dissidents expressing human rights claims often "boomeranged" back into the GDR on the nightly news (Keck and Sikkink 1998).

Above all, the newfound willingness to risk open dissent in the GDR has to be attributed largely to what has been called the "Gorbachev factor" (Kornai 1992; Ramet 1995). Encouraged by Moscow's new spirit of reform, dissident newsletters published through the churches depicted Gorbachev as the champion of a humane, democratic socialism. Where once East German activists had watched the regime co-opt their issues (such as peace and disarmament) as expressions of the official ideology, it now became easier to follow Gorbachev in using socialist icons to demand democratization. Most famously, dissidents now appropriated one of the GDR's official socialist martyrs, Rosa Luxemburg, whose maxim "Freedom is always the freedom of those who think differently" seemed in line with glasnost.

New openings in international politics were not matched by liberalization at home. As far as the Politburo was concerned, "socialist human rights" had already been realized in the GDR, and there was no "objective need" for any dialogue on reform (Honecker 1979). And yet the Stasi warned party leaders of the wide resonance of reformist ideas and appeals for human rights. As early as 1985 the secret police warned of growing interest in the "demagogic," "bourgeois-liberal" conception of human rights and feared that dissidents might mobilize a "democratic mass movement." Such a movement would "intend to put permanent pressure on the party and state leadership."[10] The analysis was essentially right. Just as the state pressed the Church to limit dissident access, human rights activists in East Berlin formed the Initiative for Peace and Human Rights (Initiative für Frieden und Menschenrechte, IFM) in 1986. The IFM declared political independence from the Church and began the publication of *Grenzfall* (Border Case), the first widely distributed dissident newsletter in East Germany. It published frequent reports on re-forms in Eastern Europe and the USSR, open letters for democracy and human rights, and the full texts of the Helsinki documents and the UN Charter on Human Rights.

The IFM's founders were clear about their purposes: "A broad public sphere must develop, one that can exercise independent control. The de-velopment of a critical public sphere is not independent of a guarantee of human and civil rights. The establishment of a rule of law, in this sense, that of political rights for everyone, is a considerable step on the road to democ-racy."[11] In addition to publishing newsletters, dissidents used West German broadcasts as an ersatz media for the alternative public sphere (Havemann 1982). Exiled dissidents established monthly broadcasts of "Radio Glasnost" from West Berlin beginning in the fall of 1986.

The aim was to create a "second public sphere" (*zweite Öffentlichkeit*), which would compete with the official media and stimulate political discus-sion. The nascent democratic movement soon demonstrated remarkable creativity. Produced with the use of Church facilities, a wide variety of information sheets, journals, literary magazines, and other unofficial mate-rials were distributed under the general disclaimer "For internal Church use only." The editors of the new Leipzig samizdat *Streiflichter* (Searchlights) boldly planned to "create an information network in the GDR" that would link dissident groups across the region and the country.[12] Despite ongoing efforts by the state to suppress the samizdat journals, de facto toleration of dissidents within the Church provided the necessary space to keep them in circulation (Poumet 1996: 69, 82). In mid-1989 the Stasi reported that there were twenty-five occasionally appearing illegal newsletters and journals in the GDR, produced in centers such as East Berlin (seven), Leipzig (five), Halle (four), and Dresden (three). *Arche nova*, an environmentalist journal, reportedly had a distribution of some two thousand copies.[13]

Opposition groups also made organizational innovations that stretched their free spaces. The most important of these were the Environmental Libraries (*Umweltbibliotheken*). The first was established in 1987 at the Zion Church in East Berlin, and it became an information center for East Berlin's alternative scene. The library's newsletter, the *Umweltblätter* (Environmental Pages), also initiated in 1987, reported on ecological conditions and environmental abuses in the GDR, as well as on glasnost, human rights, and democratization. Its success encouraged dissidents in other cities to create their own libraries where samizdat could be distributed and information meetings held. By the fall of 1989, more than twenty Environmental Libraries had sprung up in congregations across the GDR.[14] In addition to issuing dissident newsletters, the libraries made available copies of the UN Human Rights Declaration and the Helsinki accords.

In early 1989 the Stasi reported the growing ideological independence of groups linked to the Church. Activists presented a clear threat in their expanding "influence in the public sphere" and "development of strong networks" and in moving toward their ultimate goal of "the formation of countrywide political associations with legal recognition."[15] Awakening broad discussion, in 1988 Bohley, a key figure in Berlin's activist scene, urged her fellow dissidents to move away from religiously based activism and challenge the regime directly: "The 'opposition' in the GDR must go through a process of self-discovery. That goes for everyone who is interested in solving looming human rights questions and believes that only a radical critique of the established economic and social relations in the GDR can bring the movement in the direction of a solution. . . . It will be necessary for all progressive forces in the GDR to join together, be they within or outside the Church. But this process should take place outside the Church."[16] Yet moving outside the Church threatened repression that might crush the nascent movement, as had happened earlier in the decade to a fledgling independent peace movement.[17] When even small groups of protesters held protest placards, sang songs, or otherwise engaged in public activism, they were usually arrested or dispersed before they could have much of an impact. Vocal opposition groups were hampered by repression and infiltration. In November 1987 Stasi agents and police raided the Environmental Library in Berlin's Zion Church and destroyed its printing equipment (Neubert 1998: 599–600).

With the Stasi frustrating their efforts within the Church, dissidents developed new tactics. One was to hold protests in association with anniversaries and other public events.[18] Official commemorations, such as May Day, Luxemburg-Liebknecht Day, or the GDR state anniversary, had the advantage of drawing large numbers of people into the streets without dissident effort. Dissidents could piggyback on such events, and disaffected persons would turn up during these events in the hopes of encountering like-minded people. For example, in Dresden activists used the anniversary of the 1945 firebombing to stage demonstrations against the militarism of the regime. In January 1988 the IFM organized a protest against the raid on the Environmental Library, which was staged in East Berlin at the official commemoration of the martyrdom of socialists Rosa Luxemburg and Karl Liebknecht.

In such situations the state could strike back hard. In January 1988 dozens of activists were arrested as "provocative troublemakers" and counterrevolutionaries (Rüddenklau 1991; Dietrich 1994). Several IFM activists were imprisoned, and some accepted deals whereby they were expelled to the West instead of being given lengthy jail sentences. The arrests effectively undercut the IFM and delayed its attempts to organize a GDR-wide democracy movement based in East Berlin.[19] However, an SED security analysis conceded that the demonstration had come to the attention of the broader public, provoking interest and sympathy even among party members and students. It concluded that the opposition must be denied "public forums" and advised security organs that "in general political vigilance must be increased. It must be taken more seriously that hostile forces will take the opportunity to misuse cultural assemblies, historical dates, and public events."[20]

The Stasi's strategy was to bottle up the dissidents in the churches and embroil them in conflicts with religious authorities. For their part, Church leaders accepted that political activities "must be based on the foundation of the constitution and all relevant laws," but they also made clear that congregations must be protected domains.[21] After the Luxemburg-Liebknecht Day march, the State Office for Church Affairs warned the clergy that "the Church is not an opposition party and must make that clear." Bishop Gottfried Forck of the Berlin-Brandenburg synod announced that the Church sympathized with those who want "more humanity and justice" but strictly condemned illegal demonstrations. Manfred Stolpe, a high-ranking Church administrator, encouraged congregations to distance themselves from dissidents, affirming that "the Protestant Church in the GDR . . . is neither an emigration office nor an opposition club."[22] But as the space narrowed for dissidents in the capital, dissidents in Leipzig expanded their influence.

Leipzig as the Cradle of Popular Protest

The East Berlin–area human rights activist Ludwig Melhorn observed: "Leipzig acquired a much larger base for opposition activities throughout the year 1989. . . . In Berlin the opposition was pretty much confined to intellectuals. In Leipzig, on the other hand, the whole thing was more open" (Philipsen 1993: 212). This was puzzling because there were seemingly better opportunities for opposition in Berlin. In the capital Western news coverage made the regime reluctant to crack down for fear of "creating an international scandal" (213). East Berlin also had seemingly more advantageous recruiting grounds in its universities and research institutes. Leipzig was smaller, poorer, and more obscure than the capital city.

Nevertheless, Leipzig did have advantages, including a Church establishment sympathetic to dissidents and biannual East-West trade fairs that brought foreign business people and journalists to the city. It also had diverse intellectual milieus less dependent on official resources. Leipzig was the site of one of three Protestant seminaries in the GDR. Its alternative arts scene included underground cafes and art galleries (such as Club "naTO" and the Eigen+Art gallery) and punk music bands. Leipzig's well-known cabarets offered political satire, and students tested the limits of critical expression within the shell of the official *Kulturbund* and Student Union (Zwahr 1993; Rink and Hofmann 1992: 289–90).

In this climate a political subculture involving pacifists, environmentalists, writers, and activist Christians evolved. Leipzig activist Uwe Schwabe (1998: 22) recalled: "In Leipzig, no centralized structure existed in most groups. A lot happened in groups of friends who were active in a variety of circles, and a lot of things were done together besides the political. One did not sit in darkened cellars and promote 'the revolution'; we laughed and partied together. Many people shared apartments." Liberal clergymen and a few congregations let activists use their telephones, typewriters, mimeograph machines, and meeting rooms. Theology students, regarding themselves as the "left opposition" within the Church, acted as intermediaries between political subcultures and the clergy.[23] Given niches in which to operate, Leipzig's political subcultures gave birth to about thirty small political groups in the mid- to late 1980s (Dietrich and Schwabe 1994). According to Stasi estimates, in early 1989 Leipzig alone probably contained about a fifth of the total number of movement activists in the GDR (see Mitter and Wolle 1990: 46–71).

But what really made Leipzig important was that over the course of 1988–89 dissidents established the Peace Prayer services as a kind of "speaker's corner." Held at the ancient St. Nicholas Church in the city's compact urban center, the prayer services had been established as part of the short-lived peace movement in 1981 and survived the crackdown against pacifism (Dietrich and Schwabe 1994). In 1985 Pastor Wonneberger was reassigned to Leipzig from Dresden and in 1987 was given responsibility for the Peace Prayers. He immediately set about giving activists a major role in deciding their content (Schwabe 1998). He also encouraged would-be exiters to make a "noisy" exit by filing formal protest petitions explaining their decision to leave the GDR.[24]

Wonneberger established working groups for justice and human rights in 1987, and under his supervision in 1988 environmentalists and peace activists formed the Initiative Group for Life (Initiav-Gruppe-Leben, IGL), endorsing nonviolent direct action and promising to "Create publicity within and outside the Church."[25] Inevitably, these newly politicized Monday evening services became a point of contention between activists and Church authorities (Dietrich and Schwabe 1994). In August 1988 the church superintendent for Leipzig charged that the Peace Prayers were being misused for purely political reasons and called for their reorganization or abolition. In an open letter to the Saxon bishop Johannes Hempel, activists accused the hierarchy of doing the Stasi's bidding: "We must always ask the question if this action really springs from a Christian motivation or is really representing other interests." Officials relented when Pastor Christoph Führer of St. Nicholas pledged to censor the services so that activists would not "play into the hands of the state."[26] But rather than submit to pastoral censorship, activists attended religious services with gags reading "Silenced" over their mouths (Schwabe 1998). Interest surrounding the conflict increased attendance at the Peace Prayers, and people now began to linger after the services for informal political discussions.

The growing activism of Leipzig dissidents did not escape the attention of the police. The Stasi reported that the "so-called internal opposition" was exploiting the Church to "establish a countrywide political organization with legal recognition." A Stasi report on dissent in Leipzig explained: "The substance of the attacks made by 'human rights groups' is primarily composed of alleged violations of human rights and basic freedoms in the GDR, [rejection] of the principle of democratic centralism, and the functioning of socialist democracy."[27] In order to contain the threat, security officials increased the pressure on the Church to narrow the space for activism. Clergymen found themselves in the increasingly difficult position of appeasing state authorities without alienating congregations or provoking outcries from dissident groups.

For their part, dissidents now prepared to step outside the shelter of the Church. In June 1988 the IGL broke with convention and staged a public protest. The group's "Pleisse Memorial March" was designed to generate public awareness concerning Leipzig's abysmal environmental situation.[28] When its application for a march permit was rejected, the IGL simply "claimed for itself the right to have a demonstration." On the day of the protest, about two hundred people marched silently through city streets and then attended a teach-in at a local church.[29] Following the demonstration the Church establishment denounced the march as a "provocation" and warned against using faith as a "testing ground for revolution." A seminarian, Michael Arnold, rejected the charge, noting in his Peace Prayer sermon that "what happened here had nothing to do with a revolution of guns, but rather with a small revolution in thinking: openness, co-determination, and public responsibility."[30]

It was evident that activists planned to keep up the pressure, but they had few resources and uncertain support from Church officials. In order to compensate for these weaknesses, a "Democratic Initiative" composed of activists from several area congregations adopted the tactic of protest at public commemorations. In early January 1989 they distributed hundreds of flyers demanding "democratization of our socialist state" and calling on Leipzigers to demonstrate for glasnost during the official Luxemburg-Liebknecht anniversary celebrations. Although the Stasi was able to arrest several organizers before the January 15 anniversary, an estimated eight hundred people appeared in the city center and joined a silent march to the nearby Liebknecht memorial. Before they reached their destination, however, police responded in force, dispersing the crowd and making more than one hundred arrests.[31]

Several of the dissidents detained by the Stasi were threatened with lengthy imprisonment or expulsion from the country. But within the Church a campaign was swiftly set in motion to demand the release of the Leipzig activists. Crowds gathered at the Peace Prayers on January 16 and January 23 to demand their release. Through contacts with foreign journalists and the Church, activists were able to exploit international publicity with surprising success. The Organization for Security and Cooperation in Europe (OSCE) meeting in Vienna pressured the government of the GDR to show restraint in dealing with peaceful dissidents. And the U.S. secretary of state, George Schulz, specifically called for the release of Leipzig detainees. To their surprise, the organizers of the demonstration were released from custody within two weeks of their arrest.[32] Leipzig's dissidents had learned a valuable lesson: international publicity was not only the best way to attract public support but also the best defense against the police.

On March 13, 1989, dissidents exploited the annual international spring trade fair to stage a demonstration in view of Western journalists. Following Monday Peace Prayers in St. Nicholas, several hundred protesters and bystanders, the bulk of them exit-visa applicants according to police reports, began shouting democratic and anti-regime slogans. In the central market square, the protest was brutally dispersed in view of more than a dozen Western journalists and under the lens of a West German television crew.

With the Leipzig demonstration coming on the heels of the embarrassing *Sputnik* affair, the Stasi warned in earnest of a "campaign of propaganda and defamation against the GDR whipped up by the Western mass media" that could "seriously damage the relationship between the state and the Church."[33] But Stasi informants minimized the threat noting that Peace Prayers generally only involved people already integrated into Church-based subcultures.[34]

However, this underestimated a significant shift. Once congregants and activists began staging silent vigils on the steps of the church following religious services, others, including curious passersby and would-be exiters swelled their ranks. By the spring of 1989, the message had evidently reached beyond religious circles: if you want to voice your grievances, St. Nicholas on Monday evening is the assembly point.[35] Dissidents saw the government's upcoming communal elections in May as a chance to reveal the political fraud by which the SED operated. Because voting was mandatory in the

GDR, opposition groups encouraged citizens to either vote "No" or abstain from voting on the approved slate of candidates. On election day, activists monitored voting places to check for fraud and poll nonvoters, resulting in what the party described as "disruptions of public order" in several cities. In Leipzig, the Initiative for Democratic Renewal, organized by members of several Church-based groups, passed out flyers calling on Leipzigers not to vote and placed election monitors across the city. During the voting, several hundred citizens gathered at Leipzig's market square to demonstrate against dictatorship. Policemen and Stasi agents dispersed the crowd, and scores were arrested.[36] In explaining how the dissidents had pulled this off, security officials reported to party leaders that "the time of the planned demonstration was known through the broadcasts of [West Berlin–based] 'Radio Glasnost,' thus making the plans of these forces to attract public attention effective."[37]

Following the election, Leipzig democracy activists claimed that they could show that up to 10 percent of Leipzigers took the risk of voting "No" and that many others had refused to vote at all, clearly contradicting the regime's reported 98.8 percent participation and 98.5 percent "Yes" vote. In the days that followed, hundreds of people gathered to hear about the election fiasco at the St. Nicholas Peace Prayers. A silent march formed after the services; the police broke it up and made numerous arrests.

The May elections seem to have provided ordinary Leipzigers with their first concrete indication that there was organized opposition to the regime; some even went to city hall to request that local officials explain the discrepancies in reports about the vote.[38] Although declaring that elections were rigged in the GDR might appear to be only stating the obvious, that was actually the point: the dissidents wanted to document publicly what nearly everyone privately knew to be true. And they wanted to demonstrate that tiny anti-regime cliques were not the only people demanding reform, as state media continually claimed. A Leipzig district police report observed that "now there are increasingly appearing people who understand themselves to be the 'internal opposition in the GDR.' The turning point for this structural change can now be seen in the preparation and carrying out of the popular elections of 1989" (Schwabe 1998: 17). Prodded by mounting dissent among ordinary parishioners, the Conference of the Church Leadership of the GDR, meeting in early June, drafted a letter demanding that the state account for apparent electoral fraud and other political abuses. An investigation discovered that nearly half of Saxon clergymen had boycotted the May elections.[39]

In the next few weeks, buoyed by success, the pro-democracy demonstrators protested the June massacre in China and expressed revulsion at the Honecker regime's support for forceful handling of "counterrevolutionary" threats. The newsletter *Umweltblätter* warned East Germans that "China is not far off," describing both countries' leaders as "desperate," "half-fascist," and "foolish reactionaries." Citing Gorbachev's New Thinking, it described the use of violence as "bloodily and permanently betraying socialist goals."[40] And public defiance was now becoming more common. As the summer recess of the Peace Prayers approached, local activists declared that they would hold an independent "Leipzig Street Music Festival" in the city center on June 10. That day, police roughed up members of the crowd that had gathered to hear several musical groups perform. In response, a group of about one hundred and fifty marched on the police station singing protest songs. Policemen assaulted the marchers, driving them through downtown streets to the nearby St. Thomas Church.

In all, about one hundred and forty people were arrested. Most were detained for twenty-four hours and given a five-hundred-mark fine (about half of the average monthly salary). Police investigators reported that the "rowdy and disruptive elements" were composed chiefly of young people (on average twenty-three years old) and that many had come to the city from other districts specifically for this event. Police officials now worried that Leipzig's dissident scene had become so well known as to attract "political tourism" among malcontents.[41] Solidarity across social niches became evident as congregations drafted petitions in favor of detainees and took up collections to help pay their fines. A silent march for the release of political detainees was held, resulting in a further twenty arrests. By this point, the campaign had attracted considerable public attention, including the involvement of local cultural notables, among them Leipzig's world-renowned conductor, Kurt Masur.[42]

The Focal Point of Popular Unrest

As the Peace Prayers went into their usual summer hiatus in July 1989, the local opposition had done something new in the GDR: it had achieved a public profile. The St. Nicholas Church and its immediate surroundings were the known center of dissident activity, with no need of additional advertisement. Those willing to risk voice, such as political activists, and those who saw arrest as a vehicle to exit through expulsion, were regularly present on Monday evenings. In September, this made St. Nicholas on Monday night the ideal rallying point of a diverse assortment of groups activated by large-scale flight from the GDR.

To understand why dissidents and ordinary citizens came to the streets in numbers on Monday evenings in Leipzig, it is necessary to consider how blocked exit stimulated voice. Unlike the core dissidents, the would-be exiters that swelled their numbers were less motivated by the goal of reform than by improving their own personal circumstances through escape to the Federal Republic.[43] In denying most applicants their immediate aim of emigration, the state pushed many to put voice behind their individual aims. When they turned to "noisy" exiting, they found that they enjoyed the assistance of Church-based dissidents. A Politburo security briefing noted that "in increasing measure Church officials and other representatives of the Protestant Church are supporting the hostile influence and antisocialist activities of would-be emigrants and other citizens of the GDR."[44] By June 1989 the party's security office reported that an "exiting movement" had formed: "Communication is increasing among the applicants . . . in an attempt to achieve emigration."[45] Exit applicants were being recruited to join an "internal opposition with counterrevolutionary goals," which "made concerted efforts to create every possible form of association, [including] so-called working and self-help groups that through communication of information about activities such as silent demonstrations and marches, events in churches, but also in public areas, to bring together and mobilize such persons."[46]

The exit-voice linkages that security agencies described were most advanced in particular regions of the country where grievances were especially pronounced and local authorities failed to assert control. In some regions complacent party organizations not only failed to deter exit but also in effect promoted it: "To some degree local leaders, party brigades, and workshop masters support the exit applications of their colleagues. Even party members, union functionaries, and brigade leaders sometimes will declare their misunderstanding by asking why the citizens are not simply allowed to leave."[47] The industrial south was one such region. With only about 30 percent of the GDR's population, the Saxon districts contained more than half of all exit applicants.[48]

Some would-be exiters joined dissident protests in the hopes of being classified as seditious by the state, which, they reasoned, would lead to a swifter exit via political expulsion. In fact, the state did try to rid itself of vocal citizens, and the exiters, in turn, exploited the policy. In the spring of 1989, the SED's Office of Security Affairs reported that Leipzig applicants had learned that "confrontations with state authorities are more effective than moving within the limits of the law."[49] By that time, the Leipzig district contained only 8 percent of the GDR population but accounted for 20 percent of all exit visas granted, underscoring the volatility of Leipzig even within a broader region that was rife with discontent.[50] The police dossiers of fifty-two protesters arrested at a Monday demonstration outside St. Nicholas on May 22, 1989, show that about half had standing emigration applications. In subsequent interrogations some revealed that they were less interested in the struggle for democracy than they were in getting out of the GDR.[51] The fact that most exiters exhibited so little interest in building a human rights movement divided the dissidents. A Stasi informant in March 1988 reported that Peace Prayer organizers were split on whether "emigration should not be the goal of its work. [They say] people should be staying here and standing up for democracy and reform and having an effect."[52]

As conditions in the GDR deteriorated, the demand for legal exit was now growing uncontrollably. In June 1989 there were more than one hundred and twenty thousand outstanding applications for emigration—despite that, more than thirty-five thousand people were permitted to leave in the first half of the year. Security organs were forced to conclude that the policy of selective emigration was crumbling. The regime could neither satisfy the demand for emigration nor effectively suppress the voice that denying exit had created. Exit applicants no longer remained isolated from each other.[53] As demonstrations grew more strident in Leipzig between May and September 1989, exiters became an important element of street protest. An evaluation of police documents reveals that in the period between May 8 and September 11, 1989, about a fifth of those arrested at demonstrations had outstanding exit applications.

The contrast between voice motivated by exit and that motivated by reform became explicit in early September 1989. The start of the fall trade fair on September 4 coincided with the mounting exiting crisis (see chapter 5), making for a fortuitous set of circumstances for protesters. On that day, the first Peace Prayer services were held after a long summer recess, when many foreign businessmen and journalists were in the city. Dissidents assembled outside St. Nicholas with a banner reading "For an open country with free people" (*Für ein offenes Land mit freien Menschen*). According to police estimates, about two-thirds of the demonstrators in the streets outside St. Nicholas were would-be emigrants. As the police prepared to move in, hundreds of young people surrounding the church shouted, "We want out!" (*Wir wollen raus!*). Officers ordered the protesters to disperse and then forced them to comply. Stasi agents destroyed the banner—but not before Western reporters filmed the entire episode. As the plainclothes officers roughed up the demonstrators, angry youth yelling "*Stasi raus!*" became part of the West German evening news.

The regime swiftly responded with a press campaign warning the public that provocations were intolerable. The state youth organ *Junge Welt* published a call for a crackdown, denouncing dissidents as "egoists and political rowdies" and would-be émigrés as "lazy and irresponsible." The article blamed the movement growing around St. Nicholas on the Western media's imperialist "slander campaign" against socialism.[54] The *Leipziger Volkszeitung* published an editorial that implied that West German reporters were complicit in "antisocialist rioting."[55] The Leipzig party daily snarled, "A couple of hundred people wanted to disturb the peace. They were worth some big headlines in the FRG media, and, without exaggerating, we can see that they march shoulder to shoulder with them to disturb the peace. Fortunately, such manipulations could have no influence on the 550,000 citizens of Leipzig who ignored such disturbances and went peaceably about their business on Monday evening."[56]

It is unclear whether the propaganda and threats deterred Leipzigers from turning out on Mondays, but it certainly worked to raise awareness further about what was going on at St. Nicholas. On September 11 the traditional Monday Peace Prayers were packed with more than a thousand people eager to hear what the opposition had to say about the political crisis. Attempting a march following the prayers, some six hundred protesters were stopped in their tracks by riot police and Stasi agents. Scores were injured and more than one hundred arrested. Eighteen were charged with rioting and sentenced to four months in prison while others received draconian fines.[57]

But would repression halt the movement? Despite the propaganda, it was clear to the security agencies that the swelling Monday demonstrations were orchestrated neither by Church-based groups nor the Western press. A district police intelligence report of September 25 noted, "It is ever more evident that the area bordering the St. Nicholas Church will become an assembling point for hostile forces without there having to be a connection in time or place to the Peace Prayers that take place on Monday nights" (Schwabe 1998: 20). The district Stasi chief reported to the minister for state security that there was not "incitement on the part of church officials." The assemblies "do not need to be organized any longer" because "people gather completely on their own." Nevertheless, the district Stasi commandant expressed confidence he could contain the movement (Mitter and Wolle 1990: 128–29). Party officials were less convinced. The acting district party boss, Helmut Hackenberg, reported to the Central Committee, "The legal measures applied so far and the massive presence of the police did not succeed in suppressing or preventing the provocations that have taken place in the public squares and streets after the Monday services."[58]

In fact, despite the violent repression on September 11, the following Monday a crowd estimated at about fifteen hundred people attended services at St. Nicholas, and hundreds more joined them in the demonstration afterward. From the pulpit of St. Nicholas, Pastor Führer appealed for calm, urging composure and forbearance toward the agents of the state. This change of emphasis apparently had tremendous resonance.[59] For the first time, police now reported that a significant number of bystanders were joining in the protest. On September 18 a newly self-aware movement began drawing in bystanders with the slogan "We're staying here!" (*Wir bleiben hier!*). The slogan told the authorities that a loyal opposition was staying in the streets and squares until its demands were met. It told ordinary East Germans that the country was facing a moral crisis and that no government could remain indifferent when tens of thousands of citizens risked everything to escape. But neither appeals for peace nor expressions of loyalty prevented violent confrontations with the police and more than two hundred arrests.[60]

At the Peace Prayers on September 25, Pastor Wonneberger took to the pulpit. In front of an audience of thousands, he drew on prophetic inspiration to preach stirringly: "He who practices violence, who threatens violence and employs it, will himself be the victim of that violence. He who takes up the sword will die by the sword. He who takes up a Kalashnikov must reckon with a shot to his own head [loud applause]. . . . He who blinds another blinds himself. He who robs another of his freedom will soon have no place to run [laughter, applause]. . . . Against true power stands the Stasi apparatus, the army units, and the police dogs. But they are only paper tigers [applause]. Do not be afraid!"[61] Following the sermon, a human rights activist stressed the practical imperative of nonviolence: "One thing is clear—The first injured policeman will lead inevitably to an escalation of violence that we cannot at this point even imagine. Therefore, we who are assembled here must strictly promote the doctrine of nonviolence. And that also applies to [controlling] the provocateurs who come within our ranks."[62]

That Monday the demonstration burst the boundaries local authorities had been able to impose so far. Thousands of bystanders came to the city center to observe the demonstration, and some began to join in. At least four thousand citizens took part in the demonstration outside St. Nicholas, most protesting for the first time. Now the preponderant voice was of ordinary citizens shouting, "We are staying here!," "We are not rowdies!" and "Freedom, Equality, Fraternity!" Reflecting their diversity, protesters sang the Latin hymn "Dona nobis pacem" ("Lord, grant us peace") alongside the socialist anthem "Internationale" and the American spiritual "We shall overcome." As the crowd swelled, it moved northward toward the city's expansive transportation and administrative hub, Karl Marx Square.

The Turn to Voice

The demonstration of September 25 was the culmination of developments that had amplified and encouraged dissident voice. The customary Monday evening church services allowed for the legal assembly of diverse citizens: activists, exiters, church congregants, and curious bystanders, who by now had come to expect something at St. Nicholas on Monday nights. The Monday demonstrations were so well known by this point that those most ready to defy the state knew where to go if they were considering participation. One witness to the evolution of the Peace Prayers, the Saxon bishop Hempel, described demonstrations that had become "ritualized occurrences" by the end of September 1989. They were calculable enough such that participants joined in and dropped out at the moments most advantageous to them. The hard core of the demonstrations confronted the police directly while most participants slipped away. By the end of the month, Hempel reported, the informal rules of the game were "known to all."[63] As popular grievances mounted at the end of September and into early October 1989, the nucleus of a protest movement was already in place, and the Monday demonstrations had developed norms of conduct and a basic tactical repertoire. In short, the basic conditions for spontaneous mobilization were being set: a common focal point had been established; a widely known protest repertoire had taken shape; and the behavior of both protesters and police had become interpretable to bystanders.

The role of the Lutheran Church was crucial in the birth of voice, and it has even been called the driving force in a "Protestant revolution" (Neubert 1990; Moses 1993; Alsmeier 1994). However, this overstates its role; the Church was not an insurgent organization. Groups of dissidents found refuge in church structures mostly so they could retreat from society and "experience honesty" (Hildebrandt 1988). When activists became confrontational, clergymen usually withdrew their support. The Lutheran Church did not embody the national, cultural, or spiritual ambitions of the people as did the Roman Catholic Church in Poland, which, as Maryjane Osa (2003) demonstrates, became a symbol of a "solid nation" opposed to Communism and built a "movement that transcend[ed] social boundaries." Unlike the Polish Catholic Church or the Negro churches of the U.S. South of the 1950s and 1960s, the Lutheran Church in the GDR did not provide the overarching ties that would link activists, intellectuals, and the broader public.

Yet the churches in the GDR did provide a niche in which political subcultures could survive. From this weak position, the East German dissidents hoped to unleash a cascade of honest public expression. Publicity, including an "alternative" public sphere of their own devising, was their single shield and weapon. St. Nicholas proved an ideal venue: the church and the surrounding streets offered access to the compact city center and the large number of citizens who regularly worked, shopped, or passed through the downtown area. Crucially for the production of common knowledge that spurred subsequent mobilization, the Monday Peace Prayers became a public ritual of opposition to the state. Over the course of 1988–89, the site and time of the Monday protest gatherings became widely known. Once that was the case, the nucleus around which a spontaneous revolution would cohere had been established.

Triggering Insurgent Voice: The Exiting Crisis and the Rebellion against Communism

Democratic ideas and humanity's inherent demand for freedom have an explosive power.

—KARL MARX AND FRIEDRICH ENGELS, "ON EUROPE"

B efore September 1989 dissent was limited to political sub-cultures shielded by the Church. Yet in the fall of 1989 the repressive equilibrium suddenly gave way. Thousands, then hundreds of thousands, and finally millions of East Germans took to the streets, first in Leipzig and then in a widening number of cities. In fact, the pivotal Leipzig demonstration represents one of the great instances of mass mobilization into high-risk protest: on October 9 at least a tenth of the city's residents took to the streets in opposition to the Honecker regime and in bold defiance of threatened repression.[1] Collective action occurred despite the free-rider problem, resource deficits, threats, poor media of communication, and only a modest chance that protesters would achieve the desired change of regime. What disrupted the GDR's repressive equilibrium, and why was the popular response so massive? What drove this extraordinary instance of popular mobilization?

Changing international circumstances in the summer and fall of 1989 destabilized the GDR, in particular those surrounding the regime's policy of selective emigration. While they defied pressure to emulate Gorbachev's reforms, the leaders of the GDR also made clear that they would not loosen emigration policies even as growing numbers of citizens filed applications for exit visas. A Politburo member, Joachim Herrmann, stated bluntly in June 1989, "The Wall will continue to exist until the conditions leading to its construction are eliminated."[2] Although hard-liners affirmed their steadfastness, the Berlin Wall and the policies it represented were just one part of the Iron Curtain along which new holes were beginning to appear. Hungary's reformist party leadership, which was doing much to court popular support at home and foreign assistance from the West, by this time had come to regard the Iron Curtain as a "gruesome anachronism" (Zelikow and Rice 1995: 64). As part of its politics of liberalization, Hungary began to dismantle border fortifications with Austria in May 1989.[3]

Thanks to wide coverage in the Western media, East Germans learned of this new hole. The new exit route (*Fluchtweg*) led many to reason that it was getting easier to cross the border from Hungary into Austria, whence one would be sent to West Germany. At first, Hungarian authorities tried to prevent an East German exodus. More than half of those who attempted illegal border crossings were turned over to East German authorities. But on September 11 the Hungarian government announced that it would no longer restrict access to the Austrian frontier, even though this violated its treaties with the GDR (Zelikow and Rice 1995: 63–68). The shift in policy was influenced by West Germany, Hungary's largest Western investor and creditor, which pressured it to honor the human rights of East German refugees.[4] With their increasingly liberal convictions now reinforced by West German guarantees of billions of marks in new loans, Hungarian reformers withdrew their support from Honecker and, despite considerable diplomatic pressure from East Berlin, endorsed the UN Convention on Refugees. Hungarian authorities refused to cooperate any further in apprehending refugees.[5]

The effect of this hole in the Iron Curtain was electric. Between January and August 1989, the Ministry for State Security reported that only about 10 percent of migrants to the West had exited illegally (Mitter and Wolle 1990: 92). But once Hungary's borders became permeable, the trickle turned into a flood. In August and September 1989, more than forty thousand citizens illegally fled to the Federal Republic. In October another nearly fifty thousand citizens joined the exodus (see figure 8).[6] As the government and its allies in Czechoslovakia tried to stem it, exiters developed a second tactic in their efforts to flee, occupying West German embassies in neighboring socialist countries (Naimark 1992; Mueller 1999). Thousands flooded

FIGURE 8. Number of Emigrants from the GDR, January–October 1989

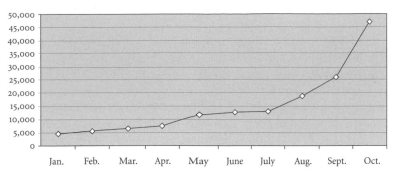

Source: Zentrales Einwohnerregister (ZER) data reported by Grundmann (1998).

embassies in Budapest, Prague, and Warsaw. The government of the GDR furiously denounced West Germany for encouraging illegal emigration and the occupation of diplomatic missions, both violations of current treaties and attacks on its sovereignty.[7] Throughout it all, Gorbachev's USSR did virtually nothing to counter this grave threat to its client.[8]

Under intense pressure, hundreds of embassy occupiers agreed to return to East Germany, but thousands more remained in Prague, Budapest, and Warsaw. On September 30, the West German foreign minister, Hans-Dietrich Genscher, and the East German foreign minister, Oskar Fischer, announced a compromise. The GDR would permit the embassy occupiers to go to the West on the condition that they be formally deprived of GDR citizenship. The refugees would travel in closed trains over GDR territory so that they could be legally "expelled" before they reached the FRG. In all more than fifteen thousand East Germans would escape by means of embassy occupation.[9]

Hoping to stop the gush of refugees, the government announced on October 3 that it was suspending visa-free travel with Czechoslovakia, the only country GDR citizens could visit without special permission—and the principal route to Hungary as well as the conduit to the FRG embassy in Prague. This step was portrayed as a joint measure of the GDR and Czechoslovakia to "normalize" travel policies and prevent imperialist schemes to destabilize and discredit the country.[10] But now, with exit routes blocked, would-be exiters were left with a stark alternative: accept their confinement in a state they opposed or risk public voice against it. Even East Germans who did not want to emigrate now saw their already strictly circumscribed opportunities for foreign travel reduced, and to many it seemed as if the government planned to imprison the entire populace.

The Honecker Regime and the Exiting Crisis

In retrospect it is striking how flat footed the East German regime was in its response to the crisis. It turned the issue, particularly the embassy affair, from a difficult diplomatic-political situation into a full-fledged domestic crisis. The regime postponed reaching a decision on Hungary for weeks and then hastily ordered a travel ban in early October. It insisted on doctrinaire measures such as having trains full of exiters cross its territory so that it could formally deprive them of citizenship as traitors to the state, an arrogant display of power that appears to have incited protest along the expulsion route.

The poor handling of the crisis can be explained, in part, by the erosion of Soviet bloc solidarity, on which the regime so clearly relied. But it may also be explained by Erich Honecker's absence, due to a serious bout with cancer, from crucial Politburo meetings between mid-August and late September 1989. Confronted by an exodus of citizens that worsened week by week, the party leadership awaited the chief's return and was divided over the severity of the problem. The expression of so much popular disapproval was disorienting, and the leadership was unsure of how to respond; Günter Schabowski recalled how a sense of "malaise" competed with outrage against this "unspeakable and unbearable manifestation of desertion" (Pond 1993: 90).

With international relations in flux, GDR diplomacy failed to adapt. As the bonds of Soviet bloc solidarity frayed, Foreign Minister Fischer pointedly denounced his Hungarian comrades for "joining the other side" (Zelikow and Rice 1995: 68). But he was forced to convey to the Politburo the sorry fact that diplomatic pressure on Hungary was no longer effective. Fully committed to economic reform, Hungary was more eager to cultivate relations with West Germany than stand by its Warsaw Pact allies. Meanwhile, in Poland, elections in the summer of 1989 had brought Solidarity to power in a government led by a non-Communist majority. The USSR had done nothing, signaling its willingness to allow change in the region.[11]

Indecision and malaise are indeed evident in the transcripts of Politburo meetings from this critical period. In the Politburo meeting of August 29, influential figures still minimized the crisis, confident that the party enjoyed the trust of the people. State Council chairman Willi Stoph argued that the regime remained strong enough for an immediate political counteroffensive. Gerhard Müller minimized the economic grievances that were driving people to exit, claiming, "We live well in the GDR. There should be no general discussion of living standards."[12] Others were not so sanguine. Joachim Hermann worried that the GDR now had its "back to the wall," and the party secretary for foreign affairs, Hermann Axen, complained about a damaging loss of public credibility, largely because Western television broadcasts had become the "enemy's strongest means" in promoting the discontent that fueled the exodus.

Again, during the September 5 meeting most Politburo leaders still seemed ready to lay full blame for the exiting crisis on a plot masterminded by Bonn and Washington, but security officials knew better. National Defense Minister Heinz Kessler reminded his comrades starkly, "One must say, that those who run away are dissatisfied with us." Erich Mielke concurred, identifying the country's serious economic deterioration as the root cause of desertion.[13] But many in the inner circle discounted reports of dire conditions within the GDR. As Honecker himself later recounted, "These reports from the Ministry of State Security . . . were just not that reliable. I myself didn't give these reports a lot of credence, because you could find everything in them in the Western media" (McAdams 1993: 196).

Egon Krenz, Honecker's trusted lieutenant and the party's security chief, drafted an internal memo on September 17 acknowledging that emigration had become a political crisis. He noted that the regime faced an unfavorable shift in international relations that it was powerless to counteract. He laid the blame on an "imperialist offensive" aimed at "dividing the socialist countries," but he also acknowledged that "bourgeois liberalism" had broken into the socialist house in Poland and Hungary. At home, confusion, resignation, and hopelessness were growing within the party. The public had real economic grievances but had been whipped into a mass hysteria by "illusionary fantasies of life in the FRG." Most worrisome to Krenz was the passivity, even approval, the Soviet regime evinced in the face of antisocialist developments. Gorbachev appeared unwilling to render any assistance to the embattled regime.[14]

In an October 3 report to Erich Honecker, who had now returned from medical treatment, Krenz outlined the crisis in terms of three political options. The first would be to liberalize travel and emigration laws contingent on a binding recognition of GDR citizenship by West Germany; the second would be the immediate closing of borders with neighboring socialist states, laying the blame for the crisis on West Germany; and the third would be to seize the political initiative by immediately granting citizens broader travel rights and thereby satisfying calls for liberalization at home and abroad. Krenz reasoned, "The third variant is the best because it is aimed at a permanent solution. It would, however, mean the further loss of tens, if not hundreds, of thousands of citizens." However, in view of the dire economic consequences of the loss of labor power in the already staggering GDR economy, Krenz felt compelled to recommend the second option.[15]

Cutting off the exit routes came at the cost of further discrediting the regime in the eyes of its citizens and the international community, an audience that Gorbachev was working hard to court. Meanwhile, the regime turned up its propaganda offensive. State media denounced exiters as instruments of Western imperialism, misled by materialism and by an illusionary faith in capitalism. On October 2, the SED leadership savaged exiters in the pages of *Neues Deutschland* as "antisocial elements" and reassured citizens: "Through their actions, they have all trampled on moral values and cut themselves off from our society. Thus no tears need be shed for them."[16] However, if these statements were intended to marginalize refugees or restore confidence in the system, they appear to have seriously misfired. In effect, ordinary East Germans were being told to turn their backs on the thousands of mostly young people—friends, children, relations, colleagues—without mourning their loss, all the while facing the material insecurity that the loss of so much labor power would undoubtedly produce. And for those who had been planning to exit, they now had no choice but to rebel or remain silently behind.

Double Jeopardy: Exit and the Fortieth Anniversary of the GDR

By coincidence, the exiting crisis overlapped with a highly symbolic, politically charged event: the long-planned celebration of the creation of the socialist GDR in 1949. If mass exit focused discontent, the GDR's birthday celebrations gave it a clear object. Coming on the heels of the decision to close the borders, the state visit of Mikhail Gorbachev raised expectations and brought forth the first countrywide rumblings of public discontent. The coincidence of the exiting crisis with the fortieth anniversary magnified the voice of dissident groups and occasioned their first concerted efforts to organize a political movement. In September and early October, numerous theater groups, musical performers, and artists issued statements condemning the government and supporting opposition groups. Even some members of the ordinarily compliant Church hierarchy criticized the Honecker government's handling of the exiting problem.

Prior to October 1989, with the partial exception of Leipzig, the opposition in the GDR was small, disorganized, and under unremitting police surveillance. In August Stasi estimates reckoned the various opposition groups as having no more than twenty-five hundred active members divided into about one hundred and sixty groups.[17] Even in Saxony, the crucible of popular protest in the GDR, the opposition still remained embryonic. The Stasi reported fifteen independent political groups in Dresden, chiefly peace and environmental groups,[18] and roughly twenty peace, environmental, and civil rights groups in the district of Karl-Marx-Stadt (Chemnitz). Leipzig had about thirty politically alternative groups, involving perhaps a thousand people. But even with thousands taking part in a demonstration on September 25, this means that before October 9 only about 1 percent of the population had any involvement at all with the opposition.[19]

Indeed, state security reports indicated that even if they did proliferate over the course of 1988–89, most Church-based groups had only a handful of active members, and their efforts were highly circumscribed by police surveillance and infiltration.[20] In fact, it was only in September 1989, in the midst of the exiting crisis, that what became known as the East German civic movement (*Bürgerbewegung*) was born. Networks of activists in Berlin, Leipzig, and other cities had been discussing plans to build a united opposition movement throughout 1989. Nevertheless, the founding of new organizations came only with the urgency of the exiting crisis and the increased attention that the Western media began to pay East German affairs (Neubert 1998; Pollack and Rink 1997; Torpey 1995; Joppke 1995; Findeis, Pollack, and Schilling 1994).

On August 31 a Social Democratic Party was formed; an appeal of the

United Left was announced on September 4; the most prominent of the organizations in the nascent civic movement, New Forum (Neues Forum), held a founding convention outside Berlin on the weekend of September 9 and 10 and issued a petition drive in favor of reform; the group Democracy Now (Demokratie Jetzt) called for a new opposition movement at a GDR-wide Church conference in Eisenach on September 15; Democratic Awakening (Demokratischer Aufbruch), organized by pastors and Church officials, appealed to the public on September 14. Distributed through the churches and broadcast over Western media, these early statements made clear that the SED finally faced an opposition with political aims. Although New Forum was still an embryonic organization, it quickly gained the most attention, and its message of socialist reform spread. In the period leading up to October 7–8, thousands of citizens signed its founding petition (see chapter 8 for a detailed analysis of the civic movement).

Despite the exiting problem and the statements of newly assertive dissident circles, the regime still expected that the long-planned celebration of the GDR's fortieth anniversary scheduled for October 7–8 would reaffirm party loyalty and serve as a public display of the regime's strength. In order to ensure that the celebrations would not be disrupted, Honecker, in his capacity as chairman of the National Defense Council (Verteidigungsrat), ordered that local police agencies be put under the emergency authority of the Ministry for State Security and that about twenty thousand army troops be mobilized for domestic security (Friedheim 1997: 245–49).

And despite signs that the regime was increasingly vulnerable because of the eroding Soviet bloc, there was no shift in domestic policy that would provide favorable opportunities for domestic challengers. Backed by the massive deployment of the security forces, the gala celebration of the GDR's achievements went ahead. In East Berlin on the evening of October 6, a hundred thousand party members, troops, and socialist youth activists assembled to celebrate four decades of victorious socialism and proclaim their loyalty to their beloved "outpost of peace and socialism in Europe." Honecker himself presided over the great torch-lit march of the party faithful, praising the country's heroic achievements, denouncing imperialist foes, and pledging to keep to the party's proven course. But everyone was really interested in what Mikhail Gorbachev would say on the occasion. Initially, Gorbachev had resisted visiting the GDR on its birthday because of his reluctance to offer Honecker support. But under pressure from hard-liners in the USSR who wanted assurances that the German outpost would not be abandoned, he agreed to attend the anniversary (Zelikow and Rice 1995: 72). Gorbachev struck a different note in his address, sending an unmistakable signal of his disapproval of the regime: "The choice among forms of development remains a sovereign decision of each people. . . . Democratization, openness, socialism, free development of all peoples and their equal participation in the country's affairs, dignified living conditions for the entire population and guaranteed rights for all, extensive opportunities for creative expression by each individual—this is what we are striving for, and we will not be diverted from these goals" (Jarausch and Gransow 1994: 54–55). Although Gorbachev made no move to oust Honecker or encourage those who would, his statements were taken as a sign that the USSR might well approve of a change of leadership.

Gorbachev's visit to the People's Republic of China earlier in the year had raised expectations among Chinese students that change was possible; now he awakened hopes for change in East Germany.[21] Dissidents knew that a visit by the prophet of reform would also bring extensive international news coverage that could be exploited. Seizing the opportunity, dissidents in East Berlin attempted a candlelight march from the Gethsemane Church to the city center on October 6. Another protest march involving some three thousand people formed parallel to the official commemorations and tried to reach the Palace of the Republic near the Alexanderplatz. As the evening progressed, some spectators at the official ceremony tried to cross over to the demonstration but faced aggressive riot policemen. Protesters shouted, "Gorby, Gorby, Gorby" and "Gorby, help us," cries audible even on the official podium. Riot police and Stasi operatives drove the protesters back into the crowded Prenzlauer Berg neighborhood, where the crowd swelled to an estimated five thousand citizens before finally being dispersed (Friedheim 1997: 262).

The unrest was widely reported in the Western media and, in turn, reached most East German households. With dissatisfied citizens newly emboldened, disturbances and clashes between the police and demonstrators continued on October 7. Stasi chief Mielke ordered that police should "aggressively disperse" crowds and authorized officers to carry firearms (Friedheim 1997: 263). Aggressive police measures during that weekend resulted in more than a thousand arrests and scores of injuries in East Berlin. But interrogations revealed that those detained were not the usual suspects. The arrested protesters were disproportionately workers less than twenty-five years old, and few of them (just 12 percent) were highly educated.[22] In fact, in their social profile these protesters were more like the exiters than the Church-based dissidents.

The East German press service blamed the debacle on imperialist provocation: "Acting alongside the Western media, rowdies rioted on the Alexanderplatz and the surrounding area shouting slogans hostile to the republic. The restraint of the police and security forces is to be praised that an international incident did not occur."[23] But it was not only in the capital that the regime's birthday party was spoiled. Strident, sometimes violent, anti-regime protests occurred in Leipzig, Dresden, Karl-Marx-Stadt, Halle, Magdeburg, Plauen, Potsdam, Arnstadt, Bischofswerda, and Dippoldiswalde. The Ministry of the Interior reported that in all at least seventeen thousand people took part in protests against the regime between October 6 and October 8 and that more than fifteen hundred citizens were arrested outside the capital during the anniversary.

In East Berlin the government restored order through the ruthless use of security forces, but in some provincial centers the rebellion spread unchecked. For the previous few years, the Ministry of the Interior granted a disproportionate share of exit visas in the Saxon districts in order to relieve domestic pressure. As was noted in chapter 4, Saxons, representing less than a third of the GDR population, received more than half of the exit visas granted in the late 1980s.[24] In 1988 residents of the Dresden district led the GDR in applications for emigration at a rate nearly three times the national average (see figure 3). Now, with illegal exit becoming easier, the real exodus began. In August and September 1989, nearly twenty thousand citizens of the Saxon districts fled the GDR, about 40 percent of the total exodus. Party officials in the city of Leipzig estimated that two thousand residents had emigrated and that more than ten thousand had filed new applications for exit visas.[25] Exit was clearly fraying the bonds of political control, and local officials warned of "sharp and impatient criticism" in Saxon districts.[26]

On September 13, the SED leadership in Dresden met to discuss the exit problem, acknowledging that socialism was in crisis and warning of its failing authority (Friedrich 1994: 5). Yet regional and local party officials still made no move to break with East Berlin. At a party conference in mid-September, the Leipzig district leadership published an open letter to Erich Honecker and the Central Committee pledging full support against "imperialist threats to the socialist fatherland."[27] Leipzig's party chief sneered that exiters were thankless dupes who "worship[ped] the Golden Calf" and promised to help halt the "panicked stampede" of selfish youths misled by the "mad slander campaign of the enemy." Rank-and-file party members were warned against talk of reform and were cautioned that human rights dissidents were out to "restore capitalist relations."[28] Officials declared that "riotous" assemblies would not be tolerated and that order and security would be restored in Leipzig.

However, in the days following the closing of the Czechoslovak border and the expulsion from the West German embassy in Prague, protests spread in the Saxon region. In Karl-Marx-Stadt a crowd estimated at eight hundred people mobbed the railway station in an effort to board the expulsion trains from Prague passing through on October 3. The riot police restored order after making dozens of arrests, but on the seventh some five hundred protesters again assembled in the city center. In the nearby industrial border town of Plauen, strident anti-regime protest also erupted along the route of the expulsion trains. Between October 2 and October 5, as sealed trains passed by, hundreds of local residents came to the railway tracks to express their solidarity with the expellees or to try to board the trains. On the evening of October 4, paramilitary riot police units under the direction of the Stasi were deployed to clear the railway by force. On October 7 angry Plaueners marched on the town hall. Riot police and paramilitary forces struck with water cannons and clubs to disperse an estimated four thousand protesters. Violent clashes resulted, and demonstrators hurled paving stones and bottles at the police, overturned police cars, and smashed the windows of the town hall. The police restored order, but the situation remained tense. A week later an estimated ten thousand people—nearly 15 percent of the city's population—protested police brutality.[29]

Among all East German cities in the fall of 1989, Dresden most clearly showed the explosive potential of exit-voice dynamics. In the first week of October, the city experienced the worst and most sustained violence of East Germany's largely peaceful revolution. Days of angry confrontations between protesters, police, and army units left hundreds injured and resulted in more than thirteen hundred arrests in the Dresden district. Like Plauen, Dresden was close to the German-Czech border and felt the effects of the exiting crisis directly. With the borders closed, many young Dresdeners reportedly thought it would be possible to board the special expulsion trains that were crossing the GDR on their way to West Germany. As the sealed trains bearing those who had occupied the FRG embassies made their way through the south of the GDR on October 3 and 4, crowds mobbed railway stations in an effort to board the westward-bound trains while peaceful demonstrators gathered along the tracks to protest the policies of the Honecker regime. On October 4 district Stasi officials in Dresden reported to Berlin that protest was erupting in Bad Schandau, a border crossing just south of Dresden. There, a crowd of some fourteen hundred people forcibly tried to board trains leaving the GDR. When policemen prevented them, the crowd swelled to an estimated two thousand young persons shouting, "We want out!" As police tried to clear the station, violent scuffles broke out; protesters threw stones and bottles at policemen; and three dozen protesters were detained. Later that day an estimated twenty-five hundred people tried to force their way into the Dresden main railway station. When riot police prevented them from reaching the tracks, several thousand people surrounding the station began shouting, "Stasi state!" "Freedom!" and "Gorby!"

In retaking the rail station, authorities deployed thousands of riot police officers, Communist militiamen (*Kampfgruppen*) and National People's Army (NVA) troops. With the help of water cannons, the protesters were dispersed, but there were numerous injuries on both sides. Police vehicles were tipped over and burned, and more than two hundred people were arrested. Finally, in the early morning hours of October 5, sealed trains bearing the expelled citizens were able to pass through the Dresden station.[30] Ominous (but ultimately false) rumors circulated that demonstrators had been killed and whisked away.[31]

For their part, local SED leaders were shocked by the news, by the visible destruction wrought on the central railway station, and by the persistence of the crowds in the face of a police crackdown. Hans Modrow, Dresden's district party chief, convened a meeting of the district defense council, including the regional directors of the police, the Stasi, and the army command. The council approved the deployment of several NVA units, including elements of the Seventh Panzer Division. However, even though Modrow pledged to restore order in the city, officials failed to reach a consensus on how much force was justified against protesters (Friedheim 1997: 293–303).

The following day, a demonstration of several thousand people whom the Stasi called the "militant core" of the opposition confronted police and troops near the train station. Shouting "We want out!" and "Stasi pigs!" demonstrators again clashed with security forces, leading to another two hundred arrests.[32] Meanwhile, in anticipation of the state anniversary celebrations, the Dresden party leadership was instructed by Berlin not to allow disturbances that might create a diplomatic crisis during Gorbachev's state visit. Modrow dutifully instructed municipal and local party officials to suppress all "hostile" and "anti-GDR" protests. On the afternoon of October 6, a demonstration of some four thousand citizens was dispersed from the city center at the cost of an additional three hundred and sixty arrests. But now the widening rebellion posed a dilemma. Despite the large numbers of police officers and troops deployed, as well as the mounting tally of arrests, there was no sign that repression was deterring protesters. Modrow told district officials that the political situation was deteriorating and that the demonstrations were resonating broadly in the population. While he noted that Church officials in Dresden were not interested in "an open confrontation with the SED" and were "distancing themselves from rioting," they were supporting the recently established New Forum. More worrisome, the exiting crisis had led to a wave of resignations from the SED and the state labor union organization (FDGB), to unauthorized work stoppages, and, on the evening of the fortieth anniversary, the cast of the Dresden State Theater "exited their roles" during a performance and read a protest resolution decrying the state and party leadership (Friedrich 1994: 31–32).

The following day, thousands of protesters marred the carefully planned celebrations of the national holiday. While most of the demonstrators marched through the city peacefully chanting "Freedom," "Gorby," and "We demand New Forum," stone-throwing youths clashed with police, leading to more than one hundred arrests.[33] A Leipziger who took part in the Dresden demonstrations was startled to find them more aggressive and polarized than the Monday demonstrations that had arisen back home. "The march was very isolated. There were not as many people joining in during the march as in Leipzig. . . . In comparison with Leipzig demonstrations, there were many more young people present." He was especially worried by the presence of rowdy teenagers.[34] Dissidents and clergymen urged nonviolent protest but could not prevent clashes between angry youths and nervous policemen. Many tried to quell violence with chants such as "No violence!" and by calling to the police, "Brothers, join us" and "Aren't you ashamed?" Church activists carried candles and urged peace and reconciliation, but despite these efforts protesters clashed with police, and bystanders were seized by the police and beaten.

The deployment of army and paramilitary riot police units in Dresden apparently failed to deter widening protest, contrary to the assurances of security officials. Some Dresdeners later reported that they joined the demonstrations precisely because they were outraged by what they considered to be the illegitimate use of force by the state.[35] After several days of protests, however, solidarity and a sense of common purpose began to emerge. On public squares and in the streets, demonstrators began to sing the same songs and chant the same protest slogans. Citizens assisted the injured and jeered when any among them were arrested. At the Fetscherplatz in the city center, police and NVA units took over three hundred people into custody. As they were herded onto trucks, fellow citizens shouted encouragements and applauded their bravery while soldiers were heckled. Even in detention demonstrators tried to maintain high spirits, share food, and tease their jailers.[36]

The rebellion in Dresden reached its crescendo on October 8, when more than five thousand protesters defied the police by staging sit-ins and candlelight marches on the central Prager Strasse. After the police failed in their attempts to clear the streets, Church officials and a handful of opposition activists intervened, insisting on absolute nonviolence. With both sides exhausted after days of confrontation, local officials were ready for compromise. Acting against the advice of the district Stasi chief, and without prior approval from his superiors in Berlin, Modrow tried to decelerate the conflict, offering demonstrators a political dialogue in exchange for clearing the streets (Friedheim 1997: 293–303). Dresden mayor Wolfgang Berghofer agreed to meet with representatives of the demonstrators and the churches. On the spot, Church officials and activists selected the "Group of Twenty" representatives from the peaceful demonstration and charged them with presenting citizen grievances (Friedrich 1994: 35).

The actions of the Dresden leadership set a dangerous precedent for the Honecker regime. The breakthrough in Dresden had occurred not only because regional officials sought an unauthorized compromise but also because the demonstrators themselves had begun to organize. The Dresden Stasi reported to Berlin:

> The vandalism on the evening of October 4 and 5 had a large public impact. . . . In this situation it can been seen that the Lutheran Church and the followers of the "New Forum" began to initiate peaceful forms of resistance by, on the one hand, denouncing the vandalism but, on the other hand, voicing intense calls for the elimination of the causes of discontent in the populace through reforms and alterations of the policies of the SED and the government. As a result, the composition of the demonstrators and of the assemblies has changed. The [subsequent] actions lost their aggression and physical violence . . . [shifting to] passive resistance against the measures of the security and defense forces.[37]

In their October 9 meeting with Berghofer, clergymen and the Group of Twenty presented demands for expanded press freedom, the legalization of New Forum in Dresden, freedom of assembly, and a state-society dialogue on necessary reforms. For their part Modrow and his advisers saw evidence of reformist loyalty in this program, hoping for a pragmatic solution to the GDR's widening crisis. In Dresden the authorities had been pushed to the brink of a bloody confrontation; they blinked and thereby helped to set a peaceful revolution in motion.

Mass Mobilization and the "Miracle" of Leipzig

As was discussed in chapter 4, over the course of September, the Leipzig Monday demonstrations had swelled from a small activist core to raucous protests involving hundreds of citizens. Up to that point, the police had not deterred noisy protesters from crowding into downtown Leipzig on Monday evenings, in spite of their brandishing billy clubs and making scores of arrests. Nevertheless, the district secret police chief was confident that the threat was manageable and that protest could be contained in the area immediately surrounding St. Nicholas Church. Yet on Monday, October 2, protesters shouting "We're staying here!" left the narrow streets around the church and marched onto Karl Marx Square. Bystanders now began to join the march, singing and shouting anti-regime slogans alongside the dissidents.

Baffled by the seeming spontaneity of the developments, the Leipzig chief of police reported to the Interior Ministry, "A clearly recognizable demonstration march began to form on Georgi Avenue in the direction of the main train station. Ringleaders and organizers could not be directly made out. During this period definite indecisiveness was discernable."[38] As the crowd swelled on Karl Marx Square, a procession began to form in the direction of the city's main ring boulevard. One Leipziger exclaimed at the sight of his fellow citizens' flooding the downtown on Monday night, "Suddenly, the country was no longer what it had previously been" (Zwahr 1993: 40). In all, as many as eight thousand people took part in the march before riot police were able to disperse it.

The demonstration on October 2 came to an end not because the police had withdrawn, or because the regime had promised concessions, or because the state had made some other indication of a new tolerance for popular dissent. As the district police report clearly indicates, "Demonstrative deployment of a company [of riot police] with body armor had [an] immediate effect. The mass of people distanced itself from the security forces and fled the streets and public squares. Police maneuvers dissolved the assembly. . . . The psychological effect of the riot equipment brought us success against the hostile forces and restored confidence in our own ranks. Self-confidence [on the side of the police] was strengthened."[39] Following this show of force, local security officials were convinced that a demonstrative police action involving special military police and army units could deter another demonstration of this magnitude.

Parallel to police measures, local officials launched a campaign of propaganda and intimidation. The *Leipziger Volkszeitung* praised the police and the armed party militia for forcefully suppressing "unlawful rioting" by "dangerous rowdies."[40] In the days leading to October 9, the threats of a crackdown became more menacing. The commander of a party militia unit published an open letter in the Leipzig daily demanding an end to "activities hostile to the state" and warning, "We are willing and able to protect effectively that which we have created through our own work and to stop these counterrevolutionary actions once and for all—If necessary with weapons in hand!"[41] Shops and business in downtown Leipzig were instructed to close early on Monday evening, and citizens were warned that they should avoid the city center at all costs. In one documented instance, a factory director advised his employees against taking part in demonstrations led by "vandals and rowdies who must be brought to reason with cudgels."[42] And on the morning of October 9 the district party daily, the *Sächsisches Tageblatt*, announced on its front page that if a "rowdy minority continues to blow a storm against the state with its reform-trumpets, then it will reap a storm in return and, if necessary, not merely a storm of verbal discouragement."[43]

Consequently, rumors of a planned "Chinese solution" to the unrest were rife in Leipzig. The sense of menace was further fueled by the deployment of military riot police and regular army units in the district and by the recent rioting along the Czechoslovakian border. All accounts make clear that citizens feared a bloodbath. One participant recalled that Leipzig "looked like an army camp" (Schneider 1990: 7), and word spread that the city was surrounded by tanks while the medical authorities were preparing blood reserves and emergency rooms (Zwahr 1993). Mobilized riot policemen and Communist militiamen were prepared to confront the "rowdies," "counter-revolutionaries," and other dangerous elements whom state authorities blamed for unrest in the GDR. As security forces gathered and crowds began to form in the narrow streets around St. Nicholas and other churches to hear Peace Prayers, an unexpected set of events transpired. First, large numbers of citizens—far beyond the numbers the police had prepared to confront—began to fill the downtown streets on Monday afternoon. Second, clergymen and dissidents made powerful appeals for peace and nonviolence, and additional churches were opened up for Peace Prayers. Finally, just before 5:00 p.m. a public appeal by the "Leipzig Six"—an ad hoc coalition of district party officials and prominent cultural figures—called on both sides to remain calm and endorsed dialogue. (For an analysis of the local government's retreat, see chapter 7).

But even at 5:00 p.m. the outcome remained uncertain as unprecedented masses—ultimately at least seventy thousand citizens and as many as one hundred twenty thousand—clogged Leipzig's compact city center. Neither the nascent civic movement nor the police were prepared to control crowds of this size, and both feared disaster. But the widely expected violence and disorder did not occur. Instead, what transpired was popularly dubbed the "miracle" of Leipzig and even the official police report of the event sent to the Interior Ministry conveys a sense of wonder:

At the end of the church services the participants assembled in the area of the Karl Marx Square/Georgi Avenue and formed into a procession. A protest march began through the city center. During it additional citizens continually joined in the march. In all, approximately 70,000 persons took part. During the march, slogans such as "We are the people" (*Wir sind das Volk!*), "Legalize New Forum," "Gorby, Gorby, Gorby," and "We are staying here, we're not rowdies," were shouted. Two banners with texts reading, "We don't want violence" and "Legalize New Forum," along with lit candles, were carried along. On marching past the police and State Security [Stasi] headquarters, there were whistles and boos as well as the call "Join in with us!" After the procession reached Karl Marx Square again, at about 9 p.m., it dissolved itself independently.[44]

In spite of prior repression and threats of worse to come, the authorities did not swing their clubs or open fire. Despite lacking adequate social movement organization, the demonstrations nevertheless proceeded in a peaceful and organized manner, unlike the chaotic scene that had unfolded in Dresden. And both of these unexpected outcomes grew from a tiny dissident core to involve tens of thousands of ordinary citizens.

Karl-Dieter Opp observes: "One of the most fascinating and puzzling features of the revolution in the GDR is the fact that the citizens took action in spite of the danger involved. How can it be that a single citizen, who certainly cannot influence the process of history, takes part in the demonstrations in Leipzig on October 9, 1989, although he had to face the risk of a bloodbath?" Drawing on a survey of more than a thousand Leipzigers and over two hundred self-declared oppositionists conducted a year after the events of 1989, Opp and his colleagues find that "spontaneous cooperation" —the uncoordinated result of many discrete individuals reacting to the same set of interests, incentives, norms, and expectations at the same time— explains the sudden appearance of mass protest.[45] Yet the cooperation Opp describes had to occur in spite of the expectation that participation could have been dangerous to the individual. Both fear and the rational temptation to follow an opportunistic wait-and-see strategy could have led individuals to remain bystanders. If enough of them had stood by the side, the "miracle" of October 9 presumably would not have taken place.

In fact, most of the evidence suggests there was a general fear that the state would make good on its threatened repression of the protest movement, including violent dispersal of crowds by the armed forces. In their accounts of the days leading up to the "miracle" on October 9, Leipzigers reported strong anticipation that the Honecker regime would not go down without a fight. Zwahr (1993: 81) has aptly summarized the situation: "On October 8 and 9 in Leipzig the fear that the Monday demonstration would be bloodily suppressed was general." This contention is supported by the available evidence. In his survey Opp (1994) found that nearly 70 percent of the respondents expected drastic measures to be used against demonstrators on October 9. For them, an attempted "Chinese solution" was credible; Opp concludes, "At least on October 9, [expected] probability and costs of repression were *larger* than before" (129, emphasis added). This seems justified. My analysis of oral histories of protest participants that were published within three years of October 1989 found that half of the Leipzigers who participated in Monday demonstrations on or before October 9 described themselves as "fearful," or "full of dread" in the face of threatened repression.[46]

It is well established in the theory of collective action that even if members of a group share a common interest, they will not necessarily make individual contributions to produce public goods. In part, this is because of the well-known problems associated with free-riding on the efforts of others, because of the obstacles to cooperation when information is incomplete or communication difficult (as in the prisoner's dilemma), and because of the difficulty of achieving effective social solidarity in large, diverse groups (Olson 1965; Hardin 1982; Taylor 1987; Hechter 1987; Coleman 1990). All of these factors should make the mobilization we observe in the fall of 1989 in the GDR unlikely. As Jack Goldstone (2003: 71) has noted, "For any individual the logical incentives were strongly in favor of not joining a revolutionary protest, as individuals faced substantial risks but were unlikely to change the outcome." Indeed, so pessimistic are the general implications of much of the literature on collective action that widespread mobilization would seem unlikely under most circumstances and particularly so in repressive regimes, where the potential costs of participation are high and the likely policy effect of protest modest (Olson 1965, 1990; Tullock 1971; Klandermans 1984; Lichbach 1994).

How then to explain the spontaneous rebellion documented by Opp? On October 9 the problem was not one of citizens' having been unsure of where and when other people would gather. As we saw in chapter 4, by this point the regular Monday evening Peace Prayers had become common knowledge in the city, and even beyond it.[47] Clearly, if individual citizens of Leipzig had been adequately motivated to protest, they would have known where to go to register opposition to the regime. Given these conditions, Opp's analysis is persuasive. But he may overestimate the spontaneity of the protest on October 9 by overlooking the role of dissidents in providing elementary means of coordination. The dilemma dissidents faced on October 9 was not how to communicate popular opposition to Honecker—people were coming into the streets in droves—but rather how to stage an effective protest that would minimize the hazards of repression. Recall that before October 9 much of the protest associated with the exiting crisis involved rioting and violent clashes with police and troops in cities like Dresden, Plauen, and Karl-Marx-Stadt. Street clashes also occurred during the celebration of the GDR's fortieth anniversary on October 6–7 in East Berlin and Leipzig. In each case, security forces struck back hard, deploying anti-riot measures against protesters and arresting thousands. As the Monday demonstrations swelled from a few score participants in September to thousands in October 1989, there was a real risk that loosely organized dissident groups would be unable to contain the resulting volatility. A Tiananmen-style military crackdown might be the result.

And yet, however eager dissidents may have been to play the role of moderating agents in Leipzig, several factors stood in the way. The New Forum manifesto provided protesters with a rallying cry in the streets of Leipzig, Dresden, and East Berlin. But this did not mean that the embryonic opposition groups had the organizational means to achieve their aims. In Leipzig, New Forum only came into being in late September and consisted of a couple of dozen activists and about a hundred supporters. It had no office space, telephones, copying machines, or any other resources of its own; communications media were limited to posters and flyers distributed at the Peace Prayers.[48]

Although activists carried a banner painted with its name on October 9, New Forum did not compose an organized presence at the Monday demonstrations until two weeks later, when it finally publicly addressed the crowds on October 23. Indeed, after the first large Monday demonstration on October 2, Michael Arnold, a leading New Forum activist, conceded to a Western reporter that there was little his tiny group could do to guide the masses toward nonviolence.[49] A Stasi informant reported in early October that New Forum activists had not mobilized the masses at the Monday demonstrations and knew no more than anyone else about what to expect on the ninth:

"He [Arnold] does not know anything specific and will not take part himself. He gave the source two leaflets from 'New Forum' that call for nonviolence. These leaflets are also to be distributed on Monday, October 9, at the St. Nicholas Church. Arnold thinks that by no means should bloody confrontations be allowed to develop on the national holiday [October 7] because "then the state will finally have the opportunity to snuff out the light."[50] Clearly the nascent civic movement lacked the influence and resources to mobilize or direct large-scale demonstrations and was vulnerable to repression. But the dissidents had resourceful allies in the Church.

Church officials were strongly committed to nonviolence on moral grounds, even if their reach into the general population was limited. Like the dissidents, the clergy in Saxony generally favored reform, but they were also interested in preserving the peace and forestalling threats to the Church's legal status and privileges.[51] As the opposition groups became more vocal, Church officials dutifully insisted on "political neutrality," but activists appealed to lay members to support "active evangelism" and "bearing public witness through protest."[52] They won sympathy by pledging "to speak the truth about the country" and to combat the "lack of political voice" that reigned in the GDR.[53] With pressure from an activated laity and with the country veering toward a crisis, Church leaders had become more assertive. For example, in conversation with city officials in March 1989, the Saxon bishop Johannes Hempel reminded them that it was the state that was to blame for the growing opposition movement because of numerous "deficits in freedom of speech and expression."[54] And by July 1989 an SED security report found that the opposition had found stable refuge in the Church.[55] At the start of the exiting crisis, local Church officials in Saxony quietly threw their support behind the dissidents, extending the Monday evening Peace Prayers to other downtown churches besides St. Nicholas. Although local party leaders demanded that the Peace Prayers be banned as the source of "all hostile activities,"[56] Hempel pointed out the apparent fact that demonstrations were forming spontaneously. Rather than canceling the services, the best way of averting radicalization was to extend the message of peace and reconciliation to the widest possible audience.[57] The Leipzig pastor Klaus Kaden acknowledged that the opposition's nonviolence and its moral objection to tyranny convinced many Christians of the necessity of quiet support even as a Chinese solution loomed (Philipsen 1993: 354).

Pastor Hans-Jürgen Sievers of the Reformed Church explained that the unexpected appearance of mass protests in early October forged the cooperation with dissidents: "It was unavoidable that October 9 forced a decision . . . and we wanted to do everything possible to prevent bloodshed."[58] Accordingly, on the ninth Peace Prayer sermons stressed three themes: courage in the face of official intimidation, the need for nonviolence, and the united will of the people (see Hanisch et al. 1996: 36–53). Clergymen also had another advantage: they were informed on the afternoon of October 9 that some moderate local party officials were trying to appeal for toleration of nonviolent protest (see chapter 7). And although riot police, militia units, and troops were surrounding the city center, participants at the Peace Prayers learned of public appeals for peace and dialogue from local leaders, the Leipzig human rights groups, Hempel, and the Catholic clergy (Hanisch et al. 1996). In the churches, New Forum activists passed out leaflets appealing for nonviolence.

And at St. Nicholas the evening's sermon insisted on absolute nonviolence: "Every one listening, every participant in these devotions has the great task of being an instrument for peace. The spirit of peace must go forth from these walls. See to it that the men in uniform are not antagonized. Make sure that no songs or slogans are shouted that would provoke the authorities. Snatch away the stones that have found their way into the balled fists of your neighbors. Only through God is there help and protection!" (Hanisch et al. 1996: 42).

Likewise, at St. Thomas, famous as J. S. Bach's church, Bishop Hempel asked that "blood not be spilled" and counseled his fellow citizens to "maintain a cool head, be reasonable, and absolutely nonviolent" (Hanisch et al. 1996: 47). Preaching from the Proverbs,[59] Church Superintendent Johannes Richter declared to the swollen congregation, "There is for us no alternative to dialogue. We have nothing other than the strength of argument. There is nothing for us except fearlessness in the truth" (50). Pastor Sievers drew on the example of Martin Luther King and the American civil rights struggle to convince his audience that the regime's militant rhetoric belied a faltering confidence. "The policemen and militiamen are afraid of the people who've taken to the streets" (46), he declared. If absolute nonviolence prevailed, the "men in uniform" would lose their will.

The church services thus provided members of the crowd with some of the prerequisites of effective cooperation. Protesters already knew of the risks of violence, but now thousands had some concrete indication that a bloodbath might be avoided. Through the Peace Prayers, the mass demonstration was seeded with citizens that knew if they helped to keep peace and order, then others would likewise restrain themselves and their fellow demonstrators. On October 9 protesters continually exhorted each other with "No violence!" and maintained order within the ranks of the marchers. Christians sang "Dona nobis pacem" and other hymns. When they encountered the ranks of riot policemen and troops, citizens chanted, "We don't want violence," "We are not rowdies," and "Brothers, join us!" (Neues Forum Leipzig 1990, 1991; Zwahr 1993). At previous Monday demonstrations, protesters had attempted to break through police lines, and a few sought to provoke the authorities. Apparently, this was not the case on October 9. Citizens surrounded rowdies to ensure that they would not tangle with the police. Remarkably, the police reported that "ringleaders and organizers" could not be identified despite the demonstration's apparent order. The peaceful, almost disciplined, behavior of the crowd seems to have provided worried security officials with no pretense for the use of force. One police official later recounted: "Many honest comrades actually thought this was the mob. Then we saw they were entirely normal people shouting *Wir sind das Volk*, and we belonged to them too" (Pond 1993: 118).

Moreover, the evidence suggests that ordinary citizens did not join the mass demonstration in a disorderly fashion. It appears that informal groups provided vehicles for mobilization. A citizen's willingness to protest may be based less on formal organizational ties than on the support of family, friends, and acquaintances. The trust that obtains in such groups may make citizens confident that if they are driven to protest, others will also be driven to it. This robust interpersonal trust is most common in smaller, intimate groups, "large enough to have an impact on the collective, yet small enough to provide a unique identity" (Brewer and Schneider 1990). Small groups like these are easier to coordinate and usually have more success deterring free-riding than larger groups (Olson 1965; Taylor 1987; Hechter 1987). Small personal circles united by "pleasure in the life of the group" (Hardin 1982) can provide real incentives for collective action; this is a point nicely illustrated by Dennis Chong (1991: 35) in his study of the U.S. civil rights movement, where he observes that "friendship and familial, religious, and professional relationships create an array of ongoing exchanges, obligations, and expectations that individual members have considerable incentive to uphold."

If we imagine the mobilization of East German society in terms of the image of the niche society depicted in chapter 3, potential sources of cooperation become clearer. In the absence of organized interest groups, loosely structured and "structurally diverse" groups often emerge as vehicles with which to pursue collective interests in times of instability or crisis (Mayer 1966; Boissevain 1971). The quasi-groups located in the "niches" may thus be seen as latent groups for the purposes of collective action (Hardin 1982). Indeed, Leipzigers *expected* solidarity because they had decided to join the protest after consultation with their peers. In Opp's survey fully 67 percent of the respondents that participated in the Leipzig demonstrations reported that they joined the demonstration accompanied by friends or close associates (Opp and Gern 1993: 676). These survey findings are reinforced by contemporary oral histories of the protests (Neues Forum Leipzig 1990, 1991; Lindner and Grüneberger 1992) and first-person observers (Schneider 1990; Tetzinger 1990; Zwahr 1993; Philipsen 1993), which consistently report that participants decided to join the protests only when it was clear to them that close associates were doing the same.

It is plausible that, rather than mobilizing as members of groups, Leipzigers simply responded at the same moment (October 9) to the same signs of opportunity (the exiting crisis, Gorbachev's visit) in the same way (by protesting).[60] Nevertheless, the empirical evidence provides strong support for a mobilization scenario premised on informal organization. Once groups of people decided among themselves to join the demonstration, an array of social incentives could be activated. Failure to take to the streets would be a betrayal of one's friends, neighbors, and fellow citizens. In other words, actors did not reach decisions to participate alone and had reason to expect that they would not be taking on risks alone. Protesters purposely exploited these sentiments, chanting to bystanders milling around the edge of Karl Marx Square, "Brothers, join us!" and "Join us, we need everyone!" and by stopping buses and streetcars to make direct appeals to fellow citizens. Oral histories reveal that groups of friends pledged to stand by one another (Lindner and Grüneberger 1992; Tetzinger 1990; Schneider 1990; Neues Forum Leipzig 1990).

Informally based mobilization may have provided an unnoticed advantage for rebellion in that there were relatively few rival claims to solidarity. The more typical categorical appeals to collective action, such as those of social class, political party, interest group, occupation, and so on have little importance in a Leninist regime since interests and identities have been organized and rhetorically appropriated by the state. Large-scale, crosscutting social appeals, on the other hand, have an advantage if they resonate with people's experiences within their immediate social niche. "Wir sind das Volk," the characteristic rallying cry of the popular rebellion against Communism in October, was surely a thin basis for solidarity. Yet what it evoked was an uncomplicated "us versus them" conflict, a claim to political identity that could bridge lines of class, education, occupation, neighborhood, and so on. Cutting across niches, populist appeals linked groups with highly generalized grievances and with few competing organizational loyalties.

Paradoxically, the "Wir sind das Volk" message helped to overcome the sense of being part of an anonymous mob and soon implied emergent rules of cooperation. The "people" insisted on nonviolence in their ranks; they exhorted each other to bravery and to wariness against agents provocateurs. The singing of hymns, anthems, and other songs reinforced the sense of collective purpose. Bystanders were encouraged to express voice by their fellow citizens who insisted, "We are staying here!" and "Join in with us, we need everyone!" Protesters reportedly shouted out, "Will you be here next week?" to which others responded with loud cheering. One woman, who participated in her first Monday demonstration on October 9 was surprised to discover that "in general the demonstration proceeded peacefully, really in a disciplined way." She reported her enthusiasm in joining in the chants of "We are the people," "We want reforms," and "No violence."[61] A middle-aged man explained: "I felt as if we had learned to walk upright. It was wonderful when we saw that many people leapt out of buses and trams and joined in with us. The barrier, the fear of the Stasi, was broken" (Zwahr 1993: 25).

The mobilization of people drawn from innumerable social "niches" alone does not make for effective protest. The informal structure of Leipzig's peaceful protest worked, in large measure, because of the familiarity and relative simplicity of the Monday demonstration repertoire. The Leipzig demonstrations were basic affairs, forming at the same time on the same day of the week (Monday at 5:00 p.m.) at the same place (the St. Nicholas

Church) throughout 1989–90. Moreover, the rapid expansion of protest was facilitated by Leipzig's highly compact, ring-shaped city center with its obvious points for assembly. A demonstrator recalled, "There was no head of the revolution, the head was the Nicholas Church and the body was the city center" (Opp, Voss, and Gern 1993: 46). The ring boulevards circling the city center passed along the Karl Marx Square, the university, opera and symphony houses, the main train station, the Stasi headquarters, and the seat of the city government (Neues Rathaus). The ring was also the traffic hub of Leipzig, where most bus and tram routes passed. Assembling on the spacious Karl Marx Square was already familiar to Leipzigers as an element of official public political rituals such as May Day. The route protesters took on October 9 was common knowledge: Official marches formed on Karl Marx Square and followed the ring avenue to end at city hall, or else to wind up again at the square. When the police retreated on October 9, protesters occupied the whole of the central square, spilled out of the city center, and were able to make a full loop of the city center (Zwahr 1993: 43). The old parade route was turned to a new purpose.

Opportunity and Threat before October 9

The explanation of the mass mobilization in Leipzig and Dresden that I have offered suggests that citizens protested in spite of considerable dangers. That might seem implausible given what we know about Gorbachev's growing reluctance to back up Soviet bloc governments with force. However, we now know what ordinary Leipzigers did not know on October 9, that is, that the Soviets refused to back up a "Chinese solution" in the GDR with troops of their own. Nor did Saxons know that regional officials had lost confidence in the security forces and were increasingly paralyzed by indecision. In fact, citizens had good reason to fear that threats of a Chinese solution were credible, particularly given warnings in the state media and Honecker's continuing grip on power. And on October 9 citizens could see that army units and paramilitary police were taking up positions ringing the downtown. Regardless of the private reservations local and regional officials may have harbored at this point, they had recently made public professions of loyalty to the regime. Balancing this generalized sense of threat, citizens had been exposed to numerous signals of Gorbachev's disapproval of the regime and his endorsement of reform—most recently expressed on October 6 during his Berlin speech on the GDR's fortieth anniversary. In a general way the "Gorbachev factor" (Kornai 1992) seemed to be opening a door for change in eastern Central Europe.

It appears that Leipzigers, in particular, may have had a particular advantage that did not obtain in other parts of the country. Their city had repeated experience with public demonstrations and the police response to them over the course of 1988–89. In early October 1989, they may well have been able to reckon the relative threat that repression posed, not from trying to divine what was going on behind the closed doors of power, but based on local experience. This experience would have suggested, at least to interested and alert citizens, an imbalance between threatened and actual repression in the weeks leading up to October 9. In Leipzig the authorities' repressive strategy was based on containment. In the early 1980s the state had managed to keep the peace movement bottled up in the Church, where it gradually waned. But the containment strategy failed in 1989 because of three factors: the Church's refusal to push out dissident groups; inadequate and tentative police measures in response to public protest; and failure to adapt repression to changing dissident repertoires. Once containment failed within the Church, the police tried to prevent public demonstrations by appearing in force in city streets. In the months leading up to October 9 police ringed St. Nicholas after the Peace Prayers, harassed bystanders, videotaped participants, and made frequent arrests. Plainclothes Stasi agents stood among the bystanders and identified instigators. These tactics proved relatively effective so long as the number of demonstrators remained manageable—no more than a few hundred protesters. But when thousands of bystanders joined in the protests beginning in late September 1989, it became difficult to contain the crowd in the narrow streets and squares surrounding St. Nicholas.

Other than driving away crowds with batons, the chief repressive means used by the police were large-scale arrests of the "hard-core protesters." However, police repression was neither consistent nor severe enough to deter the activists around whom the Monday demonstrations crystallized. According to police reports, between September 1 and October 7 in Leipzig, the number of arrests relative to the number of reported protesters varied from half of the participants to none of them. Inconsistent repression of this kind is less likely to deter subsequent protest; indeed, it may even encourage it by appearing arbitrary, uncertain, and indecisive. Examining all protest events from January 1988 through September 1989, one finds that average attendance (assuming the lowest [police] participation estimate) was about 360 persons. An average of twenty-seven arrests were made per demonstration, yielding about a 7 percent arrest rate overall. While police actions resulted in hundreds of arrests over this period, it was not a crushing proportion of the total number of participants. Moreover, most arrests did not result in long-term imprisonment, so that protestors arrested at one event would be available for future protests. Given this pattern, it is not surprising that Leipzig police forces failed to neutralize activist political subcultures or prevent zealous dissidents from staging protests.

This imbalance between threatened and actual repression in the police records became apparent when I was able to identify arrest information for demonstrations between May 8 and September 11. According to police estimates, the twelve demonstrations during that time involved a total of about 2,400 people. At these events police reported a total of 444 arrests, about a fifth of participants.[62] Those arrested were mostly men (81 percent) and young (on average about twenty-seven years old), and about a fifth had standing exit visa applications (22 percent). Most were not sentenced to prison, suffering a few days detention and a stiff fine before release (generally about a thousand marks). Although this was a substantial penalty, it was evidently not stiff enough to have deterred committed activists, risk-prone young men shut off from opportunities for improvement, or the unhappiest of would-be exiters.

Local authorities understood the dissidents to be poorly organized and incapable of mass mobilization. They thought stringent police measures would be enough to contain the protests that spilled out of the Peace Prayers and deter bystanders from joining the dissident cause. Yet when they struck hard against the mounting protest, it failed to generate the expected result. On September 18 authorities forcefully dispersed the Monday demonstration, and 242 protesters were arrested. Nevertheless, a week later the Monday demonstration involved about two thousand citizens—at that point the largest demonstration since 1953! The most aware citizens were probably increasingly cognizant of the risk of arrest or injury and thus learning to discount the possibility of a massacre. Knowing this reduced uncertainty, allowing some to estimate, if only roughly, the actual risks associated with protest.

In the first week of October 1989, police used force to disperse crowds and arrested more than three thousand people across the country. Criminal proceedings were filed against more than seven hundred of them. But, according to police estimates, some sixty-eight thousand people took part in protests across the GDR from October 1 through 8, so the incarceration rate was not especially high. Still, the declining risk experience of repression over the course of 1989 might have been calculable to well-informed activists at the core of the movement, but not necessarily to ordinary citizens. The fact that across the GDR during this critical period police, militiamen, and army troops were deployed against protesters and made thousands of arrests could have been a potent symbol of the government's resolve. For ordinary people, events in their own city may have been more influential, and the average level of repression across the country (at least as measured by arrests) could have obscured significant local differences in the severity of the state's response to protest. Indeed, comparing the magnitude of arrests across the major centers of protest during the first week of East Germany's "October revolution" (October 1–8) reveals that only 3 percent of reported participants in Dresden protests and less than 2 percent of reported participants in Leipzig protests suffered arrest and detention. By contrast, in East Berlin during the same period nearly 13 percent of protesters were apprehended.

At least in the Saxon cities, by early October citizens may well have begun to notice a gap between threatened and actual repression that led them to downgrade the expected risks associated with protest. In Leipzig, the episodic and variable level of police repression apparently lacked the consistency, certainty, and severity that are the foundations of effective deterrence (Wilson 1983). By October 9 Leipzigers, particularly those connected with the dissidents or with the churches, may have had enough experience to discount regime threats. In fact, this interpretation is supported by Opp's (1994: 114) survey research on collective action in Leipzig. Opp found that previous exposure to moderate levels of repression substantially increased one's subsequent propensity to participate in protest demonstrations. The experience of repression in Leipzig in the fall of 1989 seems to have been adequate enough to increase grievances while not decisive enough to deter participation. Even if the majority of citizens were fearful, this would not have prevented mobilization around the Peace Prayers. If bystanders were playing a wait-and-see game on October 9, the fact that a sizable core of protesters went ahead with their demonstration as usual may have been enough to spur them on. And once the police retreated from confrontation, the conditions were in place for a cascade of bystander participation. The situation would have been different in East Berlin, the center of regime

FIGURE 9. Percentage of Protesters Arrested in the Principal Cities of the GDR, October 1–8, 1989

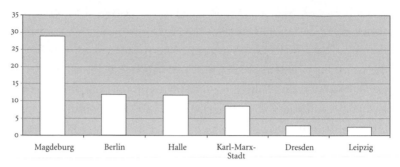

Source: GDR Interior Ministry.

power, where a show of force coordinated by the Stasi indicated that hard-liners remained in place and had not lost the will to fight.

When we compare the Saxon districts to the other regions of the GDR, it is evident that regional officials faced a much more difficult situation. Their region was both the cradle of the protest movement and the area most destabilized by the exiting wave. And although before October 9 they had followed regime orders to suppress demonstrations, comparative evidence suggests that their actions lacked the resolution apparent elsewhere. Comparing the percentage of protesters arrested by security forces in the different district capitals between October 1 and October 8, based on reports from the Interior Ministry, shows that the level of repression in the Saxon districts was considerably lower than that in Magdeburg, Berlin, and Halle. Only about 3 percent of reported demonstrators suffered arrest in Dresden, and only about 2 percent in Leipzig. (See figure 9.) It is true that the Saxon districts experienced a larger number of protest events and greater numbers of demonstrators during that week, but clearly police repression failed to keep up. Leipzigers were brave on October 9, but they were not foolhardy.

The Shifting Balance of Exit and Voice

With mass emigration surging at the time of the fortieth anniversary of the state, there was a coincidental concentration of citizen grievances. The political uncertainty created by exit and occasioned by the state visit of Mikhail

FIGURE 10. The Shifting Balance of Exit and Voice in the GDR: Comparison of Number of Exiters to Number of Protesters, August–October 1989

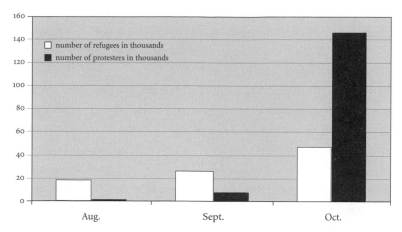

Sources: GDR Interior Ministry and Zentrales Einwohnerregister (ZER) data reported in Grundmann 1998.

Gorbachev increased the salience of voice, leading to protests in East Berlin, Leipzig, Dresden, and other cities. But it was the effort to block exit that did the most to bring diverse groups of citizens into the street. When crowds of young people in the streets of Saxon cities shouting "We want out!" made common cause with Church-based dissidents insisting "We are the people!" and "We are staying here!" the revolution began. It was only in October 1989 that the reported number of protesters exceeded the number of people leaving the country. East Germans mobilized behind a new voice-driven political insurgency. (See figure 10.)

It is possible that the exit crisis worked as effectively as it did to trigger rebellion in the first week of October because citizens had some sense that the time was ripe for change and that they might not have as much to fear from repression as in the past. There is a well-known paradox that repression may deter protest in the short term but increase it in the long run (Goldstone and Tilly 2001; Opp 1994; Rasler 1996; Moore 1978). Perhaps heavy-handed state action increases political grievances among citizens, or it may help them learn over time to evaluate the relative risk of protest more effectively. If citizens gain the sense that the actual level of repression is less intense than the threat, they may be willing to risk voice. In Leipzig, the emerging organization of the Monday demonstrations also played a role. Novel forms of organization and new norms governing protest emerged out of the demonstrations themselves and raised the cost of repression for security forces. In fact, the revolution in the GDR involved only a limited incidence of the kind of violence usually associated with psychological models of collective behavior.[63] Despite rioting in Berlin, Dresden, and Plauen in the first week of October 1989, led by the example of Leipzig, East Germany's revolution was generally a peaceful, even orderly affair. For most of the 1989–90 protest cycle, East German demonstrations consisted nearly universally of citizens assembling peacefully for a demonstration or protest march at the end of the workday or on a weekend and quietly dispersing afterward. This does not suggest crowd behavior driven by resentments or frustrated ambitions.

Ideology may have also contributed to the willingness to rebel. In the GDR social justice norms were part of the official public culture and by every indication were widely shared across the population. East Germans held to the ideal of a just society and the norm that the state must "provide a better life for all of its citizens" (Marcuse 1991: 56; Friedrich, Förster, and Starke, 1999). Official socialist ideology itself offered "unambiguous criteria for the definition of justice," promising "perfect equality" and steady economic advancement (Csepeli and Örkény 1992: 72). By 1989 official socialist ideology, along with its clear articulation of the nature of injustice, had become a threat to the system it was meant to legitimate. In this context there was little need for social movement groups to frame grievances. No dissident group needed to point out that the conditions of everyday life in the late 1980s were at odds with the socialist ideology used to justify the party dictatorship. As the majority of the people endured shortages and worsening living conditions, the privileges enjoyed by party and state functionaries "always ready to quote Karl Marx" became increasingly irritating (Philipsen 1993: 125).

The broadly populist nature of the demands shouted by protesters on October 9 reflected the highly visible crisis that (temporarily) united many categories of citizens into the same movement. In short, nearly everyone in the GDR could expect to endure both present and future losses as a result of the crisis. It is in circumstances in which grievances are widely generalized across social groups that popular rebellion is most likely to occur. Remaining a bystander and free-riding on others no longer pays off when one's direct interests are threatened. The mass exodus in 1989 exacerbated shortages and undercut health and social services. This situation could be expected to worsen the more that people exited. Since most East Germans had at least some investment in GDR society, most did not wish to abandon their homes and families. And the testimony of those left behind in the exiters' wake suggests that the regime's callous, intransigent position in the face of the crisis worsened the insecurities that most East Germans felt (Plato 1993). Later, those who stayed recalled feeling trapped and alarmed—"living in a house without doors or windows" (Zwahr 1993)—as a result of the government's desperate efforts to seal the borders in early October to stem the exodus. In their 1990 survey of Leipzigers, Opp and Gern found that 41 percent had expected economic and social conditions to worsen as a result of the exiting crisis (Opp and Gern 1993: 674). All of this means that those left behind in decaying cities like Leipzig had good reason to conclude that the failure to act might impose higher costs than participation in demonstrations.

Crisis events are well suited to focusing otherwise diffuse grievances (Schelling 1960). An event like an exiting crisis can suddenly unite a host of disparate concerns into "moral anger" if it is perceived to worsen existing grievances or generate new burdens (Moore 1978). Rank mismanagement of national crises has radicalized popular opinion against authoritarian regimes in a number of settings (Goodwin 2001; McAdam, Tarrow, and Tilly 2001). This most often occurs when those in power fail to deliver the customary or expected goods and protection commonly understood by their subjects as an obligation. Apparently, in October 1989 ordinary East Germans were faced with the distressing reality that the regime was unable to reassure them of their economic livelihoods or guarantee economic and social stability. The government's dismissive handling of the exiting crisis and its brutal attacks on peaceful protesters during the fortieth anniversary in early October probably activated what might have otherwise remained despairing, but inert, citizens. An East German worker recalled: "The straw that finally broke the camel's back was Honecker's statement [during the exiting crisis] that 'we are not going to shed a tear for these people.' We were simply outraged, everywhere, young people and old people alike. This statement was just impertinent. Every evening we saw on Western television thousands of young GDR citizens who had fled to West German embassies or had made it across the border in some way, and then this comment, 'we are not going to shed a single tear' (Philipsen 1993). The insensitivity and heedlessness of strident celebrations of socialism during an apparent crisis were probably no less galling. On the same day that the government sealed the border with Czechoslovakia, state media featured a Politburo statement declaring the GDR to be the "good fortune of our people and the peoples of Europe" (Zwahr 1993: 53).

In 1989 the SED did not enjoy a monopoly over the news. Most citizens received West German television and radio reports that reported the restraint of the crowds and the brutality of the security forces. As covered on Western television, the police attack on peaceful candlelight marchers in East Berlin on the evening of October 6–7 was a startling display of aggression and political intolerance. The brutal treatment of demonstrators in many cities on October 7 and dark threats of the bloody restoration of order stood in sharp contrast to what was supposed to be a celebration of the "Unity of the Party and the People." A middle-aged woman reported how she and her family had witnessed the police savagely beat peaceful protesters during anniversary celebrations in central Leipzig on October 7. She described the conduct of the police as "horrible" and "scandalous," adding, "Isn't it a shame that something like this happened in the GDR, and above all to have to experience it on such a holiday?" This experience drew her to join New Forum.[64] When protesters chanted, "We aren't rowdies!" and "We are the people!" on October 9, they were not only demolishing the regime's portrayal of the opposition; they were sending a message of reassurance to their fellow citizens that they had done nothing to provoke a police crackdown.

Although protesters in Dresden and Leipzig in the first week of October shouted, "Legalize New Forum!" this does not mean that social movement organizations mobilized protests. Throughout the GDR, the core membership of the first citizen's organizations was usually no more than a dozen activists. In a scene in many ways emblematic of the first stages of the East German revolution, a Western reporter covering the demonstrations in Dresden was approached by a protester who said, "Tell me, there is supposed to be a group, New Forum. I should be a part of that. What is it?"[65] People in the provinces knew little more than that a GDR-wide opposition was forming and that it had been immediately banned by the state. Yet this was enough to make it a symbol, if not an effective instrument, of voice. In Dresden, the "Group of Twenty" that negotiated an end to the standoff with state authorities was formed on the spot by protesters and clergymen on October 8. In Leipzig, the infant New Forum hardly played a role in mobilizing protest on October 9, but dissidents and clergymen connected to the Peace Prayers provided the crystallization points for mass protest in the fall of 1989.

After the "miracle" of Leipzig, the peaceful revolution spread rapidly across the country. The first weeks in the autumn of 1989 were marked by unforeseen eruptions of protest activity followed by the efforts of opposition activists to keep up with events and impose form and purpose on the mounting protest. As we have seen, mass mobilization could not make more than a localized breakthrough without some crisis, a shock to the system that would signal the vulnerability of the regime and provide a focal point for grievances around which otherwise dispersed, uncoordinated actors could direct their attention.

Fight or Flight? A Statistical Evaluation of Exit-Voice Dynamics in the East German Revolution

The role of "incidents" can thus be seen as a coordinating role; it is a substitute for overt leadership and communication. Without something like an incident, it may be difficult to get action going at all.

—THOMAS SCHELLING, *THE STRATEGY OF CONFLICT*

In the previous chapters we examined the factors that led tens of thousands of people to flee the GDR in the summer of 1989. This exodus was associated with sporadic protest in September, but in October protest mushroomed into a sweeping popular rebellion against the communist regime. Insurgent voice now vied with exit as the predominant force for change. In the first week of October, large-scale protest rocked the larger cities of the GDR. Just a week after the "miracle" that had occurred in Leipzig and Dresden, on October 16, more than one hundred thousand people again took to the streets of Leipzig. Once more, the demonstration remained peaceful and the state refrained from repression. On October 23 police reported that more than three hundred thousand people clogged the city center, many traveling by rail or automobile from the surrounding area and other regions of the GDR to be part of what was fast becoming a people's revolution.[1]

It is astounding to consider how quickly the anti-regime movement mushroomed and how little prior organization guided its expansion. Once people came into the streets across the GDR, they often simply emulated what had worked in Leipzig. The repertoire of protest developed there—a public prayer meeting or assembly followed by a peaceful march through the city center—became the standard East German demonstration across the country. In fact, a quarter of all demonstrations between September 1, 1989, and March 18, 1990, took place on a Monday, as many towns simply introduced "Montagsdemos" of their own.

The "miracle" of this revolution was that masses of ordinary citizens without prior involvement in opposition groups, social movements, or the Church took to the streets against what had seemed an immovable regime and brought it crashing down. But vying for their involvement in either an anti-regime or a pro-reform movement was the possibility of simply fleeing the GDR for the safe and prosperous haven of West Germany.

In other words, citizens faced a basic choice: to stay and fight for reform or to flee the GDR for a better life. Clearly, as least as far as initiating instability, the exiting crisis strengthened the hand of voice. In his essay on the GDR in 1989, Hirschman (1993) argued that in blocking illegal emigration the regime united the interests of dissidents and exiters in Leipzig and other cities. But apart from the generation of protest in a few influential cities, we still have not identified the specific mechanism that united exit and voice. Nor is it clear that mobilization triggered by mass exit would be sustainable. Under what conditions are exit and voice confederates and under what conditions does exit undermine voice?

The narrative evidence presented in chapter 5 indicates that exit stimulated voice in cradles of anti-regime protest like Dresden and Leipzig. But in order to arrive at a better analysis of the movement, it is necessary to specify the exit-voice dynamic in collective action and test the resulting model with data from the whole of the country. By focusing on the role of prior exit on subsequent voice, one can discern how exit, especially large-scale exit, would affect the possibility of effective collective action. The theory tested here posits that exit triggers collective action by disrupting a repressive equilibrium but, at greater magnitudes, undermines voice without making a continuous contribution to mobilization. Hence the overall effect of exit on voice should depend on how great the magnitude of exit is.

Exit-Voice Dynamics and Social Mobilization

We have already seen that in Leninist regimes the poverty of resources and the limitations placed on the exchange of information pose particularly daunting challenges to collective action. Because of the monopolization of public media, the disproportionate visibility of the regime's advocates and supporters, and the highly constrained and selective disclosure of dissent, mobilization of protest cannot be taken for granted. In dictatorial regimes we expect the distortion, misperception of circumstances, and public dissimulation that leads to the condition of "pluralistic ignorance." In other words, a citizen goes along with things as they are because he or she incorrectly assumes the majority wants it that way (or at least is indifferent to change). Overestimating another's adherence to the regime thus leads the citizen to underestimate the potential efficacy of collective action (Allport 1924; Noelle-Neumann 1984; O'Gorman 1986; Kollock 1998). Mono-organizational dictatorships like the GDR rely on such processes to atomize opponents and demobilize collective action. When we consider communication deficits of this kind alongside the general obstacles to collective action we confront a situation in which "rationality requires inaction" (Lichbach 1994: 16).

On the other hand, if the costs of participation are believed to be declining at the same time that expectations that protest will succeed are enhanced, a sudden upswing of protest can be seen as a rational response to grievances. This is a central insight of the "political opportunities" approach in polity models of social movements (Tilly 1978; McAdam 1982; Klandermans 1984; McAdam, McCarthy, and Zald 1996; Tarrow 1998). But a simple application of such logic runs into an obvious problem in accounting for the breakthrough phase of the East German revolution. In early October 1989, when repression was the predominant regime response to popular contention, protest massively expanded across a dozen GDR cities. No matter what the regime's distance from Gorbachev's Soviet Union may have been, its vulnerability was not apparent at this point; but after the events of October 9, it did indeed seem vulnerable.

In a situation like this even if everyone (or nearly everyone) would prefer a different government, no one should be willing to risk enough to initiate a movement or sustain it in the face of long odds of success and a high likelihood of repression. So long as the regime can set the balance of incentives such that potential costs outweigh the sum of individual benefits, and makes clear that it will not surrender without a fight, it can establish a repressive equilibrium such that most people will never rebel. Even a weakened regime that is still willing to use force should encourage citizens to adopt a "wait-and-see" attitude rather than join protest in massive numbers.

Recall Tocqueville's surprise at the mass mobilization during the February revolution of 1848 that seemingly came from nowhere. Why is it that even highly dissatisfied citizens do not rebel most of the time but, occasionally, join terrific upsurges of public-spirited collective action? One might begin with a basic premise opposed to Olson's (1965) free rider: let us imagine that ordinary citizens do want to force a change of regime and are willing to pay to achieve this goal. As we have seen in previous chapters, this is not an unrealistic assumption for the GDR. With the exiting crisis in full view, actors may wish to join political action if only because the cost of silently enduring continuing deterioration of public goods is also high. Siegwart Lindenberg (1989: 58) notes in his theory of revolution, "In this way, collective action is an instrumental extension of individual goal seeking. . . . At this stage free riding offers no extra incentives, but the added disadvantage that it does not contribute to loss avoidance." In a situation in which grievances are widely generalized and there is the expectation that the failure to act may lead to even worse provision of public goods in the future, a rational actor may well be willing to pay costs now to avert even greater losses later.

Even so, actors would be restrained by what they perceive as the dangers of the endeavor. Why should they believe that others will match their contribution? If their fellow citizens leave them in the lurch, either by exiting or by sitting on the sidelines, their efforts will be a costly failure. "Critical mass" and other threshold models of collective action focus try to explain how groups solve this "who goes first?" problem. A threshold represents the adoption rate of an action strategy by other actors that should be reached before an actor decides to follow suit (Marwell and Oliver 1993; Schelling 1978; Granovetter 1978). Discontent of varying levels and the willingness to pay some cost to undo it should be distributed across the population ranging from a very low threshold of involvement (committed dissidents) to a very high level (pro-regime conservatives), with most citizens falling in between these two poles.

In many situations, prudent citizens play wait-and-see games; if an adequate number of fellow citizens join the protest movement at a previous point, they will also do so at a subsequent point. The result can be rapid bandwagon effects as those citizens with higher protest thresholds are persuaded by the actions of earlier initiators that protest is viable and not too dangerous. Imagine that each Leipziger has a "voice threshold," which can vary across the population from a low to a high figure. Die-hard activists look for any opportunity to express political voice no matter how few people take part, and old regime conservatives will never join the protest no matter how large it grows. This heterogeneity concerning the willingness to protest does not necessarily prevent its emergence. A group of committed dissidents might get a bandwagon moving by paying the substantial start-up costs of collective action (Marwell and Oliver 1993; Lichbach 1994). On the other hand, there may be circles of isolated or ineffectual dissidents that express voice but fail to spread it across the population (Chwe 1999). This is exactly the situation that the Leipzig dissidents and would-be exiters described in chapter 4 faced. They routinely demonstrated after the Peace Prayers and on other advantageous occasions, but until September 1989 only a small fraction of their fellow Leipzigers responded.

Obviously, if actors think protest probably will fail or that they will probably face harsh reprisals, they will tend to avoid it. A citizen should prefer action if his or her preferences for public goods are high enough, if costs seem to be declining, or perhaps if future losses through inaction are to be expected. If the individual citizen thinks that there is a reasonable chance that he or she will suffer repression, such as injury, arrest, dismissal from a job, and so on, he or she will be reluctant to join a protest movement. Hence isolated or sporadic acts of protest are unlikely to achieve change in a determined or insensitive authoritarian regime. Under the conditions of uncertainty in which these citizens must operate, nearly everyone avoids protest because he or she lacks the information necessary to assess the likely costs and consequences of protest. However, if a considerable number of fellow citizens are expected to take part in the political activity, a citizen might also, because in larger numbers he or she can expect a smaller chance of suffering repression and because wide social mobilization is more likely to challenge or unseat a government than small-scale acts of dissent.

Hence individual citizens need to have some sense of assurance that they will not be without the support of fellow citizens no matter how great their sense of grievance (Hardin 1982; Taylor 1987; Chong 1991). As Roger Gould (1995: 18) observes of French insurgents of the nineteenth century, "Potential recruits to a social movement will only participate if they see themselves as part of a collectivity that is sufficiently large and solidary to assure some chance of success through mobilization." In the context of the GDR in 1989, without this sense of assurance, citizens have to reckon with the possibility that if others fail to show up, then not only will the protest fail, but they might also be beaten, arrested, fined, or even shot. The problem is that in a repressive society it is difficult to achieve this sense of assurance. Citizens often have difficulty judging whether others would prefer action or inaction. They have difficulty judging whether professions of uncritical loyalty to the regime by its agents are genuine; if few citizens ultimately join the protests and security officials are stalwart, the movement will be easy to crush. Why does mass emigration in 1989 appear to have overcome these problems? And what were the implications of the magnitude of the exiting wave for subsequent mobilization?

Exit and Spontaneous Coordination

Exit, especially large-scale defection that becomes "common knowledge," can signify to those left behind that the exiters, and by extension the public in general, are discontented with the system. By "voting with their feet," they publicly authenticate whatever grievances have been latent in a population under the mask of feigned loyalty (Kuran 1991, 1995b). Even in repressive mono-organizational regimes, a sense of the deteriorating performance of the system is not difficult for citizens to grasp. But what is obscure is how widely like perceptions are shared among one's neighbors, particularly where extralocal communication is difficult and actors are clustered in social niches. In the absence of such information, individual grievances remain too compartmentalized to fuel collective action.

Exiters signal to others that others share their fundamental opposition to the regime and thereby disrupt the prevailing pluralistic ignorance that has silenced them up to this point (Noelle-Neumann 1984). This newfound realization of shared grievances can motivate voice for two reasons. On the one hand, the knowledge of shared grievances enhances opportunities to coordinate voice. In repressive settings, disaffected citizens may be looking for some sign that if they act, others will act with them. A commonly understood signal of the magnitude of public grievances will likely raise the expectation that others will speak out. Spontaneous revolt relies on unambiguous signals that others are present in sufficient numbers to reduce the individual risk of participation (Lohmann 1993). Exit offers such a signal for action because large numbers of people understand it in the same way and may reach similar decisions to act without requiring extensive coordination.

Secondly, awareness of the extent of shared grievances enhances social recognition as people receive the unmistakable cue that there is general opposition to the regime. An exiting crisis can thus create the "common knowledge" theorized to enable spontaneous collective action. As Michael Chwe (1999: 136) argues of social thresholds, "It is not enough for everyone to simply know that there is sufficient discontent; what is required is 'common knowledge': everyone has to know that there is sufficient discontent, everyone has to know that everyone knows, everyone has to know that everyone knows that everyone knows, and so on." In a situation of expanding common knowledge and mutual recognition, actors may feel vulnerable to social pressure if they do not act as others like them do (Hechter 1987; Coleman 1990; Chong 1991; Calhoun 1991). This was evident in the origins of the Monday demonstrations in Leipzig in October 1989 where nonparticipants ran the risk of being shamed in the eyes of friends and neighbors if they failed to join them in the streets (see also Opp 2001; Goodwin and Pfaff 2001).

The signaling effect of exit on voice is not expected to be uniform or constant. It should vary with the magnitude of exit. That said, the signaling effect of exit need not require a mass exodus, nor need it increase monotonically with the level of exit. Rather, it is likely that as a symbolic act the signaling potential of exit follows what is often known as an S-shaped production function vis-à-vis exit (Marwell and Oliver 1993; Oberschall 1994). For exit to induce mutual recognition of discontent and grievances, it needs to take on the character of a "social phenomenon." A few scattered incidents of exit fail to disrupt pluralistic ignorance. Yet, in adequate volume, exit becomes a "crisis," signaling generalized discontent and the regime's potential vulnerability.

Tens of people quietly slipping away do not make an exiting crisis; but thousands fleeing the country do. The perception of the crisis and with it social recognition of generalized grievances and governmental incapacities intensify with further increases in the level of exit. As the level of exit increases above the crisis point, however, additional incidents of exit would have an increasingly diminished impact. It does not make much difference how many thousands of people have opted to exit. The crisis has made the message clear and unmistakable.

Exit and the Hazard of Network Erosion

While the signaling effect of exit works largely to induce voice, it is a two-edged sword. Exit has implications not only for communication among actors but also for the connectivity between them. By definition, exit removes people from a social system and the social networks they had constituted. If emigration occurs en masse, as it did in East Germany, it may undermine the relational foundation for voice. Network erosion among potential activists seems to occur when individuals ("nodes") are removed from a network (by emigration, in this instance). This has implications for the connectivity and density of a subsequent network. Diffusion of a behavior is more likely to succeed in a social network that connects nodes more closely (Rogers [1962] 1995; Marwell and Oliver 1993; Valente 1995). Some ties among individuals create "shortcuts." A "shortcut" is a specific kind of network tie that reduces the average path distance for the network as a whole.[2] If an individual's ties to a social network have the potential to enhance overall network connectivity, the removal of that node and its associated edges could reduce overall connectivity of the network among those left behind.

Students of social movements agree that the formation of interlocking networks among like-minded activists is crucial for the onset and spread of social movements: Such networks help activists coordinate action, pool resources (McAdam and Paulsen 1993), and form an "ideological envelope" that incubates the dissent that spreads across a population (Kim and Bearman 1997). A dense network into which potential activists are interlocked is crucial under highly repressive and intrusive regimes. Posing a high risk to individuals, information tends to travel within short distances in such regimes. This dynamic has been widely observed in East Germany, where the predominant social structure was the niche society characterized by dense clusters of strong social ties (Völker and Flap 2001). In this repressive social structure, networks tend to be highly clustered, making them highly vulnerable to local erosion and unable to produce the "ideological envelopes" that are the basis of an informational cascade across a social system. Studies find that cooperation in clustered networks is highly sensitive to defection, meaning that exit would tend to disrupt local structures of cooperation (Cohen, Riolo, and Axelrod 2001). Recall that previous studies of

East German dissidents found that exile suppressed the development of organized dissent (Torpey 1995; Joppke 1995). In effect, this was network erosion in operation.

Of course, the effect of removing individuals from a network varies depending on which individual is removed. On average, removal of a node from a network should not affect the density of a subsequent network. If an individual with an above average number of edges is removed, however, it decreases network density of the subsequent social network. Removal of an individual with a number of edges below the average would increase network density. Given this, the implications of exit for social erosion depend on who the exiters are: If exiters come from the ranks of alert, resourceful, would-be protesters, exit may well have the expected negative effect of eroding the relational foundation for future protest. Otherwise, it may leave the social capital of future protesters intact and thus fail to have the expected negative effect on voice.

Suppose that actors have not only a protest threshold (or "voice" threshold) but also an "exit" threshold. A potential actor with a "low" exit threshold but a "high" voice threshold would be the most likely to adopt the exit strategy; an actor with "high" exit threshold but "low" voice threshold would be the first to adopt voice (join or initiate a protest). Given this, how exit would affect the network foundation of future protest events depends on how the two thresholds are jointly distributed. If exit and voice thresholds have a perfect negative association, in which those with "lowest" exit thresholds tend to have "highest" voice thresholds and vice versa, the group of people who first opt to emigrate would not affect the activist network of subsequent protesters. In the case of a perfect positive association between exit and voice thresholds where both are low, both exiters and future protesters would have come from the same pool. Hence the potential members of the "critical mass" necessary to initiate and sustain collective action (Marwell and Oliver 1993) have gone away.

Actors embedded in networks characterized by low exit and low protest thresholds are crucial here; their exit is highly consequential for others in their network. If they exit, would-be activists' perceived efficacy of protest collapses. This is because people with low thresholds are influenced more by the actions of a few others in their network than by people with high thresholds for whom many others must act (Chwe 1999). In a scenario of joint distribution of low thresholds, exit is expected to undermine a subsequent movement. If, however, exit and voice thresholds are distributed randomly with each other, members of a critical mass would still remain to organize protest events, although the resulting protests might encounter difficulty in attracting wide support.

In the case of East Germany, the exit and voice thresholds are likely to have assumed a positive, even if weak, relationship with each other. First, available evidence suggests that both exiters and protesters shared similar socioeconomic and demographic characteristics. The emigration wave consisted largely of younger, well-informed urban residents. For them, the option of exit was probably less costly (young people have less invested in the home country), more opportune (urban residents are better informed and more resourceful), and more viable (portable skills or education make a person more likely to succeed in the host country) than for others. Protest initiators—sometimes Church-based dissidents—were also generally young and urban. In Leipzig, the first demonstrations were launched by an impromptu coalition of human rights activists and would-be exiters. So it is likely that exit probably removed some portion of the sort of people generally understood as being prone to movement participation (McAdam 1986).[3]

Second, many of the popular grievances in the GDR—concerning economic and environmental decay, political repression, rule by intransigent party hard-liners—apparently motivated both exiters and protesters (Grundmann 1998: chap. 4; Opp, Voss, and Gern 1995; Mitter and Wolle 1990). Aside from the threshold effects of loyalty (aggrieved but loyal persons may prefer voice, whereas aggrieved and disloyal persons exit), aggrieved people would not necessarily distinguish between exit and voice, behaving more "opportunistically" when exit became available. This scenario fits the unique sequence in which exit and voice occurred in East Germany. We know from the few cities, such as Leipzig, where scattered protests did occur prior to September 1989 that these were composed chiefly of Church-based dissidents and young people who had filed applications with the state to emigrate. Until the Iron Curtain was lifted, these groups made common cause. Instead of uniting them, as Hirschman (1993) suggests, the exiting wave uncoupled them.

In the context of a more or less positive association between exit and voice thresholds, exit tends to erode the relational foundation for subsequent voice and thus inhibit its occurrence. However, this network-erosion effect of exit is not uniform. As inelastic demand, loyalty retards exit and becomes a prerequisite for voice (Hirschman 1970). This implies that early exiters are more likely to come from those discontented persons with the least degree of loyalty to the state. In the case of the GDR, early exiters were generally younger, skilled workers who would have seen immediate improvement of their economic circumstances in fleeing to the West. Lacking loyalty, however, they are not among the primary candidates for sustaining the movement anyway. In sufficient degree exit becomes so generalized that highly aggrieved but partially loyal citizens may also leave the country. These defections would be a devastating blow to movement prospects. That does not mean that protest will not occur at all; exit is probably least damaging to voice by an activist core. But extensive exiting from a locality could have the effect of putting an immediate break on protest expansion. Given a high level of exit a "reverse bandwagon effect" could rob voice of its bandwagon supporters (Granovetter 1978: 1433).

If the implications of this theory are correct, exit signals the shared nature of grievances but, particularly in higher volumes, can also undermine the relational foundation of voice. If a generalized exit crisis creates the perception that the provision of desired goods is at risk, rational loyalists may join reformist mobilization. Furthermore, social ties with family, friends, and colleagues inhibit exit. This implies that in the GDR exit should have been most attractive to highly mobile people with fewer restraining ties. Those with greater social capital are likely to join the exit wave only if it becomes a mass social phenomenon undermining the stability necessary to make reforms. Given this, the network-eroding effect should be minimal when exit occurs on a small scale but should become conspicuous when exit occurs at a greater level.

How exit would affect voice in a particular historical instance depends on which dynamic of exit becomes predominant, the signaling effect or the network-erosion effect. The theory of exit and voice suggests that it is the degree of exit that matters: If exit occurs at a level large enough to be unambiguously recognizable as a "crisis," it is likely to invoke the protest-facilitating "signaling effect." If exit occurs en masse, however, its signaling effect may reach its upper limit, failing to further instigate voice. As exit reaches this point, the network-eroding effect becomes increasingly dominant with further increases in exit: the most discontented have already left, and the local networks that connect those left behind have been eroded. Although exit might leave scattered dissident groups intact, mass exit would undermine the likelihood of their expansion into a movement.

A strong test of the theory would require measuring the two intervening mechanisms of exit: shifting perceptions of system crisis as shared by the populace and the effect on social networks, especially among protest participants. Such intermediate mechanisms are rarely measurable in the social sciences, and, for understandable reasons, empirical data for both are unavailable. However, it is possible to evaluate the theory by focusing on the functional forms that the theory predicts exit and voice should have taken. The countervailing dynamics of exit imply that exit will increase the probability of protest in those localities where emigration occurs in small or moderate quantity. Where emigration occurs en masse, however, this positive effect of exit will decrease with the degree of exit due to the increasingly salient network-eroding effect of exit. Consequently, the hypothesis to be tested is a further specification of that suggested by Proposition 5 in chapter 1: *The level of exit should have an inverted-U-curve relationship with the frequency and magnitude of protest events.*

A Statistical Evaluation of the Exit-Voice Dynamic

Up to this point, the propositions offered in chapter 1 have been supported by narrative and descriptive evidence alone. Exit-voice dynamics and the rise of protest have been traced in specific cities, most notably Leipzig and Dresden. The data on the magnitude of exit and voice from September 1989 through the March 1990 elections (see especially figure 1) suggest a strong correlation between the emigration and the protest waves. However, to test the implications of exit-voice dynamics for collective action requires systematic comparison of the exit and voice relationship across the cities and counties of the GDR.

Drawing on the files of the police agencies of the GDR Interior Ministry, I assembled a data set of protest events in the counties and municipalities of the GDR and East Berlin between October 1989 and March 1990 (see the appendix).[4] Employing these data to estimate the dependent variable (voice), we can do a simple test of the central hypothesis. To evaluate the triggering effect of exit and its implications for subsequent mobilization, protest events are regressed against the degree of emigration experienced in the first wave of the exiting crisis (January–September 1989) and several other variables that might capture movement dynamics to discern exit-voice effects. Although every county was affected by the exit wave from January through September 1989, East German counties and municipalities (*Kreise* and *Stadtkreise*) varied tremendously in regard to the magnitude of exit experienced locally and the frequency of local protest events, providing a good test of the model. (See figure 11.)

The analytic strategy is straightforward: the degree of voice each of the counties/municipalities experienced after the onset of the East German revolution in September through March 1990 is regressed on the level of exit they had had prior to the onset of the revolution. This measure of "early exit" may have had a statistically significant effect on subsequent voice. In multivariate analysis one can examine how robust the exit-voice association remains when other potentially influential factors for protest such as indicators of political loyalty, economic grievances, past social movement activity, and state reactions to protest are included in the analysis. In order to avoid problems of multicollinearity, population size is controlled by calculating both exit and voice variables as proportions of a county or municipality's population size. See table A1 in the appendix for the univariate statistics of the variables in the analysis and their correlation coefficients matrix.

The time-lagged pattern in the measurement of the dependent variables and the independent variables allows a reasonable assumption to be made about the causal direction between exit and voice. Although it does not capture every time-dependent effect, this measurement strategy is a simple way to determine the causal direction of the correlation between exit and protest since subsequent events cannot affect the likelihood of exit that occurred prior to the onset of the protest wave. Following the beginning of the protest wave, declining returns to the signaling effect of exit could reflect the increasing salience of signaling through voice. Counties and municipalities with higher protest rates after September 1989 may also have had higher protest rates in the preceding period, resulting in serial correlation in the residual terms. However, the records show that no protests had occurred in the overwhelming majority of localities before September 1989, the only two significant exceptions being Leipzig and East Berlin. Even there, protests were small and sporadic before the revolution. Serial correlation is

FIGURE 11. Frequency Distributions of Protests and Exiters at the County Level

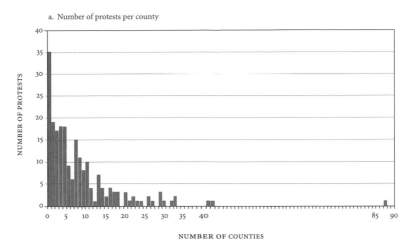

a. Number of protests per county

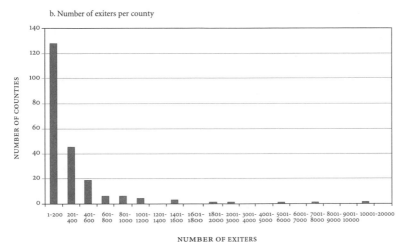

b. Number of exiters per county

Sources: GDR Interior Ministry and Zentrales Einwohnerregister (ZER) data reported in Grundmann 1998.

unlikely in this design, which divides the periods *before* and *after* the onset of the revolution.

The dependent variable is the degree of voice in a GDR county (*Kreis*) or municipality (*Stadtkreis*) during the period between September 1989 and March 1990. The concept is measured by reference to two dimensions: the frequency and magnitude of protest. To prevent overdispersion that might bias the analysis, both measures are logged. The frequency of protest is measured by a log of one plus the total number of protest events in a county per 100,000 residents (Protest Event Rate—PER). The magnitude of protest is measured by a log of one plus the average cumulative number of protesters in a county per protest event and per 1,000 residents in a county. No protest event in a county is coded 0. As such, this variable measures the degree of average protest mobilization in a county (its Average Participation Rate— APR). The measure is generated from GDR police reports of voice events occurring everywhere in the GDR between September 1989 and March 1990 (see the appendix).

The key independent variable in the analyses is the degree of exit in a county. "Exit rate" measures this by the number of exiters per 1,000 residents who migrated from a particular GDR county from January through August 1989 and took up residence in the FRG, that is, prior to the beginning of the protest wave in September 1989. The magnitude of exit before September 1989 pales in comparison with the magnitude afterward. This notwithstanding, the former is used to avoid a simultaneity issue between exit and voice.[5] The data are drawn from the nationwide county-level population register (Zentrales Einwohnerregister—ZER) based on the records of the GDR statistical agency and compiled by Siegfried Grundmann (1998). This is the most reliable and complete source of migration data available and permits observation of the key exit variable on the same level as the protest event data.

Clearly, there are alternative explanations of the East German revolution that must be considered. Multivariate analysis allows one to compare indicators of rival hypotheses alongside the proposed explanatory variable. In explaining events like the 1989 revolution in the GDR, many students of social movements and collective action propose that movement organizations constitute a key condition for the emergence of insurgency (McCarthy and Zald 1977; Tilly 1978; Jenkins 1983; McAdam, McCarthy, and Zald 1996). Even small groups of organized dissidents may provide the "critical mass" around which bandwagons form (Oliver and Marwell 2001).

In the case of East Germany, local resources increasing the prospect of successful voice could have persuaded citizens to choose voice over exit or inaction. We might expect that, more than exit, social movement organizations such as indicators of preexisting dissident networks could explain variations in voice across GDR counties. To control for this possibility, the presence of social movement organization in a county after September 1989 is measured by reference to New Forum archival materials on organizational meetings in the early autumn of 1989 (Pflugbeil 1999: 529–32). A county is coded as 1 if New Forum reported having an organization in a municipality or county at the start of the protest wave.

Another perspective in the literature on social movements emphasizes the importance of political opportunities for insurgencies. Polity theories have long argued for the central role of state facilitation or repression in affecting the emergence and success of protest activities (Tilly 1978; McAdam 1982; Tarrow 1996). Hence we would expect that powerful regime actors or elite intolerance toward dissent might affect the incidence of voice across GDR counties. Indicators of the strength of regional party organizations might capture this effect. As an indicator of the local potency of the regime, an SED density variable is measured by the proportion of the adult communist party membership in a district, drawn from a May 1989 analysis of party strength (Holzweissig 1996: 33). This measure, although not available at the county level, may be suggestive of sectional political opportunities.

Alternatively, the varying zeal of the regime's defenders might be a better indicator of opportunities. This can be captured by a local measure indicating the performance of state security agencies. Repressive actions by state authorities deter protest activities by raising the cost of participation and making protest appear unlikely to succeed. Social movement theorists have qualified this understanding of repression, however, arguing that perceived threats to welfare and liberty can instigate protest (Goldstone and Tilly 2001). We can estimate the local opportunity/threat effect, noting that while the threat of repression was present uniformly at the national level, its local implementation varied considerably across counties/municipalities. In fact, police records show that the arrest of protesters occurred mostly in large cities that spearheaded the revolution such as East Berlin and Dresden (about 1,000 persons arrested in each), Leipzig (562 arrests), and Karl-Marx-Stadt (106 arrests). In the analysis the degree of state repression is measured by the logged number of one plus the total protest arrests made by state agencies in each county during the whole period from September 1989 to March 1990. The arrest figures are drawn from files of the GDR Interior Ministry.

Finally, it is also important to measure the possible effects of variables that Hirschman (1993) considers important in his own analysis of the East German revolution. To do so, we need indicators of loyalty to see their effects on the incidence and magnitude of voice as well as an indicator that will help us determine whether blocked exit, rather than the signaling effect of exit, determined the local expression of voice. Hirschman argued that attempts to block the emigration wave spurred the rebellion in the GDR. Voice was amplified by the disappointed exiters who joined protesters in the street to oppose the regime. His argument is supported by the historical evidence that showed that in the border areas, especially those with Czechoslovakia and West Germany, heightened flight attempts, chaos at border crossing points, and clashes with police brought thousands to the streets and weakened the hold of regional and national authorities. In particular, the expulsion trains that left the GDR passed along the Czech border in southern Saxony to the West German border (Děčín-Hof route). Particularly after November 9, easy exit to the West might have reinforced voice. The *Czechoslovakia border* variable is coded 1 if any part of a county's boundaries were within 40 kilometers (18 miles: the smallest unit measured on the scale of the official atlas) of the GDR-CSR boundary; otherwise, it is coded 0. Likewise, the *West German border* variable is coded 1 if a county's boundaries were within 40 kilometers of the GDR-FRG boundary; otherwise, it is coded 0. The data are drawn from the official GDR Atlas (Lehmann 1976).

In order to capture possible loyalty effects on protest, the percentage of the labor force employed in the tertiary sector of the economy and the presence of institutions of research and higher education are included in the analysis. Economic historians of the GDR find that the relative development of the tertiary sector is a good indicator for the level of investment by the central government in a region's technology, advanced industries, and consumer sectors (Kuhrt et al. 1999). In order to capture the major cleavage between the residents of advantaged and disadvantaged regions in GDR society (see chapter 2), the measure of "economic" loyalty is the percent of the labor force in a county that was employed in the tertiary sector. The data are obtained from the last county-level GDR census in 1981 (SB 1994). While employment in the tertiary sector might indicate material investment in GDR society, university, college and research campuses might be potential reservoirs of critical loyalty—people invested in socialist ideology but disappointed by the performance of the regime. As we have seen in chapter 2, campuses seem to have played this role during the *Sputnik* incident. Measured as the number of universities and technical colleges (*Hoch- und Fachschulen*) and research science centers located within a county/municipality, this variable indicates institutional repositories of ideological loyalty. The data come from the official atlas of the GDR (Lehmann 1976).

Statistical Results

Tables A2 and A3 in the appendix report the outcomes of regressing Protest Event Rate (PER) and Average Participation Rate (APR), respectively, on selected independent variables across the sample. Note that both PER and APR are left-censored at 0 with 35 counties/municipalities having no protest event. Even for those localities with no public protest event, their residents may vary in the latent propensity to organize and mobilize an event. Police officials may have also missed small, incoherent protest events leading to mistaken non-reporting. With censoring on the dependent variables, ordinary least squares (OLS) estimates are known to be inconsistent (Long 1997). To correct for this, the model is estimated using maximum likelihood Tobit models.

Focusing on the full model specification (Model 3 in each table), the model fits the data well. The Likelihood Ratio test for each dependent variable is statistically significant at the 0.01 level. The pseudo R-squared for each of the dependent variables is low, although there is not unusual regression with limited dependent variables (Long 1997). An alternative measure of model fit, the correlation coefficient between the observed and the predicted dependent variable reaches 0.39 for PER and 0.37 for APR, indicating about 14–15 percent of the variance in the dependent variables is explained by the model. The reasons for the relatively low explanatory power of the model can probably be attributed to the largely unstructured and spontaneous nature of collective action in the revolution and to the higher level of measurement error in measuring the size of protests. The East German police gave estimates often in units of hundreds or thousands and sometimes provided range estimates. Given the limitations of historical data, the model does a good job in accounting for cross-county variations in protest.

To examine the voice effects of exit, PER was regressed on Exit Rate, then its squared term, and then all the control variables, inclusively. Models 1 and 2 suggest that the Exit Rate had a nonlinear effect on the Number of Protests, which is statistically significant at least at the 0.05 level. This pattern holds even when we enter all the control variables, one of which is statistically significant at the 0.01 level (Model 3). In the case of APR, Model 2 of table A3 shows that if we focus only on the bivariate relationship between exit and voice alone, they would appear to have formulated a linear positive relationship. A different picture emerges once we control for the effects of other factors that might have affected the East German revolution. With all the control variables in Model 3, the previously insignificant squared Exit Rate attains statistical significance at the 0.05 level. It appears that its statistical insignificance at the bivariate level is spurious, especially with regard to the voice-depressing effects of state repression: the Logged Number of Arrests variable had a large negative effect on APR, although it misses the target statistical significance level. With controls for the voice effects of these covariates, the negative coefficient of the squared Exit Rate turns statistically significant, revealing its nonlinear effect on voice.

The positive regression coefficients for Exit Rate and the negative ones for squared Exit Rate indicate that the predicted regression lines follow at least a concave form. If the signaling effect of exit at a lower level is overshadowed by its network-erosion effect at the higher level of exit, we expect exit to have an inverted-U-curve effect on voice. A key point here is whether an inflection point occurs in each of the predicted relationships within the empirically observed range of Exit Rate. Indeed, an inflection point occurred at about 9 emigrants per 1,000 residents for PER and at about 10 emigrants per 1,000 residents for APR. In other words, when exit remained below these inflection points, the marginal effect of exit on voice was positive, with decreasing marginal returns as exit approaches the inflection points. Once these inflection points were reached, however, the marginal effects of exit on voice became negative in localities where exit rate surpassed that point. In fact, there were eight localities whose exit rate was beyond these inflection points: in descending order, the municipalities of Plauen, Jena, Leipzig, Gera, Dresden, and East Berlin, and the counties of Zittau and Freiberg. Here, the network-erosion effect of exit is conspicuous.

The non-monotonic effect of exit is robust to a few seemingly influential cases. Given the spectacular events that occurred in Leipzig and East Berlin, both of which experienced an extraordinary magnitude of exit and voice, one may well suspect that the outcomes would be sensitive to their influence. Influential case diagnostics (conducted on OLS regression analyses of Model 3) suggested that the cities of Plauen, Jena, and Gera (for both dependent variables) and Leipzig (only for PER) may be influential. Interestingly, these cities also had among the highest levels of Exit Rate. With their removal, however, the inverted-U relationship becomes more conspicuous (see figure 12 and tables A2 and A3). Furthermore, the inflection points in figure 12 occur at much lower level of exit rate: about 6.5 emigrants per 1,000 residents for PER and about 6.6 emigrants per 1,000 residents for APR. Now, fully twenty-six counties/municipalities fall at or above the inflection point. Figure 12 graphically illustrates the bivariate relationship between exit and voice. This is especially true for APR: Without the outliers, the relationship between exit rate and APR is unambiguously reflective of an inverted U-curve. Apparently, a substantial number of counties/municipalities experienced a salient network-erosion effect of exit in addition to its signaling effect once we remove the few outliers that obscure the gravity of the network-erosion effect.

The statistical results provide evidence for the hypothesized effect of prior exit on voice that goes beyond a simple monotonic, linear relationship. Were we to focus only on the bivariate relationship between exit and voice, as previous studies have done, they would appear to be clear confederates. A different picture emerges when controlling for the effects of other factors that might have affected the East German revolution. The case of the GDR, where out-migration played such an apparent role in the demise of the regime, renders clear empirical support for the signaling interpretation of exit and supports the hypothesized social-erosion effect of mass migration. Exit, below a certain level, facilitates voice by sending out unambiguous signals of widespread discontent, thereby triggering collective action. As the size of exit approaches a certain point, however, the protest-facilitating signaling effect of exit starts to give way to the network-erosion effect of mass exit. At this stage, as more and more people have walked out of the game, the exodus erodes social capital among the residents of a county, thereby undermining the movement potential of the population.

The Variable Effects of Exit, Voice, and Loyalty in Revolutionary Mobilization

How much did emigration weaken the capacity of citizens to express voice, thereby determining the course of the East German revolution? We would expect that, in addition to its network-erosion effect, mass exit could also

FIGURE 12. The Effect of Exit on Voice: Predicted Regressions Lines against Empirical Observations

a. Predicting logged protest event rate

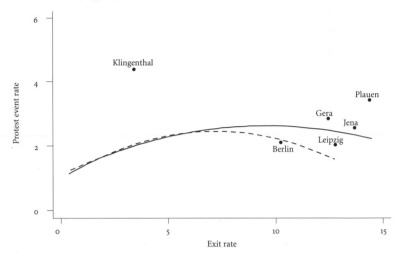

b. Predicting logged average participation rate

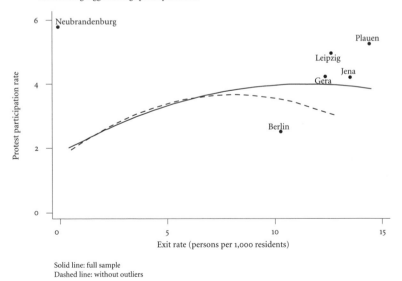

Solid line: full sample
Dashed line: without outliers

Sources: GDR Interior Ministry and Zentrales Einwohnerregister (ZER) data reported in Grundmann 1998.

impede voice by changing individuals' assessment of the likely efficacy of voice over exit. In localities suffering a large volume of exit, citizens may have lost confidence in the possibility that voice could succeed in achieving desired public goods. Such an effect would be devastating to movement prospects.

But not everyone was equally able to join the exodus. Karl-Dieter Opp points out that although the cost of exit fell in 1989, it still entailed breaking off social ties and forfeiting property and possessions, making it too costly an option for many people (Opp, Voss, and Gern 1995: 41). Accordingly, exit must have clearly been a more viable option for younger citizens of the GDR that had fewer possessions, lacked homes of their own, and had smaller investments in socialist society. Descriptive statistics on GDR exiters from 1989–90 confirm this: About 60 percent were men and 80 percent were less than forty years old (Grundmann, Müller-Hartmann, and Schmidt 1992: 1593; SJDDR 1990). Occupational data on the migrants of 1989 reveals that more than 40 percent were skilled workers (Mitter and Wolle 1990: 82–92; Ammer 1995: 443–40). This may have widened the distance between ordinary citizens and the dissidents. In the crisis of 1989–90, many younger, vocationally skilled East Germans might have seen their best hope in emigrating westward while university-trained professionals might have been more invested in reform.

We saw in chapter 5 that the effects of the exiting crisis were most evident in the Saxon border region. It was through this region that the infamous expulsion trains ceremonially passed, leading to a number of strident protests and rioting in cities like Dresden and Plauen. It was also in Saxony that state repression first gave way. Given these facts and Hirschman's (1993) argument about what propelled the East German revolution, it is noteworthy that in the statistical analysis the region bordering on Czechoslovakia did not have a significant voice effect. It appears that blocked exit may not have been as salient as the more general signals the exiting crisis sent, and no matter what the border region's initial importance may have been, there was not a strong regional dimension to the exit-voice dynamic. The signaling effect of exit was determined by its local magnitude, but this was not specific to certain regions.

Based on the archival evidence and oral histories used in chapters 4 and 5, one can see that the arbitrary and episodic repressive measures taken by local authorities in Leipzig were not successful in preventing protest events by dissidents or in keeping citizens from joining the movement once they were activated by the exiting crisis. Statistical evidence supports this interpretation across the GDR. The logged Number of Arrests did not have a significant effect at the county level.[6] Despite all the threats from regime leaders in Berlin, local police agents responded to citizens' protest activities more reactively than proactively. Still, to the extent it was carried out, even reactive repression might have effectively deterred protest. Local authorities resorted to repressive measures largely during the earlier phase of the revolution, before October 9. In cross-sectional analysis, the potential deterrent effects of police repression may have been lost. It is thus possible that, had local security forces followed the instructions of the central government to make good on threats of a "Chinese solution," mass mobilization might have been contained. Now that we know the dynamics that drove the popular rebellion against the regime, we still must understand the failed mobilization of the regime's agents. Why did state and party officials in the Saxon districts fail to act in the interests of a regime in which they had so much invested and refrain from the use of force, ultimately capitulating to the demands of unarmed protesters?

CHAPTER 7

Why Was There No "Chinese Solution" in the GDR?

> The contempt into which the governing class, and especially the men who led it, had fallen [was] a contempt so general and so profound that it paralyzed the resistance even of those who were most interested in maintaining the power that was being overthrown.
>
> —ALEXIS DE TOCQUEVILLE, *SOUVENIRS*

Leipzig's mass protest on October 9 was a turning point in the history of the GDR. Unlike all previous large-scale protest demonstrations, the massive march on October 9 was allowed to proceed without confrontations or arrests despite regime threats that the nascent opposition movement would provoke a deadly show of force from the state security apparatus. Instead, as tens of thousands of citizens peacefully demanded change—shouting "We are the People!" and "We are staying here!"—security forces simply withdrew.

Once the state failed to carry out the threatened "Chinese solution" to popular unrest, its apparent vulnerability unleashed the full force of popular mobilization. Peaceful Leipzig-style protests spread to the whole of the GDR and soon plunged the government into a tumultuous, though peaceful, political revolution. Insurgent voice on this simple model quickly achieved results. On October 18 Erich Honecker was forced to resign his state and party offices. The new party chairman, Egon Krenz, declared on state television that the GDR had a historical "turning point" and that the party was ready for "serious internal political dialogue." Yet the ruling elite remained intact, and radical reforms were immediately ruled out (Hertle and Stephan 1997; Maier 1997; Jarausch 1994). Half-measures did not mollify newly empowered citizens. In the month of November alone, the Interior Ministry reported over four hundred protest events involving a total of more than four million participants.[1]

In the month before October 9, the Interior Ministry reported a total of twenty-eight protest events involving an estimated seventy thousand people. In the following month between October 9 and the fall of the Berlin Wall on November 9, it reported some two hundred and sixty protests involving an estimated four million participants. Krenz's conservative reform program also buckled under the weight of a mobilized citizenry demanding increasingly radical reforms. Under this pressure, an open battle broke out in the ranks of the ruling party between hard-line and reform-minded elements. By the end of 1989, the old regime's back had been broken. With the fall of the Berlin Wall coming only three weeks after Krenz ascended to the party leadership, the Communist regime began a fatal spiral of concessions and retreats that led, ultimately, to its collapse.

Why did the East German regime capitulate in the face of an unarmed protest movement, particularly given the calamitous implications it had for the ruling party? The example of the People's Republic of China in 1989 stands in sharp contrast to East Germany's peaceful revolution.[2] Both regimes rejected political liberalization and repressed dissident groups. In China during the spring of 1989, students spearheaded a mass protest movement against the authoritarian party leadership demanding greater democracy, transparency, and accountability from the regime—many of the same issues embraced by the East German dissidents. In the space of just a few weeks in the spring of 1989, the student-led movement grew to involve millions of citizens. After government efforts to threaten and cajole the students and their supporters failed, Beijing's rulers decided on a decisive use of force. On June 4, 1989, army units cleared the streets and squares of the capital. Troops opened fire on demonstrators and used tanks to smash hastily constructed barricades on Tiananmen. Following the massacre the movement quickly collapsed, and conservative party leaders reasserted control (Lin 1992; Calhoun 1994; Zhao 2001).

Like their Chinese counterparts, the rulers of the GDR had appeared willing to make a decisive show of force despite Gorbachev's disapproval. Their commitment to orthodox Marxism-Leninism and threats to crush "counterrevolutionary" protest and "demagogic" human rights campaigns were public knowledge. The Politburo openly praised China's use of force against its "counterrevolutionary revolt." As protest began to appear in September and early October, the regime ordered riot police and troops into the streets of East Berlin, Dresden, and other cities to restore order. Yet, confounding expectations, the repressive strategy was abruptly abandoned on October 9.

Indeed, the East German capitulation and the peaceful revolution that resulted represent a crucial turning point in the history of the Soviet bloc, one that continues to resonate. In the past, Communist regimes in the region had ruthlessly suppressed popular unrest by means of deadly force (Ekiert 1996). Their ability to restore order in the face of a massive popular rebellion should not surprise us; the party-state enjoyed a monopoly of the means of violence, and, compared with any of its challengers, it had a superior capacity to coordinate its supporters. As Max Weber (1968: 952) observed of political crises in authoritarian regimes long before 1989, "The ruling minority can quickly reach an understanding among its members; it is thus able at any time quickly to initiate that rationally organized action which is necessary to preserve its position of power. Consequently it can easily squelch any action of the masses." More rarely, however, a regime fails to act in defense of its vital interests and is swept away. History provides examples of regimes in which divisions within ruling elites, problems of coordination and control, and the unreliability of demoralized soldiers and police did undermine collective action meant to save the status quo. The failure of a regime to rally thus demands explanation.

In the case of East Germany, as we have seen, joining the protests depended on citizens' assuring one another that they could be relied on. Presumably, citizens must also be reasonably confident that elites are vulnerable to protest and are willing to grant concessions, perhaps through the pressure of sufficiently large enough crowds or because of a perceived imbalance between threats and action. The state, for its part, must convince its citizens it will not give way, and it must inspire its own agents to be resolute in carrying out its orders. Chong (1991: 174) observes that confronted with mounting unrest a regime will "try to quash the demonstrations by convincing the activists they will not capitulate to their demands." To demonstrate this, the state first makes threats and then arrests, and finally it uses force to increase the costs of collective action beyond the point that any save the most committed dissidents will pay. The conflict becomes a "battle of wills in which each side attempts to outlast the other" (174).

Thinking about the revolutionary situation from the perspective of collective action theory thus points to an often-overlooked dimension of revolutionary situations: regimes face a dilemma in having to overcome tendencies toward inaction, defiance, and defection among their own agents (Lichbach 1994).

At first glance, it does not seem likely that the East German regime would be presented with a "State's Dilemma" in the fall of 1989. In early October the party leadership was still in the hands of an ailing but resolute Honecker and his hard-line Politburo. The GDR possessed a large and well-trained army, police forces firmly under party control, and the feared Stasi, the loyal "sword and shield" of the SED. To understand why the GDR effectively capitulated, we will need to consider Honecker's preference for repression over reform, the reliability and combat readiness of the GDR's security forces, and the reasons why regional officials in Saxony created an unanticipated revolutionary breakthrough by defecting from regime leaders.

Honecker's Repressive Strategy

For an orthodox Leninist regime, concessions that respond to popular pressure are hazardous because they suggest that the party's political monopoly is open to revision. Poland's ruling party countered popular rebellion with both harsh repression and concessions to citizen demands. The result was a spiral of increasing restiveness, popular detachment from the regime, repeated uprisings, and ever more insistent dissident demands (Ekiert 1996, 1997; Osa 2003). Hoping to avoid what they called the "Polish bacillus," Honecker and his associates rejected liberalizing concessions as a danger to party control and inherently destabilizing. They favored riding out the crisis in the Soviet bloc by remaining firmly on course and employing the apparatus of repression to quash domestic challenges (Baylis 1999; Jarausch 1994; Maier 1996). The inner circle of the regime worried that any concession to reform would lead to a "rollback" of Marxism-Leninism and reforms of the "bourgeois-democratic" variety.[3] Rather than endorse perestroika and glasnost or propose reforms of their own, Honecker and his associates stood on the achievements of the vaunted "Unity of Economic and Social Policy" and positioned themselves alongside hard-liners in the People's Republic of China, Czechoslovakia, and Romania.

This position was now undermined by the regime's lack of external backing. The Gorbachev regime made no effort to conceal its frustration with the leaders of the GDR and made fruitless efforts to convince Honecker of the merits of reform. In 1988–89 Gorbachev gave his tacit approval to reform in Poland and Hungary, increasingly distancing himself from the kind of outmoded Stalinism he saw in the GDR. Still, Soviet leaders did not wish to destabilize the GDR. In 1988 Gorbachev referred to German unification as "an incalculable and even dangerous endeavor" (Adomeit 1998: 270). Above all, Gorbachev took his repudiation of the Brezhnev doctrine seriously: the Soviet Union made no move to intervene in East Germany's domestic policies even if this meant allowing anti-reformers to retain power (Adomeit 1998; Zelikow and Rice 1995). Although there were numerous signs prior to October 9 that the USSR would not intervene to rescue Honecker, it did nothing to prevent his regime from attempting a crackdown.

In the weeks leading up to October 9, Gorbachev remained cautious with respect to the GDR. The Soviet Union announced the end of the Brezhnev doctrine in July 1989, but an unequivocal repudiation of intervention did not come until October 25, by which point Gorbachev described his posture as a "Sinatra doctrine" of letting national reformers go their own way.[4] In meetings with the East German Politburo during his visit on the occasion of the GDR's fortieth anniversary, Gorbachev stressed both reform and the Soviet Union's noninterference in domestic affairs (Zelikow and Rice 1995: 84). In effect, Gorbachev and Foreign Minister Eduard Shevardnadze sent mixed signals to would-be reformers as to whether they would be supported. But the message to those who would bring to bear a "Chinese solution" was clear: if you resort to force, you act alone.

With no intention of giving ground, the regime developed a three-part strategy to suppress mounting unrest. First, the state media denounced imperialist meddling in GDR affairs and warned citizens that the state would not tolerate "rowdiness," "disturbances of public order," and "counterrevolutionary protest." The SED-controlled parliament (Volkskammer) passed a resolution defending the actions of the Chinese government, and, on a visit to China in early October, Krenz declared that the GDR and the People's Republic were "united by common ideals."[5]

Second, the regime readied the security forces for a confrontation. Ever since 1953, the SED and the Ministry for State Security had developed contingency plans in the event of widespread popular unrest. In the event of rebellion, plans called for the mobilization of riot police backed by regular army troops, and the secret police were to "arrest and isolate" domestic enemies including "persons who could possibly represent leadership in hostile or negative groups" along with "spies, agents, saboteurs, and other state criminals." The Stasi specified that the "internal enemies of the GDR" to be rounded up in an emergency included members of independent Church groups; peace, human rights, and environmental activists; emigration applicants; "reactionary clerical forces"; as well as those advocating "democratic socialism" or "new models of socialism."[6]

Third, during the exiting crisis in September, the Politburo issued specific instructions for maintaining order in the face of "counterrevolutionary" protests. On September 22, in his capacity as chairman of the National Security Council, Honecker issued instructions to the district (*Bezirk*) party chiefs and security officials, stating, "Recently various hostile acts of our enemies have taken place on a number of levels. They are intended, in keeping with West German propaganda, to organize counterrevolutionary groups. These matters have been discussed at the last conference of district party first secretaries. There is a unanimous consensus that these hostile actions must be nipped in the bud; no mass basis for them will be permitted . . . and at the same time efforts must be taken to isolate the organizers of counterrevolutionary activities."[7] The instructions detailed the arrest of leading dissidents combined with the forceful handling of protests to prevent their widening to the general population. The National People's Army (NVA) was alerted to prepare army units to engage in crowd control. Honecker did not rule out the use of firearms.

Minister for State Security Erich Mielke drew up plans to mobilize paramilitary riot police, party militiamen, and Stasi agents in support of the conventional police forces (VP). The aggressive tactics employed in East Berlin during the anniversary protests of October 6–7 resulted in hundreds of arrests and scores of injuries. For the looming showdown in Leipzig on

October 9, Mielke mandated that local security forces have armed units at hand. However, his instructions equivocated in an important respect. Although he authorized the use of violence against rebellious crowds, he stated that "offensive measures" were to be used only in the event of "rioting" (*Zusammenrottung*) or attacks against government or party personnel and facilities.[8] The ambiguity may have been intentional. Mielke did not rule out "Chinese" methods but also did not specify their use except if protesters rioted or engaged in violence. It appears that regime leaders were hedging their bets: should repression have gone disastrously for the regime, resulting in either an embarrassing massacre or the defection of security agents to the crowd, the leadership would have been able to distance itself from the "misjudgment" of local officials.

Amid all this, there was no question that if the regime were to go against the crowds with force, it would go alone. On October 8 the Soviet ambassador to the GDR, Vyacheslav Kochemasov, directly warned Krenz that "the most important thing is to avoid bloodshed." Kochemasov also instructed the Soviet military commandant in East Germany to keep his troops clear of unrest in Leipzig, an order later confirmed by Moscow (Zelikow and Rice 1995: 84–85). Nevertheless, the regime seemed resolute. In the first week of October, Honecker's government closed the border with neighboring states and struck hard to restore order, as evidenced by the conduct of the security forces in Berlin and Dresden during the fortieth anniversary celebration (see chapter 5). Even without Soviet assurances, hard-liners in East Berlin apparently considered a forceful solution to domestic unrest a smaller risk than chancing reform. Later, various Politburo members claimed that they never intended the use of violence and had countermanded orders that would have led to a "Chinese solution" in Saxony; in fact, decisive orders from the Politburo to avoid violence came only after the breakthroughs that occurred in Leipzig and Dresden. Indeed, it was only on October 13 that Honecker issued clear instructions forbidding the use of force against peaceful demonstrations.[9]

The Soviet Union did nothing to topple Honecker, but it also discouraged the use of force. Pragmatists in the regime may have been looking for some way to remove the aging party boss, as Krenz and others later claimed they were doing. But as they considered moving against him, they received no direct support from Gorbachev's government. Their palace coup against

Honecker took place more than a week after October 9. Yet, regardless of the intentions of the ruling elite of the GDR, the apparatus of repression stood by passively and allowed the streets to fill with peaceful demonstrators on the evening of October 9 in Leipzig. To know why, we have to look more carefully at the local level.

Planning for Repression on October 9

Honecker's instructions left it up to local party and security officials to implement the crackdown on demonstrations. In Leipzig, the cradle of the protest movement, the district party leadership issued orders on September 27 to prevent a Monday demonstration from taking shape on October 2, calling for "deployment readiness" on the part of security forces and an aggressive campaign to discredit antisocialist forces. Police were ordered to prevent all unauthorized public assemblies and to cooperate with Stasi and party militia units (*Kampfgruppen*). Church officials were sternly warned to avoid the "misuse" of religious events by the opposition.[10]

In the weeks leading up to October 9, Leipzig district security officers prepared an arrest list of over one hundred "ringleaders" of counterrevolutionary activities, about half of whom were members of Church-based opposition groups.[11] But the sweep was never carried out in the days leading up to October 9, apparently because international attention was focused on the situation and—paradoxically—because the local opposition was so obviously weak in its organizational capacities. Police intelligence on the Monday demonstrations had indicated that there were no clear leaders or instigators whose arrest could have crippled the movement. Stasi informants inside the nascent civic movement reported activists were doing nothing to instigate popular rebellion and described the Leipzig dissidents as poorly informed, disorganized, and lacking effective leadership.[12] District Stasi chief Manfred Hummitzsch had acknowledged as much in a report to Mielke on August 31, in which he noted, "Our evaluation of the situation is that the 'Peace Prayers' no longer need to be organized. For months now, it has been the traditional meeting point for these [disaffected] people. They have no need of leaflets or any other [organizational] activities. The people go there completely of their own accord" (Mitter and Wolle 1990: 128). Given this, simply rounding up the "usual suspects" would have probably failed to deter protesters and come at the cost of an international embarrassment. At any rate, having decided that the Monday demonstrations were occurring spontaneously, security officials never organized a general roundup.

On October 2 security forces managed to disperse the Monday protest march with a minimum of arrests by deploying heavily armed riot police that disrupted efforts to form a procession. In light of this success, the district police commander in Leipzig calculated that a sizable deployment of riot police and Communist militiamen would be sufficient to prevent a protest march on October 9. To support the regular police forces, he mobilized three thousand military riot policemen (BPS) and five hundred militiamen to stiffen his forces. He placed three thousand regular army troops (NVA) with live ammunition in reserve on the edge of the city (Friedheim 1997: 335). Yet he insisted that he would only act if he had the clear political support of local party officials. On October 3 he wrote to the minister of the interior, "On October 9, 1989, massive oppositional forces in an even greater number are to be expected [than on October 2]. I will strive to prevent a concentration of these forces from forming around the St. Nicholas Church. . . . The forty-year history of our GDR has continually proven that a decisive and lasting political solution can be advanced by the deployment of party militiamen."[13] If a Chinese solution proved necessary, police officials would not be the only ones with bloody hands.

Police strategists planned on a massive show of force that would push the demonstrators out of the narrow confines of St. Nicholas and onto the Karl-Marx-Platz, where riot squads could be more effective than in the tangled streets of the old city. As a result, on October 9 the city bristled with security forces. Militiamen and police were outfitted with riot equipment and batons, and officers were issued pistols. The army units held in reserve were given automatic weapons. As Hummitzsch later testified, "At this moment, everything was possible."[14]

Meanwhile, in spite of the directives from East Berlin, local officials appear to have been losing their nerve in the early afternoon of October 9. Security officials became worried that they did not have support from local party leaders and that the Politburo did not fully comprehend the situation in Leipzig. Hummitzsch later explained to an examining commission,

> On the morning of October 9 in a meeting at the district headquarters
> at 7:30 a.m. under the leadership of Helmut Hackenberg [acting dis-

trict party chief], it was made absolutely clear that neither the deployment of firearms nor other so-called police resources would be possible in order to push back the demonstrations. This was also in contradiction to the central directives [from the Politburo of the SED]. But this was not so only on the ninth. I must tell you that I had already, prior to this date, expressed this opinion, this opinion that is today the official position of the leadership, that political conflicts can only be solved by political means. I was personally contacted by the former minister for state security [Mielke] on this Monday, the ninth of October, twice in the morning by telephone, and he reminded me of my duties. I was pressured to not lose my nerve, to maintain order, and to prevent anything that could lead to an escalation (*Zuspitzung*) of the situation.[15]

However self-serving Hummitzsch's account may have been, what is clear from this and other statements is that the regime had left local security officials with an uncertain mandate. They were instructed to prevent the "escalation" of the situation—if necessary, by use of deadly force. But in the context of October 9, what was an escalation? If a disaster resulted from actions taken in Leipzig, it was conceivable that regime leaders would distance themselves from the local officials, claiming that they had exceeded their orders and authority. Given the uncertainty that resulted from these conflicting imperatives, police and security officials erred on the side of caution. They prepared a forceful response in case the demonstration escalated into violence but would not initiate violence of their own unless directly ordered to do so by East Berlin.

In addition to ambiguities in their instructions, the serious underestimation of the scale of popular mobilization shook the confidence of security officials. They had expected several thousand people on October 9—not seventy thousand or more. One militia commander recounted how security forces had been told to expect between two thousand and three thousand protesters on the evening of the ninth.[16] That afternoon he and his comrades found themselves surrounded by a veritable sea of demonstrators outside St. Nicholas. "And it was clearly said (by police commanders) that we should attempt to prevent a demonstration from forming in front of St. Nicholas. But it was actually formed anyway because the sort of demonstration that we expected didn't take place. We had falsely evaluated the situation. None of us had expected such masses of people. . . . We expected provocations would come, stones would fly or Molotov cocktails. . . . We were not there to start shooting; we were there to dissolve counterrevolutionary groups. Only if they provoked us, only in this instance [would we shoot]."[17] The militia commander further claimed that both officers and men were organizationally and psychologically unprepared for crowds of this size. The evidently peaceful tone of the mass demonstration that was forming on the afternoon of the ninth and the restrained mood of the protesters quickly convinced them that the use of force was not prudent.

Once the sheer scale of mobilization became evident, Leipzig's police chief realized that he would have had to open fire on the masses to prevent a protest march, simply because he had, he later said, "no other means to break up the crowd" (Friedheim 1997: 335). It appears that the rapid, unforeseen mobilization of tens of thousands of people between October 2 and October 9 threw local security officials off balance and demoralized troops and policemen. And it was not simply a matter of the protesters' moral advantage—it was not clear that the police would prevail if shots were fired and such a large crowd became enraged. On the afternoon of October 9, the loyalty and the morale of the outnumbered security forces were questionable, and thus the prospect of instigating an angry, violent popular uprising must have been seen as a dangerous threat.

Local party officials seem to have been especially unprepared for a confrontation with the masses. The reason is as much strategic as political. In the aftermath of the unexpectedly large Monday protest march of September 25, the Leipzig district party leadership planned to reinforce police and security forces with party activists and the factory-based party militias.[18] These party militias (Kampfgruppen der Arbeiterklasse) had been organized, in Walter Ulbricht's words, to make "a repeat of the seventeenth of June [1953] or similar fascist provocation impossible." They had proven reliable when they helped seal the borders in August 1961 during the construction of the Berlin Wall. In the late 1980s tens of thousands of workers were assigned to militia units, with their oversight given to the Interior Ministry. To prepare them, militia units were outfitted with automatic weapons and armored vehicles.[19]

The mobilization of the party militia was important in signaling party resolve to the public. Party directives instructed that militiamen "must assume a high state of readiness to defend their homeland with weapons against internal and external enemies."[20] However, by September 1989 local leaders could no longer take the commitment of their comrade militiamen for granted. Party Control Commissions (PKKs) reported difficulty in mobilizing militiamen and noted the low morale and disorganization that prevailed in many units. There was also abundant evidence that the Kampfgruppen rank and file were neither uniformly party stalwarts nor as "combat ready" as their mission demanded.[21] Leipzig party officials complained of their demoralization, insubordination, and tendency to resign:

> In connection with the statement of purpose to ensure law and order in the city of Leipzig by the militia, it seems that some comrade militiamen have given into the slander of the enemy and have announced their withdrawal from the militia. In so doing, they cite the statement made by militia commander Lutz, who, on October 6, 1989, made it clear in the pages of the *Leipziger Volkszeitung* that, if necessary, members of these socialist organizations would defend the GDR with weapons in their hands. This was not acceptable to them, and they took the position that they would refuse to use weapons against so-called peaceful demonstrators.[22]

In fact, during their deployment in early October, some militia units were so undermanned they were considered unfit for deployment.[23]

As the state prepared for the showdown on October 9, militia personnel were on the verge of massive insubordination. One militia commander reported to the district leadership that he and his men were unwilling and unable to fight.[24] A report by the Leipzig PKK in the days following the events of October 9 explained that some militiamen simply failed to muster for action. Others refused to be deployed against protesters and resigned from their units. Some wondered why the state wanted them to "terrorize ordinary citizens" instead of having them simply round up the "hard core of the opposition." Many explained that "they were ready to defend property, but otherwise the demonstrations should be allowed to proceed," and they said they were "not willing to go against the demonstrators." Although mutinous members risked severe disciplinary measures, internal reports reveal that militia units were already seriously compromised by defection and disobedience in the weeks leading up to October 9.[25]

Called on to confront "counterrevolutionaries" and "political rowdies" and to "nip counterrevolutionary riots in the bud," few militiamen seem to have been ready for such a confrontation if it meant bashing unarmed protesters or chancing the full brunt of popular wrath. As an SED militia unit commander recounted,

> I knew the ninth would be the day of reckoning. I stood with my comrades, seventy-four comrade militiamen; we were present standing at the Swan Pool [near the city center], and another fifty comrades stood at the corner of Grimmaische Strasse. We would provide backup for the People's Police [DVP], not with any firearms, but with our party point of view and our very presence as party comrades. I asked if anyone was afraid. Well, they all stood their ground, but they were afraid. . . . Even our militia comrades were afraid, and they were glad that they didn't have to use their cudgels, that things could lead to a dialogue.[26]

A militia commander deployed on the edge of Karl Marx Square on October 9 was to comment later: "I can tell you that this deployment was a turning point in my life. What we experienced there . . . was a real disillusionment. We said to ourselves, we will never allow ourselves to be used like this by the party leadership again" (Zwahr 1993: 100).

Clearly, the eroding loyalty of the party rank and file made the position of district officials precarious. Former Politburo member and Magdeburg party boss Werner Eberlein (2000: 461) said of the October crisis in his memoir: "The idea of outfitting some militia units with cudgels led to some refusing their orders, because they were not prepared to beat up their colleagues. . . . The members of the militia were prepared to defend the GDR and their factories, but the very thought of having to beat up their buddies evoked dismay. The problems in the GDR could not be resolved by force." In fact there is no evidence that party militiamen were effective against peaceful civilian protest anywhere in the GDR in 1989. Although they were mobilized in support of police and army units, archival records suggest that the militia did not play an important role even on the occasions when security officials used force or where large-scale arrests were made (Koop 1997: 242–45).

However, even if the militiamen had lost their resolve, that did not necessarily mean that the state would buckle in the face of popular protest. Rather than rely on the party militia, the GDR turned principally to a highly professionalized force of police and army personnel to maintain internal security. Indeed, as we have seen, in the first week of October police and army units did use considerable force to break up demonstrations and arrested thousands of protesters in Dresden, Berlin, Plauen, Leipzig, and other cities. Yet it was not only within militia units that loyalty to the regime was faltering. On October 9 policemen had been warned that they would face a violent mob and that the use of firearms could not be ruled out, even if women and children were present. But once it became clear that these were peaceful demonstrators representing all sections of the population, police morale appears to have evaporated (Neues Forum Leipzig 1990: 92–93).

Members of military police units, although trained in anti-riot tactics, were usually neither party stalwarts nor career policemen. Most were conscripts and reservists. In early October some refused mobilization orders because they felt that they should not attack peaceful citizens or because they professed sympathy for the goals of New Forum. And even some officers had lost confidence in their mission. A ranking military police official in Dresden complained to a Western reporter that political repression damaged his status as a military professional, "I am sick of this, these people are peaceful. Now our image is completely ruined."[27] Eager for a "political solution" to the crisis, military policemen in Leipzig expressed resentment about "having to do the Party's dirty work."[28]

In Dresden some military personnel apparently risked being court-martialed and imprisoned for refusing to obey their superiors. One military policeman recalled, "Before us stood the enraged masses and behind us the officers, the Stasi, and back at the base, the military prosecutor. That which we did there among the crowds we did only out of fear and the will to survive."[29] Youthful army conscripts found themselves battling their peers in the streets and railway stations. Many objected and a few incidents of insubordination occurred. According to prosecutors, in the midst of the fighting in the Dresden train station during the night of October 3–4, more than a dozen members of the Seventh Panzer Division refused orders to clear the station.[30]

In his interviews, Karl-Dieter Opp found that Leipzig security officials realized that they faced a considerable threat of solidarity between the troops and the demonstrators should the order to open fire be given (Opp, Voss, and Gern 1995: 178). A former military state prosecutor reported of the armed forces, "And where these units gathered together, there came resistance, especially from the soldiers. They came out and said directly, 'We're not going to attack' " (220). Given evidence of the failing commitment of rank-and-file party members and the questionable loyalties of police, military, and militia units, local and regional party officials increasingly had reason to fear that a Tiananmen situation would go terribly wrong.

Privately, even some regime insiders quietly began to hedge their bets. Eberlein was to recall his fear that a "Chinese solution" might have "suicidal" consequences:

> It was forbidden [in Magdeburg] to distribute ammunition, and the Kampfgruppen were not deployed because it would have been senseless. The militia groups would not have been ready to go up against their own colleagues. It was just the kind of situation that couldn't go on any longer. And if today someone or another claims, "I prevented a bloodbath," that is nonsense. It would have been suicide. . . . Whoever tried something like that would have been immediately lynched. I cannot decide against a movement that brings 50,000 people to its feet in Magdeburg; to go against something like that is really impossible. And neither police nor Stasi can do anything about it; all such measures would be senseless.[31]

In fact, the possibility that armed personnel might go over to the crowd was acknowledged by the Stasi as early as August 1989 when it cautioned against deploying the army against civilian demonstrations because of the political unreliability of rank-and-file troops (Mitter and Wolle 1990: 53). If a violent crackdown went awry, officials and security officers might have feared a scenario not unlike that which occurred in Romania in December 1989 when rebellious soldiers turned against the secret police and helped topple the regime of Nicolae Ceausescu.

The weakened resolve of the security forces was apparently known to some protesters in Dresden and Leipzig during the tumultuous week of October 2–8. On October 9 astute civic movement activists and clergymen were convinced that the bulk of ordinary police and military personnel were dispirited. Clergymen urged sympathy for the policemen and soldiers; indeed, among the mass of the demonstrators only Stasi agents were truly despised. In Dresden on October 7, as police and NVA troops, some armed with submachine guns, lined up to disperse demonstrators, activists, linked arm in arm, shouted, "No violence!" and "Brothers, join us!" (a few also shouted, "Stasi swine!"). An activist reported to a Dresden congregation that it was obvious that "the majority of them [military policemen] were not very enthusiastic. How can the deployment of such a huge number of police to an absolutely peaceful demonstration be justified?"[32] In Leipzig, citizens approached security personnel, asking questions like "How can you beat up your own children?" or pointed out to militiamen that "you know yourselves how bad things are going in the factories, something has to change." Others called on the police and army personnel to "Join in with us!" and chided them, "Aren't you ashamed?" when they made arrests. Some protesters shouted, "Do you really want your own China?" at the assembled ranks of troops and militiamen.[33]

In the end, undermined by inadequate planning, failing morale, and the political unreliability of security forces, all the plans to prevent crowds from assembling failed. As we have seen, Leipzig's compact urban geography further undermined the police by facilitating crowd formation and bystander recruitment. The plan to force the crowd out of the tangled streets around St. Nicholas was a mistake. As riot police herded people from the area around the St. Nicholas Church, the crowd was pushed onto the much-larger Karl Marx Square where passersby, the curious, and the wavering could more easily join the protest. People on their way home from work stopped to see what was going on, and many became part of the march. Trams and buses were halted in the traffic, with marchers chanting to their fellow Leipzigers, "Join in! We need every person!" (Zwahr 1993; Neues Forum 1990), and, by the tens of thousands, they did.

Why Did Midlevel Officials Defect?

As the Monday demonstrations mushroomed in September, the Leipzig party leadership realized that its strategy of containment was faltering. In taking stock of the radicalization of the situation in Leipzig, local officials laid most of the blame on the imperialist West, but they remained divided on how forceful a response was necessary to halt the expansion of protest. In a meeting of the district party leadership on September 12, party secretary Kurt Meyer, who would later defect from the hard-liners, contended that Western media "exaggerated the impression of mass pressure against socialism" and that the protests were narrowly based among "groups of Christians." He concluded that the informal organization and lack of sophistication of the dissidents meant that the opposition had little chance of drawing popular support.[34] Acting district party boss Helmut Hackenberg concurred, claiming that "those who were really pulling the strings on Monday [September 4] at the St. Nicholas Church were more than apparent. . . . They [the Western press] had orders to put together a top story for the evening news." A handful of "rowdies" and troublemakers would never sway the party to adopt liberal reforms and make it fall victim to the "politics of surrender and rollback."[35]

Municipal officials voiced more concern and urged that forceful steps be taken. One warned that the GDR was facing an "antisocialist movement" that was "no less counterrevolutionary than, for example, it was in our republic in 1953 or in Hungary in 1957 [sic]." Leipzig municipal party boss Jochen Prag warned, "No one should forget that these antisocialist groups want to destabilize the political situation. They want to spread disorder and insecurity. . . . We declare here and now, we will not allow the enemy to get a foothold. We will nip all politically hostile actions, in whatever form, in the bud."[36] Yet, in spite of the militant rhetoric, there was no consensus among municipal and district officials on how to prevent the Monday demonstrations from widening.

District officials knew that resolve was faltering among the party rank and file. In an analysis of the influence of "hostile ideologies" in July 1989, an internal party report found that Leipzig comrades were almost universally aggrieved by economic decline, the decay of the urban infrastructure, and the impassivity of the party leadership. The report specified that "the policies of the party are said to be dogmatic and conservative and incapable of change" and that "more democracy and freedom is supported, and in this context the protection of human rights in the GDR is placed under criticism." Many party members, particularly the young, favored glasnost and even preferred "democracy and freedom of the Western conception." The report acknowledged the widespread sentiment that "in the GDR socialism [has] become worse and that perestroika would also be good for the GDR." In particular, the report noted, the aging Politburo was condemned by many as "inflexible," "dogmatic," and even "senile."[37]

Exit further challenged party discipline. Between August and October, the Leipzig party organization had lost more than three thousand members for disciplinary reasons, about five hundred of whom had illegally left the country.[38] By early October, local officials were concluding that many—perhaps the majority—of local party members could no longer be relied on to mobilize against political challengers. There was a growing sense of retreat from political confrontation among party members that made it difficult to impose order in the factories and neighborhoods.[39] Party authorities were barraged with petitions, resolutions, and protest letters during the first week of October. Open demands for reform flooded in from such diverse sources as a local machine tool factory collective and the musicians' union of the Leipzig Radio Orchestra. Many petitions denounced the Central Committee and called for constitutional reforms, investigations of official corruption, and the end of party privileges.[40]

As security officials began to draft plans for a crackdown against the Monday demonstrations, party officials met in Leipzig on October 8 to decide on what measures were to be taken the following day. The conference brought together district party secretaries, security officials, the mayor, officials from various municipal and regional branches of the party, and the commanders of militia units. The Leipzig chief of police agreed to back up city officials in carrying out the directives they had received from Berlin to suppress the demonstrations.[41] Despite the apparent sense of resolve, however, it was clear at this emergency meeting just how serious the crisis in the region really was. As the municipal party chief Joachim Prag later explained,

> A conference with around a hundred and fifty officials took place on October 8, and again this showed the secretariat very clearly what was expected of us by local party branches. . . . In evaluating this conference we developed a realistic, solid analysis of the mounting situation, which we immediately gave to the district leadership and the Central Committee of our party the next day. In this report we explained that questions were mounting, anxieties were growing, thousands and thousands of members of our party were not in a position to solve everything and to react to the attacks on the GDR. . . . [That] helped us to evaluate our situation realistically and to judge it critically.

Although local officials dared not openly defy East Berlin, there was no consensus that the repressive strategy favored by the party leadership was the appropriate one. From their later testimony, it appears that Leipzig officials were angered by the intransigence and dogmatism of the party leadership and were resentful that it was left up to them to take the riskiest steps. Further challenging their resolve, on the afternoon of October 8, news reached Leipzig that the Dresden district leadership under Hans Modrow had begun to negotiate with clergymen and activists (Friedheim 1997: 334). In the end, the Leipzig officials at the emergency meeting on October 8 failed to agree to a clear course of action, thereby creating opportunities for the pragmatists.[42]

All of the evidence suggests that a critical factor in the peaceful outcome on October 9 were last-minute defections from the hard-line policy. On the afternoon of October 9, the "Appeal of the Leipzig Six," a plea for peace and dialogue, was announced. It was the initiative of three midcareer SED district secretaries and three prominent figures from the local artistic and intellectual milieu (the famous Gewandhaus Orchestra conductor Kurt Masur, a cabaretist, and a theology professor). Agreeing to risk action without authorization from Berlin, the conspirators held a meeting on October 9 at which they drafted their call for toleration and dialogue. The eleventh-hour appeal, finished only ten minutes before four o'clock (by convention, the demonstrations began at 5:00 p.m.), was then distributed to clergymen and read over the local radio. Once they realized that local party officials were distancing themselves from repression, security officials quickly decided to avert bloodshed (Zwahr 1993: 85–86).

The "Appeal of the Leipzig Six" far exceeded the authority of those who instigated it. They were midcareer party functionaries and local cultural notables who were sympathetic to perestroika, but who before this point were neither leaders nor vocal proponents of a liberal faction in the party organization. Indeed, they took pains after the fact to deny charges of factionalism and disloyalty to the party, describing themselves as pragmatists who did not wish to see a violent confrontation that might end badly for the party and imperil socialism. As they repeatedly stated afterward, their goal in pressing for dialogue was to save the socialist system and the party's predominant role in it, not to facilitate a democratic revolution.

In explaining his part in drafting and propagating the appeal, party secretary Kurt Meyer told a meeting of party leaders two weeks after the events, "We had already experienced the 7th and 8th of October and knew there was a real danger that things could escalate. We Communists didn't want that, but the security forces were independent of us, and they were prepared for a provocation. And so facing this, I had a telephone conversation with Kurt Masur at 1:30 p.m. and said to him personally, Let's think about things together. What can one do to prevent something bad, or even the worst, from happening in our city?"[43] In explaining why they had taken the risk of drafting the appeal without authorization from the party leadership or security officials, Meyer explained that local leaders were too indecisive and divided on what course of action should be taken and that the Politburo did not have a realistic appraisal of the situation. Given the frustrating indecision that prevailed at the party conference on the eighth, it was clear that only a local intervention could be effective. Indeed, Meyer defended the conspirators' "civil courage" against charges of violating Leninist norms forbidding insubordination and factionalism:

> Personally, this civil courage stemmed from fear, from fear about what could happen if it came to blows that day. I mean that if blood had been spilled, socialism would have been swept away. We couldn't accept that. . . . I can understand that many comrades were confused [by the intervention] and that a lot of comrades didn't know how to regard this politically, if a faction was responsible for this. But we had no opportunity between 10 a.m. and 4 p.m. to call together a meeting of the district leadership and have a conference to say what we should do.[44]

As to evidence that the Leipzig Six had acted without authorization from above, Meyer explained to his comrades that the Politburo's security secretary, Egon Krenz, had only approved their appeal once it was made public, calling at midnight on the night of October 9–10 to praise the actions of the three party secretaries after learning about the initiative from West German television news. It was not until October 13, in advance of the next Monday demonstration, that Krenz went to Leipzig to endorse the politics of peaceful dialogue.[45]

   This should not imply that the Saxon districts of Leipzig and Dresden were hotbeds of reformism. Regional officials in Saxony were motivated in large part by opportunistic considerations. During the previous week street clashes in Dresden had "resembled a civil war" (Zwahr 1993: 57), and violence had also been evident in Leipzig. Modrow's district government had deployed troops against protesters and made more than thirteen hundred arrests. With conventional crowd control tactics failing to clear the streets, local military officials recommended sending in tanks against unarmed demonstrators. By October 8 the Dresden leadership concluded that a call for dialogue was the only alternative to a bloodbath. Dresden's mayor, Wolfgang Berghofer, later lamented that "the leadership under Honecker led us into a terrible situation." He added, "If one sees a hundred thousand shouting, 'We are the people,' flooding into the streets, one begins to worry, what will it all lead to? And when one experienced how the leadership of the country reacted, concerns emerged, also fear."[46] Unwilling to risk a massacre, Dresden's local authorities finally decided to engage in a dialogue that they thought would buy them the time needed to regain the political initiative.

Events in Dresden would presage the turn in Leipzig. In Leipzig, more than two hundred people had been arrested between October 2 and 8. Many on both sides of the police barricades feared that violence, perhaps on a large scale, was inevitable. For the nascent opposition movement, it is obvious that nonviolence was an essential part of any reform strategy, but it was also becoming evident to elements within the local party organization that forswearing violence might also be the best way to prevent a radicalization of the protest movement. Key officials in Leipzig, as in Dresden, favored moderate concessions that would satisfy demands for Gorbachev-style reforms. Moreover, closer to the action in the streets, pragmatic officials perceived that the nascent civic movement was led not by revolutionaries but by critical loyalists who could be co-opted as junior partners in a top-down reform process.

Indeed, in justifying his unilateral recognition of the local opposition, Dresden district leader Modrow explained to the Central Committee that the opposition movement was no threat to the GDR, but rather reflected diffuse pressure for change that was not fundamentally hostile to the state. He noted that it was the exiting problem—not the new opposition groups—that had instigated the popular rebellion. As a result, "the influence of the 'New Forum' people has taken a leap." Through cooperation with the dissidents, stability might be restored: "These groups recognize in their language the GDR and socialism, but demand changes and reforms. . . . Participants explain that they are going to the streets because otherwise nothing about the acute problems in our development will be discussed."[47]

Of course, the failure of the state to act decisively on October 9 was partially the result of the failure to coordinate national and local decision making. Had regional party officials in Leipzig been given clearer instructions from East Berlin, they might have acted in accord with Politburo goals regardless of their private preference for reform. As became clear in the wake of October 9, the failure to provide clear guidance from the center, the equivocations of Honecker and Mielke, and the weakness of hard-line elements in the Leipzig party organization made possible local initiatives by realists unwilling to hazard the risks of a "Chinese solution" and hoping instead to secure popular support through limited concessions.[48]

Local officials understood their actions not as opportunistic, which hard-liners asserted they were, but as "realistic" responses to the general crisis in the GDR. Local party and state officials were not mistaken when they observed that party leaders in East Berlin had a poorly formed view of the situation they confronted. They knew this, in part, because for years they had reinforced the naïve impression of stability and consent held by many senior regime leaders through their falsification of data and distorted reports of local conditions. Many party leaders in the Politburo persisted in the notion that living conditions in the country were good and that, save for a handful of dissidents and "reactionary clerics," most people in the GDR were satisfied with their circumstances. Even though Stasi reports generally provided a fairly accurate picture of the actual mood of the country and anticipated many of the developments in Leipzig and other cities (Mitter and Wolle 1990), Honecker, Günter Mittag, and other conservatives in the Politburo discounted these reports as exaggerations (McAdams 1993; Opp, Voss, and Gern 1995: 173–74).

The hard-liners saw a small-scale rebellion instigated by antisocialist forces that would be easily crushed by a show of force. They thought their propaganda campaign had convinced citizens to stay out of the streets and incited the party rank and file to leap to the defense of their party. Of course, local officials knew better. For Modrow, as for the Leipzig Six, the best hope of stabilizing the GDR lay in the inclusion of a loyalist civic movement in a party-led reform process. In other words, they aligned themselves with reformist voice against what they saw as the ineffective rule of the Honecker circle.

Local Coordination and the Retreat from Violence

In strategic terms the situation confronting both the nascent opposition movement and Saxon state officials on October 9 was unusual in that neither side saw itself as having much to gain from violence if the other side refrained from it. If violence continued on both sides, the situation would remain much the same as it had since the exiting crisis triggered mass mobilization. Saxon officials realized that repression was no longer deterring street protest and was probably bringing bystanders outraged by the state's heavy-handedness into a swiftly expanding movement.

Clearly, given the high stakes, dissidents had every reason to avoid a violent confrontation on October 9. No citizen movement could prevail against the regime if it exercised determined, violent repression. If the sort of violence that had occurred during the first week of October were to continue, then it would tend to justify Honecker's "Chinese solution" to political turmoil. All of this fed into a more basic Gandhian calculation of movements of the weak: if the protesters remained committed to nonviolence in the face of police provocations or brutality, their moral standing would prosper while the state damaged its own. Yet even if adopting a strategy of strict nonviolence is the most rational way to improve the efficacy of protest (assuming that the state will not simply mow down protesters), it can only be managed by a dissident leadership capable of implementing the most advantageous tactics. This is not an easy matter even for a sophisticated movement organization. As Chong (1991) has argued in the case of the U.S. civil rights movement, the strategic advantages of nonviolence were clear for Martin Luther King Jr. and his associates, but the policy of nonviolence sometimes failed and allowed the authorities to gain the upper hand (29).[49] Thus, even when nonviolence was the only feasible strategy, it still required extensive coordination and could collapse under the weight of a single defection. Indeed, this occurred in some of the failed campaigns of the U.S. civil rights movement, where "the presence of a large number of followers in a movement [made] collective action volatile and difficult to sustain" (189). Even though dissident activists and clergymen recognized the need for nonviolence in Leipzig, there was no guarantee on October 9 that it would prevail.

On the side of the state, violent tactics were much easier to employ but were not without significant costs. If the loyalty of the rank-and-file security forces were in doubt and they refused to obey orders to meet violence with violence, the result would be a disaster. And if the state were to use violence against peaceful protesters, that would create the possibility of a massacre of innocent citizens potentially ruinous to the future effectiveness of local elites, damaging to the GDR's international relations, and spurring a widening opposition to the regime. Nevertheless, Politburo member Werner Eberlein later reported that the party leadership continued to regard New Forum as a counterrevolutionary threat at exactly the moment in which co-opting it might have steered the GDR toward reform instead of collapse. By contrast, local officials apparently recognized the advantages of strategic concessions. As Eberlein (2000: 462) admitted, "It [the Politburo's position] contradicted the experience of the district secretaries, who said a useful dialogue was possible with these citizens, who are in no way hostile to socialism." In short, for local officials there were clear incentives favoring a peaceful resolution of the mounting protests.

In fact, Saxon officials were hoping for just such a shift in political strategy. Wolfgang Berghofer, the mayor of Dresden, recounted how he and Modrow abandoned the "Chinese solution" when they grasped that "events had come to a point of culmination. One had to decide: either a bloodbath or a reasonable way toward a political solution. . . . One had to prevent violence at any price. The fear that it could escalate was quite acute. That was the beginning, even though I couldn't foresee the ends to which this breakthrough would lead politically."[50] The archival evidence shows that local state agents were dealing with considerable uncertainty concerning the outcome of the "Chinese solution" favored by the party elite in Berlin. A peaceful resolution, by contrast, might give local and regional officials in Saxony enough credibility to serve as negotiating partners and perhaps broker a reform program.

Even if both dissidents and local leaders wanted to avoid violence, a mutually beneficial outcome did not have to result from strategic interaction. The situation facing dissidents and midlevel government officials in the Saxon cities of Leipzig and Dresden can be thought of as a game of "chicken." Mutual coordination would be preferable to conflict, but achieving a peaceful compact would be difficult. After nearly two weeks of mounting unrest in Leipzig and Dresden that neither dissidents nor local officials could control, both parties preferred to reach an agreement that would halt the violence, but they struggled to reach a mutually credible set of terms. Among the difficulties were doubts about each side's honesty and capacity to make independent decisions and the crucial problem of deciding who should act first. The breakthrough was made possible by two factors. First, both parties realized that external allies would not come to their rescue if violence continued to escalate. The clergy and the nascent civic movement leaders knew that they enjoyed Western support only to the extent that they were seen as responsible and peaceful agents for change that would not destabilize international relations. State officials knew that the Soviet Union would not mobilize its forces if a full-fledged rebellion broke out.

As Jon Elster (1989: 6–7) observes of such situations, "Assuming that we are facing a choice under uncertainty . . . many people then want to play it safe, by adopting the 'maxi-min' criterion for choosing the option whose worst consequence is better than the worst consequences of any other." In Leipzig and Dresden, because both sides made the choice to refrain from violence or, in other words, "disarmed," a mutually beneficial outcome was achieved. Of course, in some games of "chicken," no one blinks. Fearing betrayal, or overconfident of winning, one or both sides arm (or, in this case, employ violence), and the result is far less than optimal. In practice, what helps to avoid the unhappy outcomes of the game is a credible nonviolence bargain. In Leipzig, the Group of Six played this role, communicating the commitment to nonviolence to both sides on October 9. In Dresden, clergymen and the Group of Twenty played a similar role in their meetings with Mayor Berghofer. For the dissidents, the state's switch from violent repression to nonviolence was credible because district party secretaries and government officials risked their necks by calling for peaceful dialogue. Local officials, for their part, were reassured by the nonviolent posture of dissidents and the clergy and their clear efforts to maintain the peace.

Had there been violent clashes, the seizure of government buildings, rioting and looting, or efforts to terrorize state officials, as was the case across the GDR on June 17, 1953, Saxony might not have been the birthplace of a democratic revolution. But on October 9 the protesters remained peaceful, and Soviet forces were instructed to stay out of civilian affairs. Prestigious actors in both camps signaled their willingness to throw their support behind a compromise. Clergymen and local human rights activists clearly instructed the crowds to refrain from violence and sought out a dialogue with state officials. Local officials signaled their goodwill to dissidents and clergymen. Peace prevailed and a new kind of revolution began.

CHAPTER 8

Activists of the First Hour:
New Forum and the Mobilization of Reformist Voice

No historic class lifts itself from a subject position to a position of rule suddenly in one night, even through a night of revolution. It must already on the eve of revolution have assumed a very independent attitude towards the official ruling class; moreover, it must have focused upon itself the hopes of the intermediate classes and layers, dissatisfied with the existing state of affairs, but not capable of playing an independent role.

—LEON TROTSKY, *THE HISTORY OF THE RUSSIAN REVOLUTION*

In the study of revolutions, the presence of a "counter-elite" vying to replace the current regime with one of its own has been identified as a necessary factor. Leon Trotsky (1933) defined a revolutionary situation as one of "dual power" in which a new political class strives to replace the old elite. Curiously, in the case of East Germany, no such counter-elite evolved. Insurgent, anti-regime voice propelled the fall of Honecker and inaugurated the GDR's peaceful revolution. But, alongside this wave of protest, a reformist movement also arose. In the midst of the popular rebellion in October 1989, crowds of citizens shouted slogans supporting the new civic movement organizations, most prominently New Forum. Thousands risked arrest by publicly signing on to the illegal New Forum organization prior to November 9. Unlike those who defiantly challenged the state in relatively anonymous street protests, these citizens openly declared themselves part of the movement for reform. Over the next several months, New Forum and other civic movement organizations sought to take the lead in democratizing socialism.

After attaining legal status on the eve of the events of November 9, New Forum expanded rapidly. At the time of its founding political convention in January 1990, the organization could boast some two hundred thousand declared supporters. Yet its sudden rise was matched by its rapid decline into insignificance; New Forum won only a small share of the vote in the first democratic elections in March 1990 and lost more than 90 percent of its supporters by the end of the year. Evaluating the eclipse of the civic movement, historians argued that the "national turn" in the revolution, or as Sigrid Meuschel (1992) has dubbed it, the "transformation in the transformation," redirected the popular movement away from demands for a reform of socialism to pressure for reunification with the capitalist West. This turn was evident in the streets with the replacement, in the space of just a few weeks after October 9, of the implicitly reformist popular slogan "We are the people!" with "We are *one* people!" Civic movement leaders increasingly found themselves alienated from a *Volk* that repudiated the vision of a renewed, humane, and democratic socialism (Torpey 1995; Joppke 1995; Philipsen 1993).

Why did the civic movement—initially applauded as the activists of the first hour—fall so out of step with the majority of mobilized East German citizens and fail to take power when the pressure of the streets was behind it? Previous studies have considered how leadership and ideology affected civic movement strategies and goals. Scholars documented how antifascist ideology shaped the leading intellectuals of the civic movement and blunted their revolutionary potential (Philipsen 1993; Torpey 1995; Joppke 1995; Rucht 1996). Historical accounts have shown that movement leaders were generally dissident intellectuals, artists, and liberal clergymen unfriendly to conventional parliamentary politics (Neubert 1998). Electoral studies have probed the question of who voted for the civic movement in March 1990 (Kopstein and Richter 1992). But there has been no careful analysis of rank-and-file civic movement support in East Germany. Political sociologists have thus left a central question unanswered: in the midst of a revolution triggered by exit but propelled by insurgent voice, what made some citizens feel invested enough in the socialist system to respond to the civic movement's call for reform?

The contrast between the street protests and the efforts to build a reform movement points to two related but distinct forms of voice that characterize the East German revolution. Triggered by the exiting crisis, insurgent voice made use of elementary mobilizing structures to expand rapidly enough to overcome the state's efforts at repression and intimidation. This sort of popular insurgency is exemplified by the "miracle" of Leipzig on October 9. This was voice motivated largely by broad grievances against the regime, by rejection of the ruling elite, and by the insecurity created by a decaying socialist system. Its principal object was to remove the regime. The reformist social movement organizing of New Forum and other groups, however, was designed to protect and improve socialism. Drawing on Proposition 3 in chapter 1, one can think of this as *reformist* voice: opposition that is inspired by the hope of improving socialism and that relies on the activation of loyalty.

However, when applied to Leninist regimes it is difficult to assess the meaning of loyalty because of the opportunistic dissimulation and insincere public discourse typical of societies governed by one-party states (Kuran 1995b; Jowitt 1992). Indeed, the swift erosion and unprecedented collapse of the Communist parties of Eastern Europe in 1989 suggest the wide extent to which seemingly "loyal" comrades were actually opportunistically motivated (Hechter 1994; also see Hollander 1999). For purposes of analyzing exit-voice dynamics, loyalty can best be understood as dispositions that determine the relative attractiveness of exit and voice strategies. Based on the limited data available, there are three ways in which we might identify the effect of loyalty in political mobilization. The first is by identifying the stated motives that inform participation. Political ideals often motivate collective action, as for example the belief in the legitimacy of a polity or the rightness of an ideology (see, e.g., Weber 1978). The second way is by identifying what actions are taken by participants. Loyalty can be discerned in the object of collective action and inferred from the strategies and tactics participants adopt. A third way is to discern loyalty in the social characteristics that determine mobilization.

Up until now little has been known about the early supporters of the civic movement whose mobilization behind New Forum helped propel the reformist cause. Combining qualitative and quantitative data provides a clear understanding of the civic movement as a loyal opposition, a manifestation of voice behind the reform and improvement of a separate GDR. Analysis of New Forum support at the local level is intended to uncover the sources of support for the civic movement during the breakthrough phase of the revolution.

Ideology and the Organization of the Civic Moment

In the fall of 1989, dissident leaders in the nascent civic movement directly appealed to an awakening citizenry. The most influential of the early appeals, issued on September 19, was New Forum's "Awakening 1989." It called on GDR citizens to exercise voice through criticism, through political dialogue with reform-friendly officials, and through local chapters of a national reform movement. Those wishing to support the movement were instructed to sign a statement of support that would be used to form a national organization and assist its application for legal recognition.

The government's reaction was swift. On September 21 the Interior Ministry declared New Forum to be an "anticonstitutional and seditious organization" and declared its petition drive illegal. Dissident leaders in East Berlin filed appeals, but on September 26 the Interior Ministry cited Article 1 of the Constitution granting the SED a political monopoly and rejected any "social requirement" for independent political associations. Nevertheless, New Forum was becoming a rallying cry of protesters filling the streets of larger cities. When Stasi officials reported on the growing demonstrations in the Dresden district in early October, they noted that "the influence of the 'New Forum' people has taken a leap."[1] Indeed, in the nearly two-month period of the organization's illegality between mid-September and early November, thousands of people responded to New Forum and began forming local activist groups. Others drafted protest letters to the Interior Ministry demanding that New Forum be legally recognized.[2] A Stasi report in late October noted that grassroots New Forum cells had appeared in "churches, state enterprises, in health and higher education, research and cultural establishments, and in workshops."[3] By the time the government agreed to recognize New Forum on November 8, more than twenty-five thousand people had openly associated themselves with a local New Forum organization.

Like the inauguration of protest in the street, the exiting crisis activated voice in socialist dissidents. The exiting wave of the summer of 1989 made apparent the country's economic and political crisis and served as a call to action among the country's loosely organized dissident communities. For example, the dissident newsletter *Umweltblätter* argued that the exiting crisis showed that the Honecker government was "politically and economically bankrupt" and called true socialists into action: "We have been experiencing with deep involvement in the last days the daily mass exodus of GDR citizens over the Hungarian border to the FRG. . . . Tens of thousands of fellow citizens are ready to abandon all their social ties to experience their dream of a different Germany. . . . The SED has achieved what capitalist ideology never did; because it maintains that its bureaucratic dictatorship is the only path to socialism, the idea of socialism among the population of the GDR is fully discredited."[4] Now, *Umweltblätter* argued, only radical reforms based on "authentic democratic and left concepts that are accessible and popular" could save the GDR.

The founding manifestos of the emerging civic movement likewise declared a commitment to socialist ideals. New Forum called for a new "political platform" aimed at reforming socialism; it strongly condemned capitalism and the inevitable "degeneration into the elbow-society" that would come with a shift to market economics.[5] Imagining a "Third Way" between communism and capitalism, New Forum leaders spoke of democratization, "economic solidarity," and a new "ecological socialism."[6] Democracy Now (Demokratie Jetzt), a smaller civic movement group also founded in mid-September, advocated a "reformed socialist society" liberated from the authoritarian bureaucracy. Calling on East Germans to get "actively involved in their own affairs," it endorsed "ecology and economy joined together" and the "socialization of production."[7]

Indeed, the new civic movement was inspired more by "democratic reconstruction" in the spirit of Gorbachev than by Western-style parliamentary democracy.[8] The first joint statement of the groups composing the civic movement promoted a platform that would include protection of human rights within the framework of a democratic renewal of socialism.[9] On the eve of the fortieth anniversary of the GDR in early October, New Forum declared, "Our goal is to establish a legal and political platform on which we can bring desperately needed social dialogue into practice. No one should be excluded from this even if he or she is an SED member."[10]

The fact was that the leaders of the nascent civic movement wanted to distance themselves from opponents of socialism and made clear that they were disenchanted with the country's rulers but not with the state (Pollack and

Rink 1997; Findeis, Pollack, and Shilling 1994). They were less united on how to achieve democracy than they were in their commitment to socialism. Human rights advocate Wolfgang Templin hoped to realize Marx's "great vision of socialism" and insisted it could only be fulfilled outside a "bourgeois" parliamentary regime. By contrast Stefan Hilsberg, Templin's fellow activist in the Initiative for Peace and Human Rights (IFM), was hoping to promote social democracy.[11] For the most part, East German dissidents wanted Gorbachev-style reforms and initially believed that SED rank-and-file membership would enthusiastically join their movement (Neubert 1998). Unlike activists in other parts of Eastern Europe who already were "beyond glasnost" (Goldfarb 1991) in advocating democracy and markets, many East German dissidents premised their political activities on the persistence of a socialist state, believing with Templin that "every bad socialism was better than a good capitalism."[12]

In early October, on the fortieth anniversary of the state, New Forum eagerly declared its willingness to work with the ruling party:

> We object to regime attempts to depict us as enemies of socialism. New Forum is a platform for New Thinking. . . . Socialism, which the regime sees as so terribly threatened, cannot be endangered by a grassroots movement. Citizen movements do not threaten, but enrich social life. . . . We turn to the two million members of the SED: You are the greatest and most important political body in our country. You are an enormous reserve of specialist knowledge and leadership experience that is urgently needed for the renewal of society. You claim the leading role—so act on it! Lead the discussion in your own ranks, lead the whole party on a constructive course.[13]

However, despite their professed loyalty to socialism, New Forum and the other new civic movement groups were quickly declared by the SED regime to be illegal, "antisocialist" associations. New Forum would only be recognized when the Krenz government was on the verge of collapse in early November and desperate to regain support.

In October many ordinary East Germans expected New Forum to direct the growing protest wave and begin to act as an independent political force. But New Forum soon made clear that it was not interested in serving as a revolutionary force or pressing for a transfer of power. A New Forum organizer, Bärbel Bohley, explained in September,

New Forum does not want to be an umbrella organization; rather, it aims to be a platform where various people can meet: Christians, party comrades, nonparty members, every possible profession. We want to speak with one another. Naturally, in New Forum people from other groups will also be represented. That doesn't mean that these groups have to surrender their autonomy. They will remain independent and can represent their own positions. The purpose and goal of New Forum is to set a social dialogue—outside the Church, throughout the GDR, open for all and legal—about the economy, culture, environment, and bringing justice into motion. . . . While some groups already have a conception of goals, we are in favor of a society that can regain the desire to imagine its own goals.[14]

In a subsequent interview, another New Forum leader, Eberhard Seidel, specifically distanced the civic movement from the Leipzig protests:

New Forum does not engage itself in organizing demonstrations and leading 15,000 people on a march through the cities. New Forum is engaged in getting a dialogue started. We wish to warn emphatically against unexamined activism. . . . One must continually emphasize that New Forum represents a platform for forming political opinion and is not an organization that can organize action all over the country. That so many people in Leipzig have demanded the legalization of New Forum expresses the wish for an opposition, an opposition that they have drawn out of their own despair to give them courage.[15]

Moreover, Seidel explained, New Forum opposed demonstrations, favoring "constructive changes" over "unreflective activism." Seidel's comments may have been intended to shield the organization from repression in the event of a state crackdown, but it is clear that New Forum responded to events in the streets, rather than instigated them. It was only after demonstrators in Leipzig and Dresden had pushed out Honecker that New Forum began to appeal for action in the streets.[16]

No matter how idealistic it may have been, the civic movement soon faced unpleasant realities. Its leaders had foreseen a great movement for democratization, not the collapse of the GDR government. They were in dismay at the popular enthusiasm for ending Germany's division that was so forcefully expressed when the Berlin Wall fell on November 9. Dissident intellectuals feared that ordinary people had forgotten their "democratic awakening" in a flurry of Western consumerism and lust for the West German deutschmark. New Forum took pains to warn East German citizens, "You are the heroes of a political revolution; don't let yourselves be made passive through vacations and debt-ridden shopping sprees."[17] Movement leaders oscillated between praising the people for making a "holiday for us all" and urging their countrymen not to let themselves be "sold out" as "rent-slaves to Western capitalism."[18]

While the once-lionized *Volk* celebrated in the streets, grim warnings of a "sellout" became emblematic of a civic movement realizing its alienation from a populace in whose name it operated. When the exiled dissident songwriter Wolf Biermann was finally allowed to return to the Leipzig stage in early December, he spoke of the pain and disappointment that the expression of national passions was causing him. He pleaded for the truer, more humane socialism based on radical-democratic principles.[19] Others hoped that party and populace could be united through participation in grassroots democracy. The prominent novelist Christa Wolf appealed to the people to "help us build a truly democratic society that demonstrates the vision of a democratic socialism; it's not just a dream if you help us prevent it from being nipped in the bud."[20]

Following the fall of the Berlin Wall, Wolfgang Ullmann, one of the leading voices in Democracy Now, conceded that he was disturbed by the expression of nationalism, a "hopelessly burdened concept" as he saw it, but he was confident that there would be sufficient time to build support for reform over reunification.[21] New Forum's Bohley warned against hasty, ill-conceived plans to introduce multiparty elections.[22] New Forum advocated democratization on the local level first, calling for the empowerment of local civic committees and free elections in May 1990 limited to the communal level. Above all, it made it clear that there should be no political unification with West Germany. New Forum leaders would endorse no more than a "contractual community" (*Vertragsgemeinschaft*) between two independent German states.[23]

Despite the ongoing collapse of the socialist system and the emigration of hundreds of thousands to the West, when the founding congress of New Forum was held in Berlin in January 1990, its political program continued to promote a socialism at home and a fight for a "new world economy based on solidarity." Delegates soon had difficulty resolving their position on a number of questions, including unification, whether or not to demand the dissolution and forfeiture of assets by the Communist party (SED) and whether New Forum should evolve into a conventional political party. Chairman Jens Reich declared of the ideal state: "We want a direct democracy mediated only through a direct exchange of opinions, hence a New Forum. Forum means an open marketplace of ideas. Every citizen can put on his toga and enter the forum, but not the functionary."[24]

In his keynote address Reich seemed to realize that the prospects for the socialist, democratic revolution he had hoped for had already been snuffed out: "The romantic phase of our revolution, the wild time of excitement and movement [*Sturm und Drangzeit*], is over. It was characterized by an excited awakening through the Leipzig demonstrations, through 'We are the people!' and 'We'll remain here!' and by the wonderful, imaginative demonstration on November 4 in Berlin. But it ended on November 9, the day when the eggshell cracked and a freedom for which we were unprepared stormed in. After this first mad carnival of unleashed freedom came everyday reality, and it rules us today."[25] But political romanticism was hardly extinguished among the activists of New Forum. The founding conference resolved to field candidates for political office and encouraged involvement in local government but clung to the position activist Reinhard Schult had articulated before the fall of the Wall: "We don't want any centralized structures. The grassroots groups should be as independent as possible. . . . There should be no group of elites; there should be no circle of specialists who instruct the rest of the population on what should be done."[26] Even as the foundering GDR tilted toward the introduction of parliamentary politics, New Forum was reluctant to give up its vision. Divided between members advocating parliamentary party structures and those wanting a grassroots movement, New Forum was so divided on "bourgeois democracy" and so feared a "capitalist sellout" that it found it difficult to adapt to political pluralism. In most of its literature, the emphasis remained on direct action and extraparliamentary mobilization. Democratic citizen assemblies would be the basis of a new form of government "formed from below and democratically legitimated."[27]

All of this reflected deeply held elements of dissident ideology. As Sigrid Meuschel has observed, the idea of a democratic, self-organizing "civil society" completely negated Western-style parliamentary government. Wolf-gang Ullmann of Democracy Now described parliaments as "outdated." Democratic Awakening's Rainer Eppelmann imagined that the "awakening" of the population through grassroots participation would last for years. Templin described the ideal political system as one based on "civil disobe-dience" (Meuschel 1992: 322). Werner Fischer of New Forum later recounted, "The West German democratic model had no attraction for us. For us, parliamentary democracy was only one possibility, perhaps an intermediate step, but certainly not a model to strive for, something that could be installed with equal validity in the GDR" (Findeis, Pollack, and Schilling 1994: 105). Above all, New Forum wanted to avoid the rise of a new political elite that would threaten true socialism. Bohley explained, "No, the civic movement could not take up power in the streets because it was something totally different than a party. Its ideas and goals could not be reached strategically. They had to develop out of the movement, through what every individual wanted. . . . A civic movement has no leadership; it has no one at the top and no chairperson" (Findeis, Pollack, and Schilling 1994: 58).

New Forum and the Movement in the Streets

As the birthplace of mass popular protest, Leipzig was an important center of the unfolding revolution in the GDR. In fact, the total estimated par-ticipation in demonstrations in Leipzig over the course of the revolution was far greater than in any other district of the GDR; it was approximately double the total protest mobilization in East Berlin. (See figure 13.) But the "cradle of the revolution" was by no means a bastion of civic movement support.

Leipzig, the second largest city in the country, did appear to back New Forum's campaign for a new democratic socialism. Church-based activists had quickly established a chapter there. Two-dozen members of various opposition groups agreed to unite under the umbrella of New Forum on September 24, and the organization soon boasted about eighty declared members.[28] But, uncertain of its role in the spontaneous mass mobiliza-tion of early October, the New Forum chapter waited until after the mass Monday demonstration of October 16 to begin to develop a wider organiza-tion and recruit support beyond activist circles. Now events were outpacing

FIGURE 13. Total Protest Participation in GDR Districts, September 1989–March 1990

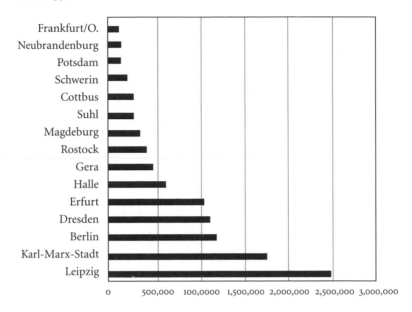

Number of Protesters reported from all events

Source: GDR Interior Ministry.

organization. At the time of the Wall's collapse on November 9, New Forum Leipzig had just 175 declared members.[29] The group was only loosely organized and was led by a steering committee of several "spokespersons," including, most prominently, longtime human rights activists such as the theology students Michael Arnold and Jochen Lässig.

From the start New Forum faced a daunting challenge in communicating its message at the Monday demonstrations, which soon became a platform for all sorts of political demands. At first, it echoed demands for a public dialogue between the regime, the Church, and citizen groups.[30] But the revolution kept widening in terms of participation and in its scope. The Monday demonstration drew more than seventy thousand people on October 9, more than one hundred thousand on October 16, two hundred thousand by the end of the month, and three hundred thousand on November 6. The New Forum chapter, with its lack of office space, printers, and telephones could not keep pace with these developments. And the content of its message did not shift with the increasingly impatient demands of the Leipzig protesters. At the end of October, with the party-state fast collapsing, Lässig said of the group at a Monday demonstration: "We don't understand ourselves as the opposition to socialism. Why not? Because we are for socialism! That is, in principle, for more socialism."[31]

The tone of the Monday demonstrations by that point suggests that the taste of many Leipzigers for socialism had become dulled, if not soured. But if New Forum was falling out of step with the radicalized political demands of an activated citizenry, it nevertheless still enjoyed popular sympathy. Police reports and journalistic coverage of the Monday demonstrations in October make clear that New Forum's influence was considerable.[32] Yet, over the next weeks, New Forum appears to have gradually surrendered its influence both because of its message and its limited organizational reach. A reporter noted of the demonstration on October 30th: "As soon as someone says, 'New Forum is speaking,' then the people break off from the march and eagerly assemble around the speaker. But no one usually speaks directly to the masses; texts drafted by New Forum are simply read off."[33] New Forum activist Frank Hocquel explained, "We are not far enough along with our organization that Leipzig should become the center of the GDR civic movement." Speaking to the crowds assembled in Karl Marx Square on Monday, October 23, Lässig declared New Forum neither willing nor prepared to play a leading role: "Please do not expect from us in the following weeks to offer ready concepts and reform programs. We don't want to form the new power elite that would try to order how everything should go forward. All of you should speak; all of you should bring your suggestions for restructuring our society and share the responsibility so that power in our country will really be shared."[34]

By the first week of November, the lack of confidence in the Krenz government had become obvious at the Monday demonstrations. On November 6 Lässig declared to crowds outside the Leipzig city hall, "If the party leaders believe that the transformation is behind them, well we think it is only about to start. A democratic transformation is only achieved . . . when complete media freedom and free elections are introduced. There must be elections with a choice of various parties, organizations, and personalities, so that the people can have a real choice."[35] But if local New Forum leaders were moving beyond the more modest demands of their counterparts in

East Berlin, they were no less dismayed by the fall of the Wall. In its newly established newsletter, New Forum Leipzig declared,

> Yes, freedom to travel, we demanded that. And this demand stands. But do we want to make ourselves the recipients of alms? To stand in long lines for 100 DM so that we can smash our noses against the shop windows of capitalism? Whoever has looked around in the West knows the shock brought on by our first impression [as GDR citizens]. But this unearthly wealth is the result of the exploitation of the Third World and is also the result of the brutal economic policies of the old GDR leadership who played into the hands of the capitalists.[36]

At the first Monday demonstration after November 9, New Forum leaders warned, "It would be easy after we allowed ourselves to be controlled by the Big Brother in the East or to just put ourselves in the hands of the West. It would be easy to sell our enterprises from the ground up at the cheapest prices to Western monopolies. But the factories and the real estate belong to us, the working people."[37]

But were the "working people" with New Forum? Police reports in October indicate that the chants and banners at Monday demonstrations were most often directed against party corruption, the regime's leaders, and the Stasi—all congruent with New Forum's program. Following the opening of the Wall, antisocialist, populist, and pro-unification themes began to appear prominently at demonstrations in Saxon cities. At the Leipzig Monday demonstration on November 13, protesters shouted not only "Never again the SED!" but also "Germany, Germany!" and joined in singing "Germany, united Fatherland" (*Deutschland einig Vaterland*), a verse from the banned stanza of the original GDR national anthem (Zwahr 1993: 139). German tricolors without the GDR's hammer and triangle icon began to appear. On December 4 protesters at Leipzig's Monday demonstrations chanted, "We are *one* people," "Reunification, yes!," and "Down with the SED!" As the Monday demonstrations grew more polarized, they remained massive but dropped from an estimated three hundred thousand participants on November 6 to about half that number or less on November 13 and November 27.

At the end of November, the West Berlin *Tageszeitung* reported that speakers from New Forum were being heckled when they spoke of unification as an "annexation." Intellectuals and students bitterly condemned the nationalism of the masses, while populists shouted at the "Reds" to get off the streets. The reporter concluded, "For some time now in Leipzig the people and the opposition have been speaking two different languages."[38] On December 4 the Monday demonstration drew an estimated one hundred and fifty thousand demonstrators. The tone was resolutely hostile to the government, with chants and slogans such as "Krenz must go!" and "The SED stinks of corruption." Demonstrators were also beginning to turn against each other. The demonstrations were crowded with placards bearing messages as diverse as "GDR + FRG = Germany," "One German state!," "Only Kohl can help us," "GDR—No part of a 4th Reich," and "Against the Right, against Reunification, and against Neo-Fascism."[39]

As the regime tottered and the survival of the GDR came into question, the civic movement was being pushed aside by the rush of developments. With the party in retreat and more and more political organizations joining the fray, the Monday demonstrations lost the "us versus them" tone that had initially been so important for their spirited atmosphere. The growing polarization of revolutionary politics was covered by the GDR's state media, which, in a belated spirit of glasnost, began to provide live coverage of demonstrations. East German television reported that Saxon crowds blamed socialism for the ruin of the country.[40] The appearance of a handful of visible young political extremists of the right and the left at the Monday demonstrations further contributed to a sense of polarization and antagonism.[41] Although they remained mass events, the Leipzig demonstrations in December and January never again exceeded one hundred and fifty thousand participants. Hoping to slow the pace of polarization in the city, Church officials in Leipzig pushed for a Christmas respite for the Monday demonstrations, and the Church superintendent Friedrich Magirius and the Gewandhaus conductor Kurt Masur appealed to the crowds to hold a silent demonstration on December 18. Asked about what Leipzigers wanted, Masur bluntly responded, "Reunification. Everyone wants the same thing, some sooner, and some later."[42]

With the situation polarizing, New Forum was slow to adapt. Its first political rally in Leipzig took place on November 18—roughly two months after the formation of the local chapter. Speakers called for democratization and dialogue and endorsed cooperation with Communist party reformists, with one speaker noting, "It doesn't help us if the SED goes under and drags us down with it." Participation was estimated at about ten thousand citizens—sizable, but tiny relative to massive Monday demonstrations. Discord within the ranks was now apparent, as vocal dissenters at the rally demanded that Communists be driven out of politics.[43]

Despite its desire to cooperate with the former ruling party, New Forum's loyalty was not readily rewarded by local officials. In a meeting with Mayor Bernd Seidel, New Forum leaders were assured of formal recognition by the city government. But in the weeks following the fall of the Wall, hostility persisted between Communist authorities still unwilling to share power and a civic movement unsure of how to exert influence. In early December the conflict escalated to the point where the movement finally took direct steps against the state's power structures. A citizens committee occupied the Stasi offices during the Monday demonstration. The Leipzig police reported to the Ministry of the Interior, "When the head of the demonstration march reached the building at about 7:00 P.M., a spokesman from New Forum announced in the name of several democratic groups from the balcony that it had been placed under their control a half an hour earlier and that the official chambers were being sealed and that the arrival of the state prosecutor was expected. . . . The announcement was greeted with applause [and] chanting slogans."[44] Staged with a fitting sense of political theater, the seizure of the Stalinist bastion temporarily restored New Forum's momentum. Press reports spoke of the enthusiasm with which demonstrators cheered the taking of the hated Stasi headquarters and the "rage against crimes committed against the people." However, the press also noted that in the initial occupation of the building reporters outnumbered civic movement activists by three to one.[45]

This was not the storming of the Bastille—New Forum seized the building to forestall the possibility of an angry crowd taking it by force. Police officials apparently had foreknowledge of the occupation and readily cooperated with the citizens committee.[46] Still, the civic movement activists had rendered a vital public service by halting the state destruction of documents and putting the dreaded Stasi out of business. Indeed, hatred of the Stasi inspired East Germans to rise to their last great peak of insurgent mobilization. In mid-January Leipzigers joined citizens around the country in protests that doomed the Modrow government's efforts to preserve party privileges and the state security service. (Concerning Krenz's ouster and Modrow's accession to leadership, see chapter 9.)

By January the transformation of the Monday demonstrations into pro-unification rallies was becoming evident. A police analysis reported of the Leipzig demonstrations: "The chief demands are directed at rapid unification of the two German states or to existing social and ecological problems. Demonstrators carry almost exclusively West German flags."[47] When confronting crowds that were vocally pro-unification, New Forum and other civic organizations found themselves being heckled.[48] As the winter continued, the demonstrations became electoral rallies for the various political parties. The broad political dialogue that New Forum had promoted had all but disappeared.[49] Civic movement activists began to feel that their revolution had been defeated. As one journalist observed in late February, "The revolution has grown tired. What began as a powerful demonstration has at last become a stage for an electoral campaign."[50]

It certainly did not help the movement's cause that in Leipzig New Forum was ill prepared for the crush of new supporters—some five thousand citizens—that signed up to support it in November and December. Only in early January did the civic movement begin to overcome its lack of resources by occupying the former district SED headquarters. Yet in the newly christened "House of Democracy," where New Forum shared office space and telephone service with fifteen new political groupings, the urgent priority soon became to prepare for March parliamentary elections.[51] In January and February 1990, demonstrations in Leipzig remained large—still in the tens of thousands—but were becoming "political flea markets" for the electoral campaigns of the various political parties and organizations.[52] The moment for grassroots politics seemed to be passing.

As democracy "from the bottom up" lost its luster, the civic movement organizations appeared ever more isolated. The *Leipziger Volkszeitung* complained in mid-February that the civic movement had "surrendered to populism."[53] Demonstrators from the right- and left-wing camps often shouted down each other's speakers and sometimes clashed on Karl Marx Square.[54] With the country's first free election now on the horizon, New Forum was largely disappearing from public view. A Leipzig activist later commented about his colleagues: "They all wandered away; they quickly freed themselves. They said now we can finally do what we want and go where we want. And one must say that the groups quickly lost momentum" (Opp 1997: 114). The most adept of the movement activists prepared for a new vocation as full-time politicians in local and regional governments, an aspiration at odds with the romantic ideals of radical democracy.[55]

Missing Marx? The Civic Movement and the Working Class

One of the most puzzling aspects of the East German civic movement was its political distance from the working class, given that it professed to be wedded to socialism. In fact, the limits imposed on the civic movement by its loyalty to socialism are especially evident in its relationship with labor. In recent decades alliances between opposition forces and labor movements have played an important role in the course of democratization in regions as diverse as Southern Europe, Latin America, Asia, and Eastern Europe (Linz and Stepan 1996). But in East Germany, according to Linda Fuller (1999), workers were no more than "passive participants" in an intraclass conflict between dissident and orthodox factions of the socialist elite. Thus the "revolution" was merely an aborted reform movement that left the workers behind.

Yet, as we have seen from the composition of the Monday demonstrations in Leipzig, workers were more than passive spectators in the peaceful revolution. Studies of the Leipzig protests have consistently revealed how the political breakthrough in October was only possible because thousands of predominantly working-class citizens joined the dissidents in the streets. The unreliability of workers' militias was a factor in the failure of state repression. Günter Roski and Peter Förster (1990) found in their surveys of Leipzig's Monday protesters that blue-collar workers were in attendance in roughly the same proportion as this category's share of the total population. In an evaluation of surveys taken at four Monday demonstrations stretching from November 1989 to January 1990, Kurt Mühler and Steffen Wilsdorf (1991) found similar proportions. And it was not just in the streets that workers mobilized. As Fuller documents, workers in some factories began to organize workers' councils (*Betriebsräte*) for collective representation independent of the party-controlled unions, and insurgent labor organizers led a revolt against the East German state union federation.

The key point is that when workers demonstrated in Leipzig and other cities, they did so principally as citizens, not as class-conscious members of a labor movement. Strikes, the emblematic form of workers' collective action, played only a minor role in the East German revolution. Of all protest events reported by police authorities between August 1989 and April 1990, only about 7 percent involved strikes (see also Schwabe 1997 and Kubik 1998). Reports from the Ministry of the Interior reveal that although strikes and other forms of workplace protest did grow far more common in the winter of 1990, most were relatively small, local in scope, and poorly coordinated. In fact, the leaders of the civic movement were not eager to mobilize labor or to bring workers' struggles into politics. Although they urged workers to build democratic councils, they warned them not to engage in job actions or stage wildcat strikes.[56]

Labor's minor role could be attributed to the fact that the unions were state controlled. But the evidence suggests that there was genuine militancy among East German workers that the civic movement could have exploited. In early December, Saxon New Forum representatives and labor activists met in Karl-Marx-Stadt (Chemnitz) to propose a general strike for December 6. Workers wanted a general strike to demand the dissolution of the party organization and its removal from all public authority. Inspired by labor's militant position, at the Monday demonstration on December 4, Saxon New Forum activists called for dissolving the SED, public disclosure of all party finances, the separation of party and state organizations, and the abolishment of all party privileges. They supported the call for a general strike, which they hoped would land a fatal blow against Leninist structures and avert a Communist countermobilization.

Nevertheless, the radical implications of a general strike could not be squared with the leadership's critical loyalism. New Forum's general steering committee in Berlin, while acknowledging that a job action was a "legitimate means to pursue nonviolent demands," refused to endorse a general strike.[57] It urged Saxon activists to rescind the strike call, fearing that work stoppages would undermine negotiations with the government and plunge the country into an economic disaster that would hasten unification. On December 12 a New Forum spokesman and union activist, Jürgen Tallig, retracted the strike call before the crowds assembled in Leipzig.[58] In the following weeks, the new workers' organizations gradually abandoned the civic movement and began organizing unions on the Western model. They found a more ready ally in the West German Social Democrats, who provided funds and expertise for reorganizing unions (Fuller 1999; Weissgerber 1995).

This turn to Social Democratic unionism was not the grassroots union-ism that activists had dreamed of in November. One of the Leipzig New Forum leaders, Jochen Lässig, bitterly recalled, "The readiness to strike was at that time greater among the workers than in the divided opposition movement in which intellectuals and pastors set the tone. . . . The call for a general strike at this time, which came from places like Plauen and Mag-deburg, was ridiculed within our own ranks. When the time was ripe we did not act, but instead watched and waited to see how the situation would develop."[59] With benefit of hindsight, Jens Reich also regretted New Forum's dealings with working-class supporters in Saxony: "Several delegations of workers approached us to support their strike call. But we tried to calm them down. Our goal was not to usurp power, but to push for elections. 'Demo-cratic legitimation' was our key concern, not power. . . . We missed the opportunity; we ducked in the decisive moment" (Joppke 1995: 163).

That Reich saw taking power from the SED as "usurpation" indicates the fundamental system loyalty behind the strategies of the civic movement's leadership. And the fact that the civic movement never attempted to use the general strike as a weapon in its struggle with the SED suggests broader weaknesses than misdirected loyalty or strategic miscalculation. It speaks to the fact that civic movement intellectuals, unlike their counterparts in Po-land, had few ties to labor before the revolution was under way and concen-trated on mobilizing the population as citizens united by universal demands rather than as workers with specific material grievances. This was true even for those elements within the civic movement, such as the United Left or the Party of Social Democrats, that most identified with working-class politics. Civic movement values had more in common with the postmaterialism of the Western New Left than it did with traditional German socialism or the independent trade unionism of neighboring Poland (Knabe 1988). With traditional working-class culture and labor's institutional milieu having long since disappeared into the niche society, workers responded to populist "us versus them" appeals, first as the *Volk* against the autocratic party elite, and later as German patriots against the "Reds" and the "unrealistic dreamers" of the civic movement.[60]

East German workers were hardly passive onlookers while the revolution unfolded. They took to the streets in small groups of friends, family, and co-workers, even if not as part of a labor movement. They came out of their niches to oppose Honecker and Krenz at crucial moments, making October

9 and November 9 possible. But for East German workers, it was not voice alone that carried the weight of redressing their grievances. Emigration, often the least costly and probably the most effective form of economic redress available, was an attractive option for blue-collar East Germans. The civic movement never managed to counter this appeal, and, as will be explored in greater detail in the next chapter, reunification as de facto "exit" from socialism enjoyed strong support among workers by February 1990.

Was the political rift between labor and the civic movement inevitable, given the different social and cultural profiles of dissidents and workers? Perhaps it was not, at least in the short run. The case of Civic Forum in Czechoslovakia in 1989 suggests that the East German opposition, even with its limitations, might have had far more success in directing the course of events had it cooperated with workers.[61] The Czechoslovak civic movement arose under repressive conditions not unlike those in the GDR and was triggered by East Germany's rebellion. On October 28, after sporadic dissident protest and the occupation of the West German embassy in Prague by East German exiters, an estimated ten thousand people gathered in Vaclav Square to protest the loss of the Czechoslovak republic's independence. The police responded with overwhelming force, but the movement continued to expand. On November 17 a government-sponsored commemoration of antifascist martyrs was overtaken by student activists. Some fifty thousand citizens joined them. This time the police response was especially brutal, resulting in scores of injuries and arrests. In response to this outrage, a loosely organized protest movement took shape and demanded real political reform. In solidarity with the students, theater workers went on strike to protest regime brutality.

On November 19 an estimated two hundred thousand people filled Vaclav Square, and on November 23 up to a third of a million occupied Prague's center. In the midst of the events, Czechoslovakia's small but well-known dissident movement cast its divisions aside to form a united front in Civic Forum in Prague and Public versus Violence in Bratislava. These were not long-standing organizations; Civic Forum was founded on November 18 in the Czech lands and Public versus Violence in Slovakia on November 23. But they were prepared to direct mass demonstrations against the government.

Up to this point, ordinary workers had played a small role in the unfolding rebellion. But the population of the capital was now turning against the government despite its vow to hold on. The regime gave way only when a general strike made a show of force on November 27. Even though the factory committees had only been hastily organized, the appeal to the workers drew millions of employees in hundreds of state enterprises into the strike.[62] Within a week of the general strike, the Communist Party of Czechoslovakia gave up its constitutionally guaranteed "leading role" in the state. And the opposition pressed its advantage, demanding a new government and the immediate replacement of both the prime minister and the president. By the end of December, a dissident playwright was the nation's president; the hero of 1968, Alexander Dubček, was the chair of the National Assembly; and the Communists were out.

Like their East German counterparts, the Czechoslovak dissidents had few resources, no grand political strategy, and no ideological program. Civic Forum was also a movement largely of intellectuals and students with few ties to workers. Yet it had the confidence to ride the crest of a growing insurgency that cut across the traditional lines of social class to appeal to workers. Rather than trying to slow down the process of transition, dissidents recognized that maximum concessions had to be won while the party was weakest, most disoriented, and most uncertain. In this, the contrast with the gradualism of the East German dissidents is particularly striking. At first both had few links to workers or labor organizations.[63] But the Czechoslovak opposition was not burdened by socialist commitments and not afraid to identify with national issues. It staved off sectarianism long enough to compose an interim government during the winter of 1989–90 and prevail in the first post-Communist elections in 1990 (Glenn 2003). Ultimately, the Czechoslovak dissidents, battered by electoral defeats and the dissolution of Czechoslovakia, declined into political insignificance.[64] But Civic Forum did not surrender to factionalism, sectarianism, or anachronistic socialist ideals in the heat of the revolution. It cemented its advantage over the party-state by forging links to workers and pressuring the regime to resign with a resounding general strike. New Forum never achieved anything close to that.

Explaining the Sources of New Forum Mobilization

Previous studies suggest that GDR citizens with higher levels of education, and thus greater exposure to Marxist ideas and values, were more committed to socialist ideology than others (Friedrich, Förster, and Starke 1999). We would expect that those citizens who had been favorably treated economically should have been more loyal to the socialist GDR than others. Put simply, economically privileged citizens should be more loyal than less-privileged citizens. Ideological convictions and economic privileges are closely related. For example, higher education had become the chief pathway for entry into the socialist middle classes in the GDR (Geissler 1983; Solga 1994; Huinink and Solga 1994; Jessen 1999). In order to succeed, students had to display not only academic merit but also ideological commitment (Solga 1994). Young people who proceeded to higher education had spent their entire lives in socialist organizations, from the Young Pioneers, to the Free German Youth, to the Circle of Young Socialists, to student leagues, and often joined the party itself.

Because all investment and development in the GDR was directed by central state planning, there are also regional implications of the loyalty hypothesis. Economic historians of the GDR find that employment in the tertiary sector of the economy is a good indicator for the level of investment by the central government in technology and advanced industries (Kuhrt, Buck, and Holzweissig 1999). Economic privileges in a region should have helped increase and sustain loyalty to socialism both by generating invest-ment in the system and by concentrating selected cadres. Loyalty should be strongest in two overlapping categories: those with higher education and those employed in the tertiary sector of the economy. The implications of this hypothesis would reverse the expected social support for socialism ac-cording to classical Marxism. It is not from the industrial provinces of the GDR—which, as we have seen in chapter 2, had become a socialist rust belt—but from the regions where blue-collar workers composed a smaller share of the workforce that we should expect the strongest support for socialism. Once the regime faced a grave political crisis, people living in economically privileged localities may have been more likely to mobilize to save the GDR through reform. For them exit would have been a less attractive option than trying to improve socialism at home. They would have had substantial ideo-logical, material, and relational investments in the system. Therefore, we would expect an occupational distribution among New Forum supporters titled toward the socialist middle class and more New Forum support origi-nating outside industrial districts.

Does the social structure of New Forum support correspond to the loy-alty interpretation of reformist voice? Answering this question relies on exploiting a previously untapped data source. Movement leaders in East

Berlin collected all of the petitions seeking to establish local New Forum chapters throughout the GDR from the middle of September through November 9—at which point the movement achieved legal recognition. New Forum's archive also contains the lists of people who signed statements of public support for New Forum during the autumn of 1989.[65] Coding the petitions and lists permits an analysis of more than twenty-five thousand citizens who declared themselves partisans of reformist voice during the breakthrough phase of the revolution.[66]

Movement leaders hoped to use the petition drive, with its lists of the names, addresses, and occupations of declared supporters as the nucleus for a GDR-wide network of local New Forum chapters. Sign-up lists were distributed in churches, at workplaces, and among the crowds at some large demonstrations. Although the New Forum's appeals were becoming widely known in the autumn of 1989 thanks to Western news broadcasts, the membership list of the first twenty-five thousand members suggests that the civic movement expanded not through isolated recruitment but largely through networks of church congregants, members of factory collectives, artistic communities, and neighborhood residents. Strong social ties were plainly evident in motivating involvement: at least 20 percent of New Forum supporters signed up with a relative or with someone sharing the same home address.[67] In other words, the structure of early New Forum mobilization seems to have reflected the organization of the "niche society" so important in bringing people into the streets in October 1989.

The descriptive statistics drawn from these lists provide a unique portrait of New Forum's core support. As one might expect given the risks involved and the disproportionate burden placed on women in the care of children, men outnumbered women (60:40) in the early rolls of New Forum supporters. New Forum supporters were relatively young, averaging about thirty-two years of age. They were drawn heavily from the educated strata of society, particularly from the category of technically trained professionals. Blue-collar workers were underrepresented among New Forum activists, as were citizens with agricultural occupations. In fact, citizens with working-class occupations (*Arbeiter* and *Facharbeiter*) were about 40 percent of the membership, even though such workers accounted for more than 50 percent of total employment in the GDR.

White-collar, professional, and service sector employees were overrepresented in New Forum. More than a quarter of its early supporters were

FIGURE 14. Comparison of the Early New Forum Organization with the
Occupational Structure of the GDR, September 15–November 8, 1989

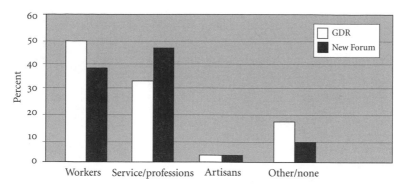

Source: Mathias-Domaschk-Archiv, NFO; and *SJDDR* 1990.
Note: Workers include apprentices; service/professional includes students; other/none includes farmers, housewives, and the unemployed.

technically trained employees in information services, health care, and clerical and administrative occupations (*Angestellten, Techniker, Krankenpfleger,*
and the like). Professionals and intellectuals—such as physicians, engineers,
academics, and clergymen—made up an additional 15 percent of signatories,
while students in universities and colleges constituted a further 7 percent. If
we combine these categories to reflect the service and professional class in
the occupational structure of the GDR, we see that New Forum drew nearly
half of its supporters from the socialist middle classes, although these categories accounted for only a third of the employed in the GDR. Craftspeople
and artisans independent of state employment composed 4 percent of the
New Forum support, with the remainder composed of farmers, the unemployed, and those failing to report an occupation. (See figure 14.)

The New Forum data further demonstrate that it was largely an urban
movement, with the metropolis of East Berlin at its center. More than half
of its early supporters resided in East Berlin and the capital's surrounding
nine counties. However, outside of Berlin and its suburbs early support for
New Forum does not suggest a simple pattern of core-periphery diffusion
when we evaluate the regional distribution of support in terms of a mobilization rate generated by calculating the number of supporters per 10,000
population in a district. After Berlin, the high-tech belt in the far southwest
centered in the Erfurt district and the northern district of Rostock on the
Baltic coast had the highest concentrations of New Forum support. The

FIGURE 15. Density of Early Support for New Forum by Regional District,
September 15–November 8, 1989

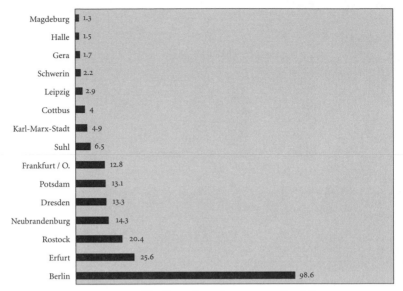

New Forum Supporters per 10,000 Population

Sources: Mathias-Domaschk-Archiv, NFO; and *SJDDR* 1990.

Neubrandenburg, Dresden, and Frankfurt an der Oder districts also had
strong concentrations of early civic movement support. The weakest support was registered in the heavily industrialized Magdeburg, Halle, Gera,
and Schwerin districts and, despite its role as a cradle of anti-regime protest,
in the city of Leipzig (also heavily industrialized) and its surrounding counties. The density of involvement in the nascent civic movement in Berlin and
its environs should not surprise us, given that the capital was the educational, administrative, and economic center of the country. The greater
Berlin area and Rostock in the north were centers of modern industry, and
Erfurt and Dresden specialized in microelectronics.[68] (See figure 15.)

A Statistical Evaluation of New Forum Mobilization

The description of the social basis of New Forum supports a loyalty interpretation of civic movement mobilization. However, the descriptive data
alone do not provide a means of evaluating whether exit was responsible for

activating reformist voice, as the theory of exit-voice dynamics claims. Unlike insurgent voice, loyalist voice should have been less sensitive to mass exit's threat to the social basis of collective action. New Forum supporters would be expected to have high exit thresholds and low voice thresholds, making them ideal candidates for reformist mobilization in 1989. The testable hypothesis that can be drawn from these propositions can be stated as follows: *The level of support for New Forum in a county/municipality should be determined by indicators of economic investment and will be insensitive to the network-erosion effects identified in chapter 6.*

In order to evaluate the role of exit in triggering reformist voice, I take a statistical approach similar to that which appears in chapter 6 in the analysis of insurgent voice. In analyzing the factors propelling loyalist voice, I make the dependent variable the level of New Forum mobilization in a GDR county (*Kreis*) or municipality (*Stadtkreis*) during the period between September 1, 1989, and November 9, 1989, that is, between the point at which the civic movement was in formation and the point when it was legalized in the midst of the collapse of the Krenz government. New Forum mobilization rate measures the concept of loyalist voice by the total number of people that signed a New Forum supporter list in a county or municipality per 10,000 residents. To control for the highly skewed distribution of the variable, which ranges from 0 (34 cases) to 110 (East Berlin), it is log-transformed. Because New Forum mobilization rate is a continuous variable and because there is no possibility of censoring in a complete membership list, OLS regression was employed instead of the Tobit model used in chapter 6. See table A4 for the univariate statistics of the variables and their correlation coefficients matrix.

As in the analysis of protest event rate and average participation rate, New Forum mobilization rate as a measure of loyalist voice during the revolution is regressed against the *Exit Rate* experienced in a locality before the onset of the revolution, the variables SED *Density*, *% Employed in Tertiary Sector*, and *Institutions of Research and Higher Education* employed in chapter 6, and other control variables. Hirschman (1970) suggested that loyalty deters exit and can motivate voice behind reform. In the absence of individual measures of subjective loyalty, the question one faces is which counties/municipalities would have had residents most invested in the survival and reform of the GDR? It is fair to presume that localities best integrated into the socialist system and that had benefited most from Communist rule were probably more likely to remain loyal. Hence I focus on three possible repositories of loyalty: SED Density, % Employed in Tertiary Sector, and *Institutions of Research and Higher Education* present in a locality. Recall that in 1989 the SED had more than two million members, many of whom were employed in administration, services, and the professions. An intransigent regime threatened the possibility of socialist reforms that were apparently favored by many in the party rank and file (see chapter 2). Although in East Germany protest against the regime was not instigated by reformist factions or by party dissidents, it is worth noting that "loyalty does not normally mean a mere reluctance to leave a collectivity but rather a positive commitment to further its welfare" by various means, including protest (Dowding et al. 2000: 477). For analytical purposes, the density of party organization could have several implications. It could be a source of defensive countermobilization by loyalists in the face of the threat to their privileges, or it could possibly be a source of vigorous reformist sentiment. Prudential loyalty that saw the need for reform over reaction may have found repositories in strong regional party organizations.

Another possibility is that people were loyal simply because they were economic beneficiaries of the system. The GDR clearly exhibited what Andrew Walder (1994) calls the "organized dependence" of citizens on the party-state for the allocation of goods and opportunities. It is reasonable to assume that citizens who enjoyed a relatively privileged position in society may have been more attached to the socialist system than those that might have regarded themselves as its "losers." Although income differences in the GDR were relatively small (Atkinson and Micklewright 1992), this does not mean there was an equal distribution of life chances. In chapter 2 we saw that working in the tertiary sector in the GDR economy generally meant being a part of the most modern and differentiated part of the economy. Employment in this sector was often linked to technical and professional training, so it is a good indication of opportunities for social mobility. In the 1980s the regime expended large sums in modernizing the economy, chiefly through investment in microtechnologies (Gutmann, 1999; Maier, 1997; Dennis, 1993). For East Germans lucky enough to benefit from the shift in development priorities to the tertiary sector, there were far better opportunities for career advancement and development of human capital than in other sectors. Hence I expect that on average economically privileged counties/municipalities should be more loyal than less privileged ones. Of course, this variable might also reflect the varying degree of local grievances residents of a county had on account of failing economic conditions.

In addition to the distribution of cultural and educational privileges (captured by the tertiary sector variable), the presence of college campuses and research institutes in a county or municipality might have provided a different reservoir of loyalist support or the site for the formation and mobilization of loyalist networks. Based on the limited public opinion data available on citizens of the GDR, it is evident that students in higher education consistently reported a greater commitment to socialism and the state than other young people (Friedrich, Förster, and Starke 1999). And numerous scholars have documented that, in contrast with other intellectuals in Eastern Europe, the East German intelligentsia was generally loyal to socialism (Torpey 1995; Joppke 1995; Jarausch, 1991).

In order to control for alternative explanations of New Forum mobilization rate, the logged *Number of Arrests* is included to control for possible opportunity/threat effects as in chapter 6. New Forum was founded by activist networks based in the East Berlin area and spread rapidly through its widely publicized appeals, attracting supporters in every district of the GDR. Yet we have seen that about half of New Forum's declared supporters resided in the district of East Berlin and nine surrounding counties. Hence it is possible that variations in New Forum mobilization are related to proximity to East Berlin. People in counties or municipalities closer to the capital might have simply had a greater opportunity to encounter New Forum activists. To control for possible proximity effects, the variable is coded 1 if a county's boundaries were within 40 kilometers of the city of East Berlin; otherwise, it is 0. The data are drawn from the official GDR atlas (Lehmann 1976).

Social movement theory would probably account for variations in New Forum mobilization in terms of varying resources of collective action across localities. Narrative evidence suggests that New Forum mobilization might have grown out of the activities of the dissident intelligentsia and Church-based activists. In order to control for the possible effects of local dissident Church organizing on New Forum mobilization, two indicator variables are included in the analysis: whether or not a chapter of the lay activist organization "Solidarity Church" was present in a locality and whether or not it had had a "samizdat press," that is, regularly appearing alternative newsletters and information bulletins printed by Church-based dissidents (Neubert 1998).

The Solidarity Church (Solidarische Kirche) in the GDR was a network of pastors, seminarians, and lay members in the Lutheran Church (BEK) committed to the democratization and reform of the Church, serving as a "left opposition" against the state-accommodating religious hierarchy. Church organizations in the GDR were one of the few resources available to dissidents. In order to control for whether dissidents had a foothold in local religious organizations in a county or a municipality that could have served as a vehicle for New Forum mobilization, a county or municipality is coded 1 if the Solidarity Church organization was active, as measured by published Church documents (Goertz 1999: 334–35).

As we have seen in Chapter 4, the most important source of dissident communication in the GDR was the samizdat press. Illegal newsletters, journals, and information bulletins were printed in alternative media centers, usually established under the roof of sympathetic religious congregations. From the mid-1980s onward, alternative political cultures tied to these media centers thrived in East Berlin, Leipzig, and other cities. According to social movement theory, alternative media centers could have served as assembly points for dissidents and allowed communication vital to dissident mobilization in 1989. In order to control for the effect of alternative media on New Forum mobilization, a county or municipality is coded 1 if the Stasi reported the operation of a samizdat press in a county in 1989 (Neubert 1998: 756–66).

The results of the analysis point to the effects of exit-voice dynamics on reformist mobilization (see the appendix, table A5). In OLS regression the effect of Exit Rate on the dependent variable NF *Mobilization Rate* in Model 1 is positive, as expected, and highly significant, rendering support to the signaling interpretation of exit for collective action described in chapter 6. In Model 2, in which Exit Rate and its squared term are regressed against mobilization rate, *Exit Rate* achieves significance but not its squared term. This finding, which does not support an interpretation of Exit Rate having nonlinear effects on Mobilization Rate, suggests that the network-erosion mechanism hypothesized to undercut insurgent voice at the highest volumes of exit did not influence this different expression of political voice. In Model 3, in which the *Tertiary Sector Employment* variable is added to the model alongside control variables capturing political, cultural, and organizational characteristics of localities, exit rate remains significant while only the tertiary employment variable achieves significance. In Model 4, the full model is again estimated without East Berlin, a potentially influential outlier in terms of *Mobilization Rate*. Again, only exit rate and tertiary employment achieve significance with the East Berlin case removed. Although it is surprising that neither the presence of grassroots Church organizations nor a samizdat press in a locality significantly increased mobilization rate despite the fact that pastors and religious congregations seem to have played a role in launching New Forum, the reason for this result may be that these variables fail to capture the underlying social network structure of the oppositional milieu on the eve of the East German revolution. The R-squared value achieved by Model 3 is .170, indicating that about 17 percent of the variation in the Mobilization Rate is explained by the model, a proportion similar to that achieved in the Tobit models reported in chapter 6.

The analysis suggests crucial differences in insurgent and loyalist voice. Insurgent voice was largely spontaneous, popular street protest in which the satisfaction of economic and social grievances was the predominant object. Reformist voice was organized collective action with a declared object, the reform and democratic revitalization of the socialist state. Both of these forms of voice responded to the exiting crisis. For both insurgent protesters and civic movement supporters, the crisis signaled the extent of the GDR's deterioration and vulnerability. Without exit, neither insurgents nor loyalists could coordinate their actions in the repressive and resource-poor context of the GDR. But while network erosion seems to have prominently undermined protest in localities at higher levels of exit, loyalist voice does not appear to have been undercut by exit through the erosion of social capital through flight.

The reason for the differing effects of exit on these two forms of voice can probably be explained by the different motives that seem to have informed protest mobilization as against civic movement mobilization. While I theorized that protesters and early exiters probably had positively correlated exit and voice thresholds to some extent, this would not be true for loyalists. Civic movement activists wanted to reform the GDR rather than simply improve their life chances. As a result the exit and voice thresholds of critical loyalists at the individual level were probably negatively correlated. This negative correlation has its probable roots in greater material and ideological investment in GDR society and greater integration into its occupations and institutions. This is clear when we bring the social origins of the civic movement's critical loyalty into focus. The descriptive statistics of New Forum supporters as compared with those who exited the GDR in 1989 are illustrative. Recall from chapter 6 that studies of GDR emigrants from the 1989–90 exit wave suggested they were not much different in sociodemographic terms than protesters. In some regards civic movement supporters were also not so different from exiters: about 60 percent of exiters were men and about 80 percent were less than forty years old (Grundmann, Müller-Hartmann, and Schmidt 1992: 1593; SJDDDR 1990; Bundestag 1995). More than half of the migrants in 1989 were semiskilled or technically skilled workers (Mitter and Wolle 1990: 82–92; Bundestag 1995). By contrast, New Forum supporters were heavily drawn from the educated, white-collar, and professional strata. It seems that in the crisis of 1989–90, many younger, ambitious East German workers apparently saw their best hope in emigrating westward, not in joining a civic movement aimed at reforming the socialist state. Compared with skilled workers, however, citizens with higher education in the GDR system confronted an obstacle to exit in the lower relative portability of socialist educational credentials and the fact that equivalent professional and administrative positions were not always available in the West.

Thus it appears that the differential appeal of exit for workers because of more favorable labor market conditions in the West had important implications for civic movement mobilization.[69] As Hirschman's model would predict, loyalty to socialism, either as a result of ideological commitment or as an economically motivated "loyalty to the paychecks," or, perhaps, driven by both at once, seems to have activated voice among alert citizens occupying middle-class social roles and residing in economically advantaged localities. As a result, the political aspirations of many of the most resourceful and politically aware members of the GDR's socialist middle class might have been different from those that typified their working-class compatriots. This cleavage appears to be as evident in New Forum's ideology and political goals as it is in the structure and dynamics of its support.

No Way for the Third Way?

The founding and rapid diffusion of New Forum would suggest that these activists of the first hour may have played the role of the highly interested and resourceful actors theorized to be essential in early phases of collective action (Oliver and Marwell 2001, Marwell and Oliver 1993). That is certainly the impression one gets from the evolution of opposition demonstrations in cities such as Leipzig, Dresden, and Berlin, where protest often crystallized around Church-based groups and civic movement activists. However, the resonance of New Forum early in the protest wave provided many observers inside and outside the country with two mistaken impressions: first, that the civic movement was responsible for the mass mobilization of September and October, and, second, that the civic movement would be motivated to steer mass protests against the regime in order to achieve its political goals.

Historical evidence shows that the pace of mobilization in East Germany was not continuous with increasing organization. Instead, the movement was characterized by abrupt and unforeseen jumps in protest activity followed by the attempts of civic movement activists to keep up and try to give form and purpose to the protest wave. In fact, New Forum organized itself as a protest movement only after the first large protests in many cities. Its primary importance at the local level was usually symbolic during the breakthroughs of late September and early October 1989. The narrative evidence of New Forum in Leipzig shows that for a time the civic movement rode the crest of popular mobilization, but it never really propelled it or exploited its advantages to make a revolution. The famous Leipzig Monday demonstrations became indicative of a revolution without revolutionaries. In the middle of December 1989, West Berlin's *Tageszeitung* observed of Monday demonstrations in the "capital city" of the revolution: "They [the Leipzigers] have made it in a true German style, virtuous and restrained. . . . The revolution is made only in the evenings, after work, and only so long as they can make it in to work the next morning."[70] Somehow, the democratic socialists of the civic movement had missed Marx entirely.

The statistical analysis of insurgent and loyalist forms of political voice also casts doubt on the centrality of the civic movement in mobilizing the popular revolution. The social structure of New Forum mobilization reflected not only the informal organization of society characteristic of the niche society but also the differential appeal of its loyalist message. Its supporters were drawn disproportionately from the educated middle classes and from parts of the country where the benefits of the socialist system were the most apparent. New Forum failed to exploit working-class support and offered working-class citizens little reason to join its movement. The movement never offered an expeditious route to achieving the public goods—economic welfare, social stability, and political liberties—that most ordinary citizens desired. As the dissident pastor Rainer Eppelmann explained, "We wanted a democratic, an open and pluralistic GDR. Until November 9 there was no publicly stated wish among us—and not only in Democratic Awakening but among any group—no publicly stated desire for German unification."[71]

As their early manifestos and programs make clear, the dissidents first looked for allies within the ruling party, not among ordinary East Germans, whose loyalty, in the sense of a positive commitment to GDR socialism, could not be relied on. For their part, workers seem to have often regarded civic movement leaders as "unrealistic dreamers" who were too impractical and ideological to help them. Some disappointed intellectuals such as André Brie mourned in proper Leninist fashion that the masses had been mobilized at all, claiming that the revolution took its "wrong turn" because there was too much popular participation and that "change did not emanate from the top" (Philipsen 1993: 173).

Of course, the East German civic movement had not chosen the historical circumstances that put it at such a profound disadvantage. The presence of a prosperous West German alternative next door did its part to shape an opposition movement that had to reject popular aspirations that might lead to reunification. In the summer of 1989, Otto Reinhold of the GDR Academy of Sciences had warned dissidents that the liberalization they were clamoring for would destroy socialism: "What right to exist would a capitalist GDR have alongside a capitalist Federal Republic? In other words, what justification would there be for two German states once ideology no longer separated them?" The prominent dissident author Stefan Heym shared that opinion: "The fact is that two capitalist German states are unnecessary. The raison d'être of the GDR is to offer socialism, whatever form it takes, as an alternative to the free-booter state with the harmless name of the Federal Republic. There's no other reason for the existence of a separate East German state."[72] No matter how much the authoritarianism of the Marxist-Leninist system may have been despised, without it the GDR itself was in jeopardy so long as the gap widened between economic conditions in the East and those in the West.

Loyalty led New Forum to avoid the central issue every movement faces in a collapsing state, namely, the transfer of power to a new authority. Despite its public prominence, New Forum, as well as other opposition groups, never exploited popular protest to establish a political force parallel to the government or prepare for a transfer of power. As Jochen Lässig, one of the principal figures in the Leipzig chapter of New Forum, conceded in a speech at the University of Leipzig on October 9, 1990: "The month of October [1989] was the most hopeful of our revolution. . . . Hundreds of thousands came together and cried, 'We are the people!' . . . Sadly what never happened was what must happen in a revolution: the transfer of power. It should have been the task of the opposition movement to form a provisional government. . . . When the time was ripe, we didn't act but simply stood by and waited to see how things would develop. And they developed too quickly."[73] It is only in viewing the civic movement as an expression of loyalist voice that much of what it did—and did not do—becomes explicable.

CHAPTER 9

Reunification as the Collective Exit from Socialism

> *In the concept of the nation, historical reality and political will are united. Nation embraces more and means more than common language and culture, than state and society. The nation is based upon the enduring feeling of togetherness shared by the members of a people. No one can deny that, in this sense, there is still a single German nation and that there will be one for the foreseeable future.*
>
> —WILLY BRANDT, SPEECH TO THE PARLIAMENT
> ON THE STATE OF GERMANY, 1970

In January 1989 Erich Honecker had mused that the Wall might last another fifty or one hundred years—as long as it was necessary to protect socialism (Hertle and Stephan 1997: 42). History moved its great hand, and by January 1990 his defiant party dictatorship had been expelled from power; the borders to the West had been flung open; and a transitional government began preparing for the country's first free elections, leading to German reunification in October 1990.

These swift and decisive events seem to contradict much of what we have learned about democratic transitions during the last two decades. Studies of political transition generally identify two-party negotiations and "brokering" as the crucial mechanisms of democratic transition and consolidation.[1] These brokered, or "pacted," transitions are marked by oppositionists capable of pressing for change but moderate enough to compromise and by reformist elements within a regime that have the autonomy and desire to negotiate a transition with the moderate opposition. In the case of the GDR, we have a regime collapse in which popular mobilization pushed hard-liners out of power but did not propel the transfer of power to a new regime. What explains the rapid collapse of the GDR, instead of some negotiated, gradual transfer of power or the formation of a stable, reformist regime? And why were democratic challengers unable to counter popular protest demanding German reunification?

The Wende and the Failure of Communist Countermobilization

After the "miracle of Leipzig," the question of reform became inescapable. Although desperate for a change of course that might blunt the protest movement, the party elite could only rid itself of Honecker through a palace coup. After more than a week of maneuvering, the revolt was led by his former protégé, Egon Krenz. With the blessing of the Soviets, Krenz and his co-conspirators confronted Honecker on October 17, declaring that his policies had failed and demanding his resignation. Disoriented, betrayed, and obviously detested by the masses at the demonstrations in Leipzig on October 9 and again on October 16, the ailing dictator relented, making a face-saving resignation before the Central Committee on the following day (Hertle and Stephan 1997; Maier 1997; Jarausch 1994; Przybylski 1992). Declaring that the GDR had reached a *Wende*—a "turning point"—Krenz announced in a televised speech that he was embarking on a program of regeneration that would include "serious internal political dialogue."

From the outset it appeared that Krenz was ill suited to play the reformer. Popular neither with the party rank and file nor with the citizenry in general, Krenz enjoyed even less credibility in dissident circles. Long regarded as the regime's "crown prince," Krenz served as the security chief in the Politburo and had overseen the fraudulent communal elections of May 1989. After the Tiananmen crackdown, he had made highly publicized visits to Beijing, where he praised his comrades' handling of "counterrevolution."

A much more popular figure, and the more credible reformer, was Dresden's Hans Modrow, declared by West Germany's influential newsweekly *Der Spiegel* to be the "German Gorbachev" and the "bearer of the GDR's hopes."[2] Having previously favored reform, Modrow won public attention when he courageously broke with the party leadership and called for dialogue on October 8. He commanded genuine sympathy among the party rank and file and among civic movement leaders, making him an ideal candidate to lead a top-down reform program. However, his ascent was blocked by Honecker's prior manipulations, which had prevented Modrow's candidacy for the Politburo. He therefore did not have the formal qualifications to be party chair, and Krenz and his associates had no intention of giving power to an unreliable upstart.

The party elite Krenz inherited was of little help in setting new policies in motion or selling them to a skeptical public. The party's top functionaries were an aging and conservative lot: the 213 members of the Central Committee averaged sixty years of age. The average age of Politburo members and candidates was somewhat older at sixty-six years (Hertle and Stephan 1997: 25). The effective transfer of power was also hampered by the secretiveness and cronyism of Honecker's inner circle (Hertle and Stephan 1997; Maier 1997; Przyblski 1992). Critical economic data and information on fiscal affairs had long been kept hidden by Honecker, economics chief Günter Mittag, and Erich Mielke. Senior party and state functionaries were largely ignorant of the desperate plight of the country and thus unprepared for the daunting challenges the government faced.[3]

The new regime immediately sought Western loans and increased Soviet subsidies. Politically, it hoped that by leading the "change of course" toward top-down economic reforms the constitutionally mandated "leading role" of the party could be preserved. But in order for his agenda to succeed, Krenz needed to buy time and win foreign support. He hoped to gain time by stalling the wave of protests that was battering the party's confidence and by stifling the prospects of a renewed surge in emigration. Although he promised a series of public dialogues to involve citizens in the reform question, Krenz continued to forbid visa-free travel and refused to recognize New Forum and other civic movement groups.

Mimicking the spirit of glasnost, party officials and prominent intellectuals organized a "dialogue offensive" on such themes as "Socialist Democracy," "Economy and Ecology," and "The GDR in the 1990s."[4] In the resulting forums the government showed no interest in meaningful political pluralism. The dialogues did not feature structured talks between the government and the opposition groups that had become a standard part of democratic reform in Hungary and Poland. Meanwhile, the state-controlled media continued to denounce demonstrations as "provocations" and to insist that the street was no place to pursue reform.

Given its tepid agenda, the dialogue offensive did little to silence dissidents or demobilize the masses. And division was spreading within the SED as a widening fraction of party members began to favor cooperation with the civic movement. In an effort to convince reform-minded party members that the civic movement must be suppressed, the Krenz government denounced New Forum as a hostile and anticonstitutional force that had exploited the exiting crisis for its own benefit: "Did it [the founding declaration of New Forum] occur merely coincidentally at the same time that considerable imperialist forces led a hate-filled campaign against the GDR in order to defame socialism and to cast doubt on its perspectives?" The new government could not "put the socialist disposition of our country into question" through any sort of direct relationship with the civic movement.[5]

Central Committee reports soon concluded that the *Wende* was failing to regain public trust, to halt the protest wave, or to reaffirm party discipline. By the end of the third week of Krenz's tenure, internal political analysts expressed grave doubts: "Many comrades are worried about the existence of the party. . . . The collapse of trust at the grass roots is in many ways impossible to overlook. There is no shortage of questions in the party apparatus— even in the Central Committee—as to whether the party is capable of reacting to the new challenges with flexibility."[6] Meanwhile, the erosion of basic party structures was making effective political control impossible in the regional districts.[7] Krenz was widely viewed as a hypocrite who had "gone along for over ten years with policies now considered false" and had "welcomed the actions of the Chinese leadership against the students."[8]

In the month between October 9 and the opening of the Berlin Wall on November 9, the Interior Ministry reported some 260 demonstrations throughout the GDR involving an estimated four million protesters.[9] By the first week of November, the Krenz government seemed paralyzed. It was unable to stem mass protests, to repair its eroding party control apparatus, or to co-opt the opposition—all essential if the party-led *Wende* were to succeed.

In the provinces officials were now openly divided between moderates and hard-liners. Eager to support Krenz, district party leaders in Leipzig instructed local officials, "We are not prepared to engage in discussions with the organizers of the 'New Forum' and other oppositional and antisocialist groups."[10] The party leadership demanded that there be no movement toward political pluralism: "Let no views be brought into the newspapers that make things harder for the government side and are intended to mobilize the people."[11] Prominent scientists and physicians issued a statement distributed to the crowds at the Monday demonstration on October 16 urging them to disband: "Don't demonstrate! Dialogue, understanding, working together—that is the way forward. . . . Together we must have the strength to learn how to advance the dialogue so that peace will be guaranteed and socialism will again become attractive." On October 17 the *Leipziger Volkszeitung* warned citizens, "Our party recognizes the need for change and wants it. But the street offers neither the place nor the means for this." District officials publicly raised the alarm of impending "chaos" and an "uncontrolled escalation" of demands because of New Forum's activities.[12]

But party leaders in the Saxon districts faced a growing insurgency within the ranks. Ignoring Stasi officers who characterized the civic movement as a "reactionary force," midlevel officials were increasingly in favor of cooperating with the opposition.[13] At a meeting of the Leipzig district leadership on October 24, party secretary Jochen Pommert (one of the "Leipzig Six") argued that cooperation with the civic movement was both inevitable and desirable since its leaders agreed that the loss of a socialist GDR would be "a historic catastrophe for humankind."[14] One official warned that Krenz's *Wende* "wouldn't get even one person off of the streets," while others began to speak openly of political pluralism.[15] In Dresden Hans Modrow rebuked the Krenz regime, saying that his comrades were "ready to take part in democratic changes; if the party leadership in Berlin continues to remain silent, then the loss of trust will continue" (Friedrich 1994: 46).

However, even many party reformists had no intention of entering into the power-sharing arrangement that New Forum wanted. District party secretary Roland Wötzel declared, "If we let them in too quickly, then we will have our own 'Solidarity' in the GDR."[16] Even so, in the month following the revolutionary breakthrough, it was becoming impossible to ignore the faltering of the Krenz line as economic chaos spread and the party organization frayed. Leipzig officials warned that the campaign was foundering on "the broad doubts expressed in our party and the rejection of the policies of our party" and concluded that "the leading role of the party has never been subject to so much discussion as it has been in the days since October 9."[17] On October 26, party control officers reported that many members had "lost their link to the party" and "in general no longer agree[d]" with the leadership.[18]

And at the end of October, Leipzig officials conceded that New Forum was winning the battle for public opinion, even within the ranks of the party: "It is not to be overlooked that individual comrades consciously or unconsciously share the ideas of the New Forum. This can be seen in their requests for the legalization of this group and their demand for proof of this group's actual hostility to the state [*Staatsfeindlichkeit*]. . . . Some comrades want to get a picture of the New Forum for themselves and don't want it to be discredited."[19] Leipzig's municipal party boss Jochen Prag now began talks with local opposition figures. He justified his initiative by pointing to the political loyalty of the opposition and at its curious lack of interest in seizing power: "They say that they don't want to become a party; they want to be a broadly based democratic platform for political discussion."[20] Prag believed that New Forum was willing to cooperate with the government, which he thought would blunt its appeal among the masses, noting, "As soon as these groups are involved in matters of concrete political responsibility, it will no longer be possible for them to find fault with every step we take and demand more and more from us so that we are continually on the defensive."[21]

This pragmatic outlook was not yet shared in East Berlin. On November 5 the Politburo instructed Leipzig district officials that reform could only mean a "higher, different measure of genuine democracy in socialism" and a "fight for a real democracy and against bourgeois democracy." There could be debate—"in the spirit of glasnost"—but no "deformation" that would lead to the "triumph of counterrevolution."[22] Yet what party reformers were now offering was too little and too late for the crowds at the Leipzig Monday demonstrations. When the newly appointed district party leader brought his message to the Monday demonstration on November 6, he was jeered by a crowd shouting, "You're at fault!" "Too late, too late!" and "Resign!"[23]

On November 10, responding to the catastrophic course of Krenz's *Wende* policies, the Leipzig party leadership abandoned the Politburo and endorsed calls for a special party congress to preside over a transformation of the SED.[24] In hopes of regrouping demoralized supporters, the Leipzig party reformists organized a "mass party rally" for the following day. Assembled beneath red flags, twenty-eight speakers from the municipal and district party organizations denounced nationalism, called for a new "party of perestroika," and affirmed the existing GDR as the "only chance to unite democracy and socialism."[25] However, when the reformists promised to preserve the "Marxist-Leninist" system, they drew jeers. Perhaps worst of all, only about six thousand supporters turned out to back the reformers, an anemic showing compared with the hundreds of thousands taking part in the weekly Monday demonstrations.[26]

A few days later, Leipzig's dejected reformers openly expressed the fear that their moment had passed and that the regime was finished.[27] Wötzel lamented at a district party conference, "Comrades, we are in a situation that has never existed before. . . . When you face every Monday demonstrations of two hundred thousand people and are living from week to week you become tense, like scared rabbits."[28] Admonishing his comrades to accept that "attempts to develop and lead socialism through a bureaucracy have failed," he argued that it was time to separate the state and party apparatuses and abolish the "leading role" of the SED.[29]

The End of the Party Dictatorship

In spite of developments unfolding in Leipzig and the provinces, the notion that socialism could only be regenerated by activating the party itself was widely shared among reformists; indeed, this was essentially the policy that Gorbachev was allegedly pursuing with success in the Soviet Union (Hanson 1991; Bunce 1999). That Gorbachev's strategy was leading inexorably to the dissolution of the party of Lenin and to the unraveling of the USSR (see Solnick 1998) was not clear to East German party leaders, nor did they seem to appreciate fully how far beyond glasnost their country had come since October 9.

Rather than working with the nascent civic movement leadership, party leaders had tried to mobilize what proved to be a moribund party organization. But all efforts at restabilization were undermined by the widening economic crisis. The Krenz government had inherited a state debt worth more than $26 billion in convertible currencies. Servicing it would cost $4.5 billion in 1989 alone, a sum representing over 60 percent of the GDR's annual export earnings (Hertle and Stephan 1997: 63). The government needed to offer economic improvement or, at least, a short-term enhancement of living standards in order to win popular support. The means to do so, however, were fast shrinking. State economists calculated that if the GDR were forced to sustain current debt payments in the context of declining output, average household consumption would have to decrease by about a third throughout the 1990s (Hertle and Stephan 1997: 63).

Desperate for an economic bailout, Krenz turned both eastward and westward. On November 1 he visited Moscow hoping to gain the political blessing and financial backing of the patron of socialist reform. But he found Gorbachev willing to offer little in the way of financial assistance or increased subsidies of critical raw materials. With its own economic woes, the USSR did not wish to forgo Western export earnings in favor of subsidizing a ramshackle GDR (Zelikow and Rice 1995; Kotkin 2001). At least on one issue, the German question, Gorbachev buttressed Krenz by assuring him that unification was simply "not an issue of contemporary politics." But he also warned Krenz not to delay any longer in bringing prominent dissidents into the government.

Krenz next turned westward, dispatching agents to begin negotiations with Bonn for an emergency credit of twelve billion to thirteen billion West German marks. The government also proposed that Bonn subsidize a liberalized travel policy for GDR citizens with hard-currency payments. It was soon apparent that Chancellor Helmut Kohl's government wanted to avert a catastrophic collapse of the GDR, but it aimed to link assistance to substantial political reforms, including the legal recognition of the opposition, the end of the SED's political monopoly, and free elections. Even worse for Krenz's cause, in a speech on November 8 Kohl publicly announced his government's plan to tie economic aid to conditions ensuring meaningful political pluralism. The new government was now effectively boxed in: while Moscow offered no bailout, Bonn's conditions imperiled the future of the socialist state.

Domestically, the situation was scarcely more favorable. At the time of Honecker's fall, few East Germans had a clear idea of how shaky state finances had become. When the Krenz government began to discuss the GDR's economy and its looming financial crisis in early November, it proved a shock to the political elite that had convinced itself of the country's "world-class" economic status (Hollander 1999). On November 2, in a new effort to gain credibility as a reformer, Krenz sacrificed unpopular Honecker cronies, including Kurt Hager, Hermann Axen, and Erich Mielke (Jarausch 1994: 61). By ridding itself of these crooked figures, his government now claimed it had

"joined the working people" in the struggle for socialism built on the foundation of the rule of law.[30]

What proved truly destabilizing was Krenz's effort to win support by
liberalizing restrictions on travel. As early as September 1989, Krenz considered liberalizing travel policies as the best way of neutralizing the political
threat of exit (see chapter 5). Now, desperate to regain the initiative, he acted
on his earlier plan. On November 1 the travel ban against visa-free travel
with Eastern European countries imposed on October 3 was lifted. Yet, far
from satisfying the populace, this measure initiated a second exiting crisis as
East Germans fled through neighboring countries to reach Austria. Between
November 1 and November 9, tens of thousands of East Germans fled the
GDR over the exit routes used in the summer of 1989. This second wave of
exit was a devastating blow to confidence in the reform project and hinted at
just how vulnerable the state had become.

In the midst of the deepening crisis, the largest demonstration of the East
German revolution took place in East Berlin on November 4. Organized by
New Forum leaders, it was a show of support for socialist reform. Incredibly,
despite being able to draw more than half a million people, New Forum did
not use the event as an occasion to demand Krenz's resignation or a transfer
of power. Rather, the tone remained one of firm loyalty to the state. Dissident leaders shared the podium with famous intellectuals, such as the writers
Christa Wolf, Christoph Hein, and Stefan Heym, but also with government
officials, including Berlin party chief Günter Schabowski and the former
Stasi spymaster Markus Wolf. For many, this had the taste of a government
rally. Angry crowds reportedly jeered state officials and chanted antigovern-
ment slogans, clearly revealing fissures between the civic movement and
public. An analysis of police intelligence reports indicates that nearly half of
the banners and placards displayed in the crowd bitterly assailed the government and the SED, a greater proportion than those that promoted the civic
movement and its goals.[31]

Meanwhile, Krenz was now facing a growing insurgency within the ranks
of the party. While many disillusioned SED members simply dropped out of
the organization during the first months of the revolution—about a third of
the party's 2.3 million members quit by the end of 1989—a vocal minority
pressed for fundamental reforms. Intellectuals and academics in East Berlin
reform circles began to organize a new reformist faction.[32] They hoped to

shake off the "absolute stagnation" of the Honecker era and promote a "new social strategy" (Neugebauer 1997; Klein 1997). Desperate to stem defections and silence his restive comrades, Krenz finally invited a number of reform-minded party intellectuals into the Central Committee.

By this point, however, there was no easy way forward for Krenz. As the Central Committee drafted the new program between November 8 and 10, it was disrupted by a demonstration of thousands of party members demanding the right to elect a new leadership. With his own party increasingly against him, Krenz turned to a slate of major concessions. Now buckling under the combined pressure of exit and voice, the Central Committee dismantled the foundations of Communist power. The GDR's entire Council of Ministers, the state administrative executive, was forced to resign on November 8. The reorganized Politburo shed conservative members associated with the old guard. Finally, the Central Committee announced sweeping political reforms, including the long postponed recognition of New Forum as a legitimate "political association."

But it was the travel reform initiative that proved the most explosive item of the new action program. Travel to the "nonsocialist world" would be permitted but just for those with valid travel documents, a measure that would constrict the flow of exiters because only four million citizens, a large share of them party members, had passports. Krenz's advisers reckoned applications for new passports would take between four and six weeks to process, offering a welcome pause to the renewed exodus that had begun on November 1. Moreover, citizens would have to document possession of Western currency to qualify for travel, an enormous obstacle to most.

The plan was to announce the new travel policy on November 10 as the capstone of the action program, but events did not unfold as planned. During an evening press conference on November 9, Schabowski, still a member of the Politburo, prematurely announced the new travel regulations. Confusion broke out at the live televised event as reporters hounded him to explain when the new measures would go into force. Unprepared, Schabowski scanned his briefing for an answer and replied, "Immediately, without delay." The simplified message that went out over the West German television news was that the GDR had "opened the borders." Over the next several hours, tens of thousands of excited East Berliners began to assemble at border crossings with West Berlin, particularly in the vicinity of the densely populated Bornholmer Strasse crossing near the city center. Border police and troops, unaware of the details of the new regulations, were under orders to maintain security and prevent border crossings. There was a real danger that violent confrontations could develop as the crowds swelled and police and army units grew nervous. At 11:30 p.m. the sheer number of agitated citizens at the border crossings and the disorientation of the security forces persuaded the authorities to relent: shortly before midnight on November 9, the dam erected in August 1961 finally burst (see Hertle 1996).

The next day an alarmed Defense Ministry report spoke of populist euphoria: "During violations of border regulations, encounters between citizens from West Berlin and the capital of the GDR [East Berlin] in the area near the Brandenburg Gate occurred. There developed scenes of fraternization and celebrations with champagne. There were consistent expressions of 'joy' concerning the new regulations being imposed by the government."[33] In fact, the two Berlins had become a "gigantic popular festival" that was "completely unorganized, entirely spontaneous" (Vogel 1990: 59). In the following week nearly three million people crossed into West Berlin, enjoying shopping sprees funded by hundred-mark "greeting" gifts the government in Bonn offered its Eastern cousins. Young Berliners on both sides of the Wall took to it with hammers and chisels, and at the Brandenburg Gate police had to disperse citizens attempting to demolish barriers around the famous national icon.

The opening of the Berlin Wall took all parties by surprise. The Central Committee tried to make the best of the disaster, promising "free, democratic elections" and a "socialist planned economy oriented to market conditions." Krenz declared to the party faithful that he had opened the Wall to prove that "we are serious in our policy of renewal," and he assured citizens, "We plan great work, a revolution on German soil that will bring us a socialism that is economically effective, politically democratic, morally clean, and will turn to the people for everything."[34] But it was becoming evident that the revolution—driven not by the party but by the people—had surged past him. Kohl, on a visit to Poland during the dramatic hours of the breakthrough, rushed to Berlin and told crowds near the Brandenburg Gate, "Long live a free German fatherland! Long live united Europe!" Although criticized for raising the German question without consulting his allies, Kohl had expressed a sentiment that struck a chord with ordinary East Germans.

The West German government swiftly announced that financial assistance was linked to "thorough change" in the GDR, including political pluralism and economic decentralization.[35]

The National Turn and the Repluralization of Politics

While the opening of the Wall disoriented the leaders of the civic movement, it absolutely shattered the cohesion of the party. On November 10 the Central Committee approved a new program that included the legalization of opposition parties, the endorsement of market reforms, and the separation of state and party structures. Though these measures were close to those that had been demanded by the civic movement since September, they now seemed desperately out of step with the pace of events. With the Wall toppled, loyalist reformers soon faced a shameful truth: blocked exit was a vital condition for the reform process. The socialist intellectual Michael Brie recalled his shock that the regime had "committed suicide" on November 9. He explained, "I took [the Wall] to be an evil, but a necessary evil for the existence of the GDR. . . . Whoever wants to tear down the Wall must also be clear that he is at the same time tearing down the basis of the existence of the GDR."[36] With mass exit a threat to every attempt to stabilize the polity, the reform process was stricken.

Further undermining the reform process was a shock treatment in glasnost. In November investigative reporters began to be on hand for demonstrations, often providing live coverage of protests almost entirely directed against the party and Krenz (Ludes 1993). On November 14 the GDR's finance minister, Ernst Hofner, disclosed a ballooning state budget deficit and admitted that total foreign indebtedness had reached a per capita rate close to that of notoriously debt-ridden Poland and Hungary. At the same time, planners reported that export production had fallen by nearly half compared with what it was in 1988. Health care and social services were being crippled by mass emigration. If the economic news was not nightmare enough for the SED, reports detailing the party elite's privileges, access to Western luxury goods, and unseemly efforts to sell the country's cultural treasures for foreign currency fueled populist attacks and undercut whatever remained of the party's egalitarian image.[37]

Desperate to restore confidence in the government, the party finally replaced aging state premier Willi Stoph with Hans Modrow, who was readily confirmed by a newly assertive parliament (Volkskammer) on November 13. Modrow promised that he would rule not as a party boss but as prime minister of the parties and organizations represented in the parliament's National Front. Meanwhile, various parties in the National Front, especially the Christian Democrats (CDU) and Liberal Democrats (LDPD), saw the decline of the SED as an opportunity to reorganize and assert their independence (Jarausch 1994). And at the end of the month the Politburo finally declared it was ready to support the formation of a "Round Table" for a structured dialogue between the regime, the bloc parties, and the civic movement.

On December 1 the Volkskammer, with the approval of Modrow, officially removed the first article of the constitution, which had mandated the leading role of the SED. On December 2 Gregor Gysi and other reformist speakers at a meeting of the Central Committee demanded the dissolution of the Politburo and the reorganization of the Central Committee, promising continuing insurrection "until Krenz and company are gone." Attempting to defend himself before the assembly, Krenz was shouted down by comrades no longer willing to accept him as their leader (Hertle and Stephan 1997: 91). The next day, thousands of party members gathered outside the Central Committee, threatening to storm the house. As dissension within the party reached critical proportions, reformist party secretaries from the provinces demanded the resignation of Krenz and a criminal investigation of the leading figures of the Honecker regime. On December 3 Krenz complied with demands that he step down as party head, and every member of the Central Committee resigned. On December 6 Krenz gave up his positions on all state and national defense committees.

With the old regime in tatters, the Modrow government had two immediate priorities: first, to stabilize the economic and political situation and, second, to shore up the state so as to prevent rapid reunification. Looking to the East, it appeared that Modrow had Soviet support. Gorbachev's government dismissed all talk of reunification as a threat to peace and progress in Europe. At the same time, however, the Gorbachev regime quietly began to pursue the idea of a German confederation in exchange for Western economic aid. Looking to the West, Modrow confronted in Kohl an adversary who had cooled on cooperation with the rulers of the GDR. Yet unification, at least by a rapid timetable, was still out of the question. In a speech before

the Volkskammer, Modrow proposed a confederation of "mutual responsibility" on the basis of the sovereignty of the two German states.[38] Even with
the Wall opened, a *New York Times* editorial of November 19 summed up the
prevailing wisdom: "One Germany: Not Likely Now."

Nonetheless, in the uncertain period following the fall of the Wall, Kohl's
government began to change its policy on the German question. In his own
"Ten-Point Program" for reunification, Kohl drew on Modrow's ideas but
elaborated them to propose confederative structures and economic inter-
reliance as soon as possible. At this point, although he had clearly seized the
initiative, even Kohl suggested that the process of unification would last
from five to ten years. Shocked by what they saw as Kohl's attack on GDR
sovereignty, prominent intellectuals, civic movement activists, and reform
Communists responded with a public appeal, "For Our Country," on November 26. They warned against a "sellout" of "our material and moral
values due to harsh economic realities and unreasonable conditions . . .
leading sooner or later to a West German takeover of East Germany," and
they assembled a petition defending GDR sovereignty that drew hundreds of
thousands of signatures (Jarausch and Gransow 1994: 85).

Nevertheless, the masses in the streets seemed eager to be rid of the
Communists. Efforts to hold together structures of the old Marxist-Leninist
regime were battered by protest. Modrow announced the reorganization of
the Stasi as the "Office for National Security." Rumors of Stasi plotting
and systematic destruction of incriminating documents began to circulate,
prompting actions in several provincial cities on December 4. In Leipzig a
citizen's committee seized control of Stasi offices to prevent the destruction
of documents and turn them over to the public prosecutor. Ten days later,
Modrow reversed himself and announced plans to dissolve the Stasi, but still
insisting on the need to retain a state security agency.

Now Modrow's great concern was to rescue GDR sovereignty. The civic
movement's loyalty to socialism made it an attractive partner, particularly
given Kohl's insistence on political pluralism as precondition for aid. With
Volkskammer elections planned for the spring of 1990, Modrow's caretaker
government saw that the restabilization of the GDR was essential to the
prospects of the socialist left in the elections and bet on cooperation with the
opposition impaneled at the Round Table. But what each side hoped to gain
from such cooperation was different. Modrow would make East Germany
reliant on the West for economic subsidies and investments but preserve an

autonomous GDR in a German confederation. Civic movement leaders wanted reform of the socialist economy based chiefly on the resources and abilities of East Germans united in a new model of socialist democracy. They criticized Modrow's government as too obliging in its efforts to secure Western aid and investment and called for a new form of socialism, combining the market, public ownership, and workers' councils.

The civic movement's role as the left opposition came under new pressure when the reformist insurgency within the SED triumphed. Hastily organized in mid-December, the reform congress of the SED marked the start of a remarkable process of political regeneration. The post-Communists were led by a cadre of youthful, dynamic intellectuals, among them the brilliant Gregor Gysi, an attorney with a history of sympathy for dissident causes. Gysi advocated a political program based on "social democratic, socialist, and pacifist ideals." He became the new party leader, winning a resounding 95 percent of the votes cast for chairman.[39] Gysi embraced demands first articulated by the civic movement and adopted many of the opposition's political idioms. At the conclusion of the special party congress, he declared, "This socialist Third Way which we seek is characterized by radical democracy and the rule of law, humanism, social justice, environmental protection and the achievement of real equality between men and women" (Jarausch 1994: 84). He again echoed New Forum when he said, "We must not gamble away the democratic awakening and the right of self-determination of the people of the GDR," and he warned against a "new regime of capitalist magnates" (93). The party reformist further pledged full support to the government so as to "steer clear of the reefs of anarchy and annexation by West Germany."[40]

Civic movement leaders were quick to point out that the newly energized party still reflected a split between old-line Stalinists and Gysi's socialism with a human face. Although it refused to repudiate Marxism-Leninism, the newly minted "Party of Democratic Socialism" (Partei des Demokratischen Sozialismus, PDS) evoked a new "socialist pluralism" (Neugebauer 1997: 107). At the same time, however, Gysi denounced cooperation with New Forum as an "ideological swindle" that would weaken the socialist cause.[41] Claiming the antifascist mantle, the PDS organized demonstrations of its own, most prominently one in the Treptow section of East Berlin in early January that drew an estimated two hundred thousand people. Under the slogan "Yes to Perestroika—No to Nazis!" an animated Gysi warned against a "Fourth

Reich" and the "brown plague" of nationalism. To avert unification with the capitalist West, he called for a socialist "united front" to be led by the PDS.[42]

The ascendance of the PDS reformists was finalized in early February 1990 when Gysi visited Gorbachev and received his blessing. In February the party dropped the SED name altogether, eventually changing its name to PDS. The first PDS party congress positioned it as the true East German party that alone defended the people from Western "colonization," "annexation," the "sellout" of socialism, and the erasure of the "bright pages" of GDR history. Over the course of 1990, the PDS successfully co-opted issues drawn from the civic movement—including environmentalism, feminism, and radical democracy—and blurred the lines between the old regime and its opposition. Going into the March 1990 election campaign, New Forum's Jens Reich complained of the PDS, "I wouldn't call it a program at all. . . . It is a collection of all these phrases which are in vogue now and which everybody uses and you can scarcely distinguish them from the Social Democrats or Democratic Awakening . . . and they have the same words, the same "ecological," "social," "dynamic," "efficient"; always flexible. . . . On this level Gysi cannot be distinguished."[43]

The PDS leadership rapidly transformed the Marxist-Leninist ruling party into an electoral party even as the civic movement could not manage the self-transformation that would lead it from movement to party. Exit from the party ranks continued—by the summer of 1990 the SED/PDS shrank from more than two million members to fewer than half a million—but reorganization prepared it for the rigors of electoral competition. Although the party continued to lose membership, it found a stable basis of support among retirees nervous about their pensions, former state and party functionaries, academics, and state administrative employees—groups that would continue to give the PDS about a fifth of the East German vote for the next decade of post-Communist elections (Neugebauer 1997: 114; see also Bortfeldt 1990).

The Civic Movement and the Round Table Talks

The profound crisis in the GDR that was manifest by the end of October 1989 raised problems for a loyalist opposition movement undecided about how it would exercise power. Unlike their counterparts in Eastern Europe, who desired above all a "return to Europe" and the restoration of democracy and the market (Garton Ash 1990), the East German dissidents spoke of a democratic "Third Way" between market and socialism. Loyalty to the GDR and distrust of political power meant not only that the civic movement shied away from striking a death blow against the Communist state or seizing power but also that movement leaders opposed the introduction of conventional parliamentary government.

Part of the dilemma civic movement leaders faced was that the collapse of the party-state occurred so quickly that the opposition could keep pace in organizing itself. The activist Erhart Neubert recalls that "communication between the initiators in Berlin and the activists in other cities was so poor, even into October, that in much of the country most everything had to be improvised . . . even the material requirements for an opposition were unthinkably bad" (1998: 834). Although New Forum claimed some two hundred thousand members by the end of 1989, the vast majority of them were not integrated into the movement in any way. The civic movement could not mobilize its newly found support, negotiate with the government as a single voice, or communicate a consistent message to the domestic and foreign press. Civic movement leaders were put in the uncomfortable position of calling for the revolution to decelerate. In November Bärbel Bohley objected to demands for free elections, noting, "In immediate elections we would be left behind. We have too few prominent personalities. We need to take our time until we have an alternative."[44]

Indeed, from early on the East German opposition had declared that its intention was not to wrest power from the party but rather to join it in a democratic transformation of socialism.[45] Had Krenz been more politically astute, he might well have instituted the civic movement as a junior partner weeks earlier. It was only at the end of November 1989 that the Central Committee constituted a central "Round Table," a platform for various parties and movements to discuss the transformation of the state. With the benefit of hindsight, Krenz claimed that he should have replaced the entire Politburo right away and brought the civic movement into the government on October 18. He recalled, "We had a mistaken relationship, or no relationship at all, with the opposition. In retrospect, it seems as if New Forum, which was on the streets at the time and was in the opposition, was actually [composed of] people who were for an independent GDR."[46]

Modrow recognized the advantages of cooperation with the civic move-

TABLE 5. Public Opinion of Leipzig Demonstrators, November 1989–February 1990

% Favorable	11/13/89	11/20/89	12/11/89	1/15/90	2/12/90
Modrow	56	48	62	38	61
Kohl	19	26	26	49	56
Gysi	—	—	36	4	11
New Forum	70	69	54	64	47
SED/PDS	—	—	9	2	5
CDU/Alliance for Germany	—	—	—	—	53
"Unity now"	—	—	18	31	59
"Unity later"	—	—	55	52	33

Source: Mühler and Wilsdorf 1991.

Note: Percent of participants reporting favorable opinion of the politician, organization, or issue by date of demonstration.

ment, and in early December his optimism was buoyed by opinion polls that reported a third of the population still supported the SED and that about half were still against unification.[47] Rapid unification on a Bonn timetable was anything but inevitable in December 1989 or January 1990. Popular confidence in the reformist cause was Modrow's and the opposition's to lose, as opinions expressed at the Leipzig Monday demonstrations suggest. (See table 5.)

East Germany's Round Table evoked Eastern European experience but was actually closer to the style of the ongoing meetings of the "Group of Twenty" that Modrow had begun on October 9 in Dresden. Round Tables were constituted at the district and city levels throughout the GDR, but they could not enact legislation; they could only play a consultative role and propose reforms. In its first session on December 7, the Central Round Table in East Berlin announced ambitious plans to draft a new GDR constitution, to propose new electoral rules for the Volkskammer elections in the spring of 1990, and to investigate corruption and abuse of power by the old regime (Süss 1991: 471; Jarausch and Gransow 1994: 90–91). But the Round Table and the Modrow government did not move quickly enough to satisfy popular demands to abolish the last elements of the old regime.

Exit, or the threat of exit, continued to be the sharpest weapon against the government. On January 8 the Leipzig protest slogan of the day was "SED—If you don't go, we will" (Pollack 1990: 306). On January 15, dissatisfied with steps taken to eliminate the police state, New Forum called for a demonstration at the Stasi headquarters in Berlin's Normannen Strasse. But the peaceful demonstration soon escalated. Angry crowds shouting "Down with the Stasi!" and "No pardon for Stasi criminals!" surged through the gates and began to ransack the offices. Civic movement activists and the state prosecutor tried to seal police records and reassert order. Modrow and representatives of the Round Table appealed for calm, warning that violence would "endanger the democratic awakening." Nonetheless, by the time the demonstration had ended, the Stasi headquarters had indeed been ransacked.[48] Although it was not the storming of the Winter Palace, the events of January 15 marked another turning point. Modrow now knew that efforts to preserve elements of the old order or the political advantages of the SED risked full-fledged rebellion.

The weeks surrounding January 15 marked a second peak in the protest wave that drove the East German revolution. Despite Modrow's efforts to stabilize the GDR and institute a gradual transition, a great majority of East Germans had evidently lost faith in socialism and in the reformists. Between January 14 and 28, the Interior Ministry reported more than two hundred demonstrations around the country, involving more than a million citizens. Had the civic movement been prepared to exploit the situation in mid-January, it is likely that the government could have been compelled to surrender power directly to the Round Table. Instead, Modrow invited eight prominent dissidents seated at the Round Table to join a "government of national responsibility" as ministers without portfolio. Recognizing that the country was becoming ungovernable, the government advanced the date of the first free parliamentary (Volkskammer) elections from May to March 1990. But for civic movement leaders this felt like a betrayal that would give their largely inexperienced, disorganized, and disunited movement precious little time to prepare for electoral competition.[49]

The SED had instituted the Round Table only as a last resort, when its power had been negated in the streets and its political monopoly overturned by the resurgent bloc parties in the Volkskammer. This meant that one of the Round Table's original purposes—to introduce political pluralism—had already been achieved. What would have been the next step, the transfer of power from a dissolving party-state to the civic movement was never taken.

Composed of both the "old" and the "new" political forces, Round Table seats were divided among the SED, the former "bloc" parties and mass organizations and associations, and the representatives of the civic movement organizations. A number of small, fractious opposition groups were represented, as were several other largely moribund GDR bloc parties, all enjoying a level of influence far beyond their popular support. These splinter groups were often the most uncompromising in debates. The Round Table proved a blunt instrument to advance civic movement interests so long as there was no party or personality able to unite it behind seizing real executive power.

In televised Round Table sessions, civic movement representatives—many of them dissident artists, bearded academics, or idealistic clergymen—came across as "unrealistic dreamers" and political neophytes, especially in comparison with the polished appearance of Western politicians (Süss 1991: 474). Moreover, the clearly transitional nature of the Round Table convinced many that it was unworthy of much investment. As the elections approached, ever fewer prominent politicians bothered to attend sessions of the Round Table. Still, in serving as the institutionalized voice of the civic movement, the Round Table was not without successes. It raised questions regarding the pace of unification, advocated for a wholly new German republic, and rejected a hasty proposal to merge with West Germany before the March elections. And it promoted a new electoral law for the Volkskammer elections that did not include a 5 percent or 3 percent electoral hurdle, which the reformed "bloc" parties had demanded. The Round Table also successfully pushed for the dissolution of the Stasi and fought to preserve state archives and open them to public oversight, even guaranteeing that victims of the police state could gain access to their dossiers. The Round Table's parliamentary commission drafted an impressive charter of social and human rights that influenced subsequent negotiations on unity (Quint 2001). Yet because the Round Table never expanded its powers beyond those of an advisory council, none of its resolutions were binding. The Round Table, like the civic movement, missed the opportunity to play a leading role.

Kohl-onization, or the Rush to German Unity

For reformers eager to rescue the foundering GDR, the economic situation was appalling. The party under Honecker had led the country into the

abyss: massive foreign indebtedness, an enormous public deficit, an economy with a per capita GDP only a third as great as West Germany's and
saddled with only half of its labor productivity levels. The crippling effects
of out-migration left reformers in a difficult bind. How could the search
for an elusive "Third Way" of democratic socialism be reconciled with demands for individual liberty and welfare without halting out-migration?
The civic movement reasoned that the protections offered by the socialist
welfare system would keep citizens in the GDR. The Round Table pushed
for the expansion of welfare benefits, job guarantees and management-labor
"administrative councils" as part of a new social contract with GDR citizens. However, warning that such proposals threatened market reform and
would discourage foreign investment, the government rejected the program.
Modrow hoped to secure West German transfers that would, in effect, pay
East Germans to remain at home. But on this point Kohl's government was
coming to a clearer resolution: instead of transferring huge sums to keep
East Germans in a reformed GDR, it might be simpler to bring the Federal
Republic to them.

Civic movement leaders attacked Kohl's populism, his hostility to socialism, and his disrupting the search for a Third Way by hastening the timetable
for reunification. The historical record is somewhat more complex. Initially,
Kohl was caught off guard by the revolution in East Germany. In immediately speaking of "one German fatherland" and proclaiming "We are and
remain a nation" following the fall of the Wall on November 9, Kohl was
roundly criticized by New Forum, his domestic opposition, and by the foreign and domestic press. What is often overlooked is that former chancellor
Willy Brandt, dean of the Social Democrats and the architect of Ostpolitik,
made similar statements at that time, which were widely applauded.[50] Kohl
was certainly shrewd enough to perceive an incipient political vacuum that
no domestic East German party or movement seemed prepared to fill. Yet he
moved slowly at first. At the end of November he announced his "Ten-Point
Plan" for German unity, which envisioned a gradual, stepwise approach on
the basis of mutual cooperation and eventually a confederation of the two
German states. Even though the plan built on Modrow's proposals, it was
denounced by the civic movement and the post-Communists as a plot to
"annex" the GDR.

In fact, Kohl remained tentative about pushing for unification until a summit meeting in Dresden on December 19. During the visit Kohl recognized how weak Modrow's government was and how much public support he himself enjoyed in the industrial heartland of the GDR. In the same streets where Saxons had shouted, "Gorby, Gorby!" in October, "Helmut, Helmut!" rang out in December. The chancellor seized the day, greeting an enormous crowd waving the German tricolor before the ruins of the bombed-out Church of Our Lady (Frauenkirche) and promising to come to East Germany's rescue. He declared to cheering throngs, "My goal remains— if the historic hour permits—our nation's unity." After the overwhelming outpouring of emotion and support he experienced in Dresden, Kohl confided to his aides, "I believe that we will achieve unity. It will happen. I believe it can no longer be held back. The people want it. This regime is definitely at its end."[51]

Neues Deutschland decried what it considered to be Kohl's reckless populism. The paper chided the crowds that applauded Kohl for thinking that he could "liberate us all from our problems and troubles with his magic dust."[52] Yet regardless of the unrealistic expectations Kohl may have awakened, it was not mystical thinking that was persuading the masses of East Germans that the best route to reconstruction lay through unity with the larger, more prosperous, and democratic Federal Republic. Kohl's enthusiasm stood in sharp contrast to the disdain that the socialist intelligentsia began to pour out against a *Volk* that had "sold out" the revolution for "D-marks and foreign vacations."

Kohl's government moved events along by skillfully managing the international dimensions of the German question. Foreign Minister Hans-Dietrich Genscher succeeded masterfully in selling unification to the USSR, reassuring Eastern European governments, and securing the support of U.S. president George H. W. Bush (Zelikow and Rice 1995). Although Gorbachev made repeated statements discouraging unification, the Soviet Union's deep indebtedness to West Germany gave Kohl enormous leverage. On February 10, having secured Washington's support, Kohl visited Moscow with a pledge of economic aid. Gorbachev, impressed by the grim situation in East Berlin and desperate for economic assistance, assented to unification according to the "timing and manner" dictated by the democratic will of the Germans (Jarausch 1994: 109). His flexibility secured for the USSR loans and credits worth about fifteen billion deutschmarks (Maier 1997). With Soviet approval now assured, Kohl proposed an "economic and social union," including a currency union based on the Western mark, as the first step toward political unification.

The PDS and the civic movement joined in denouncing Bonn's "colonization" (or "*Kohl-onisation*") of the East. But the nagging issues of ongoing out-migration from a faltering GDR, their own lack of concrete alternatives to unification, and the deepening economic crisis provided little leverage for those opposing the march of political events, and any realistic reform program would have to rely on Bonn's goodwill as creditor and economic benefactor.

Choosing Unity: The March Elections and the Eclipse of the Civic Movement

In early December 1989—just as the SED's "leading role" was struck from the GDR constitution—more than forty parties, social movement organizations, and other political associations were registered with the Ministry of the Interior.[53] They were joined by more than one hundred and fifty interest groups promoting occupational, religious, scientific, cultural, and educational issues. Suddenly, the East German polity was pluralized. In the civic movement continuing political differentiation threatened to produce crippling sectarianism. To cite just one example, in November 1989 environmentalists founded the East German Green Party to fight for "ecological reconstruction," social justice, tolerance, and women's rights and against "materialist values." These goals were close to those of New Forum and, soon, to those of a "Green League" organized in December that was remarkably similar to the new Green Party.[54]

Civic movement fragmentation threatened electoral disaster in the March voting. But the New Forum leadership explicitly rejected transforming the organization into a political party for fear that the democratic revolution would be "corrupted." As New Forum activist Rolf Heinrich explained, "If you speak of a party then you must also speak of an *apparat*. And we would rather organize from below."[55] Not all of the civic movement organizations agreed. The Initiative for Social Democracy accepted the principle of "parliamentary democracy with a plurality of parties"[56] and founded a party with support from its Western sister party. The dissident group Democratic

Awakening (Demokratischer Aufbruch) was also quick to break ranks with the civic movement by pledging to organize a political party. At its founding convention in mid-December, Democratic Awakening declared the group ready to enter multiparty elections, pronounced socialism "dead," and condemned "experiments intended to revive the corpse."[57]

At the organizing convention of the Saxon New Forum in January 1990, advocates of grassroots politics declared that as the "conscience and healthy humane consciousness of the people," New Forum could not stoop to party politics. The majority remained committed to "democracy from below" and a "new political culture" in the GDR. A third of the delegates opposed this course, warning that New Forum was unprepared to compete with the resurgent bloc parties in the Volkskammer elections. A delegate from Dresden derided the majority position, noting, "We are not in a position to practice radical democracy"; he warned that a vague, disorganized movement would be swept aside at the polls.[58] Civic movement leaders continued to advocate an informal, participatory democracy long after other political actors with firmer models were drawing support. New Forum leaders explained, "Our land needs strong associations independent of parties in the process of democratization. They can—free from political-party pressure— best represent demands and interests of the electorate and can monitor whether or not electoral promises are kept."[59] As Dieter Rucht (1996: 51) observes, the civic movement's electoral platform was undercut by a mixture of impracticality, a "strong moral orientation," and "conceptual vagueness."

Alongside civic movement organizations, thirteen competing parties were registered for the Volkskammer elections, ranging in ideology from the radical left to the center-right.[60] The most prominent were newly reorganized "bloc" parties offering concrete programs and highly visible leaders; they tended to bundle the various aspirations of East Germans into a single aim: reunification. In particular, operating from its parliamentary perch the East German Christian Democrats rebuilt the CDU into a powerful organization and campaigned as the leading anti-Communist force.[61] Aligning itself with its Western sister party, the CDU proclaimed socialism a "fully discredited doctrine" and championed German unity.[62] With more than one hundred thousand members, the Eastern CDU soon proved a potent force for unification. While the civic movement splintered over matters of strategy and doctrine during the winter of 1990, the CDU went looking for coalition partners. The center-right Democratic Awakening, one of the original civic movement organizations, and the newly organized conservative German Social Union (DSU) became junior partners in an "Alliance for Germany" (Bündnis für Deutschland) advocating rapid unification on the basis of existing provisions of the West German Basic Law (Grundgesetz). The Liberal Democratic Party (LDPD), also a former bloc party, allied itself with the Western Free Democrats and breakaway New Forum factions.

Of course, unlike the former bloc parties, the civic movement had to start largely from scratch. It lacked organization, experience, a professional staff, and office space, making it unprepared for a modern political campaign. And the civic movement could no longer rely on a mass membership to carry it through the elections. After having an estimated two hundred thousand declared supporters in December 1989, New Forum retained fewer than thirty thousand by March 1990. New Forum also formed an electoral alliance, but its partners in the Bündnis 90 (Alliance 90) electoral coalition were much smaller; Democracy Now had only a few thousand supporters, and the Initiative for Peace and Human Rights (IFM) only a few hundred (Jarausch 1994: 120).

The legislation developed by the Round Table for the Volkskammer elections proved crucial for the limited electoral success the civic movement did manage to achieve in March 1990. To the advantage of the bloc parties, the new electoral law allowed foreign financial contributions to GDR political parties. This permitted the West German Christian Democrats (CDU), Free Democrats (FDP), and Social Democrats (SPD) to provide generous financial assistance to their sister parties. However, the electoral law did not restrict competition solely to formally constituted political parties (as would be the case in the FRG). Alongside parties, "political associations" could present slates of candidates on the ballot. The Round Table also prevented the introduction of West Germany's 5 percent electoral hurdle, allowing even small parties to win at least one seat.

During the few weeks of the electoral campaign, Kohl offered consoling promises that things would be "much better for most, and worse for no one," and that the blasted East German economy would soon be a "blossoming landscape" thanks to Western capital and expertise. Other West German parties, especially the West German Social Democrats and Greens, were sympathetic to the East German civic movement and thus much more reluctant to involve themselves in GDR politics (Markovits and Gorski 1993). Indeed, some Western intellectuals endorsed the idea of a Third Way and warned of the dangerous consequences of a united Germany (see, for example, Grass 1990). Others cautioned against national unity based less on civic consensus than on Bonn's economic muscle (see, for instance, Habermas 1990).

As was typical of the first open elections in much of post-Communist Eastern Europe, the political field in East Germany was divided among many poorly organized and narrowly focused parties. Bündnis 90 ran on a diverse platform of democratic socialism, ecological activism, feminism, and human rights, but it competed for votes and public attention with the Independent Women's Organization (UFV), the United Left (VL), and two Green parties. The failure of the civic movement to establish a single political platform proved to be damaging error, dividing the opposition into a variety of competing groups fighting for narrow segments of the electorate. The Polish Solidarity leader Adam Michnik now seemed prescient for having warned his East German friends, "You are crazy if you don't stand together as a bloc."[63]

Of an astounding twenty-four parties and political organizations appearing on the March 18 ballot, twelve were eventually seated in the Volkskammer. The election served as a virtual referendum on reunification on the terms Kohl proposed, with the Alliance for Germany bloc winning just under half of the total GDR vote. Counting the returns for the liberal Free Democrats, who were affiliated with the junior partner in Kohl's ruling coalition (the FDP), parties allied with West Germany's government won 53 percent of votes. The Social Democrats suffered a surprising defeat, winning just over a fifth of the vote in a part of the old German Reich that had once been a bastion of social democracy. Rescued from oblivion by Gysi and his reform team, the PDS ensured its survival with 16 percent of the Volkskammer vote. The combined vote for the various organizations of the civic movement—bitter rivals of the CDU and PDS alike—amounted to just 7 percent (SJDDR 1990: 449–450).

The March elections inaugurated a dramatic post-Communist political realignment that would shape politics in reunified Germany through the election of 1998. Nearly 60 percent of working-class voters chose the CDU-led Alliance for Germany. The educated and privileged classes of GDR society,

FIGURE 16. Percentage of Vote by GDR District for Alliance for Germany Bloc, Volkskammer Elections of March 18, 1990

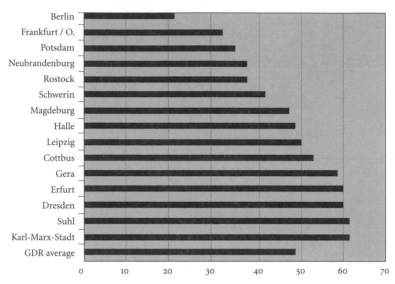

Source: *SJDDR* 1990.

including intellectuals, state and party functionaries, and socialist professionals, voted for chiefly the left, dividing their support among the PDS, the SPD, and the civic movement (see Kopstein and Richter 1992). But what has been overlooked in explaining the results is the extent to which they reflected exit-voice dynamics. In the same regions where mass exit had triggered the mass protest wave that had toppled Honecker in early October, there was the strongest support for German unification. That was especially evident in decaying industrial regions, where the vote heavily favored pro-unification parties. The regional pattern of voting for the Alliance for Germany reveals that the industrial south was the main locus of support for rapid unification. The two Saxon districts of Dresden and Karl-Marx-Stadt (Chemnitz) and the Thuringian districts of Erfurt and Suhl gave 60 percent of their votes to Kohl's allies. (See figure 16.)

If the vote for Kohl's allies can be interpreted as a vote for rapid unification, we might go a step further and regard the results as a vote for exit, that is, the demand that East Germany be allowed collectively to "exit" socialism by joining the Federal Republic. We can see this more clearly if we compare

FIGURE 17. Exit Rate per 100 Population by GDR District, January 1989–March 1990

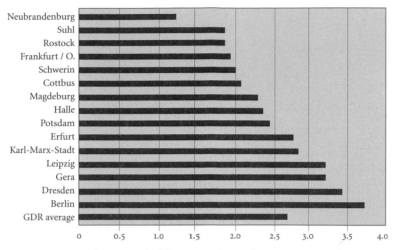

Source: Zentrales Einwohnerregister (ZER) data reported in Grundmann 1998.

the regional pattern in the vote for the Alliance for Germany with the regional pattern of emigration during the period leading up to the March 18 elections. With the exception of East Berlin, where after the Wall gave way exit was the simplest to achieve, Alliance voting matches surprisingly well with the exit rate of GDR districts. Excluding Berlin, which had the lowest level of support for the Alliance but the highest exit rate in the GDR, total exit rate and Alliance voting are significantly and highly correlated (Pearson's correlation = .61). (See figure 17.)

Over the course of 1989–90, emigration was more clearly associated with the goals of insurgent voice than with reform. In the months leading up to the March elections, many protesters in Leipzig and other cities had reinforced their demands with the threat of exit. "If the D-mark doesn't come to us, we will go to it" became a rallying cry at Leipzig's Monday demonstrations in the winter of 1990. The CDU and its allies recognized the implications clearly, promising, in effect, to bring the East Germans into the West German system as quickly as possible. The Alliance platform thus managed to encapsulate the basic aim of an active share of the electorate, particularly in the industrial heartland of the GDR.

Not having recognized the implications of exit and its link to insurgent voice, observers in both Germanys were stunned by the magnitude of Kohl's victory. Democracy Now warned bitterly of an "orgy of national feelings," while Gregor Gysi promised to make the PDS a protest party against Western colonization and "monopoly rule" by big corporations.[64] Nevertheless, the March elections made German reunification a certainty—what needed to be determined were the terms under which it would happen. Article 146 of the West German Basic Law stated that in the case of reunification a constitutional assembly should frame a new constitution to be ratified by the entire German people. It was in this spirit that the Round Table had drafted a model constitution and passed a nonbinding resolution calling for a new constitution as a precondition for unification. However, the option favored by Kohl's government was reunification under Article 23 of the Basic Law, which provided for the accession of German *Länder* (states) to the existing Federal Republic. Under Article 23, the sovereign GDR would disappear; its territorial districts would be recombined into the provinces dissolved in 1952 and would then be admitted as federal states of the FRG.

Advocates of Article 146 were convinced that a public dialogue would motivate ordinary citizens in both states to consider the benefits and drawbacks of unification and allow them to forge an all-German civic identity. New Forum wanted a new constitution to have significant provisions for popular rule, including the right to have referenda on many issues. The West German Greens endorsed this position, warning in a joint statement that "unity is not merely an economic question. It is more than anything else a democratic and political question. It cannot be given from above, over the head of the people, and only shaped by the government and economic interest groups."[65] The left-of-center West Berlin *Tageszeitung* warned against treating unification as an "administrative exercise."[66]

A broad-based "Democratic Initiative 90" interest group sponsored a petition drive demanding that the CDU-led government of the GDR not "capitulate" to Bonn by accepting unification on the basis of Article 23. The campaign gathered wide attention but only assembled about thirty thousand signatures for a petition against Kohl's route to unification. The Alliance for Germany government went ahead with a state treaty with the Federal Republic, providing for reunification under Article 23. It was passed in the Volkskammer by a two-thirds majority. With the "Economic and Social Union" that began in the summer of 1990, which included the introduction of the West German mark as the currency, the GDR as a sovereign state was disappearing even before the official date of unification.

New Forum bitterly denounced the unification treaty as a "capitulation" to Bonn and likened the new order to the old: "The Autumn Revolution has led to an exchange of rulers, but the methods remain the same."[67] Observers sympathetic to the "crushingly defeated" ideals of the civic movement still maintain that dreams of a new socialism were "ruthlessly outflanked" by a cynical Kohl, who "dangled the bait of monetary union and large-scale funding" (Eley 2002: 448–49). Yet, by the time voters endorsed German unification, there was precious little of the GDR that could have been saved. Pledging to continue the fight, Bündnis 90 and the West German Greens developed in common a program calling for a new constitution and a popular referendum on German unity as the central plank in their platform for the December 1990 all-German Bundestag elections.[68] The initiative drew wide support among intellectuals in both East and West Germany, with forty prominent West German social scientists and legal experts endorsing the demand for "extending representative democracy" and "ending the spectator democracy" in the Federal Republic.[69]

On October 3, 1990, the GDR was abolished and replaced by five reconstituted Länder, which then joined the Federal Republic under Article 23. However bitterly denounced by the left, the national political turn was confirmed in the state elections in the new Länder in the summer of 1990 and again ratified by the clear victory of Kohl's center-right coalition in the all-German federal elections in December 1990. In spite of the best efforts of the civic movement to reform socialism and the attempts by the PDS to preserve the GDR, German unification was achieved under the terms that Kohl—and, one might argue, the *Volk* of 1989—favored. The wounds resulting from the divided path to reunification are still evident in the great social and political divisions that burden the new Germany.

Conclusion

With closer communication, easy circulation of capital, and unprecedented international mobility of high-level manpower, states are today exposed to more exit pressures than ever before. Small states are particularly vulnerable to these pressures: a large country can often rather easily accommodate an inflow of capital or manpower from a small country, while an outflow of resources may represent a critical loss for the small country.

—ALBERT O. HIRSCHMAN, "EXIT, VOICE, AND THE STATE"

Full-fledged revolutions are rare events, but instances of unarmed citizens defying their rulers by means of fight or by means of flight are not uncommon. In the fifteen years following the collapse of East Germany, tens of thousands of *balseros* took to rafts and leaky boats to escape Castro's Cuba; Suharto's regime was upended by mass protest in Indonesia; a massive, if long postponed, campaign of civil resistance toppled Milosevic in Yugoslavia; students staged demonstrations against clerical rule in Iran; a broad civic movement challenged the caesarism of Colonel Chavez in Venezuela; and popular pressure secured democracy in the Ukraine. Even North Korea, perhaps the most tightly controlled totalitarian regime in the world, proved it was not completely immune to popular discontent as hundreds of thousands of oppressed and hungry citizens fled over the northern border into China, apparently persuading even this most immovable regime to experiment with economic reform.

In some instances emigration and protest are not alternatives but directly linked. How the opportunity to emigrate affects protest in a particular historical instance depends on institutional conditions that determine the balance of incentives between exit and voice and which effect of exit becomes predominant, its signaling or its network-erosion effect. The theory of exit-voice dynamics suggests that it is the volume of exit that matters most directly in how protest movements fare. If exit occurs to an extent large enough to be unambiguously recognizable as a crisis, it is likely to have a protest-facilitating effect even in a repressive polity. If exit occurs en masse, however, additional flight beyond the recognizable crisis level will undermine the further expansion of the movement by reducing a community's social capital. If a movement is to expand after this point, other processes must supplant exit-voice dynamics.

The propositions drawn from the theory of exit-voice dynamics in chapter 1 have largely been confirmed in the empirical study of the East German revolution, both in the narrative evidence and in the statistical analysis of demographic and protest event data.

Exit versus Voice

Proposition 1: All things being equal, the lower their cost of an exit option relative to voice options, the more actors will choose exit over voice.

East Germany belonged to that group of unhappy nations—among them Ireland and Korea—dominated by the problem of political division. For the East German regimes of Walter Ulbricht and Erich Honecker, this necessitated a close relationship with the Soviet Union, intensive surveillance, and the walling off of the country so as to prevent a mass migration that would impoverish, if not topple, the socialist state. Throughout this book, it is evident that emigrating from the GDR competed with collective action either to overturn the state or to compel its reform. With opportunities for voice so constrained by the mono-organizational dictatorship of the SED, millions of citizens abandoned the GDR for the haven of West Germany until August 1961. As chapter 3 documents, after walling itself off from the West, the GDR was compelled to invest heavily in "security and welfare," its system of social benefits combined with coercive surveillance. But the stability secured by the system was fragile: when opportunities to exit the country again became available with new holes in the Iron Curtain in 1989, tens of thousands fled. Yet because exit was less appealing and more expensive for some, and created such an obvious political crisis for Honecker's hard-line regime, it triggered widespread mobilization among those left behind.

The differential appeal of exit and voice is supported by evidence regarding the composition of the exit and protest waves. It appears that in the crisis of 1989–90 many young, ambitious East German workers saw their best hope in emigrating westward while older, more settled, and more professionally oriented citizens may have remained behind in order to protect their investments.

Albert O. Hirschman proposed that loyalty offsets the appeal of exit as a way of redressing grievances. The results of regression analyses in chapters 6 and 8 suggest that while exit may be an important signaling mechanism, if the degree of exit is too great it will run the risk of robbing insurgent networks of crucial support. The same effect, however, is not conspicuous in the analysis of what I have dubbed reformist voice, that is, mobilization into the New Forum organization. Voice born of loyalty does not appear to have been sensitive to the network-erosion effects conspicuous in insurgent voice because individual exit and voice thresholds were probably negatively correlated among civic movement supporters. For them, owing to material, philosophical, and professional investments in the GDR, the cost of exit was apparently higher than for the mass of East Germans; nor was it in their interest to see the socialist system overturned. The regression analyses presented in chapters 6 and 8 show that economically privileged regions produced a greater magnitude of both insurgent and reformist voice, indicating a variable distribution of the loyalist sentiment that may have deterred, or at least delayed, emigration.

The Effects of Loyalty on Collective Action

Proposition 2: All things being equal, the greater an actor's subjective loyalty to an organization or a state, the less likely he or she should be to exit it.
And
Proposition 3: If loyalists are dissatisfied, they will be more likely to join collective action and they will be more likely than other citizens to engage in reformist voice.

In social movement research, loyalty is ordinarily seen in terms of how it depresses protest or inspires reactionary countermobilization. However, loyalty can have diverse sources and consequences. It implies commitment to and investment in an organization, which can deter exit and inspire voice behind the preservation or reform of an organization or a state. There are various dimensions of the study that reinforce this understanding of loyalty's effect on voice.

In the absence of detailed data on individuals, the research and higher education campuses variable might be taken as an indicator of local concentrations of loyalty to socialism because access to higher education was influenced by political recruitment and because students were the clear beneficiaries of the socialist system. In the analyses in chapters 6 and 8, the lack of impact of this variable as an indicator of either voice or, for that matter, countermobilization suggests that even if the composition of the civic movement was heavily influenced by professionals and academics, on average highly educated citizens probably played an opportunist's game during the revolution; areas with universities and research institutes showed no greater than average commitment to the revolution or to the old order.

The loyalty effect on voice does find support in that the share of tertiary sector employment in a county did have a positive effect on the incidence, if not the magnitude, of protest (chapter 6) and New Forum mobilization (chapter 8). This suggests that the voice effect of loyalty is most robust where it is rooted in economic interests. Employment in the more modern sector of the economy thus seems to capture the "economic" loyalty to socialism that recipients of benefits provided by the central government would have developed. The fact that this variable did not influence the magnitude of protest suggests that loyalists saw little to be gained through crushing displays of opposition. Loyalists were divided on whether or not protest would improve the state's prospects or undermine them. Indeed, as is evident from chapter 8, New Forum often distanced itself from mass protests. This finding supports the argument for a broadened conception of loyalty vis-à-vis protest activities.

Moreover, the analysis of New Forum's ideology and tactics reveals the deep ambivalence of the "activists of the first hour" toward the popular protest movement. In most cases one would expect that loyalists would be unlikely to initiate protests; but if we broaden our conception of loyalty, then it need not mean silent assent to the status quo or mute toleration of worsening conditions. Loyalty may be necessary to inspire collective action behind a state in crisis. Understanding the sources and consequences of loyalty for the civic movement helps explain the ironies of East Germany's peculiar revolution. Although the civic movement claimed to be the leading force of the popular breakthrough in the GDR, it failed to exploit its advantages and watched its vision of the radically reformed, genuinely democratic East Germany ebb away. From the start it was betrayed by an SED unable to cooperate with a loyal opposition and thus guilty of helping to turn a movement for reform into a full-fledged political revolution. Brokerage between political players and interest groups, so important in the negotiated transitions elsewhere behind the Iron Curtain, could not function in the GDR, where party reformists organized too late, where the dissidents were so profoundly ambivalent on the way ahead, and where citizens could vote with their feet against efforts to thwart popular demands.

The exiting crisis was thus a mixed blessing for the reformists in the GDR. While the crisis triggered the uprising that led to Honecker's fall and mobilized reform-minded East Germans into the civic movement, the presence of an exit option terribly complicated the task of both the loyal opposition and regime moderates. They had to not only take concrete steps toward reforming the socialist state but also somehow maintain stability in the face of a debilitating exit wave. In other instances of democratization in the region, mass mobilization promoted democratic reform by undermining authoritarianism, pushing hard-liners out of power, and creating a large opposition movement united in its rejection of the old regime, thus lending dissident leaders the clout to negotiate a transitional government (Bunce 2003). In the case of the GDR, however, exit weakened the reformers and divided the populace into segments favoring reform and those favoring reunification. Once the Wall fell on November 9, reformist voice and insurgent voice no longer made common cause.

The subsequent vote for reunification can be understood as aligning the goals of insurgent voice with those of exit. Chapter 9 shows how the election was an expression of the widespread preference finally to exit the socialist GDR. Reunification on Kohl's terms brought the Federal Republic to the East Germans without their having to go to it. For loyalists, this was a staggering defeat. In the wake of unity, the PDS made itself the party representing those disappointed by reunification and promoting the interests and ideals of defeated GDR loyalists.

A Repressive Equilibrium and Its Erosion

Proposition 4: In a consolidated mono-organizational dictatorship, a repressive equilibrium can be instituted such that political voice (insurgent and reformist) will be too costly for most citizens no matter how dissatisfied.

As long as a mono-organizational regime maintains its political monopoly and punishes heterodoxy, voice will be rare compared with passive and opportunistic conformity that gradually neutralizes the organization through pervasive free-riding. Indeed, in the late 1980s many socialist leaders realized loyalist voice had been silenced, deepening the prevailing stagnation that afflicted socialism. Gorbachev's policies of glasnost and democratization were designed to activate reformist voice so as to revitalize the party and correct the pathologies of the Leninist system (Hanson 1991).

In contrast to some other socialist states during the 1980s, the Honecker regime banished all talk of reform and attacked every source of instability. Nevertheless, already suffering internal decay by the late 1980s, the system began to fray with the advent of Gorbachev's new approach to socialism. Chapter 2 shows how prolonged economic stagnation strained the bonds of loyalty while Gorbachev's calls for reform decertified the authority of GDR hard-liners and encouraged expression of dissent within the party ranks. Even so, open rebellion against the Honecker regime was stifled. The *Sputnik* affair of November 1988 demonstrated the breadth of dissatisfaction, but the party's apparatus of control quickly managed to still reformist voice. Behind the scenes, however, creeping political demobilization at the local level made it difficult for officials to act decisively when confronted with the exiting crisis in the summer and fall of 1989. The regime had become satisfied with the simulation of compliance as the returns to loyalty diminished.

Without some elite-led opening to voice, ideologically committed loyalists will not dare to press for reform against orthodox elites until an unmistakable crisis point has been reached. But by that point the system may already be in mortal jeopardy. Drawing on threshold models in collective action theory, Michael Hechter (1994: 163) notes of the revolutions of 1989, "The key to the party's fate lies with the middle-of-the-roaders who are motivated both by personal gain and by ideology. Party collapse is imminent when large numbers of these cadres defect; under these conditions a tipping point is reached that threatens the convictions of even the true believers."

The ironic implication is that no initial manifestation of collective action can be expected of the "loyal" majority until a bandwagon of defection gathers such rapid momentum that it cripples any subsequent effort at reform by genuine loyalists.

Because the regime in the GDR was able to maintain coercive surveillance up until the end, it prevented the party factionalism, the widening corruption, and the "bank run" on state assets that occurred to varying extents in China's economic reform process and during the decay of Gorbachev's Soviet Union. In the GDR economic decline and eroding confidence in the legitimacy of Marxism-Leninism did not result in either widespread defection from the party or internal opposition. Instead, the party apparatus was progressively neutralized as passive and disguised forms of withdrawal proliferated. This was nowhere more pronounced than in the rust belt of industrial districts in the GDR's south.

The robustness of the party was put to the test when the Honecker regime decided to use force to crush the nascent rebellion in the fall of 1989. Chapter 7 traces how a substantially demobilized party cadre was capable of no more than halfhearted repression. Pragmatic midlevel officials in Saxony defected from the regime's policy to seek a compromise with popular forces. That the unintended effect of Leninist institutions would be the demobilization of the regime's own cadres was a danger long recognized by socialist critics of Lenin. Rosa Luxemburg (1961) contended in her critique of Bolshevism that so long as Leninist norms are enforced, loyalty cannot promote reform or regenerate socialism no matter how pathological it becomes. Hirschman extended the insight to consider the perverse effects of blocking exit as well as voice. In a mono-organizational society, the discontented have nowhere to go. As this book shows, neither voice nor exit could be effective vehicles of change in the GDR without an external trigger.

Exit and Mobilization

Proposition 5: Exit can trigger voice, but during an episode of political contention propelled by exit, beyond a certain point mass exit should depress the occurrence of voice.

Previous studies have observed that the revolution in the GDR was largely spontaneous, with social movement organizations and political elites playing a small role. Theories of spontaneous mobilization, however, require a triggering mechanism that can activate the dynamics of mobilization. Building on Hirschman, this book shows why exit—in the form of an emigration crisis—can provide such a signal.

For exit to do more than act as a safety valve, it has to induce mutual recognition of discontent and aggravate grievances. Exit becomes a threat to the state when it takes on the character of a social phenomenon that generates mutual recognition and common expectations that one's fellow citizens will act if one acts. A trickle of exiters fails to break through the collective ignorance produced by a culture of dissimulation, but the communication of grievances is expected to intensify as the exit wave gains momentum. Now popular protest can commence, because as the volume of exit increases those left behind are affected in two ways. First, they start to appreciate the extent of generalized grievances and begin to look for opportunities to express opposition to the government. Second, since the provision of most public goods relies on the contributions of the many, the increasing volume of exit threatens the welfare of the remaining population.

The result will be a self-reinforcing dynamic; as more people leave, the more others decide they will leave too. However, all are not equally willing and able to join the exodus. Some citizens are less mobile because of the possession of fixed properties, their family situation, or their material and philosophical investments in the state. Citizens in these circumstances may forgo exit, even if only temporarily, in favor of voice. They need not have the same goals in mind in order to take action; they only need prefer revolution or reform of the current state to abandoning it for another. Beyond crisis proportions the effect of additional exit is of diminishing importance for generating protest. When people exit, they remove themselves from the social networks in which they were embedded. So, as the magnitude of exit approaches a certain point, the protest-facilitating effect of exit starts to give way to a protest-impeding effect. Where exit has become a mass phenomenon, too many people have "walked out of the game"; the exodus depletes social capital, thereby undermining the protest potential of a local population.

This theory of exit-voice dynamics does much to explain the structure of the East German revolution. The most conspicuous is that while exit exerted a systematic impact on the frequency and magnitude of protest in East Germany, as well as on the loyalist mobilization typified by New Forum, social movement dynamics evolved largely in an unstructured and spontaneous manner. Chapter 5 details how the "exit crisis" functioned as a focal point uniting dispersed actors and grievances around a single, universal cause. Given the local sources of solidarity and cooperation that existed in the "niche society" structure of East Germany, loosely coordinated responses could take shape.

Chapter 6 presents statistical support for the proposed model, finding that a strongly curvilinear pattern between exit and protest is observable across GDR counties. The message that can be drawn from the finding is clear: Exit, below a certain level, facilitates voice by triggering collective action through the signaling mechanism. As the size of exit approaches a certain point, however, the signaling effect of exit starts to give way to the network-erosion effect of mass exit. In short, exit may be an important signaling mechanism, but if the degree of exit is too great, it will run the risk of robbing insurgent networks of crucial support. The same suppressive effect, however, is not conspicuous in the estimation of loyalist voice in chapter 8. Although exit has the expected positive effect on New Forum mobilization, its squared term does not have this effect, reinforcing the interpretation that loyalist voice was not sensitive to the network-erosion effects conspicuous in insurgent voice.

As noted in chapter 5, the "exiting crisis" was most evident in the border regions with Czechoslovakia because the famous expulsion trains crossed this area amid great popular unrest. And the Dresden area was one of the first in which state repression gave way. Cross-sectional analysis in chapter 6 indicates that, regardless of its initial importance, there was not, overall, a strong regional dimension to the exit-voice dynamic in the East German revolution. The signaling effect of exit was determined by its local magnitude, not by larger regional factors. Proximity effects also failed to achieve significance in the analysis of New Forum mobilization. Although there appears to have been spillover between the capital and its surrounding region as New Forum expanded, being close to Berlin did not determine whether a locality would have citizens rallying behind its call for reform.

Although exit exerted a systematic impact on both the frequency and magnitude of protest, as well as on loyalist mobilization, statistical results confirm the basic argument of this book that social movements in the GDR evolved largely spontaneously, in a manner different from what we have come to expect from the literature. Identifying the social mechanisms that propel exit-voice dynamics contributes to our understanding of processes and structure in high-risk collective action.

Comparative Implications

The GDR, where the decay of the Soviet bloc created opportunities for flight that triggered a popular rebellion the state could not contain, is an extraordinary example of the combustive potential of exit-voice dynamics.

The GDR's peaceful collapse was hardly inevitable and stands in sharp contrast to the fate of the democracy movement in the People's Republic of China. As in other instances of revolution, it was not the strength of the insurgent challenge that toppled the Honecker regime but the weaknesses of the state's response (Goodwin 2001). The East German case confirms the position taken by sociologists of revolution that government officials need not join the opposition or openly defy their rulers in order for a state to collapse. All that needs to happen is that a critical portion of the regime's security apparatus remain neutral. This occurred in a string of states between 1989 and 1991. Steven Solnick and Valerie Bunce suggest that the Soviet Union collapsed, in large part, because officials were neutralized when they began to worry about what would come next and what would be their place in it. Evidently in the GDR no one wanted to enter an uncertain future as the "Butcher" of Leipzig or Dresden. In such a situation inaction is the most reasonable course, and it may be enough to tip the revolution in insurgents' favor.

As the historian Eric Hobsbawm pointedly observed of the demise of Soviet-type regimes, "No groups of communist ultras anywhere prepared to die in the bunker for their faith. . . . The communists, who had once been sustained by the old convictions, were now a generation of the past" (1994: 488–89). An especially curious feature of the GDR in 1989 was the absence of both counterrevolutionaries and revolutionaries. East Germany lacked not only a determined ruling class willing to kill and die for socialism but also a decisive group of oppositionists prepared to take power. Trapped by their loyalty to a socialist GDR in the context of national division, dissidents never became the leaders of popular aspirations or seized the reins of power once Honecker stumbled.

This book has also shown that East Germany's revolution was largely a populist rebellion. Although loosely organized populist rebellions are not the focus of much of the recent writing on social movements, historical sociologists have explored their implications. With the failed rebellions in Hungary in 1956 and in Czechoslovakia in 1968 in mind, Anthony Oberschall (1973) observed that Communist governments had such a high capacity for surveillance and control that organized challenges—revolutionary cadres, armed insurgencies, and opposition parties—were hopeless prospects. He suggested that egalitarianism and generalized grievances could be "the foundation for leaderless, spontaneous collective protest, despite the absence of strong community organization or associations for pursuing common interests" (133). Studies in historical sociology reinforce the impression that local sources of solidarity and the absence of civil society ties promote populist protest rather than organized social movements. Craig Calhoun (1982) argued that densely knit communities and not workers' parties were the basis of radicalism in England's Industrial Revolution. He showed how radicals employed "us-versus-them" rhetoric to widen the resistance to changes seen as threats to local interests and craft traditions. Roger Gould (1995) found that urban communities mobilized based on broad appeals to collective identity in the Paris Commune. The Communards were potent where citizens joined in as members of neighborhood groups rather than as members of a social class, pitting the cause of a broad, loosely defined coalition of heroic Parisians against the forces of a treacherous state and the ignorant peasants that backed it.

For East Germans too, a populist protest identity gave the movement its radical edge. After decades of submission and silence, protesters declared themselves the authentic people that had the right to be seen and heard. The activation of the dense local networks of the niche society provided assurance of mutual support and helped overcome the free-rider problem. The slogan *Wir sind das Volk!* shouted by hundreds of thousands of people across the towns and cities of the GDR was an unmistakable repudiation of the "dictatorship of the workers and peasants"—and, ultimately, of the division of Germany itself.

Populism in the East German case helps to explain why revolution was experienced so differently there compared with elsewhere in the region. Throughout Eastern Europe and the USSR, popular mobilization gave liberal reformists considerable bargaining power in negotiations with the old regime (Linz and Stepan 1996; Bunce 2003). However, in East Germany, once the prospect of unification became possible, the predominant message of voice was not anti-regime but antistate protest. With the survival of the state in question, the dissidents became divided from the mass of protesters in the streets and lost their bargaining power. Meanwhile, representatives of the old order reorganized in hopes of securing the most favorable post-Communist future for their party or faction, fully displacing the civic movement, which never managed to harness the populism of the peaceful revolution.

Reunification on Kohl's terms ensured that East Germany's post-Communist transition would be as a dependency of a formerly rival state. Even so, the institutional legacies of Communism may be just as profound in their enduring consequences as this peculiar route to transition. Despite the GDR's seemingly advantageous path to democracy and market, the legacies of its mono-organizational social order are still evident in the new states of the Federal Republic of Germany, just as they are in other postsocialist societies (Howard 2003). Yet the GDR's unusual route to transition created enormous opportunities for protest parties, a potential effectively exploited by the PDS, which embraced eastern German interests and loyalties. With joblessness still so common and civil society still so weak, in eastern Germany populism remains a powerful political idiom.

Although we often focus only on outspoken dissidents when trying to understand opposition in repressive regimes, a more profound source of vulnerability may be the opportunity to exit. If neighboring or nearby states lower the costs of exit, it may activate the exit-voice dynamic demonstrated in this book. Although this book makes no pretense to prediction, the link between migration and protest as forces for change has obvious relevance for a world that continues to be shaped by political exile, labor migrations, civil wars, refugee crises, forced resettlements, and failed states (Zhao 1996; Herbst 1990; Adas 1986; Pedraza 1985). Exit-voice dynamics have even larger implications for understanding those contemporary authoritarian regimes in which exit is the principal form of opposition available to ordinary citizens.

Above all in Cuba and North Korea, those two Leninist stalwarts that resisted the trend that led to political transition and economic reform in the Soviet bloc, the exit issue is of special relevance. In both of these countries, given the prevailing economic difficulties, uncertain leadership, and evidence of widespread political disaffection, the potential exists for a devastating mass exodus. As with the GDR in 1989, potential host countries for refugees are not far off: the island of Cuba lies ninety miles from Florida, and the haven of South Korea lies on the other side of Korea's demilitarized zone.[1]

As Hirschman's (1978) reflection on exit as a feature of world politics foresaw, the routine movement of peoples, the near-universal diffusion of ideas, and the fluidity of capital and expertise that characterize contemporary processes of globalization should raise the political salience of exit. It is becoming harder for states, large and small, to control their citizens' movements, their capital, and their loyalties. Of course, the theory of exit voice-dynamics is of the greatest importance for explaining the genesis of revolt under specific conditions. The implications for political change are most obvious in a state where (1) grievances born of poor economic performance and political despotism are widely shared; where (2) a repressive regime imposes coercive restraints on the exercise of exit and voice such that citizens can neither openly communicate nor coordinate collective action to seek redress; but where (3) neighboring states can disturb the repressive equilibrium in the despotic state by lowering the costs of exit. This does not mean rebellion or revolution will occur; it only means that protest will be affected by the possibility and magnitude of exit. East Germany serves as an extraordinary historical example of the combustive potential of exit-voice dynamics.

Quantitative Data and the Statistical Analysis of County-Level Exit and Voice Relationships

Protest Event Data

For the analysis of voice, detailed data—especially on protest and state repression—are difficult to come by for socialist states. Many existing studies rely on secondary source materials such as Western newspapers and previously published accounts or on retrospective, self-reported survey data. However, state-controlled media are notoriously unreliable, and Western newspaper stories are limited by the fact that reporters cannot venture wherever they wish (in the GDR, they were generally only present in larger cities such as East Berlin, Leipzig, or Dresden). Self-reported data on individual participation often suffer from social-desirability and retrospective biases. Because of these considerations, in the quantitative study in this book, secondary source materials were not employed to code the dependent variables Protest Event Rate (PER) and Average Participation Rate (APR). Instead, a powerful, if not perfect, county-level dataset was assembled from summary police reports in the archives of the GDR Interior Ministry. These records cover the whole of the country during the period from September 1989 to March 1990; thus the events statistically analyzed in this book range from the first popular demonstrations against the regime to the free elections on March 18, 1990.

The documents coded were composed of crisis reports made by GDR People's Police (*Volkspolizei*) at the county/municipal level (*Kreis* or *Stadtkreis*) to the Interior Ministry in East Berlin. The reports list politically motivated illegal assemblies, demonstrations, and violations of public order (*Störungen der öffentlichen Ordnung und Sicherheit*) occurring within a county. These crisis reports are complete for the period between September 1989 and April 1990 (see Bundesarchiv der Bundesrepublik Deutschland [Berlin-Lichterfelde], files BARCH DO 1 2.3/053614, DO 1 2.3/052445, and DO 1 2.3/052449). Only those events that involved public manifestations of voice—such as demonstrations, assemblies, marches, the seizure of public buildings, strikes, rallies, riots, and picketing—were coded in calculating the dependent variables. This means that, to prevent inflation, those activities deemed suspicious by the police but did not result in public events—such as church services, meetings of dissidents, or regime-sponsored propaganda events—are not coded as protest events. In order to prevent inflation in the APR, when local police agencies offered an estimate of protest participation in a range (e.g., 1,000–2,000 persons), the lowest figure in that range was consistently chosen.

Comparing the resulting list of protest events and participation estimates with reliable studies of protest in particular cities (Opp, Voss, and Gern 1995), with newspaper reports of protest in GDR (e.g., the West Berlin *Tageszeitung*), and with archival tabulations published by historians (Lindner 1998; Schwabe 1999) suggests that the data are accurate and complete. The only apparent discrepancy is that GDR police estimates of protest participation are more conservative than other estimates. Nevertheless, drawing on police reports helps to overcome the selective biases of mass media coverage of protest events and the tendency of activists to make exaggerated reports. Police reports, particularly in a relatively small, highly bureaucratic and centralized state, can be assumed to yield fairly standard reporting of events and estimates of protest participation (Titarenko et al. 2001). Most importantly, these data have the advantage of comprehensive national coverage that no other data source can offer.

In order to analyze the effect of exit on insurgent voice, I assessed how the level of exit was associated with the frequency and magnitude of protest events in each locality. The analysis includes the capital city of East Berlin and all of the 214 counties and municipalities that composed the former GDR, save three (Kalbe, Saalkreis, and Tangerhütte), which are missing in Grundmann's (1998) estimate of out-migration. Counties and municipalities varied greatly in their experience of the emigration crisis and subsequent protests. Counties and municipalities experienced on average about 7.6 protest events; however, a large share (35) saw no protest event, while a few localities experienced a large number (40 or more). The average number of protest participants for those counties and municipalities with protest events was about 38 persons per 1,000 residents with a median of 30 per 1,000. The average participation rate varied enormously, between 1.3 and 339, with a standard deviation of 36.6.

Likewise, although every county was affected by the emigration crisis during the period of January–August 1989, counties and municipalities varied in the degree of exit experienced. The median number of persons who emigrated from a GDR county before the onset of the revolution was a meager 148, with a mean of about 366. While the minimum number of emigrants a county experienced was only 17 persons, the maximum number reached 12,057.

TABLE A1. Univariate Statistics and Pearson's Correlation Coefficients of the Variables in the Analysis

Variables	$\bar{X}$	s.d.	correlation coefficient with variable								
			(2)	(3)	(4)	(5)	(6)	(7)	(8)	(9)	(10)
(1) Protest Event Rate	1.92	1.09	*0.81*	*0.28*	0.13	−0.03	*0.19*	0.04	0.11	*0.12*	0.04
(2) Average Participation Rate	2.82	1.45		*0.31*	0.07	−0.07	*0.14*	0.01	*0.16*	*0.12*	0.05
(3) Exit Rate	3.21	2.63			*0.43*	−0.11	*0.15*	−0.09	*0.47*	*0.28*	*0.39*
(4) CSR Border	0.23	0.42				*−0.19*	*−0.30*	−0.19	−0.03	0.02	0.05
(5) FRG Border	0.48	0.50					0.08	0.08	−0.03	0.01	−0.02
(6) % Employed in Tertiary Sector	37.15	7.61						−0.05	*0.38*	*0.20*	*0.27*
(7) SED Density	15.96	1.84							0.10	0.05	−0.00
(8) Research and Higher Education	1.34	3.51								*0.30*	*0.76*
(9) Past New Forum Dummy	0.23	0.42									*0.30*
(10) Logged Number of Arrests	0.26	1.12									

Note: Statistical significance of the coefficients at 0.05 level is indicated by italics.

TABLE A2. Tobit Coefficients for Regression of Protest Event Rate on Selected Independent Variables[a]

	Model 1		Model 2		Model 3		w/o 4 Outliers	
	β	(s.e.)	β	(s.e.)	β	(s.e.)	β	(s.e.)
Intercept	1.40	(0.13)**	1.11	(0.19)**	−1.26	(0.97)	−1.38	(0.97)
Exit Rate	0.14	(0.03)**	0.32	(0.09)**	0.34	(0.10)**	0.45	(0.12)**
Exit Rate, Squared			−0.02	(0.01)*	−0.02	(0.01)*	−0.03	(0.01)**
CSR Border					0.16	(0.25)	0.10	(0.25)
FRG Border					−0.07	(0.17)	−0.07	(0.17)
% Employed in Tertiary Sector					0.04	(0.01)**	0.03	(0.01)**
SED Density					0.07	(0.05)	0.07	(0.05)
Research and Higher Education					0.01	(0.04)	0.04	(0.04)
Past New Forum Dummy					0.06	(0.21)	0.10	(0.21)
Logged Number of Arrests					−0.15	(0.11)	−0.15	(0.11)
Sigma	1.22	(0.07)**	1.21	(0.07)**	1.17	(0.06)**	1.15	(0.06)**
Likelihood Ratio Chi-square	17.61**		22.12**		33.83**		34.54**	
Pseudo R-squared	0.03		0.03		0.05		0.05	
corr $(Y_p \hat{Y}I)$[b]	0.28		0.31		0.39		0.35	

Notes: [a] Identified as potentially influential are the cities of Plauen, Jena, Gera, and Leipzig.
[b] Reported are Pearson's correlation coefficients between observed and predicted Protest Event Rate.
* p<0.05; ** p<0.01

TABLE A3. Tobit Regression of Average Participation Rate on Selected Independent Variables[a]

	Model 1 β (s.e.)	Model 2 β (s.e.)	Model 3 β (s.e.)	w/o 3 Outliers β (s.e.)
Intercept	2.08 (0.18)**	1.79 (0.26)**	0.49 (1.30)	0.51 (1.32)
Exit Rate	0.19 (0.04)**	0.37 (0.12)**	0.46 (0.13)**	0.62 (0.16)**
Exit Rate, Squared		−0.02 (0.01)	−0.02 (0.01)*	−0.05 (0.02)**
CSR Border			−0.26 (0.33)	−0.26 (0.34)
FRG Border			−0.22 (0.22)	−0.25 (0.23)
% Employed in Tertiary Sector			0.02 (0.02)	0.02 (0.02)
SED Density			0.03 (0.06)	0.02 (0.06)
Research and Higher Education			0.07 (0.05)	0.11 (0.06)
Past New Forum Dummy			0.08 (0.28)	0.14 (0.28)
Logged Number of Arrests			−0.29 (0.15)	−0.29 (0.15)
Sigma	1.62 (0.09)**	1.61 (0.09)**	1.57 (0.09)**	1.57 (0.09)**
Likelihood Ratio Chi-square	20.34**	22.77**	31.67**	31.64**
Pseudo R-squared	0.03	0.03	0.04	0.04
$corr(Y_i, \acute{Y}_i)$[b]	0.31	0.32	0.37	0.37

Notes: [a]Identified as potentially influential are the cities of Plauen, Jena, and Gera. The inverted-U-shaped effect of Exit Rate holds true even if Leipzig and Berlin are also removed.

[b] Reported are Pearson's correlation coefficients between observed and predicted Average Participation Rate.

*p<0.05; ** p<0.01

New Forum Mobilization

The analysis of loyalist voice also draws on a unique archival source. The New Forum Organization (NFO) preserved its original list of declared supporters during the period between its founding in September 1989 and its legalization on November 8, 1989. This source provides a good picture of citizens willing to identify with the movement during its period of illegality, thus avoiding the later short-term bandwagon support that swelled the organization with new, often marginally involved supporters after November 1989. The data can thus be taken as a measure of the early activist core around which civic movement organizations took root across the country.

The NFO lists preserve the identities of about 25,800 New Forum supporters who signed their names in support of the organization and provided their place of residence. Some supporters (66 percent) also provided their occupation and a few (3.3 percent) provided their age (see Mathias-Domaschk-Archiv, Archiv der Robert-Havemann-Gesellschaft, Bestand Bürgerbewegung, NFO 047–055). The New Forum Mobilization dependent variable analyzed in chapter 8 was calculated by taking the total number of declared NFO supporters in a county/municipality per 10,000 residents. The mean mobilization rate was 8.15 with a standard deviation of 17.45, with values varying in a range between 0 and 98.6 (East Berlin).

The analysis of loyalist voice as measured by New Forum Mobilization Rate applied the same logic as the analysis of the data reported above for insurgent voice. However, there was no evidence of censoring effects in the measurement of the dependent variable, and thus no need for a Tobit analysis of APR and PER, so that an OLS regression model was estimated for the analysis of the continuous New Forum Mobilization Rate variable. In order to evaluate the robustness of the model presented, the same independent variables were regressed against a dichotomous measure of New Forum mobilization in a locality. The results of the logistic regression found that the same factors that increased the odds of New Forum mobilization can also be found to predict mobilization levels in the ordinary least squares (OLS) estimation.

TABLE A4. Univariate Statistics and Pearson's Correlation Coefficients of the Variables in the Analysis

Variables	$\overline{X}$	s.d.	(9)	(8)	(7)	(6)	(5)	(4)	(3)	(2)
(1) New Forum Mobilization Rate	0.87	1.53	.216	.148	.141	.120	.188	−.180	.311	.217
(2) Exit Rate	3.2	2.63	−.020	.386	.357	.287	.469	−.090	.490	
(3) % Employed in Tertiary Sector	37.15	7.60	.245	.268	.283	.302	.383	−.059		
(4) SED Density	15.96	1.84	−.488	−.008	.195	.188	.094			
(5) Research and Higher Education	1.3	3.51	−.005	.757	.409	.500				
(6) Solidarity Church Organization	0.09	0.29	−.024	.451	.324					
(7) Samizdat Press in Churches	0.12	0.33	−.100	.296						
(8) Logged Number of Arrests	0.26	1.12	.015							
(9) Proximity to Berlin	0.07	0.26								

Note: Statistical significance of the coefficients at 0.05 level is indicated by italics.

TABLE A5. OLS Coefficients for Regression of New Forum Mobilization Rate on Selected Independent Variables

	Model 1		Model 2		Model 3		w/o Berlin[a]	
	β	(s.e.)	β	(s.e.)	β	(s.e.)	β	(s.e.)
Constant	.464	(.162)**	.182	(.235)*	−.425	(1.247)	−.249	(1.244)
Exit Rate	.126	(.039)**	.299	(.112)**	.284	(.110)*	.282	(.110)*
Exit Rate, Squared			−.016	(.010)	−.019	(.010)	−.018	(.010)
% Employed in Tertiary Sector					.049	(.015)**	.049	(.015)**
SED Density					−.076	(.065)	−.086	(.065)
Research and Higher Education					.027	(.049)	−.005	(.052)
Solidarity Church Organization					.067	(.406)	.118	(.405)
Samizdat Press in Churches					.168	(.350)	.184	(.348)
Logged Number of Arrests					−.038	(.137)	−.048	(.137)
Berlin Proximity					.617	(.458)	.599	(.455)
R-squared[b]	.047		.059		.170		.159	

Notes: [a] Berlin is removed as a potentially influential case.
[b] Reported are Pearson's correlation coefficients between observed and predicted Protest Event Rate.
* p<0.05; ** p<0.01

Notes

Preface

1. See Alexis de Tocqueville's *Recollections* (1987) and *Old Regime and the French Revolution* (1955). See also Raymond Aron's (1968) interesting interpretation of Tocqueville's attitude toward revolution. For recent treatments of the difficulties of predicting revolutions, see Goldstone 1993; Kuran 1995; Collins 1995; Tilly 2001.

2. For historical accounts of German revolution and reunification, see Jarausch 1994; Zelikow and Rice 1995; Maier 1997; Lindner 1998; Zwahr 1991. Excellent studies of the history of the GDR and East German Communism are found in Staritz 1985; Weber 1999, 2000; Weitz 1997; Ross 2000, 2002; Fulbrook 1995; Meuschel 1992; Mitter and Wolle 1993.

3. For a clear statement on the methods of process tracing, see Goldstone 1997.

4. In 1988 Leipzig was the GDR's second city, with a population of about 550,000 inhabitants. It was a manufacturing center and the administrative seat of a regional district. See "Zahlen und Fakten zur Verwirklichung der Politik zum Wohle des Volkes in der Stadt Leipzig," September 1988, Archiv Bürgerbewegung e.V., Stadtgeschichtliches Museum Leipzig (ABL) H15. Also compare the Leipzig district with the rest of the GDR in *SJDDR* 1990.

Introduction

1. The comparisons are based on the depiction of each case in the case-specific secondary literature. For Czechoslovakia, see Garton Ash 1990; Judt 1992; Wheaton and Kavan 1992; Glenn 1999, 2001; Saxonberg 2001. For Poland, see Osa 2003; Ost 1990; Garton Ash 1993; Fehr 1992; Ekiert 1996, 1997; Goldfarb 1991; Touraine et al. 1983. For Hungary, see Bruszt 1990; Bruszt and Stark 1992; Arato 1994; Agocs 1993; Szabo 1994; Szelenyi and Szelenyi 1994. For Romania, see Chirot 1978, 1994; Jowitt 1991; Verdery 1996; Bachman 1991. For the People's Republic of China, see Lin 1992; Calhoun 1994; Guthrie 1995; Zhao 2001.

2. The GDR experienced the collapse of a Communist regime based on the political monopoly of the Leninist party, the Sozialistische Einheitspartei Deutschlands (SED), which had emerged after World War II as the forced union of Social Democrats and Communists in the Soviet Occupied Zone. The SED became incapable of rule and

could not enforce the mono-organizational dictatorship that was at the center of the polity. The state, however, did not collapse. Throughout 1989–90 the routine administrative functions of the state remained intact. Indeed, throughout the period GDR civilian ministries functioned continuously; hence this book employs data collected by East German police and census agencies throughout the revolution.

3. See among others O'Donnell and Schmitter 1986; O'Donnell, Schmitter, and Whitehead 1991; Przeworski 1991; Linz and Stepan 1996; Offe 1997; Stark and Bruszt 1998; Anderson 1999; Bunce 1999, 2003.

4. In general, the political process theory of social movements tries to capture changes in the institutional structure and power relations of a political system to explain movement dynamics. Such variables as the relative openness or closure of a polity, the stability or instability of its ruling elite, the presence or absence of elite support for challengers, and the state's capacity and willingness to inflict repression are included (McAdam 1996: 26–28).

5. See Ministry of Interior figures in Bundesarchiv der Bundesrepublik Deutschland (BArch) DO 1 2.3/052449.

6. The advocates of the "mechanisms of contention" approach declare that they wish to identify "some specific mechanisms and processes that recur across contentious politics' many forms" (McAdam, Tarrow, and Tilly 2001: 13), but there is notable imprecision in the conception and application of mechanisms. Dozens of relational, cognitive, and environmental mechanisms are suggested, and there are varying levels of abstraction (Tilly 2001: 34; Tilly 2000: 9; also McAdam, Tarrow and Tilly 2001).

7. By "public goods," I mean goods that are nonexcludable (noncontributors cannot be denied its enjoyment), jointly supplied (no individual can produce the good for himself or herself without the contributions of others), and nonsubtractable (no "crowding" effect). Hence, no matter how many people enjoy it, the utility of the good is not reduced. A change of unpopular regime (or its fundamental reform) is such a public good. Multiple contributors (a very large number in this instance) must act together to produce the desired change of government, yet once it is achieved the benefits can be enjoyed by anyone without reducing someone else's ability to enjoy it. "Free riders," those who made no contribution to achieving the change, also get the benefits. Because of the difficulties in achieving extensive collective action and the difficulty of overcoming free-riding tendencies, it can be notoriously difficult (but neither unlikely nor impossible, *pace* Olson [1965]) to produce public goods voluntarily.

1. Exit-Voice Dynamics

1. I do not mean to suggest a fatal flaw. Brian Barry (1974) rightly noted in a critical review of *Exit, Voice, and Loyalty* that while it suffers from "obscurities and ambiguities which become apparent on close examination," it also "stimulate[s] and repay[s] this degree of careful attention" with a simple, widely applicable theory (85).

2. In an interview Hirschman asserted, "Mancur Olson's idea of collective action just struck me as nonsensical. He argues for the impossibility—not the logic but the illogic—of collective action. According to him, collective action should never happen

since people act like rational actors: they always want a free ride and so on. . . . There is of course some amount of evidence to the contrary. And over the years I have tried to develop, in various forms, a counter explanation to this version of rational choice explanation" (Hirschman quoted in Swedberg 1990: 159). In *Shifting Involvements* (1982), Hirschman explained public-spirited collective action by arguing that the benefits (pleasures) of collective action had been misidentified as "costs" by Olson and others.

3. For discussion of loyalty in Hirschman's schema, see Barry 1974 and Dowding et al. 2000. For a discussion of how state-provided public goods may increase citizen loyalty, see Hirschman 1978.

2. The Crisis of East German Communism

1. Stiftung Archiv Parteien und Massenorganisationen der Deutschen Demokratischen Republik im Bundesarchiv (SAPMO-BArch) DY 30/J IV 2/50/30/2935.

2. See Central Committee of the SED 1981: 41.

3. Erich Honecker reportedly told a stunned Olof Palme during a state visit by the Swedish prime minister that "we have never experienced acid rain." See *Tageszeitung* (*Taz*), 1/5/87. Meanwhile, state enterprises paid a "mortality bonus" to workers in the most polluted areas.

4. See report of 6/15/89 in SAPMO-BArch DY 30/IV 2/2.039/74.

5. The archival record indicates that from the early 1980s the planned economy was not able to meet the demand for foodstuffs and other basic consumer goods (Weber 2000: 98). Between 1970 and 1989 the proportion of East Germans who reported that living standards were bad climbed from 13 percent to 37 percent, and the proportion that thought they were good fell from 25 percent to 14 percent (Bundestag 1995 v/1:723). See also firsthand accounts of shortages in the GDR in "Das droht die DDR zu vernichten," *Der Spiegel*, 8/14/89, and John Tagliabue "Leaving behind a Land of Shortages," *New York Times*, 10/4/89.

6. Speech of Erich Honecker at the XI Party Congress of the SED Berlin, 2/6/87. SAPMO-BArch DY 30/2175, pp. 107–13.

7. Address of Hannes Hoernig in Sächsisches Staatsarchiv Leipzig (stAL) SED IV F-2/2/029, p. 121.

8. The economist Joseph Stiglitz (1994: 200) observes: "In industries in which close monitoring can be instituted, and where there is little scope for quality variability, the socialist economies attained some success. Nonetheless, in many industries of modern economies, in service sectors like computer programming, these techniques are of little avail."

9. In November 1989 it was reported that it cost the GDR 40 East marks to produce a 64-kilobit chip and 534 marks to produce a 256-kilobit chip. At the same time the comparable technology on the world market cost 1.50 DM and 4–5 DM respectively (Hertle and Stephan 1997: 78). See also Pirker et al. 1995; Jürgen Schulz, "Wir bauen die grössten Mikrochips der Welt: DDR-Computerindustrie auf dem Vormarsch," *Taz*, 12/23/86; Maier 1996.

10. For the SED, such reforms were only justified in China, where the party remained

in complete political control and Western investment was needed to stimulate "backward productive forces," as in Lenin's strategic "New Economic Policy." See SAPMO-BArch DY 30/J IV 2/50/30/2935.

11. SAPMO-BArch DY 30/IV 2/2.039/74.

12. See Politburo discussion on 6/15/89 in SAPMO-BArch DY 30/IV 2/2.039/74.

13. Author's interview with Christa Pürschel, Leipzig, 7/22/98.

14. StAL SED IV F-5/1/058.

15. StAL SED IV F-5/1/059.

16. StAL SED IV F-5/1/058.

17. Report on municipal conditions dated 7/5/88 in StAL SED IV F-5/2/062.

18. Untitled reports of the SBPKK-Mitte, 4/9/87 and 8/4/87, StAL SED IV F-5/2/052.

19. See StAL SED IV F-5/1/065, especially p. 14.

20. StAL SED IV F-2/2/027, p. 16.

21. These numbers are based on the finding of the 1986 SED party conference (see Weber 2000: 100–102). With more than two million members, or about 14 percent of the total population, the SED had a very high party density comparable only to other Leninist stalwarts such as North Korea (15 percent) and Romania (15 percent).

22. See report on cadre politics of 1/8/86 in SAPMO-BArch 86 A 987a; and Thomas Ammer, "Abschluss der Parteiwahlen in der SED 1988/Mitgliederbewegung in der SED 1988," SAPMO-BArch 94C 281c.

23. StAL SED IV F-5/1/058.

24. See, e.g., the report on teaching college students in StAL SED IV F-5/1/057.

25. Summarized from reports in StAL IV F-5/7/060 and StAL IV F-5/2/054.

26. See report in SAPMO-BArch DY 30/IV 2/2.039/336, pp. 2–14.

27. StAL SED IV F-5/1/065.

28. StAL SED IV F-5/1/065.

29. StAL SED IV F-5/1/059.

30. Interview with Michael Brie, professor for social philosophy at Humboldt University in Berlin, GDR Oral History Collection, Hoover Institution Archives, pp. 6–7.

31. The SED's leading ideologist, Kurt Hager (a member of the Politburo), used this expression to distance the GDR from Gorbachev's reforms in an interview. He later maintained that he had been misrepresented. See interview with Hager, GDR Oral History Project.

32. This fact comes across clearly in interviews with a number of prominent SED leaders. Regional party secretaries such as Werner Eberlein and Hans Modrow, as well as regime insiders such as Kurt Hager, Werner Fischer, and Egon Krenz, make it clear that Honecker's Politburo remained implacably opposed to liberalization. See interviews with Eberlein, Modrow, Hager, Fischer, and Krenz in the GDR Oral History Project.

33. My archival findings are consistent with a retrospective micro-survey (N=117) of GDR party and state functionaries reported by Daniel V. Friedheim (1997). Friedheim found that 35 percent of midranking officials reported having serious doubts concerning the superiority of the socialist system even before the fall of 1989. More than two-thirds saw economic failure as the largest factor in the decline of the GDR,

although ideological disaffection was pronounced among younger officials most interested in the rise of Gorbachev.

34. *Taz*, 11/23/88.
35. Honecker's address of 2/6/87 in stAL sed iv f-2/1/013.
36. *Sputnik* was a kind of Soviet *Reader's Digest*. Although hardly subversive, it represented a good source of information about reforms in the USSR. See Deess 1997b: 221.
37. *Taz*, 11/21/88.
38. *Neues Deutschland* (ND), 11/19/1988.
39. See ND, 11/25/88, and coverage in *Taz*, 11/24/88.
40. In stAL sed iv f-5/2/054.
41. See stAL sed iv f-5/2/054, especially "Aktennotiz Aussprache mit Genossen Dr. S."
42. See pkk reports in stAL sed iv f-5/2/054.
43. "Gespräch mit Herrn Thomas H. am 12.28.1988." stAL sed iv f-5/2/054.
44. *Taz*, 11/23/88.
45. See report in sapmo-barch dy 30/2182.
46. stAL sed iv f-5/2/054. The same point was made to me in an interview with a Leipzig woman employed as a librarian in a medical institute; she reported that it was only after the ban that everyone began passing around copies of *Sputnik*. Author's interview with Pürschel, Leipzig, 7/22/1998.
47. sapmo-barch dy 30/iv/2/2.039/336, pp. 37–40.
48. sapmo-barch dy 30/2182.
49. See stAL sed iv f-2/2/027, p. 53.
50. Ibid., p. 85.
51. stAL sed iv f-5/1/065.
52. stAL sed iv f-5/2/054.
53. Ibid.
54. stAL sed iv f-5/1/063, pp. 187–90.
55. sapmo-barch, dy 30/iv/2/2.039/330.
56. See Werner 1996: 47. For protest in technical schools, see sapmo-barch dy 30/2182.
57. Walder explains: "Within the party-state apparatus and between the lower rungs of this apparatus and the citizenry—party power has depended upon, and varied according to, the dependence of subordinates upon superiors for the satisfaction of needs (organized dependence), the capacity of superiors to obtain information about the activities of subordinates (monitoring capacity), and the capacity of superiors to reward or punish the political behavior or utterances of subordinates (sanctioning capacity)" (1994: 300–301).
58. Solnick argues that, in an effort to institute bureaucratic decentralization, Gorbachev's reforms unintentionally weakened the monitoring capacity of the state. Reform encouraged lower-ranking officials and technical experts to attack their superiors and denounce official ideology as a rationalization for the exploitation of organizations by officialdom.
59. In this, there is a long line of German Communists including Wolfgang Leonard, Rudolf Bahro, Robert Havemann, and Wolf Biermann, whose ideologically inspired

dissidence led to their exclusion from the party. The loyalty of East Germany's best novelists—such as Christa Wolf, Stefan Heym, and Christoph Hein—did not preclude conflict with the party leadership, which condemned their explorations of the problems of socialist society. Similar tendencies can be observed in the history of the USSR (Trotsky, Sakharov), Eastern Europe (Jacek Kuron), and the People's Republic of China (Wei Jingsheng).

60. As Anthony Oberschall posited in light of the Hungarian rebellion of 1956, "In a totalitarian society, opposition movements can occur only when mobilization is initiated by dissidents from within the Party who gain temporary control of some organizations and associations normally under Party control and use this base for further mobilization" (1973: 128).

3. No Exit

1. For an insider account of how Soviet-style Communism was imposed on the GDR, see Wolfgang Leonhard's (1955) memoir of his work with the returning Moscow émigrés.

2. For a good account of the history of emigration from the GDR, see Hertle 1996. On exit and its implications for political control in the GDR, see Hirschman 1993; Ross 1998; Mueller 1999; Tietzel and Welser 1994; Zapf 1991; Hardin 1974. About 2.7 million East Germans fled the GDR from 1949 to 1961, and during the same period an estimated 500,000 people (some of them previous exiters) moved from West to East. See Klessmann 1988: 321.

3. In May 1956 Erich Apel, the minister for heavy industry, reported that the exit of engineers and technicians threatened "incalculable damage in the area of research and development" and jeopardized the industrial program of the GDR. Apel advocated harsh restrictions on travel, but he also increased salaries, benefits, and privileges for educated cadres. See his letter of 5/26/1956 in Bundesarchiv der Bundesrepublik Deutschland (BArch) DO 1 34/54134 (Bd. 72), pp. 1–3.

4. *Berliner Zeitung* (BZ), 8/11–12/01.

5. See Ministry of the Interior (MdI) report dated 2/13/61 in BArch DO 1 34/54134 (Bd. 60).

6. See official reports printed in BZ, 8/14/61.

7. See report of February 1984 in Stiftung Archiv Parteien und Massenorganisationen der Deutschen Demokratischen Republik im Bundesarchiv (SAPMO-BArch) DY 30/IV/2/2.039/308, p. 48. It was estimated that in the late 1980s the annual cost of maintaining closed borders reached about $2.2 billion a year (*Die Tageszeitung*, 8/13/01).

8. Order of August 3, 1967, in BArch DO 1 34/54135 (Bd. 20), pp. 8–10.

9. MdI report in BArch DO 1 34/54136 (Bd. C), p. 11.

10. See BArch DO 1 34/54135, pp. 9–13, and ibid., p. 1.

11. Ibid., pp. 11.

12. See ibid., pp. 1–4. In all, between 1963 and 1989 33,755 prisoners were ransomed by West Germany. These "sales" netted the GDR a total of about 3.5 billion DM

(Przyblyski 1992: 294). In using forced emigration as a tactic of political control, the GDR was not alone. In Czechoslovakia during the mid-1980s, the secret police compelled or induced about 300 of the 1,200 signatories of Charter 77 to emigrate to the West (Swain and Swain 1993: 173).

13. For historical discussions of the post-totalitarian or "welfarist" dictatorship in the GDR, see Ross 2002; Fulbrook 1995; Jarausch 1999; Kocka 1999.

14. There is an enormous literature on the Stasi. See, among others, Fricke 1991; Bundesbeauftragte 1995; Siebenmorgen 1993; Müller-Engbergs 1996; Wawryzn 1990; Bürgerkomitee Leipzig 1992.

15. Similar trends could be observed elsewhere in the Soviet bloc, discussed under the rubric of "post-Stalinism" or "post-totalitarianism" (Havel 1986; Ekiert 1996).

16. Quoted from Stasi records in MFS Abt. XX (BV-Leipzig) in Archiv Bürgerbewegung e.V., Stadtgeschichtliches Museum Leipzig (ABL) H8.

17. For estimates of comparative militarization rates, see U.S. Arms Control and Disarmament Agency 1984; U.S. Army Country Studies 1987.

18. Wheaton and Kavan note of Czechoslovakia: "An apt if symbolic example of this state of affairs was the preoccupation with country cottages. These modest, largely wooden structures represented not simply temporary flight from city life . . . [but] the relentless confrontation with the ideological" (1992: 9).

19. Allotment gardens (*Schrebergarten* or *Kleingarten*) were a legacy of nineteenth-century social reformers. In the GDR the gardens were treasured as locations of sociability.

20. The North Korean defector Kang Chol-Hwan (2001) recalled what could be gleaned from clandestine listening to South Korean radio broadcasts: "We hungered for a discourse to break the monopoly of lies. In North Korea, all reality is filtered through a single mind-set. Listening to the radio gave us words we needed to express our dissatisfaction. . . . We had plenty of evidence by which to judge the regime—and judge it harshly. What we lacked were the connective elements we needed to tie it all together. The programs furnished us with an overview of the system as a whole: its origins, the reasons for its current difficulties, the absurdity of its official boasting of self-sufficiency in light of its pleading for international aid."

21. See the report of July 1, 1987, Sächsisches Staatsarchiv Leipzig (StAL) SED IV F-5/1/063.

22. StAL SED IV F-5/1/064.

23. See SAPMO-BArch DO 30/IV/2/2.039/309.

24. SAPMO-BArch DY 30/IV/2/2.039/308, pp. 31–33. In the Helsinki accords of the CSCE, the right to emigrate as such was not directly specified (see documents in Stokes 1991: 160–62).

25. See SAPMO-BArch DY 30/IV/2/2.039/308, pp. 112–13, and ibid., pp. 35, 137.

4. *The Birth of Dissident Voice*

1. Our concern is with collective efforts to oppose an authoritarian regime, rather than with individual acts of defiance. Ramet (1995) usefully distinguishes among dissatisfaction, disaffection, and dissent. Dissatisfaction represents grievances with the per-

formance of the system or with certain policies, without necessarily challenging the system or calling its legitimacy into question. Disaffection is discontent more clearly directed at the system itself but is not connected to a program of change. Dissent is political voice aimed at effecting change (35–36).

2. Linz and Stepan (1996) have called the GDR a "frozen" post-totalitarian state. In other socialist regimes, most notably Hungary, movement emergence was facilitated by open struggles between hardliners and reformers (Agocs 1993; Bruszt and Stark 1992; Bruszt 1990; Szabo 1994; Szelenyi and Szelenyi 1994). Where Leninist regimes experimented with various strategies of reform, the relaxation of political control helped to stimulate organized opposition (Zdravomyslova 1996; Walder 1994; Calhoun 1994; Zhao 1997; Guthrie 1995).

3. My focus is on the Union of Protestant [Lutheran] Churches in East Germany (Bund der evangelischen Kirchen in der DDR, BEK), the largest denominational organization, which had about five million members (about 30 percent of the population) in 1986. There were also about one million Catholics and around two hundred thousand members of other religious groups in the GDR (Nowak 1996: 665; SJDDR 1990: 451). Although the Catholic Church served as another pocket of cultural nonconformity in the GDR, the Catholic Church, along with other religious sects, did not sponsor political activism; it mostly worked to maintain ties to the Vatican and preserve the Catholic milieu.

4. From Hempel's address "Tätigkeitsbericht Teil III. Herbstsynode 1989," 10/20/1989, in Bundesarchiv der Bundesrepublik Deutschland (BArch) DO 4 1488, p. 1.

5. See interview with Rainer Eppelmann, GDR Oral History Project, Hoover Institution Archives, pp. 7–8.

6. See the revealing accounts of activist pastors Eppelmann (East Berlin) and Joachim Gauck (Rostock) in the GDR Oral History Project.

7. Interview with Gauck, GDR Oral History Project, p. 17.

8. See report of February 25, 1988, in BArch DO 1 34/54135.

9. Author's interview with Leipzig activist Rainer Müller, 7/18/98.

10. See "MfS JHS Nr. 134/85 (1985)" in Archiv Bürgerbewegung e.V., Stadtgeschichtliches Museum Leipzig (ABL) H9.

11. *Grenzfall*, 11/12/1987.

12. *Streiflichter*, 3/15/1988, in ABL Box 6.

13. "MfS Information Nr. 168/89" in ABL H8. See also Poumet 1996.

14. *Umweltblätter*, 9/27/1989.

15. See "Anlage zur Information Nr. 150/89. Kirchliche Basisgruppen" in Archiv Bürgerbewegung e.V., Stadtgeschichtliches Museum Leipzig, Bestand Arnold (ABL BA) H MfS-PB II, p. 4.

16. *Grenzfall*, 1/12/1988.

17. On peace movements, see Büscher, Wensierski, and Wolschner 1982; Fricke 1984; Neubert 1998.

18. For a detailed analysis of the role of official commemorations in protest, see Pfaff and Yang 2001; but see also Zhou 1993.

19. A decade later, a former IFM activist, Reinhard Schult, expressed the view that the Luxemburg-Liebknecht demonstration was a "catastrophe" for the opposition

movement because repression postponed the development of a GDR-wide opposition (Zweigler 1998: 3). Flam (1998) argues that the willingness of prominent dissidents to accept the deal that sent them to the West instead of risking prison may have undercut the legitimacy of the East German opposition.

20. Stiftung Archiv Parteien und Massenorganisationen der Deutschen Demokratischen Republik im Bundesarchiv (SAPMO-BArch) DY 30/IV/2/2.039/336.

21. See *Die Kirche*, 12/6/1987, in BArch DO 4.

22. See document dated 1/7/88 in BArch DO 4 767, p. 167; also documents in BArch DO 4 768, pp. 17–18.

23. Author's interviews with Church activist Hans-Ulrich Langner, Leipzig, 6/29/98, and with IFM activist Rainer Müller, 7/15/98.

24. Author's interview with Pastor Wonneberger, Leipzig, 6/8/98. See also Wonneberger 1994.

25. Author's interview with IGL activist Uwe Schwabe, Leipzig, 6/8/98. See also notices in *Umweltblätter*, January–February 1989, in ABL Box 4. On the history of nonviolent direct action in Western democracies, see Epstein (1991) and Markovits and Gorski (1993).

26. See the exchange of letters from August–September 1988 in ABL H1.

27. See "Kirchliche Basisgruppen" in ABL BA H Mfs-PB II.

28. The Pleisse was so badly polluted it became a symbol of reckless industrial policy.

29. See "Mfs Hauptabt. xx. Übersicht zu den 4.6.89 geplanten Provokation in Leipzig" in ABL H8.

30. "Der erste Pleisse-Gedenkumzug 1988" in ABL H1.

31. For Stasi reports on the protest, see "Mfs Information über Aktivitäten feindlich-negativer Kräfte in Leipzig im Zusammenhang mit dem 70. Jahrestag der Ermordung von Karl Liebknecht und Rosa Luxemburg, Berlin 16. Jan. 1989. Nr. 25/89" in ABL BA H Mfs-PB II. The original call to protest and first-person accounts can be found in ABL H1.

32. See report of 1/18/89 in BArch DO 4 767, p. 34. See also materials collected in Dietrich and Schwabe (1998) and author's interview with Uwe Schwabe, 6/8/1998.

33. See "Mfs Information über Aktivitäten feindlich-negativer Kräfte in Leipzig" in ABL H8.

34. In "Mfs Hauptabt. xx. Bericht über das 'Friedensgebet' in der Leipziger Nikolaikirche am Montag, 21.03.1988" in ABL H8.

35. "Mfs Bezirksverwaltung Leipzig. Information über eine provokatorische Personenbewegung am 13.3.1989 im Stadtzentrum von Leipzig," Leipzig, 3/14/89, in ABL H8. See also documents concerning activist strategies in Initiative Freiheit und Menschenrechte e.V./Forschungszentrum zu den Verbrechen des Stalinismus, Dresden.

36. See SED security report from August 1989 in SAPMO-BArch DY 30/IV/2/2.039/309, pp. 102–4. On events in Leipzig, see "Mfs Information Nr. 229/89" in ABL BA H Mfs-PB II.

37. "Info.des 1. Sek.der BL Leipzig," Berlin, 5/8/89, in SAPMO-BArch DY 30/2182, p. 84.

38. See report of the Leipzig Round Table investigation in ABL H2.

39. See report of the "Tagung der Konferenz der evangelischen Kirchenleitung in der DDR," 6/2–3/89, in ABL H1. See also "Information und Schlussfolgerung zu einigen aktuellen Fragen der feindlichen Entwicklung auf Bürger der DDR," SAPMO-BArch

DY 30/IV/2/2.039/309, p. 104, and the report of the Saxon State Parliament, "Beschlussempfehlung und Bericht des Sonderausschusses zur Untersuchung von Amts- und Machtmissbrauch infolge der SED Herrschaft," p. 53, in ABL BA.

40. "Erklärung.12.6.1989" in ABL H1, and "China ist nicht fern!" *Umweltblätter*, 6–7/89, ABL Box 4.

41. Mfs Abt. XX, "BDVP. Mfs KD Stadt, VPKA, Kreisdienst. Leipzig, den 10.06.89" in ABL H8.

42. See documents relating to "Leipziger Strassenmusikfestival 1989" in ABL H1.

43. Exit applicants were among the GDR's most valuable citizens: about 70 percent were skilled workers; 17 percent had higher education; and fully 87 percent were under the age of forty. See SED report of 1/16/89 in SAPMO-BArch DY 30/IV/2/2.039/309, p. 9, and report of 6/30/89 in ibid., p. 52.

44. See security report in SAPMO-BArch DY 30/IV/2/2.039/308, p. 64.

45. See SAPMO-BArch DY 30/IV/2/2.039/309, p. 33.

46. BArch DO 1 34/54135, Bd. 8, pp. 9–18.

47. SAPMO-BArch DY 30/IV/2/2.039/308, pp. 95, 108.

48. SAPMO-BArch DY 30/IV/2/2.039/308, p. 115. For the district of origin of legal exiters in 1988, see BArch DO 1 34/29282, I/88–XVII/88. For analysis of patterns of internal and external migration, see Grundmann 1998.

49. SAPMO-BArch DY 30/IV/2/2.039/309, p. 28.

50. Ibid., p. 36.

51. See Stasi report "BV für Staatssicherheit Abt. IX. Bericht über die Untersuchung des Vorkommnises im Anschluss an das Friedensgebet am 22.5.1989 in der Leipziger Innenstadt" in ABL H8.

52. "Mfs Hauptabt. XX. Bericht über das 'Friedensgebet' in der Leipziger Nikolaikirche am Montag, 21.03.1988" in ABL H8.

53. SAPMO-BArch DY 30/IV/2/2.039/308, p. 95, and SAPMO-BArch DY 30/IV/2/2.039/309.

54. *Junge Welt*, 9/6/89.

55. *Leipziger Volkszeitung (LVZ)*, 9/7/89.

56. *LVZ*, 9/8/89.

57. *Umweltblätter*, 9/20/89, in ABL Box 3.

58. See report of September 12, "SED-BL Leipzig, 2. Sek. an ZK der SED, Mitglied des Politbüros und Sek. des ZK, Gen. Horst Dohlus" in ABL BA H MDI 15.

59. See "SED-BL Leipzig, 2. Sek. Empfänger: ZK der SED, Mitglied des Politbüros und Sek. des ZK, Genossen Horst Dohlus" in ABL H15. The pastor's sermon drew on Luke 12:11–12; see Hanisch et al. 1996.

60. See participant account in "Montagsdemo am 18. September 1989" in ABL H1.

61. Sermon in Dietrich and Schwabe 1994: 419.

62. Hanisch et al. 1996: 28.

63. "Konferenzbericht Landesbischof Dr. Johannes Hempel," 9/18/89, in ABL H1.

5. Triggering Insurgent Voice

1. The Leipzig protest on October 9 is one of the greatest instances of urban rebellion. Gould (1995: 9) argues that "the [Paris] Commune mobilized more people [around

100,000] than has any urban movement before or since." In spite of real threats, on October 9 in Leipzig between 70,000 (police estimate) and 120,000 (Opp, Voss and Gern's [1995] estimate) people took part in protest, or roughly between 13 and 22 percent of the city's population (550,000 in 1989). That is significantly higher than the mobilization rate Gould observed (in 1870 the Paris population was around 1.8 million, yielding a mobilization rate of about 6 percent for the Commune). Even if we assume that the Leipzig protests probably drew in participants from the greater Leipzig district (population of approximately 1.3 million), that still yields a mobilization rate of between 5 and 9 percent on October 9. In the case of Beijing in 1989, an estimated one million people took part in anti-regime protest on May 16, 1989, or about 8 percent of the city's population (around 12 million in 1989). In Prague on November 17, 1989, some 55,000 protesters, or about 4.6 percent of the city's population (about 1.2 million in 1989), protested in spite of an aggressive deployment of police and troops. Although the Paris Commune involved armed insurgency, with an obviously greater risk of death, the revolutions of 1989 call into doubt Gould's claim for the unsurpassed level of Communard mobilization. For a comparison of protest in Eastern Europe and China in 1989, see Pfaff and Yang 2001.

2. Quoted in Jarausch and Gransow 1994: 35.

3. On reform in Hungary and its negotiated "exchange of systems," see, among others, Bruszt and Stark 1992, 1998; Kornai 1992; Agocs 1993; Arato 1994; Szabo 1994; Szelenyi and Szelenyi 1994.

4. See Henry Kamm, "East Germans Put Hungary in a Bind," *New York Times* (NYT), 9/1/89.

5. See internal SED report of 7/14/89 in Stiftung Archiv Parteien und Massenorganisationen der Deutschen Demokratischen Republik im Bundesarchiv (SAPMO-BArch) DY 30/IV/2/2.039/309, pp. 41–48.

6. See the SED security report of 10/24/89 in SAPMO-BArch DY 30/IV/2/2.039/309, pp. 147–48.

7. See, e.g., "Mit internationalem Recht unvereinbar" and "Wortbuch und völkerrechtswidriges Handeln," *Sächsisches Tageblatt* (ST), 10/5/89.

8. Privately, the Soviet foreign minister, Eduard Shevardnadze, was willing to accept the flight of one or two million East Germans rather than try to stop them by force. Soviet reformists were certainly not trying to topple the GDR, but they regarded Honecker as a burden they were unwilling to prop up. See Zelikow and Rice 1995: 74–75; also Kotkin 2001.

9. Special expulsion trains carried 15,598 exiters through the middle of October. See MdI reports in Bundesarchiv der Bundesrepublik Deutschland (BArch) DO 1 34/55247 and report of 10/24/89 in SAPMO-BArch DY 30/IV/2/2.039/309, pp. 146–47. See also Serge Schmemann, "More than 6,000 East Germans Swell Tide of Refugees to the West," NYT, 10/1/89.

10. "Zur zeitweiligen Aussetzung des pass- und visafreien Verkehrs mit der CSSR," ST, 10/5/89.

11. Interview with Oskar Fischer, GDR Oral History Project, Hoover Institution Archives.

12. See SAPMO-BArch DY 30/IV/2/2.039/76, pp. 45–53.

13. See SAPMO-BArch DY 30/IV/2/2.039/77, pp. 1–5.

14. See "Notizen, 17.9.1989." in ibid., pp. 30–36.

15. See memo to Honecker in SAPMO-BArch DY 30/IV/2/2.039/309, pp. 142–3.

16. *Neues Deutschland*, 10/2/1989.

17. See SAPMO-BArch DY 30/IV/2/2.039/309, pp. 99–107. See also Mitter and Wolle 1990: 46–71. A greater estimate has been made by the German sociologist Detlef Pollack (1990), who estimated the number as being as many as 10,000–15,000 activists and sympathizers scattered across the GDR. Even if Pollack's estimate is more accurate, this is a minuscule percentage of the population.

18. Cited in Sächsischer Landtag (SL), appendix, p. 5.

19. See documents collected in SL, "Bericht des Sonderausschusses zur Untersuchung von Amts- und Machtmissbrauch infolge der SED-Herrschaft," pp. 1–35 and 737–67. Archiv Bürgerbewegung e.V., Stadtgeschichtliches Museum Leipzig, Bestand Arnold (ABL BA). Based on survey results from a year after the events of 1989, Karl-Dieter Opp and his colleagues report that approximately 5 percent of Leipzigers were involved in the opposition *before* October 9 (Opp, Voss, and Gern 1995: 21). Given a population of approximately 530,000 people, this would mean that there were more than 25,000 people involved in opposition groups in Leipzig. The actual percentage of people involved in alternative political groups before the breakthrough must have been much smaller—probably no more than 1 percent. Rink and Hofmann (1991) and Pollack (1990) suggest that no more than 1 percent of East Germans, fewer than 5,000 in Leipzig, had any connection at all to alternative political groups and movements. Even if we were to take as "members of opposition groups" the minimum definition of people who had done no more than attend a demonstration or sign the petition endorsing the founding statement of New Forum, this would still yield far fewer people prior to October 9. As late as that date, for example, fewer than 20,000 people in the entire GDR had signed the New Forum petition. Hartmann and Pollack (1998) found that about 5 percent of Leipzigers were churchgoers. It may be that anyone associated with the Church before October 9 considered himself or herself a member of the opposition, thereby accounting for Opp's findings. In either case, only a small fraction of Leipzigers could have been involved in oppositional activities of any kind before the exiting crisis.

20. SL, appendix, pp. 737–79.

21. Gorbachev's visit to China raised expectations that reform was possible, amplified dissident voices, and was interpreted as a reproach to Communist leaders (see Calhoun 1994: 65–67).

22. See BArch DO 1 2.3/052449.

23. Report of the East German news service, A.D.N., 10/8/89.

24. With 29.8 percent of the total GDR population in 1988, Saxon districts accounted for 53 percent of exit visas granted; calculated from figures provided in MdI in BArch DO 1 34/29282.

25. Sächsisches Staatsarchiv Leipzig (StAL) SED IV F-2/3/118, pp. 38–39.

26. SAPMO-BArch DY 30/2182, pp. 103–6.

27. StAL SED IV F-2/2/029.

28. stAL SED IV F-5/1/08.
29. See police reports on riots and "provocative" assemblies in October in BArch DO 1/2.3/052445. See also Lindner 1994.
30. Stasi reports in SL, appendix, pp. 101–2 and 126–28.
31. See "Bericht zu den Ereignissen am Dresdner Hauptbahnhof in der Nacht vom 04. u. 05. Oktober 1989," Archiv Bürgerbewegung e.V., Stadtgeschichtliches Museum Leipzig (ABL) H1.
32. See telegram to the MfS headquarters in SL, appendix, pp. 160–70.
33. BArch DO 1 2.3/052449.
34. Report of Klaus Kurske, "Augenzeugenbericht über die Demonstration in Dresden am 7.10.1989," October 9, 1989, ABL H1.
35. One bystander reported, "Something so outrageous I had never seen before and, as if possessed, I began to shout with all my strength, 'We don't want violence!' I had to shout that—it had to come out. Two seconds later I started to receive blows from a billy club and everything went black." "Erlebnisbericht 7.10–12.10.89," 10/17/89, ABL H1.
36. See "Augenzeugenbericht der Demonstration in Dresden am 8.10.89" and "Erlebnisbericht über meine Zuführung am 8.10.89 auf Fetscherplatz in Dresden gegen 17:30 Uhr," ABL H1.
37. SL, appendix, p. 251.
38. BArch DO 1 2.3/052449.
39. Ibid., p. 1469.
40. See Leipziger Volkszeitung (LVZ), 10/3/89.
41. LVZ, 10/6/1989.
42. stAL SED IV F-5/1/070, p. 6.
43. ST 10/9/89.
44. MdI BArch DO1 2.3/052449.
45. Opp and his colleagues (Opp 1991, 1992; Opp and Gern 1993; Opp, Voss, and Gern 1993, 1995) have provided us with the most complete sociological picture of the Leipzig protests based on the evaluation of survey, interview, and secondary data.
46. Analysis of participant narratives in the October Monday demonstrations found in Neues Forum Leipzig 1991 and Lindner and Grüneberger 1992 (270 pages of text, ca. 74,000 words, with thirty-three participants [23 rank-and-file protesters, 10 activists]) reveals widespread fear even among these "activists of the first hour." For a full discussion, see Goodwin and Pfaff 2001.
47. On October 16, between 10,000 and 20,000 people traveled to the city to take part in the Monday demonstration according to the district transit police, see stAL SED IV F-2/1/14, p. 92.
48. As an example of the elementary mobilizing efforts of New Forum during this nascent period, see "Offener Brief des NF Leipzig: An die Bürger der DDR!" Neues Forum Leipzig, September 17, 1989, ABL H17.
49. See interview in Die Tageszeitung (Taz), 10/4/89.
50. MfS Bezirksverwaltung, Abt. II, "Information Nr. 812/89," Leipzig, 10/7/89, ABL H8.
51. See planning report for MfS activities in the Leipzig district for 1989 in "BV

für Staatssicherheit Abt. xx. Jahresplan des Leiters der Abt. xx. Leipzig, 28.12.1988," ABL H9.

52. Michael Arnold, IGL, "Friedensgebet in der Nikolaikirche. Thema: Auftrag and Dienst der Kirche," Leipzig, 5/8/89, in ABL H1.

53. See "Wir, die Arbeitsgruppe Menschenrechte," Leipzig, 9/12/89, in ABL H2.

54. See report "Rat des Bezirkes Leipzig. Stellvertreter des Vorsitzenden des Rates für Inneres. Leipzig, den 16.03.1989," in ABL H15.

55. SAPMO-BArch DY 30/IV/2/2.039/330, pp. 23–30.

56. See BL–SED, "Information über eine erneute Provokation feindlich-negativer Kräfte im Abschluss an das Montagsgebet in der Nikolaikirche Leipzig am 2.10.1989," 10/3/89, in ABL H15.

57. MfS, "Auswertungs- und Kontrolgruppe, Leipzig 05.10.89: Aufstellung der Hinweise über konkrete Aktivitäten und Auswertung des Einflusses des 'Neuen Forums,' " in ABL H8.

58. See Siever's recollections in the manuscript "Eine zweite Kirche öffnet sich" in ABL H1.

59. Proverbs 25:15, 28: "With patience a prince is overcome, and a mild tongue can break bones." "A man lacking self-control is like a fallen city without walls."

60. Max Weber (1978: 23) observed, "Social action is not identical either with similar actions of many persons or with every action influenced by other persons. Thus, if at the beginning of a rain shower a number of people on the street put up their umbrellas at the same time, this would not ordinarily be a case of action mutually oriented to that of each other, but rather of all reacting in the same way to the like need for protection from the rain."

61. See the anonymous testimonial "Erlebnisbericht vom 9.10.89, Leipzig," in ABL H1.

62. These data are compiled from Stasi reports in ABL H8 on demonstrations and arrests at nine demonstrations between 5/8/89 and 9/11/89. The data permit partial reconstruction of the social profile of the protesters: 81 percent were male; the protesters were on average 26.8 years old; 22 percent were exit applicants; 65 percent were skilled and unskilled workers; and in all 435 were arrested.

63. Psychologically oriented theories of collective behavior posit a relationship between frustrated goals at the individual level and social unrest. Rebellions are born of social grievances, frustration of individual interests and expectations, and the collapsing enforcement of norms (Useem 1998; Smelser 1962; Davies 1962; Gurr 1970). Citizens rebel after experiencing long periods of economic and social progress followed by a short period of reversal, famously expressed as Davies's (1962) J-curve theory of revolution. Gurr (1970) argued that the greater the relative deprivation, the greater the likelihood and intensity of violence. In chapter 2 we saw evidence to support the possibility of relative deprivation, as a relatively wealthy socialist state suffered severe economic reverses beginning in the mid-1980s. However, frustration-aggression and related breakdown theories of collective behavior typically predict violence, which was notably absent in the East German case.

64. See the testimonial of Kersten K., "Es geschah am 7. Oktober," in ABL H1.

65. Quoted in *Taz*, 10/10/89.

6. Fight or Flight?

1. *Leipziger Volkszeitung*, 10/28–29/89.
2. Duncan J. Watts (1999: 511) notes that "the introduction of a single shortcut is likely to connect vertices that were previously widely separated. This shortcut then contracts the distance not only between that pair of vertices but also between their immediate neighborhoods, their neighborhoods' neighborhoods, and so on."
3. Demographic data suggest differences between exiters and protesters: the latter tended to be more college educated than the former. Data from Leipzig protests show that workers were underrepresented in demonstrations (Mühler and Wilsdorf 1991). This may have been a result of prior emigration, as skilled technical and craft workers could expect immediate improvement in their labor market position. But people with higher education confronted an obstacle in the lower relative portability of socialist educational credentials. And equivalent professional and administrative positions were rarely available in the West (Hardin 1974). For descriptive data on emigrants, see Grundmann 1998; *SJDDR* 1990; Bundestag 1995.
4. The data are inclusive of all counties and municipalities of the GDR plus the city of (East) Berlin, for a total of 215 counties and municipalities. Three counties (Kalbe, Saalkreis, and Tangerhütte) had missing estimates for emigration and were therefore excluded from the analysis.
5. Results from measuring exit based on the total number of exiters throughout the whole period were also determined through statistical analyses and largely correspond to those reported here.
6. One may argue for a non-monotonous relationship (such as an inverted-U, see Gurr 1970) between state coercion and political rebellion. A squared "Logged Number of Arrests," however, had no statistically significant effects on either the Number of Protests or Logged Average Participation Rate. Nor did its inclusion affect the inverted-U relationship between each of the dependent variables and exit rate.

7. Why Was There No "Chinese Solution"?

1. In September 1989 there had been just 7 protest events recorded by the Interior Ministry. In October there were 139 protest events; in November, 530; in December, 428; in January 1990, 248; in February, 386; and in the weeks leading up to the March 1990 elections, 35, as revolutionary mass mobilization subsided with the ouster of the Communist government. The same pattern can be observed in protest participation. From a total of fewer than 8,000 participants in protests in the month of September, there grew to be 800,000 in October; 4.2 million in November; 1.7 million in December 1989 and January 1990; and 1.6 million in February, rapidly dwindling to 56,000 in the first two weeks of March.
2. Both the People's Republic of China and the GDR explicitly rejected Gorbachev's calls for democratization and continued to harass, jail, and exile prominent dissidents. In China, however, extensive market reforms appear to have weakened political control at universities and other institutions, though the party rejected calls for

political pluralism. Recent documentation suggests that beneath the surface unity of party leaders a split developed between advocates and opponents of liberalization. The division may account for why it took the regime so long to respond with effective repression against the student movement. However, as Dingxin Zhao (2001) notes, no major party leader openly encouraged or facilitated the Beijing student movement. The chief difference of opinion within the party elite appears to have concerned how the movement should be suppressed. In the end, the threat of "turmoil" and the memory of the student-led Cultural Revolution seem to have persuaded the party leadership to heed Deng Xiaoping's call to quash the movement. See Zhang Liang 2001. For official versions of events, see Che Muqi 1990 and Jian Shi et al. 1993. See also Zhao 2000; Lin 1992; Calhoun 1994.

3. See the first-person accounts by Politburo members Egon Krenz, Werner Eberlein, Oskar Fischer, and Kurt Hager in the GDR Oral History Project, Hoover Institution Archives, as well as published recollections in Schabowski 1991 and Eberlein 2000.

4. "Gorbachev in Finland Disavows Any Right of Regional Intervention," *New York Times* (NYT), 10/25/89.

5. See, e.g., the statement of Joachim Herrmann in Jarausch and Gransow 1994: 35 and "Egon Krenz in Peking: Vereint durch gleiche Ideale," *Sächsisches Tageblatt*, 10/3/89.

6. See the final report of the Sächsischer Landtag (Saxon State Parliament) on the abuse of official power in the GDR, "Beschlussempfehlung und Bericht des Sonderausschusses zur Untersuchung von Amts- und Machtmissbrauch infolge der SED-Herrschaft" (hereafter abbreviated as SL), pp. 23–25.

7. See Sächsisches Staatsarchiv Leipzig (STAL) SED IV F-2/3/118, p. 41. On the role of the National Security Council and district security committees in October 1989, see Friedheim 1997.

8. MfS directives of 10/8/89, in Archiv Bürgerbewegung e.V., Stadtgeschichtliches Museum Leipzig (ABL) H8.

9. National Defense Council directive Nr. 9/89, 10/13/89, in Archiv Bürgerbewegung e.V., Stadtgeschichtliches Museum Leipzig, Bestand Arnold (ABL BA) H NVR O.

10. STAL SED IV F-2/3/118.

11. SL, p. 163, pp. 93–115.

12. MfS Leipzig memo of 10/7/89 in ABL H8.

13. See district police directives of 10/3/89 in Bundesarchiv der Bundesrepublik Deutschland (BArch) DO 1 2.3/052449, p. 1469.

14. Hummitzsch's statement in STAL SED IV F-2/1/017, p. 89.

15. Ibid., pp. 55–56.

16. Statement of Comrade Rosch in STAL SED IV F-2/1/017, p. 87.

17. Ibid., pp. 85–87.

18. See district party instructions of 9/27/89 in STAL SED IV F-2/3/118.

19. On the history of the militias, see Koop 1997. See also coverage in *Die Tageszeitung* (*Taz*) 10/7/89.

20. Koop 1997: 20.

21. Party militia units often resembled volunteer fire departments more than militant Leninist cadres. For example, the Leipzig PKK reported that during a training session

a battalion commander allowed "a great quantity of alcohol to be brought along," creating widespread drunkenness and leading to one militiaman going missing. See PKK report of 5/23/89 in StAL SED IV F-5/07/060.

22. SPKK Leipzig, StAL SED IV F-5/01/063, pp. 205–6.

23. See police memo of October 13, 1989, in BArch DO 1 2.3/052445, p. 742.

24. See the account of Rainer Klepzig, militia unit commander in StAL SED IV F-2/1/017.

25. StaL SED IV F-5/2/051.

26. See comments of Peter Zetscher in StAL SED IV F-5/1/008, pp. 165–66.

27. Quoted in *Taz*, 10/10/89.

28. See SED situation report of 10/9/89 in ABL H15.

29. See "Auszüge aus dem Brief einer Bereitschaftspolizisten in seiner Seelsorge," Dresdner Kreuzkirche, 10/10/89, in ABL H1.

30. SL, p. 36.

31. Interview with Eberlein, GDR Oral History Project, p. 25.

32. "Erlebnisbericht der Demonstration in Dresden am 7.10.1989" in ABL H1.

33. See the accounts of Western reporters in *Taz*, 10/9/89 and 10/11/89; see also Zwahr 1993.

34. Meyer in StAL SED IV F-2/1/013, pp. 55, 57.

35. Hackenberg in StAL SED IV F-2/2/029, p. 16.

36. See statements of Heinz Fröhlich and Joachim Prag in StAL SED IV F-5/1/08, pp. 12–13.

37. See report on "hostile influences" of 7/7/89 in StAL SED IV F-5/01/063, p. 189. Figure cited in StAL SED IV F-2/3/118.

38. StAL SED IV F-2/3/118.

39. See "SED Bezirksleitung Leipzig. Information zur politischen Lage im Bezirk," 10/10/89, in StAL SED IV F-5/2/053, p. 3.

40. See the letters and petitions from October 1989 collected in ABL H1 and StAL SED IV F-5/1/069 and SED IV F-5/1/070.

41. See resolution of the SED municipal organization of 10/8/89 in StAL SED IV F-5/1/039.

42. For details of the crumbling consensus among regional officials as the prologue to October 9, see StAL SED IV F-5/1/08, p. 41.

43. Meyer's account in StAL SED IV F-5/1/09, p. 54.

44. Ibid., p. 55.

45. Ibid., p. 56. Note that the historical evidence contradicts Krenz's later claim that it was his personal intervention that prevented violence on October 9. In fact, Krenz journeyed to Leipzig on October 13—that is, after the critical moment. Apparently, the conservative "reformers" within the SED had played an opportunist's game, only moving against Honecker when assured of the complete failure of his political line (see also Neubert 1998: 853–55). News reporters unwittingly created the impression that party elites in East Berlin had made the Saxon miracle possible. See, e.g., Craig Whitney, "How the Wall Was Cracked—A Special Report; Party Coup Turned East Germany's Tide," NYT, 11/17/89. Reporters on the scene in Saxony, however, noted that Politburo orders to stop protest by "all necessary means" remained in force until after the events of October 9; see, e.g., A. Smoltcyzck, "Feuert's Magazine leer bis zur

letzen Mumpel! Als am 9. Oktober in Leipzig Tausende demonstrieren, wird um 15 Uhr 30 Munition an bewaffnete Einheiten verteilt," *Taz*, 11/24/89. Krenz was not the first old-regime figure to masquerade as a reformist; once Louis XVI was at the mercy of the mob, he too donned the revolutionary cockade.

46. "Berghofer: In Dresden waren die Panzer bereits aufgefahren," *Volksblatt* (East Berlin), 11/30/89, and "In Dresden waren im Oktober schon Panzer aufgefahren," *Der Tagesspiegel* (West Berlin), 11/30/89.

47. See Modrow's letter explaining his actions to the Central Committee in SL, p. 231.

48. See "Protokoll 22. Sitzung der Bezirksleitung am 21. November 1989," in STAL SED IV F-5/2/039, especially pp. 90–91.

49. Chong (1991: 22–23) makes the following observations of this strategy: "From the protesters' perspective, it is obvious that the best outcome is realized when they choose nonviolence while the authorities use unjustified force. A nonviolent strategy only works if the protesters are seen as blameless victims. . . . The worst fear of the protesters is that they will be the ones to perpetrate violence while the authorities behave in a lawful, responsible fashion. . . . Only less slightly undesirable is an outbreak of violence between the two parties, since the protesters likely would be routed and yet would be seen to be at least partially responsible for the bloodshed."

50. See Berghofer's recollections in *Der Tagesspiegel*, 11/30/89.

8. Activists of the First Hour

1. "BV Staatssicherheit, Dresden, Info. Nr. 136/89," 10/9/89, Sächsischer Landtag (SL), p. 251.

2. See internal affairs report on petitions to legalize New Forum in Bundesarchiv der Bundesrepublik Deutschland (BARCH) DO 1 34/40845–40847.

3. See MFS report of 10/30/89 in Archiv Bürgerbewegung e.V., Stadtgeschichtliches Museum Leipzig (ABL), Bestand Arnold (BA) H MFS-PB Teil II.

4. Quoted in *Umweltblätter*, 9/89, in ABL B4.

5. "Aufbruch 89—Neues Forum," in Michaelis 1990.

6. See "Argumente für den Dialog," NF Berlin, 10/28/89, in ABL H17.

7. Founding declaration of Democracy Now (Demokratie Jetzt), titled "Aufruf zur Einmischung in eigener Sachen!" 9/12/89, in ABL H4.

8. See pamphlets "Bürgerbewegung Demokratie Jetzt: Was können wir tun?" 10/89, and "Demokratie Jetzt: Zeitung der Bürgerbewegung, No. 2," 10/89, in ABL H4.

9. See "Gemeinsame Erklärung," 10/4/89, in ABL H1.

10. See "Liebe Freunde und Freundinnen des Neues Forum!" Berlin, 10/1/89, in ABL H17. Erich Mielke noted in a report to the Politburo that New Forum leaders were committed to the GDR and would not threaten the "leading role of the party." See Mielke's appraisal in the MFS report of 10/30/89, in ABL BA H MFS-PB Teil II.

11. See interviews with IFM activists Wolfgang Templin and Stefan Hilsberg, GDR Oral History Project, Hoover Institution Archives.

12. Interview with Templin, GDR Oral History Project, p. 8.

13. "Erklärung des Neuen Forums zum 40. Jahrestag der DDR: An alle Mitglieder der SED!" 10/7/89, in ABL H17.

14. *Tageszeitung (Taz)*, 9/26/89.

15. *Taz*, 10/5/89.

16. *Taz*, 10/16/89.

17. See "Die Mauer ist gefallen," New Forum, Berlin, 11/12/89, in ABL H17.

18. *Taz*, 11/11/89.

19. *Taz*, 12/4/89.

20. Ibid.

21. Interview with Ullmann in *Taz*, 12/15/89; see also *Taz*, 11/18/89.

22. *Taz*, 11/13/89.

23. "Programmerklärung des Neuen Forum," 1/27/89, in Mathias-Domaschk-Archiv, Robert-Havemann-Gesellschaft e.V. Berlin, NFO 135/136.

24. See transcript of the founding congress of New Forum, "Protokoll der NF-Gründungskonferenz, 27–26 Januar 1999," in Mathias-Domaschk-Archiv, NFO 135/136.

25. Ibid.

26. "Neues Forum Nr. 1 1989: Was tun? Was tun!" 11/7/89, in ABL H17.

27. See, e.g., New Forum Berlin, "Ansätze zur Basisdemokratie," 10/23/89, in ABL H17.

28. Author's interviews with Uwe Schwabe and Rainer Müller, 7/18/98.

29. See Mathias-Domaschk-Archiv, NFO 047–055.

30. "Aufruf des Neuen Forums," 10/12/89, in ABL H17.

31. "Neues Forum Informationsblatt Nr. 3." Leipzig, 10/30/89, in ABL H17.

32. Interior Ministry report of 1/5/90, in BARCH DO 1 2.3/052455.

33. *Taz*, 11/1/89.

34. Lässig, "Rede nach der Demo. am 23.10.1989," in ABL H17.

35. "Rede vor dem Rathaus zur Demonstration am 6.11.89," in ABL H17.

36. "Neues Forum Leipzig: Informationsblatt Nr. 5," Leipzig, 11/14/89, in ABL H17.

37. "Rede zur Demonstration am 13.11.1989 in Leipzig," in ABL H17.

38. *Taz*, 11/29/89.

39. See report in BARCH DO 1 2.3/052449.

40. *Panorama*, Nr. 455/89, 12/12/1989, in ABL H17.

41. *Leipziger Volkszeitung (LVZ)*, 12/12/1989.

42. *Taz*, 12/20/89.

43. LVZ, 11/20/1989, and *Taz*, 11/20/89.

44. BARCH DO 1 2.3/052449; see also state security report in ABL BA H MFS-PB II.

45. LVZ, 12/5/1989.

46. Author's interview with participant Hans-Ulrich Langner, Leipzig, 7/22/98.

47. See report of 2/15/90 in BARCH DO 1 2.3/052445.

48. See coverage in LVZ, 1/30/1990 and 2/6/1990; see also *Taz*, 2/7/90.

49. LVZ, 2/13/1990.

50. *Sächsisches Tageblatt*, 2/20/1990; see also *Taz*, 2/14/90.

51. See coverage in LVZ, 1/11/90.

52. *Taz*, 3/14/90.

53. The Monday demonstration on 2/19/90 still drew about 50,000 people; see LVZ, 2/20/1990.

54. Report of 3/12/90 in BARCH DO 1 2.3/052445.

55. *Taz*, 3/12/90.

56. Labor activist Roland May in *lvz*, 1/22/90; and "Zur Arbeit und Bildung von Betriebsräten," Bürgerkomitee Leipzig, 2/13/90, in ABL H4.

57. *Taz*, 12/4/89.

58. *lvz*, 12/12/89.

59. See "Herbst '89—ein Jahr danach: Ursachen und Folgen einer gescheiterten Revolution," address at the University of Leipzig, 10/8/90, in ABL H16.

60. As Sigrid Meuschel (1992: 319–20) observes, "Workers demonstrated after quitting time; technicians and engineers did not seize the plants; students did not take over their universities. The revolution broke out along the lines of rulers and ruled, between society and party-state, between the 'we' and the 'them.'"

61. For detailed accounts of the "Velvet Revolution" in Prague, see Garton Ash 1993; Judt 1992; Wheaton and Kavan 1992; Glenn 1999.

62. See *Taz*, 11/27/89; see also "Millions of Czechoslovaks Increase Pressure on Party with Two-Hour General Strike," *New York Times*, 11/27/89.

63. See Judt 1992 and Wheaton and Kavan 1992; see also insightful reporting in *Taz*, 11/29/89.

64. On the role of the dissidents in the post-Communist transition, see Linz and Stepan 1996. As the dissident Jan Urban noted on the eve of the dissolution of Czechoslovakia, "Because of our anti-political way of existing as political creatures before the change, we were bound to lose—unless we ourselves changed into politicians. By now we know we have failed" (Linz and Stepan 1996: 321).

65. See Mathias-Domaschk-Archiv, NFO 047–055: "Unterschriftenlister der Unterstützungserklärungen zum Neuen Forum."

66. My focus will be on New Forum, the largest and best organized of the various social movement organizations that composed the East German civic movement. The next largest civic movement organization, Democracy Now, had only about four thousand members as late as January 1990, falling to about six hundred in June 1991 (see Wielgohs 1994).

67. The original petition and membership lists are collected in Mathias-Domaschk-Archiv, NFO 047–055.

68. In the Rostock district, shipbuilding and transportation were the major industries; each of the districts of Berlin, Dresden, and Erfurt accounted for about 15 percent or more of the total GDR production of microelectronics (*sjDDR* 1989).

69. For an early reflection on the economic contradictions of democratic reform in Leninist societies, see Hardin 1974.

70. *Taz*, 12/19/89.

71. Interview with Rainer Eppelmann, GDR Oral History Project, p. 26.

72. Reinhold and Heym quoted in Volker and Jarausch 1994.

73. Lässig, "Herbst '89—ein Jahr danach," in ABL H 16.

9. Reunification as Collective Exit

1. For a first-rate survey of the state of transition research, see Bunce 2003.

2. Modrow was on an official visit to Stuttgart in late September 1989 when *Der Spiegel*

(10/2/89) praised him; at that time, the *Stuttgarter Zeitung* described him as "open to reforms" and a leader who "rejects Stalinist methods in dealing with dissidents" (Friedrich 1994: 17).

3. See interviews with regime insiders Werner Eberlein, Oskar Fischer, Kurt Hager and Egon Krenz in the GDR Oral History Project, Hoover Institution Archives.

4. See *Leipziger Volkszeitung* (LVZ), 10/28−29/89.

5. "Informationen: Zum Neuen Forum und zu anderen illegaler oppositionellen Gruppierungen in der DDR," SED Infoblatt, October 1989, 1989/7, Nr. 261, in Archiv Bürgerbewegung e.V., Stadtgeschichtliches Museum Leipzig (ABL) H17.

6. See report of 11/2/89 in Stiftung Archiv Parteien und Massenorganisationen der Deutschen Demokratischen Republik im Bundesarchiv (SAPMO-BArch) DY 30/IV/2/2.039/330, pp. 65−66.

7. Report of 11/13/89 in SAPMO-BArch DY 30/IV/2/2.039/330, pp. 71−72.

8. Central Committee briefing of 10/2089 in SAPMO-BArch DY 30/IV/2/2.039/330, p. 60.

9. Bundesarchiv der Bundesrepublik Deutschland (BArch) DO 1 2.3/052445.

10. See district situation briefing of 9/11/89 in Sächsisches Staatsarchiv Leipzig (StAL) SED IV F-5/1/051, pp. 11−14.

11. StAL SED IV F-2/3/117, p. 18.

12. *LVZ*, 10/17/89, 10/24/89, and 10/31/89.

13. See memo of 10/14/89 in Sächsischer Landtag (SL), p. 469.

14. StAL SED IV F-2/1/014, p. 32.

15. Comments of Ludwig Schwarzbauer, ibid., p. 76.

16. Ibid., pp. 90−91.

17. Ibid., p. 63.

18. See PKK report of 10/26/89 in StAL SED IV F-5/1/054, p. 2.

19. StAL SED IV F-2/3/118, p. 19.

20. Ibid., p. 51.

21. Comments of Bernd Seidel, ibid., p. 142.

22. StAL SED IV F-2/1/015, pp. 8−59.

23. *Die Tageszeitung (Taz)*, 11/8/89.

24. StAL SED IV F-5/1/009, p. 53.

25. *LVZ*, 11/13/89.

26. Ibid.

27. StAL IV F-2/1/016.

28. Ibid., pp. 63−64.

29. StAL IV F-2/1/017, p. 3.

30. *Taz*, 11/3/89.

31. Content analysis of the larger banners displayed by groups of citizens documented by police surveillance on November 4 (N=76) reveals that 25 clearly expressed anti-party positions, 16 promoted democracy and human rights, 6 attacked official corruption, 5 attacked the Stasi, 9 promoted specific democratic opposition groups, 4 promoted environmental issues, 2 promoted peace and disarmament, and 9 addressed a variety of other issues. Report in MdI, "Information vom 05.11.1989," in BArch DO 1 2.3/052449.

32. See interview with Michael Brie, a PDS founder and philosopher, 12/23/91, GDR Oral History Project.

33. NVR Berlin, 11/10/89, in ABL BA H NVR O.

34. "The border is open; Joyous East Germans pour through the Wall; Party pledges Freedoms, and the city exults," *New York Times* (NYT), 11/10/89.

35. Henry Kamm, "Bonn Outlines Aid for East Germany," NYT, 11/14/89.

36. Interview with Brie, GDR Oral History Project, p. 16.

37. See David Binder, "Grim State of East Germany's Economy Is Disclosed to Parliament," NYT, 11/15/89, and "Reports of Corruption in East Berlin Shock Even the Party Rank and File," NYT, 11/24/89.

38. See text in *Neues Deutschland* (ND), 11/17–18/89.

39. Interview with Gregor Gysi, GDR Oral History Project.

40. NYT, 11/17/89.

41. Interview with Gysi, GDR Oral History Project.

42. See coverage in ND, 1/4/90.

43. Interview with Jens Reich, GDR Oral History Project, p. 6.

44. *Taz*, 11/13/89.

45. "Our goal is to establish a legal and political platform on which we can bring desperately needed social dialogue into practice. No one should be excluded from this if he or she is an SED member or belongs to another organization." See "Liebe Freunde und Freundinnen des Neues Forum!" Berlin, 10/1/89, ABL H17.

46. Interview with Egon Krenz, GDR Oral History Project, p. 8.

47. *Taz*, 12/8/89.

48. ND, 1/16/90.

49. NYT, 1/28/90.

50. See, e.g., "Brandts Come-Back—Kohls Reinfall," *Taz*, 11/11/89.

51. Joachim Riecker, "Auferstand an Ruine: Die Dresdner Rede vor der Einheit," *Frankfurter Hefte*, January/February 2001, 75–80; see also Jarausch 1994: 89.

52. See ND, 12/20/89.

53. LVZ, 12/5/1989.

54. *Taz*, 11/7/89 and 12/15/89.

55. *Taz*, 11/13/89.

56. "Statut der SDP—Sozialdemokratische Partei in der DDR," 10/25/89, in ABL H4.

57. *Taz*, 12/18/89.

58. See coverage in *Taz*, 1/8/90 and 1/22/89.

59. LVZ, 1/11/1990.

60. "Chronik des MdI vom 01. Januar bis 31. Dezember 1989" in BARCH DO 1 2.3/053614.

61. One of the four postwar political parties initially permitted by Soviet authorities in the East, the CDU was completely subordinated within the SED's "antifascist bloc" of parties and mass organizations (Naimark 1995; Weber 1993).

62. LVZ, 12/16/1989.

63. Michnik quoted in *Taz*, 1/9/90.

64. *Taz*, 3/19/90. It was not just in East Germany that parties of the center-right fared the best in the post-Communist elections. Indeed, throughout Central Europe,

Christian-Democratic and Liberal-Democratic parties, promising a return to democracy and the market, generally fared better than the heirs of dissidents, the former ruling parties, and hastily reorganized Social Democrats (Lemke and Marks 1992).

65. See Bündnis 90/Greens "Gemeinsame Erklärung zum Staatsvertrag der Fraktion Bündnis 90/Grünen in der Volkskammer und die Grünen im Bundestag," 6/6/90, in ABL H16.

66. *Taz*, 7/20/89.

67. New Forum Berlin, "Presseerklärung: Dieser Staatsvertrag besiegelt die Kapitulation der DDR," June 1990, in ABL H16.

68. "Mehr farben braucht das Land. Wofür wir eintreten. Bündnis 90/Grünen" in ABL H4.

69. See "Beendet die Zuschauerdemokratie!" in ABL H4.

Conclusion

1. In fact, despite strenuous efforts to prevent emigration to neighboring capitalist states, both Cubans and North Koreans have found and exploited exit routes. In the years between 1981 and 1996, some quarter million Cubans took up residence in the United States. In the last decade thousands of *balseros* have built rafts, outfitted boats, hijacked ferries, and even embarked on the Straits of Florida in inflatable inner tubes. They do so despite the risk of severe legal penalties and the hazards of the sea. In 2001 thousands tried to cross the Straits of Florida illegally, and estimates tell us that at least a third of them failed. In the last decade tens of thousands of North Koreans have fled across the Yalu and Tumen Rivers into northern China to escape famine and political repression. They reside there illegally, often abetted by local ethnic Korean communities and religious organizations. A fortunate few eventually make their way to South Korea. According to conservative estimates, with the continued economic erosion of their native country, in June 2002 more than a hundred thousand North Koreans were living in China. It is difficult to judge whether the explosive exit-voice dynamics observed in the case of the GDR could occur in Cuba or North Korea, but it is conceivable if the balance of incentives that maintain the repressive equilibrium in both countries should change, perhaps as a result of geopolitical realignments.

For details concerning exit from Cuba, see Silvia Pedraza, "Cuba's Refugees: Manifold Migrations," paper presented at the American Sociological Association annual conference, 1995; Immigration and Refugee Services of America, *World Refugee Survey* (Washington, D.C., 1998); U.S. Immigration and Naturalization Service, "Cuban Migration Interdiction Process," November 14, 2001, and "Cuba: Systematic Repression of Dissent" (INS Resource Information Center, 1998); CIA, *World Factbook 2002*; see also "3 Hijackers Were Killed to Deter U.S.-Backed Exodus, Castro Says," *New York Times* (NYT), 4/27/2003. For illegal migration from North Korea, see Marcus Noland, "Why North Korea Will Muddle Through," *Foreign Affairs* 76/4 (1997); "Report from the Icy Frontier," *The Economist*, 12/7/2002; "Defying Crackdown, North Koreans Stream Into China," *NYT*, 6/6/2002; "North Koreans in China Now Live in Fear of Dragnet," *NYT*, 7/18/2002; "China Seeks a Delicate Balance with North Korea," *Wall Street Journal*, 5/24/2002; and "China Reinforces North Korea Border," *Washington Post*, 9/16/2003. For an unusual first-person account by a successful North Korean "exiter," see Chol-Hwan 2001.

Bibliography

The primary sources for this study are drawn chiefly from archival research conducted in Leipzig and Berlin in the summers of 1993 and 1995, between January and August 1998, and in the summers of 2001 and 2003. I consulted the Civic Movement Archive in Leipzig (Archiv Bürgerbewegung Leipzig), affiliated with Leipzig's municipal archives; the Saxon State Archives in Leipzig (Sächsisches Staatsarchiv Leipzig), where the primary holdings of the municipal and district SED party archives are held; the German Federal Archives and the Archive of the Parties and Mass Organizations of the former German Democratic Republic in Berlin-Lichterfelde; and the New Forum Archive of the Robert Havemann Society (Robert-Havemann-Gesellschaft e.V. Berlin). I have listed the specific files consulted and provided an abbreviation key below. In addition I consulted the "Final Recommendation and Report of the Special Committee for the Investigation of the Abuse of Office and Power in the SED Government of the Saxon State Parliament," which includes both the committee's final report and more than one thousand pages of supporting documents. The report proved an invaluable source, particularly on the developments in the Dresden district.

In addition I made abundant use of the holdings of the GDR Oral History Project housed at the Hoover Institution Archives at Stanford University. The project includes hundreds of pages of typed transcripts and taped interviews with prominent dissidents and state officials. The list of interviews consulted is provided below. Newspapers proved an invaluable source on the process of transformation in East Germany. Particularly useful was West Berlin's *Die Tageszeitung*, a left-wing daily with the most extensive and insightful coverage of dissident politics in the revolution and reunification; it was the paper of choice for East German intellectuals and dissidents in making press statements and granting interviews. The *Leipziger Volkszeitung* is the standard journalistic source for the city of Leipzig. The SED's official mouthpiece, *Neues Deutschland*, was a primary outlet for public statements by the GDR leadership. Finally, the *New York Times* offered excellent coverage of the East German revolution, the debates surrounding unification, and reports on events elsewhere in Eastern Europe.

Archival Sources

Archiv Bürgerbewegung e.V., Stadtgeschichtliches Museum Leipzig (ABL) [Civic Movement Archive of the Municipal Historical Museum of Leipzig]

ABL H1: Events in Leipzig, 1953–1990
ABL H2: Opposition Groups in Leipzig
ABL H3: Materials on GDR Opposition
ABL H4: Parties and movements in Leipzig
ABL H8: Information from MFS Abt. XX (BV-Leipzig)
ABL H9: Information from MFS Abt. XX (BV-Leipzig)
ABL H11: Information on the dissolution of the MFS
ABL H16: New Forum 1990
ABL H17: New Forum 1989
ABL H24: Material on Alliance90/The Greens
ABL H46: Material on Alliance90/The Greens in the Bundestag
ABL SH D: Events in Dresden 1989

Bestand Arnold (ABL BA) [Michael Arnold MdI in Sachsen]

ABL BA H NVR 0: Materials of the NVR der DDR, Oct–Nov. 1989
ABL BA H MDI 12: Materials of the Ministerium des Innern der Deutschen Demokratischen Republik, 1984–1988
ABL BA H MDI 13: Materials of the MdI der DDR, Oct. 1989
ABL BA H MDI 14: Materials of the MdI der DDR, Nov. 1989
ABL BA H MDI 15: Materials of the MdI der DDR, Nov. 1989
ABL BA H MDI 16: Materials of the MdI der DDR, Dec. 1989
ABL BA H MFS-PB I: Materials of the MFS der DDR, 1970–1987
ABL BA H MFS-PB II: Materials of the MFS der DDR, 1988–1989

Dissident publications

ABL Box 2: *Grenzfall* (Berlin), 1986–1989
ABL Box 4: *Umweltblätter* (Berlin), 1986–1989
ABL Box 6: *Streiflichter* (Leipzig), 1982–1989

Bundesarchiv der Bundesrepublik Deutschland, Berlin (BArch) [National Archives of the Federal Republic of Germany]

BArch DO 1. Ministerium des Innern der Deutschen Demokratischen Republik [Ministry of the Interior, GDR]

DO 1 2.3/052445: Information on public safety and security, October 1989–May 1990
DO 1 2.3/052449: Information on public safety and security, October 1989–December 1989
DO 1 2.3/053613: Chronik, 1987–1988
DO 1 2.3/053614: Chronik, 1989

BArch DO 1 34. Ministerium des Innern der DDR, Hauptabteilung Innere Angelegenheiten [Ministry of the Interior, Department of Internal Affairs]

DO 1 34/29282–29301: Released emigrants to the FRG and West Berlin, 1988–1989

DO 1 34/40845–40847: Petitions on behalf of New Forum, 1989

DO 1 34/53268: Persons released from citizenship of the GDR (Special trains to the FRG)

DO 1 34/54134: Emigration, 1954–1961

DO 1 34/54135: Emigration, 1961–1988

DO 1 34/55243–55248: Emigration and Special Trains, 1989

DO 1 34/55068: Emigration

BArch DO 4. Staatssekretär für Kirchenfragen. 6. Abteilung II Evangelische Kirche und Religionsgemeinschaften [State Secretary for Church Questions. Division 6/II Protestant Church and Religious Congregations]

DO 4 753: Evangelical Lutheran Church of Saxony/Synods, 1987–1988

DO 4 767: Hostile Activities, 1987–1988

DO 4 768: Hostile Activities, 1989

DO 4 1488: Evangelical Lutheran Church of Saxony/Synods, 1989

Hoover Institution Archives, Stanford University.
GDR Oral History Project

Printed transcripts of interviews

Bisky, Lothar. Socialist intellectual and PDS leader. Interviewed by H. Bortfeldt, April 6, 1993.

Brie, Michael. Professor of social philosophy and PDS leader. Interviewed by M. Siena, December 23, 1991.

Eberlein, Werner. Former Politburo member and district chair for Magdeburg. Interviewed by J. Torpey, February 2, 1992.

Eppelmann, Rainer. Former pastor in East Berlin. Interviewed by T. Banchoff, December 5, 1991.

Fischer, Oskar. Former Politburo member and GDR foreign minister. Interviewed by J. McAdams, March 9, 1993.

Gauck, Joachim. Pastor in Rostock, New Forum activist. Interviewed by J. Torpey, April 23, 1993.

Gysi, Gregor. Attorney and PDS leader. Interviewed by H. Bortfeldt, July 6, 1993.

Hager, Kurt. Former Politburo member. Interviewed by J. McAdams and C. Epstein, December 3, 1990; July 11, 1991; August 6, 1993.

Hilsberg, Stefan. IFM activist and SPD member. Interviewed by T. Banchoff, June 14, 1991.

Krenz, Egon. Former Politburo member and state premier. Interviewed by H. Bortfeldt, May 31, 1990.

Meckel, Markus. Former pastor in East Berlin. Interviewed by T. Banchoff, June 10, 1991.

Modrow, Hans. Former Dresden district chief and GDR state premier. Interviewed by H. Bortfeldt, March 17, 1993.

Reich, Jens. Physicist and New Forum leader. Interviewed by M. Siena, December 28, 1989; December 23, 1991.

Templin, Wolfgang, and Regina ("Lotte") Templin. Human rights activists. Interviewed by J. Torpey, August 29, 1991; February 3, 1992.

Ullmann, Wolfgang. Theologian and Democracy Now leader. Interviewed by T. Banchoff, November 12, 1991.

Mathias-Domaschk-Archiv, Robert-Havemann-Gesellschaft e.V. Berlin. Bestand Bürgerbeweung [New Forum Archive in the Robert-Havemann-Society]

New Forum Organization

NFO 047–055 Original Unterschriftenlister der Unterstützungserklärungen zum Neuen Forum (September–October 1989).

NFO 135/136 Protokoll der Gründungskonferenz des Neuen Forums, 27–28 January 1990.

Sächsischer Landtag (SL). Beschlussempfehlung und Bericht des Sonderausschusses Zur Untersuchung Von AMTS- und Machtmissbrauch Infolge Der Sed-Herrschaft [Saxon State Parliament. Final Recommendation and Report of the Special Committee for the Investigation of the Abuse of Offices and Power in the SED Government]. Dresden, July 1994.

Sächsisches Staatsarchiv Leipzig (Stal) [Saxon State Archives at Leipzig]. Bezirksparteiarchiv der SED Leipzig [Leipzig District Party Archive]

Bezirksleitung der SED Leipzig, Büro des Sekretariats [Leipzig District SED Leadership, Office of the Secrateriat]

SED IV F-2/1/013-017: Protokolle Tagungen der Bezirksleitung

SED IV F-2/2/029: Protokoll der Bezirksaktivtagung zu der politischen-ideologischen Arbeit an der Karl-Marx-Universität und an Hoch- und Fachhochschulen (9.3.89)

SED IV F-2/2/029: Protokoll der Bezirksaktivtagung zur Eröffnung des Parteilehrjahres (12.9.89)

SED IV F-2/2/030: Protokoll der Bezirksaktivtagung zur Auswertung der 10. Tagung des ZK der SED (23.11.89)

SED IV F-2/3/116–121: Protokolle Sitzungen der Bezirksleitung

Stadtleitung der SED [City Leadership of SED]

SED IV F-5/1/08–09: Protokolle der Tagungen der Stadtleitung

SED IV F-5/1/051–052: Protokolle der Sitzungen des Sekretariats

Stadtparteikontrolkommission der SED Leipzig [Municipal Party Control Commission of the SED Leipzig]

SED IV F-5/1/057–059: Berichte und Prüfungen, Apparat und Grundorganisationen

SED IV F-5/1/062: Protokolle Sitzungen, 1989

SED IV F-5/1/063: Analysen, Information über feindliche Einflüsse, Verletzungen Leninistischen Normen

SED IV F-5/1/063: Analysen, Information über feindliche Einflüsse, Verletzungen der Leninistischen Normen, Gesetzverstösse, 1987–1989

SED IV F-5/1/064–065: Stadtparteikontrolkommission Untersuchungen in Grundorganisationen, 1987–1989

SED IV F-5/1/069–070: Stadtparteikontrolkommission. Eingaben an die leitende Parteiorgane, 1988–1989

SED IV F-5/1/076: Information, Stimmungen, Meinungen, Argumente

SED-Stadtbezirksleitung Leipzig-Mitte [SED Municipal District Leadership– Center]

SED IV F-5/2/039: Protokolle Sitzungen des Sekretariats. Fortsetzung Oct–Nov. 1989

SED IV F-5/2/039: Stadtbezirksparteikontrolkommission Protokolle Sitzungen, Oct.– Nov. 1989

SED IV F-5/2/052–054: Information über feindliche Einflüsse, 1987–1989

SED IV F-5/2/052–054: Stadtbezirksparteikontrolkommission Analysen, Information über feindliche Einflüsse, Verletzung der Leninistischen Normen, Gesetzverletzung, 1987–1989

SED IV F-2/2/062: Information und Berichte der Stadtbezirksleitung über Stimmungen und Argumente der Bevölkerung, 1987–1988

SED-Stadtbezirksleitung Leipzig-Südwest [SED Municipal District Leadership– Leipzig–Southwest]

SED IV F-5/7/060: Information über feindliche Einflüsse auf Parteimitglieder, Verletzungen der Leninistischen Normen und Gesetzverletzungen, 1987–1989

Stiftung Archiv Parteien und Massenorganisationen der Deutschen Demokratischen Republik im Bundesarchiv (SAPMO-BArch), Berlin [Archive of the Parties and Mass Organizations of the GDR in the German National Archive]

DY 30. Zentralkomitee der SED. Abteilung Sicherheitsfragen des ZK der SED (1981–1989) [Central Committee of the SED. Division for Security Affairs]

DY 30/825: Sitzungen des Politbüros des ZK der SED, 1981–1989

DY 30/840: ZK der SED. Abt. Sicherheitsfragen. Tätigkeit der Abt. SF. Bd.5, 1989

DY 30. Bestand Büro Erich Honecker [Holdings of the Office of Erich Honecker]

DY 30/2175: Entwicklung der DDR Kreisen

DY 30/2182: Berichte über politische Probleme in der DDR

DY 30/IV/2/2.039. Bestand Büro Egon Krenz [Holdings of the Office of Egon Krenz]

DY 30/IV/2/2.039/74: Sitzungen Politbüro des ZK der SED. 1989.06

DY 30/IV/2/2.039/76: Sitzungen Politbüro des ZK der SED. 1989.08

DY 30/IV/2/2.039/77: Sitzungen Politbüro des ZK der SED. 1989.09

DY 30/IV/2/2.039/308: Ausreisen nach BRD, 1984–1988

DY 30/IV/2/2.039/309: Übersiedlungen, ständige Ausreisen nach BRD

DY 30/IV/2/2.039/326: Haltung Bürgerbewegungen, neue Parteien in der DDR

DY 30/IV/2/2.039/330: Information Abt. Parteiorgane des ZK der SED an E. Krenz, 1989

DY 30/IV/2/2.039/336: Information Zentralrat der FDJ/Abt. Jugend des ZK der SED an E. Krenz

Other files

J IV/2/3/4350/7: Protokoll der Sitzung des Sekretariats am 18.1.1989

J IV 2/50/30: Abteilung Parteiorgane der SED beim ZK der SED

J IV 2/50/30/2040: Eingaben an die Partei

J IV 2/50/30/2935: Information über Versorgung des Volkes

Documentary Sources

BfG (Bundesministerium für Gesamtdeutschen Fragen). *Tätigkeitsbericht der Bundesregierung: Deutsche Politik 1961.* Bonn.

Bundestag der Bundesrepublik Deutschland. 1995. *Materialien der Enquete-Kommission "Aufarbeitung von Geschichte und Folgen der SED-Diktatur in Deutschland."* 18 vols. Frankfurt am Main: Suhrkamp.

Büscher, Wolfgang, Peter Wensierski, and Klaus Wolschner, eds. 1982. *Friedensbewegung in der DDR:. Texte 1978–1982.* Hattingen: Edition Transit.

Central Committee of the SED. 1981. *Successful Path of Developing an Advanced Socialist Society in the GDR: Facts and Figures.* From the report of the Tenth Party Congress of the SED.

Daniels, Robert V., ed. 1994. *Documentary History of Communism and the World.* Hanover, N.H.: University Press of New England.

Jarausch, Konrad H., and Volker Gransow, eds. 1994. *Uniting Germany: Documents and Debates.* Providence, R.I.: Berghahn Books.

Michaelis, Julia, ed. 1990. *Die ersten Texte des Neuen Forums.* Berlin: Forum Verlag.

Mitter, Stefan, and Stefan Wolle, eds. 1990. *Ich liebe euch doch alle . . . Befehle und Lageberichte des MfS, Januar–November 1989.* Berlin: Basis.

Neues Forum Leipzig. 1990. *Jetzt oder nie—Demokratie: Leipziger Herbst '89.* Edited by Reinhard Bose, Grit Hartmann, and Ulla Huse. Frankfurt am Main: Bertelsmann.

Neues Forum Leipzig, ed. 1991. *Von Leipzig nach Deutschland.* Leipzig: Forum Verlag.

SB [Statistisches Bundesamt]. 1994. *Sonderreihe mit Beiträgen für das Gebiet der ehemaligen DDR.* Multiple vols. Wiesbaden: Federal Statistical Agency.

SJDDR (*Statistisches Jahrbuch der Deutschen Demokratischen Republik*). 1980–1990. Berlin: Staatliche Zentralverwaltung für Statistik der DDR.

Stokes, Gale, ed. 1991. *From Stalinism to Pluralism: A Documentary History of Eastern Europe since 1945*. New York: Oxford University Press.

Tetzinger, Reiner, ed. 1990. *Leipziger Ring: Aufzeichnen eines Montagsdemonstranten, Oktober 1989 bis 1. Mai 1990*. Frankfurt am Main: Luchterhand.

Newspapers

Berliner Zeitung [East Berlin daily]

Leipziger Volkszeitung [Leipzig daily]

Neues Deutschland [GDR daily]

New York Times [New York daily]

Sächsisches Tageblatt [Leipzig district daily]

Der Tagesspiegel [West Berlin daily]

Die Tageszeitung [West Berlin daily]

Secondary Sources

Adas, Michael. 1986. "From Footdragging to Flight: The Evasive History of Peasant Avoidance in South and South-East Asia." *Journal of Peasant Studies* 13/2: 64–86.

Adomeit, Hannes. 1998. *Imperial Overstretch: Germany in Soviet Policy from Stalin to Gorbachev*. Baden-Baden: Nomos Verlag.

Agocs, Sandor. 1993. "The Collapse of Communist Ideology in Hungary: November 1988 to February 1989." *East European Quarterly* 27/2: 187–210.

Allport, Floyd H. 1924. *Social Psychology*. Boston: Houghton Mifflin.

Alsmeier, Bernd. 1994. *Wegbereiter der Wende: Die Rolle der evangelischen Kirchen in der Ausgangsphase der DDR*. Pfaffenweiler: Centaurus.

Anderson, Lisa, ed. 1999. *Transitions to Democracy*. New York: Columbia University Press.

Arato, Andrew. 1994. "Revolution, Restoration, and Legitimation." *Imagining Eastern Europe*, edited by M. Kennedy. Ann Arbor: University of Michigan Press.

Aron, Raymond. 1968. "The Sociologists and the Revolution of 1848." In *Main Currents in Sociological Thought*. Vol. 1. Translated by Richard Howard and Helen Weaver. Garden City, N.Y.: Doubleday.

Atkinson, Anthony, and John Micklewright. 1992. *Economic Transformation and the Distribution of Income*. Cambridge: Cambridge University Press.

Bachman, Ronald D., ed. 1991. *Romania: A Country Study*. Washington: Library of Congress.

Barry, Brian. 1974. "Review Article: Exit, Voice and Loyalty." *British Journal of Political Science* 4/1: 79–107.

Baylis, Thomas A. 1999. "The GDR 'on the Eve.'" *Communist and Post-Communist Studies* 32: 127–38.

Bernhard, Michael H. 1993. *The Origins of Democratization in Poland*. New York: Columbia University Press.

Blair, Irene, and John Tost. 2003. "Exit, Loyalty, and Collective Action among Workers in a Simulated Business Environment." *Social Justice Research* 16/2: 95–108.

Boissevain, Jeremy. 1971. "Second Thoughts on Quasi-Groups, Categories and Coalitions." *Man* 6/3: 468–72.

Bornstein, Morris, ed. 1973. *Plan and Market: Economic Reform in Eastern Europe*. New Haven: Yale University Press.

Bortfeldt, Heinrich. 1990. "Die Ostdeutschen und die PDS." *Deutschland Archiv* 27/12: 1283–87.

Bramstedt, Ernest K. 1945. *Dictatorship and Political Police: The Technique of Control by Fear*. London: Paul, Trench, and Trubner.

Braun, Norman. 1994. "Das Schwellenmodell und die Leipziger Montagsdemonstrationen." *Kölner Zeitschrift für Soziologie und Sozialpsychologie* 46/3: 482–500.

———. 1995. "Individual Thresholds and Social Diffusion." *Rationality and Society* 7/2: 167–182.

Brewer, Marilynn, and Sherry Schneider. 1990. "Social identity and Social Dilemmas." In *Social Identity Theory*, edited by D. Abrams and M. Hogg. London: Springer.

Briese, Käthe, et al. 1970. *Deutsch-Englisches Wörterbuch*. 11th ed. Leipzig: Verlag Enzyklopädie.

Brubaker, Rogers. 1990. "Frontier Theses: Exit, Voice and Loyalty in East Germany." *Migration World Magazine* 18/3–4: 12–17.

Brus, Wlodzimierz. 1986. *The Economic History of Eastern Europe, 1919–1975*. Oxford: Clarendon Press.

Bruszt, Laszlo. 1990. "Hungary's Negotiated Revolution." *Social Research* 57/2: 365–87.

Bruszt, Laszlo, and David Stark. 1992. "Remaking the Political Field in Hungary: From the Politics of Confrontation to the Politics of Competition." In *Eastern Europe in Revolution*, edited by Ivo Banac. Ithaca: Cornell University Press.

Buchholz, Erich, et al. 1974. *Socialist Criminology*. Translated by E. Osers. London: Saxon House.

Bunce, Valerie. 1999. *Subversive Institutions: The Design and Destruction of Socialism and the State*. New York: Cambridge University Press.

———. 2003. "Rethinking Recent Democratization: Lesson from Postcommunist Experience." *World Politics* 55/2: 167–92.

Burawoy, Michael, and János Lukács. 1992. *The Radiant Past*. Chicago: University of Chicago Press.

Bürgerkomitee Leipzig. 1992. *Stasi intern: Macht und Banalität*. Leipzig: Forum Verlag.

Caldwell, Peter C. 2003. *Dictatorship, State Planning, and Social Theory in the German Democratic Republic*. New York: Cambridge University Press.

Calhoun, Craig. 1982. *The Question of Class Struggle: Social Foundations of Popular Radicalism during the Industrial Revolution*. Chicago: University of Chicago Press.

———. 1991. "The Problem of Identity in Collective Action." In *Macro-Micro Linkages in Sociology*, edited by J. Huber, 51–75. Newbury Park, Calif.: Sage.

———. 1994. *Neither Gods nor Emperors: Students and the Struggle for Democracy in China.* Berkeley: University of California Press.

Che Muqi. 1990. *Beijing Turmoil: More Than Meets the Eye.* Beijing: Beijing Foreign Languages Press.

Chirot, Daniel. 1978. "Social Change in Communist Romania." *Social Forces* 57/2: 457–99.

———. 1991. "What Happened in Eastern Europe in 1989?" In *The Crisis of Leninism and the Decline of the Left*, edited by D. Chirot, 3–32. Seattle: University of Washington Press.

———. 1994. *Modern Tyrants.* Princeton: Princeton University Press.

Chol-Hwan, Kang, and Pierre Rigoulot. 2001. *Aquariums of Pyongyang: Ten Years in the North Korean Gulag.* Translated by Yair Reiner. New York: Basic.

Chong, Dennis. 1991. *Collective Action and the Civil Rights Movement.* Chicago: University of Chicago Press.

Chwe, Michael Suk-Young. 1999. "Structure and Strategy in Collective Action." *American Journal of Sociology* 105/1: 128–56.

———. 2001. *Rational Ritual.* Princeton: Princeton University Press.

Cohen, Michael D., Rick L. Riolo, and Robert Axelrod. 2001. "The Role of Social Structure in the Maintenance of Cooperative Regimes." *Rationality and Society* 13/1: 5–32.

Coleman, James S. 1990. *The Foundations of Social Theory.* Cambridge, Mass.: Harvard University Press.

Collins, Randall. 1995. "Prediction in Macrosociology: The Case of the Soviet Collapse." *American Journal of Sociology* 100/6: 1552–93.

Coser, Lewis A. 1990. "The Intellectuals in Soviet Reform: On 'Pluralistic Ignorance' and Mass Communications." *Dissent* (spring): 181–83.

Csepeli, Gyorgy, and Antal Orkeny. 1992. "From Unjust Equality to Just Inequality." *New Hungarian Quarterly* 33: 71–76.

Davies, James C. 1962. "Toward a Theory of Revolution." *American Sociological Review* 27 (Feb.): 5–18.

Deess, E. Pierre. 1997a. "Collective Life and Social Change in the GDR." *Mobilization* 2/2: 207–25.

———. 1997b. "The Socialist Ethic and the Spirit of Revolution: Institutional Practices and the Collapse of East Germany in 1989." Ph.D. diss., University of California, San Diego.

Dennis, Mike. 1993. *Social and Economic Modernization in Eastern Germany from Honecker to Kohl.* New York: St. Martin's Press.

Denouex, Guillaume. 1993. *Urban Unrest in the Middle East.* Albany: State University of New York Press.

Derbyshire, Ian. 1991. *Politics in Germany from Division to Reunification.* Edinburgh: Chambers.

Dietrich, Christian. 1994. "Der Protest formiert sich . . . : Zur Entwicklung der Opposition in der DDR in den 80er Jahren." In *Für ein offenes Land mit freien Menschen*, edited by B. Lindner. Leipzig: Forum Verlag.

Dietrich, Christian, and Uwe Schwabe, eds. 1994. *Freunde oder Feinde: Dokumente zu den Friedensgebeten in Leipzig.* Leipzig: Evangelische Verlagsanstalt.

Djilas, Milovan. 1957. *The New Class*. New York: Praeger.

Dowding, Keith, Peter John, Thanos Mergoupis, and Mark Van Vugt. 2000. "Exit, Voice, and Loyalty: Analytic and Empirical Developments." *European Journal of Political Research* 37: 469–95.

Eberlein, Werner. 2000. *Geboren am 9. November: Erinnerungen*. Berlin: Das Neue Berlin.

ECE [Economic Commission of Europe]. 1990. *Economic Survey of Europe in 1989–1990*. New York: Economic Commission of Europe.

Eckstein, Susan, ed. 1989. *Power and Popular Protest: Latin American Social Movements*. Berkeley: University of California Press.

Ekiert, Grzegorz. 1996. *The State against Society: Political Crises and Their Aftermath in East Central Europe*. Princeton: Princeton University Press.

——. 1997. "Rebellious Poles: Popular Protest under State Socialism, 1945–1989." *East European Politics and Societies*. 11/2: 299–338.

Ekiert, Grzegorz, and Jan Kubik. 1999. *Rebellious Civil Society: Popular Protest and Democratic Consolidation in Poland, 1989–1993*. Ann Arbor: University of Michigan Press.

Eley, Geoff. *Forging Democracy: The History of the Left in Europe, 1850–2000*. New York: Oxford University Press.

Elster, Jon. 1989. *Nuts and Bolts for the Social Sciences*. New York: Cambridge University Press.

——. 1998. "A Plea for Mechanisms." In *Social Mechanisms: An Analytical Approach to Social Theory*, edited by Peter Hedstrom and Richard Swedberg. New York: Cambridge University Press.

Epstein, Barbara. 1991. *Political Protest and Cultural Revolution: Nonviolent Direct Action in the 1970s and 1980s*. Berkeley: University of California Press.

Fehr, Helmut. 1992. "Mobilisierungsprozesse und neue politische Konfliktlinien in Polen." In *Soziologie in Deutschland und die Transformation grosser gesellschaftlicher Systeme*, edited by H. Meyer. Berlin: Akademie.

Findeis, Hagen, Detlef Pollack, and Manuel Schilling. 1994. *Die Entzauberung des Politischen*. Leipzig: Evangelische Verlagsanstalt.

Flam, Helena. 1998. *Mosaic of Fear: Poland and East Germany before 1989*. New York: Columbia University Press.

Fricke, Karl-Wilhelm. 1984. *Opposition und Widerstand in der DDR*. Cologne: Deutschland Archiv.

——. 1993. "Politische Strafjustiz im SED-Staat." *Aus Politik und Zeitgeschichte* 4/93: 13–22.

Friedheim, Daniel V. 1997. "Democratic Transition through Regime Collapse: East Germany in 1989." Ph.D. diss., Yale University.

Friedrich, Michael. 1994. *Stürmischer Herbst: Chronik der Ereignisse in der Stadt und Bezirk Dresden, September bis November 1989*. Dresden: Sächischer Landtag.

Friedrich, Walter, Peter Förster, and Kurt Starke. 1999. *Das Zentralinstitut für Jugendforschung Leipzig, 1966–1970: Geschichte, Methoden, Erkenntnisse*. Berlin: Edition Ost.

Froese, Paul. 2003. "The Great Secularization Experiment: Assessing the Communist Attempt to Eliminate Religion." Ph.D. diss., University of Washington, Seattle.

Froese, Paul, and Steven Pfaff. 2001. "Replete and Desolate Markets: Poland, East Germany, and the New Religious Paradigm." *Social Forces* 80/2: 481–507.

Fulbrook, Mary. 1995. *Anatomy of a Dictatorship: Inside the GDR, 1945–1989.* New York: Cambridge University Press.

Fuller, Linda. 1999. *Where Was the Working Class? Revolution in Eastern Germany.* Urbana: University of Illinois Press.

Garcelon, Marc. 1997a. "The Estate of Change: The Specialist Rebellion and the Democratic Movement in Moscow, 1989–1991." *Theory and Society* 26/1: 39–85.

———. 1997b. "The Shadow of the Leviathan: Public and Private in Communist and Post-Communist Society." In *Public and Private in Thought and Practice*, edited by J. Weintraub and K. Kumar. Chicago: University of Chicago Press.

Garcia, Margarita. 1983. "The Last Days in Cuba: Personal Accounts of the Circumstances of Exit." *Migration Today* 11/4–5: 13–22.

Garton Ash, Timothy. 1990. *The Magic Lantern: The Revolution of '89 Witnessed in Warsaw, Budapest, Berlin and Prague.* 1st U.S. ed. New York: Random House.

———. 1993. *In Europe's Name: Germany and the Divided Continent.* New York: Random House.

Gauss, Günter. 1983. *Wo Deutschland liegt.* Frankfurt am Main: Hoffman und Campe.

Gedmin, Jeffrey. 1993. *The Hidden Hand: Gorbachev and the Collapse of East Germany.* Washington: AIE Press.

Geissler, R. 1983. "Bildungschancen und Statusvererbung in der DDR." *Kölner Zeitschrift für Soziologie und Sozialpsychologie* 35: 735–54.

Glaessner, Gert-Joachim. 1996. "Political Culture and the Aftershocks of Revolution: Change in East Germany." In *Change after Unification*, edited by G. Glaessner. Amsterdam: German Monitor Press.

Glenn, John K. 1999. "Competing Challengers and Contested Outcomes to State Breakdown: The Velvet Revolution in Czechoslovakia." *Social Forces* 78/1: 187–212.

———. 2003. "Parties out of Movements: Party Emergence in Postcommunist Eastern Europe." In *States, Parties, and Social Movements*, edited by J. Goldstone. New York: Cambridge University Press.

Goeckel, Robert F. 1990. *The Lutheran Church and the East German State.* Ithaca: Cornell University Press.

Goertz, Joachim, ed. 1999. *Die Solidarische Kirche in der DDR.* Berlin: Basis.

Goffman, Erving. 1961. "On the Characteristics of Total Institutions." In *Asylums: Essays on the Social Situation of Mental Patients and Other Inmates*, 1–124. New York: Anchor.

Goldfarb, Jeffrey C. 1991. *Beyond Glasnost: The Post-Totalitarian Mind.* 2d ed. Chicago: University of Chicago Press.

Goldstone, Jack. 1994a. "Is Revolution Individually Rational?" *Rationality and Society* 6/1: 139–66.

———. 1994b. "Why We Could (and Should) Have Foreseen the Revolutions of 1989–1991 in the U.S.S.R. and Eastern Europe." *Contention* 2/2: 127–52.

———. 1997. "Methodological Issues in Comparative Macrosociology." *Comparative Social Research* 16: 107–20.

——. 2001. "Toward a Fourth Generation of Revolutionary Theory." *Annual Review of Political Science* 4: 139–87.

Goldstone, Jack, and Karl-Dieter Opp. 1994. "Rationality, Revolution and 1989 in Eastern Europe." *Rationality and Society* 6/1: 5–7.

Goldstone, Jack, and Charles Tilly. 2001. "Threat (and Opportunity): Popular Action and State Response in the Dynamics of Collective Action." In *Silence and Voice in the Study of Contentious Politics*, edited by R. Aminzade et al., 179–94. New York: Cambridge University Press.

Goodwin, Jeff. 1997. "State-Centered Approaches to Social Revolutions." In *Theorizing Revolutions*, edited by J. Foran. New York: Routledge.

——. 2001. *No Other Way Out: States and Revolutionary Movements, 1945–1991*. New York: Cambridge University Press.

Goodwin, Jeff, and Steven Pfaff. 2001. "Emotion Work in High-Risk Social Movements." In *Passionate Politics*, edited by Jeff Goodwin, James M. Jasper, and Francesca Polletta, 282–302. Chicago: Chicago University Press.

Gould, Roger. 1995. *Insurgent Identities: Class, Community, and Protest in Paris from 1848 to the Commune*. Chicago: University of Chicago Press.

Granovetter, Mark. 1978. "Threshhold Models of Collective Behavior." *American Journal of Sociology* 83/6: 1420–43.

Grass, Günter. 1990. *Deutscher Lastenausgleich*. Frankfurt am Main: Luchterhand.

Gritsch, Eric W. 2002. *History of Lutheranism*. Minneapolis: Fortress Press.

Grundmann, Siegfried. 1998. *Bevölkerungsentwicklung in Ostdeutschland: Demographische Strukturen und räumliche Wandlungsprozesse seit 1945*. Opladen: Leske und Budrich.

——. 2001. "Der DDR-Alltag im Jahre 1987." In *Die DDR-Analysen eines aufgegebenen Staates*, edited by H. Timmermann. Berlin: Dunker und Humboldt.

Grundmann, Siegfried, Manfred Lötsch, and Rudi Weidig. 1976. *Zur Entwicklung der Arbeiterklasse und ihrer Struktur in der DDR*. Berlin: Dietz.

Grundmann, Siegfried, Irene Müller-Hartmann, and Ines Schmidt. 1992. "Migration in, aus und nach Ostdeutschland." In *Soziologie in Deutschland und die Transformation grosser gesellschaftlichter Systeme*, edited by Hansgünter Meyer, 1577–1609. Berlin: Akademie.

Gurr, Ted. 1970. *Why Men Rebel*. Princeton: Princeton University Press.

Guthrie, Douglas J. 1995. "Political Theater and Student Organizations in the 1989 Chinese Movement: A Multivariate Analysis of Tiananmen." *Sociological Forum* 10: 419–54.

Gutmann, Gernot. 1999. "In der Wirtschaftsordnung der DDR angelegte Blockaden und Effizienzhindernisse für die Prozesse der Modernisierung, des Strukturwandels und des Wirtschaftswachstum." In *Die Endzeit der DDR-Wirtschaft: Analysen zur Wirtschafts-, Sozial- und Umweltpolitik*, edited by E. Kuhrt et al. Opladen: Leske und Budrich.

Habermas, Jürgen. 1990. "Critique of D-Mark Nationalism." In *Uniting Germany: Documents and Debates, 1943–1993*, edited by K. Jarausch and V. Gransow. Providence, R.I.: Berghahn.

Hall, John A. 1998. "A View of a Death: On Communism, Ancient and Modern." *Theory and Society* 27: 509–34.

Hanisch, Gunter, Gottfried Haenisch, Friedrich Magirius, and Johannes Richter, eds. 1996. *Dona Nobis Pacem: Herbst '89 in Leipzig: Friedensgebete, Predigten und Fürbitten*. 2d ed. Leipzig: Evangelische Verlags-Anstalt.

Hanson, Stephen E. 1991. "Gorbachev: The Last True Leninist Believer?" In *The Crisis of Leninism and the Decline of the Left*, edited by D. Chirot. Seattle: University of Washington Press.

Hardin, Russell. 1974. "Western Approaches to East German History." *New German Critique* 1/2: 115–23.

———. 1982. *Collective Action*. Baltimore: Johns Hopkins University Press.

Hartmann, Klaus, and Detlef Pollack. 1998. *Gegen den Strom: Kircheneintritte in Ostdeutschland nach der Wende*. Opladen: Leske und Budrich.

Havel, Vaclav. 1986. *Vaclav Havel: Living in Truth*. Edited by Jan Vladislau. Boston: Faber and Faber.

Havemann, Robert. 1982. "Für eine unabhänige Friedensbewegung in der DDR." Reprinted in *Friedensbewegung in der DDR*, edited by W. Buescher, P. Wesnierksi, and K. Wolschner. Hattingen: Transit.

Hechter, Michael. 1987. *Principles of Group Solidarity*. Berkeley: University of California Press.

———. 1994. "Theoretical Implications of the Demise of State Socialism." *Theory and Society* 23: 155–67.

Heckathorn, Douglas D. 1988. "Collective Sanctions and Creation of Prisoner's Dilemma Norms." *American Journal of Sociology* 94/3: 535–62.

———. 1990. "Collective Sanctions and Compliance Norms." *American Sociological Review* 55/3: 366–84.

Hedström, Peter, and Richard Swedberg, eds. 1998. *Social mechanisms: An Analytical Approach to Social Theory*. Cambridge: Cambridge University Press.

Henkys, Reinhard. 1982. "Zwischen Militarismus und Pazifismus: Friedensarbeit der evangelischen Kirchen." In *Friedensbewegung in der DDR*, edited by W. Buescher, P. Wensierski and K. Wolschner, 14–28. Hattingen: Edition Transit.

Herbst, Andreas, Gerd-Rüdiger Stephan, and Jürgen Winkler, eds. 1997. *Die SED: Geshichte, Organisation, Politik*. Berlin: Dietz.

Herbst, Jeffrey. 1990. "Migration, the Politics of Protest, and State Consolidation in Africa." *African Affairs* 89: 183–203.

Hertle, Hans-Hermann. 1996. *Chronik des Mauerfalls*. Berlin: Christoph Links.

Hertle, Hans-Hermann, and Gerd-Rüdiger Stephan, eds. 1997. *Das Ende der SED: Die letzten Tage des Zentralkomitees*. Berlin: Christoph Links.

Hildebrandt, Rainer. 1988. "Das gemeinsame Erlebnis der Ehrlichkeit." *Der Tagesspiegel*, November 2.

Hirschman, Albert O. 1970. *Exit, Voice, and Loyalty*. Cambridge, Mass.: Harvard University Press.

———. 1978. "Exit, Voice, and the State." *World Politics* 31/1: 90–107.

———. 1982. *Shifting Involvements: Private Interest and Public Action*. Princeton: Princeton University Press.

———. 1993. "Exit, Voice, and the Fate of the German Democratic Republic: An Essay in Conceptual History." *World Politics* 45/2: 173–202.

Hobsbawm, Eric. 1994. *The Age of Extremes*. London: Little, Brown.

Hollander, Paul. 1999. *Political Will and Personal Belief: The Decline and Fall of Soviet Communism*. New Haven: Yale University Press.

Holzweissig, Gunter. 1996. "Die führende Rolle der Partei in SED-Staat." In *Die SED-Herrschaft und Ihr Zussamenbruch*, edited by E. Kuhrt. Opladen: Leske und Budrich.

Honecker, Erich. 1979. *The German Democratic Republic, Pillar of Peace and Socialism*. New York: International.

Howard, Marc M. 2003. *The Weaknesses of Civil Society in Post-Communist Europe*. New York: Cambridge University Press.

Huinink, Johannes, and Heike Solga. 1994. "Occupational Opportunities in the GDR." *Kölner Zeitschrift für Soziologie und Sozialpsychologie* 23/3: 237–53.

Huntington, Samuel P. 1968. *Political Order in Changing Societies*. New Haven: Yale University Press.

Jarausch, Konrad, 1991. "The Failure of East German Antifascism: Some Ironies of History as Politics." *German Studies Review* 14: 85–96.

———. 1994. *The Rush to German Unity*. New York: Oxford University Press.

———, ed. 1999. *Dictatorship as Experience*. New York: Berghahn.

Jenkins, J. Craig. 1983. "Resource Mobilization Theory and the Study of Social Movements." *Annual Review of Sociology* 9: 527–53.

Jessen, Ralph. 1999. "Mobility and Blockage during the 1970s." In *Dictatorship as Experience*, edited by K. Jarausch. New York: Berghahn.

Jian Shi et al. 1993. *The Truth about the Beijing Turmoil 1989*. Edited by Board of Truth about the Beijing Turmoil. Beijing: Beijing Publishing House.

Johnston, Hank, and Carol Mueller. 2001. "Unobtrusive Practices of Contention in Leninist Regimes." *Sociological Perspectives* 44/3: 351–75.

Johnston, Hank, and David A. Snow. 1998. "Subcultures and the Emergence of the Estonian Nationalist Opposition, 1945–1990." *Sociological Perspectives* 41/3: 473–97.

Joppke, Christian. 1995. *East German Dissidents and the Revolution of 1989*. New York: New York University Press.

Jowitt, Ken. 1992. *New World Disorder: The Leninist Extinction*. Berkeley: University of California Press.

Judt, Tony. 1992. "Metamorphosis: The Democratic Revolution in Czechoslovakia." In *Eastern Europe in Revolution*, edited by I. Banac, 96–116. Ithaca: Cornell University Press.

Kaser, M. C. 1986. *The Economic History of Eastern Europe, 1919–1975*. Oxford: Clarendon Press.

Keck, Margaret E., and Kathryn Sikkink. 1998. *Activists beyond Borders*. Ithaca: Cornell University Press.

Kharkhordin, Oleg. 1997. "Reveal and Dissimulate: A Genealogy of Private Life in Soviet

Russia." In *Public and Private in Thought and Practice*, edited by J. Weintraub and K. Kumar. Chicago: University of Chicago Press.

Kim, Hyojoung, and Peter S. Bearman. 1997. "The Structure and Dynamics of Movement Participation." *American Sociological Review* 62/1: 70–93.

King, Gary, Robert O. Keohane, and Sidney Verba. 1994. *Designing Social Inquiry*. Princeton: Princeton University Press.

Kiser, Edgar. 1999. "Comparing Varieties of Agency Theory in Economics, Political Science, and Sociology: An Illustration from State Policy Implementation." *Sociological Theory* 17/2: 146–70.

Kiser, Edgar, and Michael Hechter. 1991. "The Role of General Theory in Comparative-Historical Sociology." *American Journal of Sociology* 107/1: 183–222.

Klandermans, Bert. 1984. "Mobilization and Participation: Social-Psychological Expansions of Resource Mobilization Theory." *American Sociological Review* 49: 583–600.

Klein, Thomas. 1997. "Zu Opposition und Widerstand in der SED." In *Die SED: Geschichte, Organisation, Politik*, edited by A. Herbst, G. Stephan, and J. Winkler. Berlin: Dietz.

Klessmann, Christoph. 1988. *Zwei Staaten, eine Nation: Deutsche Geschichte 1955–1970*. Göttingen: Vandenhoek und Ruprecht.

———. 1993. "Zur sozialgeschichte des protestantischen Milieus in der DDR." *Geschichte und Gesellschaft* 19/1: 29–53.

Kluegel, James, and David Mason. 1999. "Political Involvement in Transition: Who Participated in Central and Eastern Europe?" *International Journal of Comparative Sociology* 40/1: 41–60.

Knabe, Hubertus. 1988. "Neue soziale Bewegungen im Sozialismus: Zur Genesis alternativer politischer Orientierungen in der DDR." *Kölner Zeitschrift für Soziologie und Sozialspsychologie* 40/3: 551–69.

Koch, Willy, and Uwe Mathes. 1993. "Political-Cultural Aspects of the System Transformation." In *Political Culture in Germany*, edited by D. Berg-Schlosser and R. Rytlewski. New York: St. Martin's Press.

Kollock, Peter. 1998. "Social Dilemmas: The Anatomy of Cooperation." *Annual Review of Sociology* 24: 183–214.

Koop, Volker. 1997. *Armee oder Freizeitclub? Die Kampfgruppen der Arbeiterklasse in der DDR*. Bonn: Bouvier.

Kopstein, Jeffrey. 1996. "Chipping Away at the State: Worker's Resistance and the Demise of East Germany." *World Politics* 48: 391–423.

———. 1997. *The Politics of Economic Decline*. Chapel Hill: University of North Carolina Press.

Kopstein, Jeffrey, and Karl Otto Richter. 1992. "Communist Social Structure and Post-Communist Elections: Voting for Unification in East Germany." *Studies in Comparative Communism* 25: 363–80.

Kornai, Janos. 1992. *The Socialist System: The Political Economy of Communism*. Princeton: Princeton University Press.

Kotkin, Stephen. 2001. *Armageddon Averted: The Soviet Collapse, 1970–2000*. New York: Oxford University Press.

Kubik, Jan. 1998. "Institutionalization of Protest during Democratic Consolidation in Central Europe." In *The Social Movement Society*, edited by D. Meyer and S. Tarrow. Lanham, Md.: Rowman and Littlefield.

Kuhrt, Eberhard. 1996. *Die SED Herrschaft und ihr Zusammenbruch*. Opladen: Leske und Budrich.

Kuhrt, Eberhard, Hannsjörg Buck, and Gunter Holzweissig, eds. 1999. *Die Endzeit der DDR-Wirtschaft: Analysen zur Wirtschafts-, Sozial- und Umweltpolitik*. Opladen: Leske und Budrich.

Kuran, Timur. 1991. "Now out of Never: The Element of Surprise in the East European Revolutions in 1989." *World Politics* 44/1: 7–48.

——. 1995a. "The Inevitability of Future Revolutionary Surprises." *American Journal of Sociology* 100/6: 1528–51.

——. 1995b. *Private Truths, Public Lies: The Social Consequences of Preference Falsification*. Cambridge, Mass.: Harvard University Press.

Kuvacic, Ivan. 1993. "The Rise and Fall of the New Class." *International Journal of Politics, Culture, and Society* 7/1: 5–18.

Lehmann, Edgar, ed. 1976. *Atlas D.D.R.* Academy of Sciences of the GDR. Gotha: Haack.

Lemke, Christiane. 1991. *Die Ursachen des Umbruchs 1989: Politische Sozialisation in der ehemaligen DDR*. Opladen: Westdeutscher Verlag.

Lemke, Christiane and Gary Marks, eds. 1992. *The Crisis of Socialism in Europe*. Durham, N.C.: Duke University Press.

Lenski, Gerhard. 1978. "Marxist Experiments in Destratification: An Appraisal." *Social Forces* 57/2: 364–83.

Leonhard, Wolfgang. 1955. *Die Revolution entlässt ihre Kinder*. Cologne: Kiepenheuer und Witsch.

Levi, Margaret. 1997. *Consent, Dissent, and Patriotism*. New York: Cambridge University Press.

Liang, Zhang, ed. 2001. *The Tiananmen Papers: The Chinese Leadership's Decision to Use Force against Their Own People*. New York: Public Affairs.

Lichbach, Mark Irving. 1994. *The Rebel's Dilemma*. Ann Arbor: Michigan University Press.

Lin, Nan. 1992. *The Struggle for Tiananmen: Anatomy of the 1989 Mass Movement*. Westport, Conn.: Praeger.

Lindenberg, Siegwart. 1989. "Social Production Functions, Deficits, and Social Revolutions." *Rationality and Society* 1/1: 51–77.

Lindner, Bernd. 1994. *Für ein offenes Land mit freien Menschen*. Leipzig: Forum.

——. 1998. *Die demokratische Revolution in der DDR 1989/90*. Bonn: Bundeszentrale für politische Bildung.

Lindner, Bernd, and Ralph Grüneberger, eds. 1992. *Demonteure: Biographien des Leipziger Herbsts*. Bielefeld: Aisthesis.

Linz, Juan, and Alfred Stepan. 1996. *Problems of Democratic Transition and Consolidation*. Baltimore: Johns Hopkins University Press.

Lippe, Peter von der. 1999. "The Political Role of Official Statistics in the Former GDR." *Historical Social Research* 24/4: 3–28.

Lipset, Seymour Martin, and Bence, Gyorgy. 1994. "Anticipations of the Failure of Communism." *Theory and Society* 23/2: 169–210.

Lohmann, Susanne. 1994. "The Dynamics of Informational Cascades: The Monday Demonstrations in Leipzig, 1989–1991." *World Politics* 47: 42–101.

Long, J. Scott. 1997. *Regression Models for Categorical and Limited Dependent Variables.* Thousand Oaks, Calif.: Sage.

Ludes, Peter. 1993. "Journalismus als Klassenkampf." In *Von der Nachricht zur News Show.* Munich: Wilhelm Fink.

Luxemburg, Rosa. 1961 [1919]. *The Russian Revolution and Leninism or Marxism?* Ann Arbor: University of Michigan Press.

MacDonald, J. S. 1963. "Agricultural Organization, Migration and Labour Militancy in Rural Italy." *Economic History Review* 16: 61–75.

Macy, Michael. 1991. "Chains of Cooperation: Threshold Effects in Collective Action." *American Sociological Review* 56/6: 730–47.

Mahoney, James, and Dietrich Rueschemeyer, eds. 2003. *Comparative Historical Analysis in the Social Sciences.* New York: Cambridge University Press.

Maier, Charles. 1997. *Dissolution: The Crisis of Communism and the End of East Germany.* Princeton: Princeton University Press.

Marcuse, Peter. 1991. *Missing Marx: A Personal and Political Journal of a Year in East Germany, 1989–1990.* New York: Monthly Review Press.

Markovits, Andrei S., and Philip T. Gorski. 1993. *The German Left: Red, Green and Beyond.* New York: Oxford University Press.

Marwell, Gerald, and Pamela Oliver. 1993. *The Critical Mass in Collective Action.* New York: Cambridge University Press.

Marx, Karl. 1972. "Debatten über die Pressfreiheit." In K. Marx and F. Engels, *Werke,* vol. 1. Dietz: Berlin.

Maser, Peter. 1999. "Kirchen." In *Handbuch zur deutschen Einheit,* edited by Werner Weidenfeld and Karl-Rudloff Korte. Bonn: Bundeszentrale für politische Bildung.

Mayer, Adrian C. 1966. "The Significance of Quasi-Groups in the Study of Complex Societies." In *The Social Anthropology of Complex Societies,* edited by Michael Banton. London: Tavistock.

McAdam, Doug. 1982. *Political Process and the Development of Black Insurgency, 1930–1970.* Chicago: Chicago University Press.

——. 1986. "Recruitment to High-Risk Activism: The Case of Freedom Summer." *American Journal of Sociology* 92: 64–90.

——. 1996. "Conceptual Origins, Current Problems, Future Directions." In *Comparative Perspectives on Social Movements,* edited by D. McAdam, J. McCarthy, and M. Zald. New York: Cambridge University Press.

McAdam, Doug, John McCarthy, and Mayer Zald, eds. 1996. *Comparative Perspectives on Social Movements.* New York: Cambridge University Press.

McAdam, Doug, and Ronnelle Paulsen. 1993. "Specifying the Relationship between Social Ties and Activism." *American Journal of Sociology* 99: 640–67.

McAdam, Doug, Sidney Tarrow, and Charles Tilly, eds. 2001. *Dynamics of Contention.* New York: Cambridge University Press.

McAdams, A. James. 1993. *Germany Divided: From the Wall to Reunification*. Princeton: Princeton University Press.

McCarthy, John, and Mayer Zald. 1977. "Resource Mobilization and Social Movements." *American Journal of Sociology* 82/6: 1112–41.

McPherson, Miller, Lynn Smith-Lovin, and James M. Cook. 2001. "Birds of a Feather: Homophily in Social Networks." *Annual Review of Sociology* 27: 415–44.

Meuschel, Sigrid. 1992. *Legitimation und Parteiherrschaft in der DDR*. Frankfurt am Main: Suhrkamp.

Moore, Barrington. 1978. *Injustice*. White Plains, N.Y.: M. E. Sharpe.

Moses, John A. 1993. "The Collapse of the GDR 1989/1990: A Protestant Revolution?" *European Studies Journal* 10/1–2: 147–60.

Mueller, Carol. 1999. "Escape from the GDR, 1961–1989: Hybrid Exit Repertoires in a Disintegrating Leninist Regime." *American Journal of Sociology* 105/3: 697–735.

Mühler, Kurt, and Stefan Wilsdorf. 1991. "Die Leipziger Montagsdemonstrationen 1989/90." *Berliner Journal für Soziologie* 1/5: 37–45.

Müller, Birgit. 1995. "The Wall in the Heads: East-West German Stereotypes and the Problem of Transition in Three Enterprises in East Berlin." In *Europe: Central and East*, edited by M. Mendell and K. Nielsen. Montreal: Black Rose Press.

Müller, Klaus-Dieter. 1997. "Haftbedingungen für politische Häftlinge in der sbz und der DDR und ihre Veränderungen von 1945–1989." In *Die Verangenheit lässt uns nicht los*, edited by A. Stephan and K.-D. Mueller. Berlin: Oktoberdruck Berlin.

Müller-Engbergs, Helmut. 1996. *Inoffizielle Mitarbeiter des Ministeriums für Staatssicherheit*. Berlin: Links.

Munck, Gerardo, and Carol Skalnick Leff. 1999. "Modes of Transition and Democratization: South America and Eastern Europe in Comparative Perspective." In *Transitions to Democracy*, edited by L. Anderson. New York: Columbia University Press.

Naimark, Norman. 1992. " 'Ich will hier raus': Emmigration and the Collapse of the German Democratic Republic." In *Eastern Europe in Revolution*, edited by I. Banac. Ithaca: Cornell University Press.

———. 1995. *The Russians in Germany*. Cambridge, Mass.: Harvard University Press.

Neubert, Ehrhart. 1990. *Eine Protestantische Revolution*. Berlin: Kontext.

———. 1998. *Geschichte der Opposition in der DDR, 1949–1989*. Berlin: Links.

Neugebauer, Gero. 1997. "Von der SED zur PDS 1989–1990." In *Die SED: Geschichte, Organisation, Politik*, edited by A. Herbst, G. Stephan, and J. Winkler. Berlin: Dietz.

Niethammer, Lutz. 1991. *Die volkseigene Erfahrung*. Berlin: Rowohlt.

———. 1995. "Zeroing in on Change: In Search of Popular Experience in the Industrial Province in the German Democratic Republic." In *The History of Everyday Life*, edited by A. Lüdtke. Princeton: Princeton University Press.

Nissen, Sylke. 1992. *Modernisierung nach dem Sozialismus: Ökologische und ökonomische Probleme der Transformation*. Marburg: Metropolis.

Noelle-Neumann, Elisabeth. 1984. *The Spiral of Silence*. Chicago: University of Chicago Press.

North, Douglass. 1981. *Structure and Change in Economic History*. New York: Norton.

Nove, Alec. 1989. *Stalinism and After: The Road to Gorbachev*. 3d ed. London: Unwin Hyman.

Nowak, Kurt. 1996. "Historische Wurzeln der Entkirchlichung in der DDR." *Gesellschaften im Umbruch* 27: 665–69.

Oberschall, Anthony. 1973. *Social Conflict and Social Movements*. New York: Prentice-Hall.

——. 1996. "Opportunities and Framing in the East European Revolts of 1989." In *Comparative Perspectives on Social Movements*, edited by D. McAdam, J. McCarthy, and M. Zald. Cambridge: Cambridge University Press.

O'Donnell, Guillermo, and Philippe Schmitter. 1986. *Transitions from Authoritarian Rule: Uncertain Conclusions regarding Unstable Democracies*. Baltimore: Johns Hopkins University Press.

O'Donnell, Guillermo, Philippe Schmitter, and Lawrence Whitehead, eds. 1991. *Transitions from Authoritarian Rule: Comparative Perspectives*. Baltimore: Johns Hopkins University Press.

Offe, Claus. 1994. *Der Tunnel am Ende des Lichtes*. Frankfurt am Main: Suhrkamp.

——. 1997. *Varieties of Transition: The East European and the East German Experience*. Cambridge, Mass.: MIT Press.

O'Gorman, Hubert J. 1986. "The Discovery of Pluralistic Ignorance: An Ironic Lesson." *Journal of the History of the Behavioral Sciences* 22: 333–47.

Oliver, Pamela. 1984. "If You Don't Do It, Nobody Else Will: Active and Token Contributors to Collective Action." *American Sociological Review* 49/5: 601–10.

Oliver, Pamela E., and Gerald Marwell. 2001. "Whatever Happened to Critical Mass Theory? A Retrospective and Assessment." *Sociological Theory* 19/3: 292–311.

Olson, Mancur. 1965. *The Logic of Collective Action*. Cambridge, Mass.: Harvard University Press.

——. 1990. "The Logic of Collective Action in Soviet-Type Societies." *Journal of Soviet Nationalities* 1: 8–27.

Opp, Karl-Dieter. 1994. "Repression and Revolutionary Action: East Germany in 1989." *Rationality and Society* 6/1: 101–38.

——. 1997. *Die enttäuschten Revolutionäre: Politisches Engagement vor und nach der Wende*. Opladen: Leske und Budrich.

——. 2001. "Social Networks and the Emergence of Protest Norms." In *Social Norms*, edited by M. Hechter and K.-D. Opps, 234–66. New York: Russell Sage.

Opp, Karl-Dieter, and Christiane Gern. 1993. "Dissident Groups, Personal Networks, and Spontaneous Cooperation: The East German Revolution of 1989." *American Sociological Review* 58/5: 659–80.

Opp, Karl-Dieter, Peter Voss, and Christiane Gern. 1995. *Origins of a Spontaneous Revolution: East Germany in 1989*. Ann Arbor: University of Michigan Press.

Osa, Maryjane. 2003. *Solidarity and Contention: Networks of Polish Opposition*. Minneapolis: University of Minnesota Press.

Ost, David. 1990. *Solidarity and the Politics of Anti-Politics*. Philadelphia: Temple University Press.

Otto, Wilfried. 1995. "Widerspruch und abweichendes Verhalten der SED." In *Materialen der Enquete-Kommission "Aufarbeitung von Geschichte und Folgen der SED-Diktatur in Deutschland,"* edited by T. Ammer. Frankfurt am Main: Suhrkamp.

Pedraza, Silvia. 1985. *Political and Economic Migration to the Americas: Cubans and Mexicans*. Austin: University of Texas Press.

Petschow, Ulrich, Jürgen Meyerhoff, and Claus Thomasberger, eds. 1990. *Umweltreport DDR: Bilanz der Zerstörung, Kosten der Sanierung, Stratagien für den ökologischen Umbau.* Frankfurt am Main: Fischer.

Pfaff, Steven. 1996. "Collective Identity and Informal Groups in Revolutionary Mobilization: East Germany in 1989." *Social Forces* 75/1: 91–118.

Pfaff, Steven, and Hyojoung Kim. 2003. "Exit-Voice Dynamics in Collective Action: An Analysis of Emigration and Protest in the East German Revolution." *American Journal of Sociology* 109/2: 401–44.

Pfaff, Steven, and Guobin Yang. 2001. "Double-Edged Rituals and the Symbolic Resources of Collective Action: Political Commemorations and the Mobilization of Protest in 1989." *Theory and Society* 30: 539–589.

Pflugbeil, Sebastian. 1999. "Das Neue Forum." In *Opposition in der DDR von den 70er bis zum Zusammenbruch der SED Herrschaft*, edited by E. Kuhrt et al. Opladen: Leske und Budrich.

Philipsen, Dirk. 1993. *We Were the People: Voices from East Germany's Revolutionary Autumn of 1989.* Durham: Duke University Press.

Plato, Alexander von. 1993. "An Unfamiliar Germany: Some Remarks on the Past and Present Relationships between East and West Germans." *Oral History* 21/1: 35–42.

Pollack, Detlef. 1990. "Aussenseiter oder Repräsentanten? Zur Rolle der politisch alternativen Gruppen." *Deutschland Archiv* 23/8: 1216–23.

———. 1994. *Kirche in der Organisationsgesellschaft.* Stuttgart: W. Kohlhammer.

———. 1997. *Politischer Protest: Politisch alternative Gruppen in der DDR.* Leske und Budrich.

Pollack, Detlef, and Dieter Rink, eds. 1997. *Zwischen Verweigerung und Opposition: Politischer Protest in der DDR, 1970–1989.* Frankfurt am Main: Campus.

Pond, Elisabeth. 1993. *Beyond the Wall: Germany's Road to Unification.* Washington: Brookings.

Poumet, Jacques. 1996. "Die Leipziger Untergrundzeitschriften aus der Sicht der Staatssicherheit." *Deutschland Archiv* 29/1: 67–85.

Przeworski, Adam. 1991. *Democracy and the Market.* Cambridge: Cambridge University Press.

Przybylski. Peter. 1992. *Tatort Politbüro.* Vol. 2: *Honecker, Mittag, und Schalck-Godlowski.* Berlin: Rowohlt.

Quint, Peter. 1997. *The Imperfect Union: Constitutional Structures of German Unification.* Princeton: Princeton University Press.

Ramet, Sabrina P. 1995. *Social Currents in Eastern Europe: The Sources and Meaning of the Great Transformation.* Durham: Duke University Press.

———. 1998. *Nihil Obstat: Religion, Politics, and Social Change in East-Central Europe and Russia.* Durham: Duke University Press.

Raschka, Johannes. 1997. "Staatsverbrechen werden nicht genannt: Zur Zahl politischer Häftlinge während der Amtszeit Honeckers." *Deutschland Archiv* 30/2: 196–208.

Rasler, Karen. 1996. "Concession, Repression, and Political Protest in the Iranian Revolution." *American Sociological Review* 61/1: 132–52.

Reich, Jens. 2002. "Das Schneckenhaus: Freiheit nach innen. Anpassung nach aussen." *Berliner Zeitung* 15/16 June: 4–5.

Reissig, Rolf, and Gert-Joachim Glaessner, eds. 1991. *Das Ende eines Experiments: Umbruch in der DDR und die deutsche Einheit*. Berlin: Dietz.

Richter, Karl-Otto. 1991. "Regionale Disproportionen: Soziologische Anmerkungen zu den Volkskammer und Kommunalwahlen 1990 in der DDR." *Politologie und Soziologie* 1: 16.

Rink, Dieter, and Michael Hofmann. 1991. "Oppositionelle Gruppen und alternative Milieus in Leipzig im Prozess der Umgestaltung in Ostdeutschland." *Deutschland Archiv* 24/9: 940–49.

Rogers, Everett M. 1995 [1962]. *Diffusion of Innovations*. New York: Free Press.

Roski, Günter, and Peter Förster. 1990. "Leipziger Demoskopie." In *Leipziger Demontagebuch*, edited by W. Schneider. Leipzig: Kiepenheuer.

Ross, Corey. 2000. *Constructing Socialism at the Grass Roots*. New York: St. Martin's Press.

———. 2002. *The East German Dictatorship*. London: Arnold.

Rucht, Dieter. 1996. "German Unification, Democratization, and the Role of Social Movements: A Missed Opportunity?" *Mobilization* 1/1: 35–62.

Rüddenklau, Wolfgang. 1992. *Störenfried: DDR-Opposition 1986–1989*. Berlin: Basis-Druck.

Rusbult, Caryl E., and Isabella Zembrodt. 1983. "Responses to Dissatisfaction in Romantic Involvement." *Journal of Experimental Social Psychology* 19/3: 274–93.

Rusbult, Caryl E., Isabella Zembrodt, and Lawanna Gunn. 1982. "Exit, Voice, Loyalty, and Neglect: Responses to Dissatisfaction in Romantic Involvements." *Journal of Personality and Social Psychology* 43/6: 1230–42.

Saxonberg, Steven. 2001. *The Fall: A Comparative Study of the End of Communism in Czechoslovakia, East Germany, Hungary and Poland*. London: Harwood.

Schabowski, Günter. 1991. *Der Sturz*. Berlin: Rowohlt.

Schelling, Thomas C. 1960. *The Strategy of Conflict*. Cambridge, Mass.: Harvard University Press.

———. 1978. *Micromotives and Macrobehavior*. New York: Norton.

Schlegelmilch, Cordia. 1996. "Für das Volk oder mit dem Volk? Über Schwierigkeiten mit der Demokratie in der sächsichen Kleinstadt Wurzen." *Deutschland Archiv* 29/4: 535–42.

Schluchter, Wolfgang. 1996. *Neubeginn durch Anpassung?* Frankfurt am Main: Suhrkamp.

Schneider, Wolfgang. 1990. *Leipziger Demontagebuch*. Leipzig: Kiepenheuer.

Schoepflin, Georg. 1993. *The Politics of Eastern Europe*. Cambridge: Blackwell.

Schreiber, Helmut, ed. 1989. *Umweltprobleme in Mittel- und Osteuropa*. Frankfurt am Main: Campus.

Schuessler, Rudolf. 1989. "Exit Threats and Cooperation under Anonymity." *Journal of Conflict Resolution* 33/4: 728–49.

Schürer, Gerhard. 1999. "Planung und Lenkung der Volkswirtschaft in der DDR: Ein Zeitzeugenbericht aus dem Zentrum der DDR-Wirtschaftslenkung." In *Die Endzeit* der DDR-Wirtschaft: Analysen zur Wirtschafts-, Sozial- und Umweltpolitik, edited by E. Kuhrt, et al. Opladen: Leske und Budrich.

Schwabe, Uwe. 1997. "Wir waren das Volk!" Unpublished manuscript. Haus der Geschichte der Bundesrepublik Deutschland, Projektgruppe Leipzig.

———. 1998. "Friedensgebete in Leipzig: Symbol der Befreiung." In *Am Ende des realen Sozialismus*, edited by E. Kuhrt and G. Holzweissig. Opladen: Laske und Budrich.

Scott, James C. 1990. *Domination and the Arts of Resistance: Hidden Transcripts*. New Haven: Yale University Press.

Shi, Jian, ed. 1993. *The Truth about the Beijing Turmoil 1989*. Beijing: Beijing Publishing House.

Shlapentokh, Valdimir. 1989. *Public and Private Life of the Soviet People: Changing Values in Post-Stalin Russia*. New York: Oxford University Press.

Siebenmorgen, Peter. 1993. *"Staatsicherheit" der DDR: Der Westen im fadenkreuz der Stasi*. Bonn: Bouvier.

Šik, Ota. 1981. *The Communist Power System*. Translated by M. G. Freidberg. New York: Praeger.

Skocpol, Theda. 1979. *States and Social Revolutions*. Cambridge: Cambridge University Press.

Smelser, Neil J. 1963. *Theory of Collective Behavior*. New York: Free Press.

Smith, Roland. 1985. "The Church in the GDR." In *Honecker's Germany*, edited by David Childs. London: Allen and Unwin.

Solga, Heike. 1994. "Systemloyalität als Bedingung sozialer Mobilität im Staatsozialismus am Beispiel der DDR." *Berliner Journal für Soziologie* 4/4: 523–42.

Solnick, Steven L. 1998. *Stealing the State: Control and Collapse in Soviet Institutions*. Cambridge, Mass.: Harvard University Press.

Staritz, Dietrich. 1996. *Geschichte der DDR*. Frankfurt am Main: Suhrkamp.

Stark, David, and Laszlo Bruszt. 1998. *Postsocialist Pathways: Transforming Politics and Prosperity in East Central Europe*. Cambridge: Cambridge University Press.

Stepan, Alfred. 1986. "Paths toward Redemocratization: Theoretical and Comparative Considerations." In *Transitions from Authoritarian Rule*, edited by G. O'Donnell, P. Schmitter and L. Whitehead. Baltimore: Johns Hopkins University Press.

Stephan, Annegret, and Klaus-Dieter Muller, eds. 1997. *Haftbedingungen politischer Gefangener in der SBZ/DDR und deren gesundheitlichen Folgen*. Berlin: Oktoberdruck.

Stiglitz, Joseph E. 1995. *Whither Socialism?* Cambridge, Mass.: MIT Press.

Stoever, Bernd. 1997. "Leben im Deutschen Diktaturen: Historiographische und methodologische Aspekte der Erforschung von Widerstand und Opposition im Dritten Reich und in der DDR." In *Zwischen Verweigerung und Opposition: Politischer Protest in der DDR, 1970–1989*, edited by D. Pollack and D. Rink, 3–53. Frankfurt am Main: Campus.

Süss, Walter. 1991. "Mit Unwillen zur Macht: Der Runde Tisch in der DDR der Übergangszeit." *Deutschland Archiv*, 24/5: 470–79.

Swain, Geoffrey, and Nigel Swain. 1993. *Eastern Europe since 1945*. New York: St. Martin's Press.

Swedberg, Richard. 1990. *Economics and Sociology: Refining their Boundaries: Conversations with Economists and Sociologists*. Princeton: Princeton University Press.

Sykes, Gresham. 1958. *The Society of Captives*. Princeton: Princeton University Press.

Szabo, Mate. 1994. "Greens, Cabbies, and Anti-Communists: Collective Action during Regime Transition in Hungary." In *New Social Movements: From Ideology to Identity*, edited by E. Larana, H. Johnston, and J. Gusfield. Philadelphia: Temple University Press.

Szelenyi, Ivan, and Balasz Szelenyi. 1994. "Why Socialism Failed: Toward a Theory of System Breakdown." *Theory and Society* 23/2: 211–31.

Szelenyi, Szonja. 1987. "Social Inequality and Party Mobility." *American Sociological Review* 52/5: 559–73.

Tarrow, Sidney. 1991. *Struggle, Politics, and Reform: Collective Identity, Social Movements, and Cycles of Protest*. Ithaca: Cornell Studies in International Affairs Western Societies Paper #21.

———. 1994. *Power in Movement*. New York: Cambridge University Press.

———. 1996. "States and Opportunities: The Political Structuring of Social Movements." In *Comparative Perspectives on Social Movements*, edited by D. McAdam, J. McCarthy, and M. Zald. New York: Cambridge University Press.

Taylor, Michael. 1987. *The Possibility of Cooperation*. Cambridge: Cambridge University Press.

Tietzel, Manfred, and Marion Welser. 1994. "The Economics of the Iron Curtain and the Berlin Wall." *Rationality and Society* 6/1: 58–78.

Tilly, Charles. 1978. *From Mobilization to Revolution*. Reading, Mass.: Addison-Wesley.

———. 2000. "Processes and Mechanisms of Democratization." *Sociological Theory* 18/1: 1–16.

Titarenko, Larissa, John D. McCarthy, Clark McPhail, and Boguslaw Augustyn. 2001. "The Interaction of State Repression, Protest Form and Protest Sponsor Strength during the Transition from Communism in Minsk, Belarus, 1990–1995." *Mobilization* 6/2: 129–150.

Tocqueville, Alexis de. 1955 [1856]. *The Old Regime and the French Revolution*. Translated by Stuart Gilbert. New York: Doubleday.

———. 1987. *Recollections: The French Revolution of 1848*. Edited by J. P. Taylor and A. P. Kerr. New Brunswick, N.J.: Transaction.

Tolnay, Stewart E., and E. M. Beck. 1992. "Racial Violence and Black Migration in the American South, 1910–1930." *American Sociological Review* 57/1: 103–16.

Torpey, John C. 1995. *Intellectuals, Socialism, and Dissent: The East German Opposition and Its Legacy*. Minneapolis: University of Minnesota Press.

Touraine, Alain, François Dubet, Michel Wieviorka, and Jan Strzelecki. 1983. *Solidarity: Poland, 1980–1981*. Translated by David Denby. Cambridge: Cambridge University Press.

Trotsky, Leon. 1936 [1933]. *The History of the Russian Revolution*. Translated by Max Eastman. New York: Simon and Schuster.

Tullock, Gordon. 1971. "The Paradox of Revolution." *Public Choice* 11 (fall): 89–99.

United States Arms Control and Disarmament Agency. 1984. *World Military Expendi-*

tures. Washington: Bureau of Economic Affairs, Arms Control and Disarmament Agency.

Useem, Bert. 1998. "Breakdown Theories of Collective Action." *Annual Review of Sociology* 24: 215–38.

Valente, Thomas W. 1995. *Network Models of the Diffusion of Innovations*. Cresskill, N.J.: Hampton.

Vanberg, Viktor J., and Roger D. Congleton. 1992. "Rationality, Morality, and Exit." *American Political Science Review* 86/2: 418–31.

Van Lange, P. A. M. 1994. "Toward More Locomotion in Experimental Games." In *Social Dilemmas and Cooperation*, edited by U. Schulz, W. Albers, and U. Mueller. Berlin: Springer.

Verdery, Katherine. 1996. *What Was Socialism, and What Comes Next?* Princeton: Princeton University Press.

Vobruba, Georg. 1997. "Legitimationsprobleme des Sozialismus: Das Scheitern des intentionalistischen Gesellschaftsprojekts und das Erbe des Sozialismus." In *Autonomiegewinne*. Vienna: Passagen.

Vogel, Amos. 1990. "Two Weeks in November." *New Politics* 9/1: 57–64.

Völker, Beate, and Henk Flap. 2001. "Weak Ties as a Liability: The Case of East Germany." *Rationality and Society* 13/4: 397–428.

Walder, Andrew. 1994. "The Decline of Communist Power: Elements of a Theory of Institutional Change." *Theory and Society* 23/2: 297–323.

Walter, Franz, Tobias Dürr, and Klaus Schmidtke. 1993. *Die SPD in Sachsen und Thüringen zwischen Hochburg und Diaspora*. Berlin: Dietz.

Watts, Duncan J. 1999. "Networks, Dynamics, and the Small-World Phenomenon. *American Journal of Sociology* 105/2: 493–527.

Wawrzyn, Liehard. 1990. *Der Blaue*. Berlin: P. Wagenbach.

Weber, Hermann. 1993. *Die DDR, 1945–1990*. 2d expanded ed. Munich: Oldenbourg.

——. 1999. *Geschichte der DDR*. Munich: Deutscher Taschenbuch Verlag.

Weber, Max. 1978. *Economy and Society*. Translated by Gunther Roth and Claus Wittich. Berkeley: University of California Press.

Wedeen, Lisa. 1998. "Acting 'As If': Symbolic Politics and Social Control in Syria." *Comparative Studies in Society and History* 40/3: 503–23.

Weiss, Konrad. 1990. "Die Bürgerbewegung als Erinnerungsvereine an den deutschen Herbst." *Demokratie Jetzt: Wochenzeitung der Basisgruppen von IFM und Demokratie Jetzt* (October): 3.

Weissgerber, Günter. 1995. "Zwischen Montagsdemonstration und Deutscher Einheit: Mein erstes Jahr in der Politik." Unpublished manuscript. Leipzig: Citizen's Movement Archive.

Wheaton, Bernard, and Zdenek Kavan. 1992. *The Velvet Revolution: Czechoslovakia, 1988–1991*. Boulder, Colo.: Westview, 1992.

Wickham-Crowley, Thomas. 1992. *Guerrillas and Revolution in Latin America*. Princeton: Princeton University Press.

Wilson, James Q. 1983. *Thinking about Crime*. New York: Basic.

Wolfe, Nancy T. 1992. *Policing a Socialist Society: The German Democratic Republic*. New York: Greenwood Press.

Wonneberger, Christoph. 1994. "Ich habe immer tun müssen, was ich für richtig hielt." In *Für ein offenes Land mit freien Menschen*, edited by Bernd Lindner. Leipzig: Forum.

Yamagishi, Toshio. 1988. "Exit from the Group as an Individualistic Solution to the Free-Rider Problem in the United States and Japan." *Journal of Experimental Social Psychology* 24: 530–42.

Yurchak, Alexei. 1997. "The Cynical Reason of Late Socialism: Power, Pretense and the Anekdot." *Public Culture* 9/2: 161–88.

Zapf, Wolfgang. 1993. "Die DDR 1989/1990: Zusammenbruch einer Sozialstruktur?" In *Der Zusammenbruch der DDR*, edited by Hans Joas and Martin Kohli, 29–48. Frankurt am Main: Suhrkamp.

Zdravomyslova, Elena. 1996. "Opportunities and Framing in the Transition to Democracy: The Case of Russia." In *Comparative Perspectives on Social Movements*, edited by D. McAdam, J. McCarthy, and M. Zald, 122–37. New York: Cambridge University Press.

Zelikow, Philip, and Condoleezza Rice. 1995. *Germany Unified and Europe Transformed*. Cambridge, Mass.: Harvard.

Zhang Liang, comp. 2001. *The Tiananmen Papers: The Chinese Leadership's Decision to Use Force against Their Own People*. Edited by Andrew J. Nathan and Perry Linx. New York: Public Affairs.

Zhao, Dingxin. 1996. "Foreign Study as a Safety Valve: The Experience of China's University Students Going Abroad in the Eighties." *Higher Education* 31/2: 145–63.

———. 1997. "Decline of Political Control in Chinese Universities and the Rise of the 1989 Chinese Student Movement." *Sociological Perspectives* 40/2: 159–82.

———. 2001. *The Power of Tiananmen: State-Society Relations and the 1989 Beijing Student Movement*. Chicago: Chicago University Press.

Zhou, Xueguang. 1993. "Unorganized Interests and Collective Action in Communist China." *American Sociological Review* 58/1: 54–73.

Zwahr, Hartmut. 1993. *Ende einer Selbstzerstörung: Leipzig und die Revolution in der DDR*. Göttingen: Vandenhoeck und Ruprecht.

Zweigler, Reinhard. 1998. "Ein bürgerbewegter Trauerabend um das Erbe und die alten Träume." *Leipziger Volkszeitung*, January 19, p. 3.

Index

Churches (*continued*)
    olic Church; Church role in socialism;
    Jugendweihe; Peace Prayers; Protestant
    Church; Reformed Church; Solidarity
    Church; St. Nicholas Church; Union of
    Evangelical Lutheran Churches; Zion
    Church
Church role in socialism, 83–84
Civic movement: elections and, 247–250;
    ideology and organization of, 11, 13, 114,
    189, 190–199, 204–205, 219–242, 247,
    253, 256–258, 265; Loyalists and, 185, 189,
    220, 223; origin of, 22, 113, 215; regime
    and, 127, 185–186, 195, 226–228, 230, 232,
    236; Round Table and, 236, 239–246;
    weaknesses of, 123, 127, 172, 191, 197, 199,
    203–205, 220–222, 235, 239, 242, 258;
    working class and, 206–210, 222. *See*
    also Democracy Now; New Forum
Collective action theory, 8–9, 168, 259. *See*
    also Free rider; High-risk collective
    action; Networks; Rebel's Dilemma;
    State's Dilemma
Communism, 2, 4, 59, 61, 76, 80, 105; East
    Germany and, 32–60; institutional
    legacies of, 265; rebellion against, 107–
    141. *See also* Anti-Communist move-
    ment; Post-Communists
Communist militiamen (*Kampfgruppen*),
    118, 172, 175–176, 179
Conference on Security and Cooperation
    in Europe (CSCE), 67, 78
Constitution (GDR), 70, 93, 193, 236, 241,
    246
Convention on Refugees, 108
Council of Ministers, 65, 233
Counter-elite, 3–5, 190
Counterespionage, 69–70
Countermobilization, 10, 13
"Critical mass," 150, 151, 156
Cuba, 27, 254, 265–266,
Czechoslovakia, 2, 169; border and, 108–
    109, 123, 140, 158, 163, 262; Civic Forum
    in, 209–210; dissident movement in, 15,

89, 210, 264; exit to, 109, 117, 209; transi-
    tion to democracy in, 2, 210

Declaration of Human Rights, 90
D-mark, 245, 251
Democracy Now, 114, 194, 197, 199, 248, 252
Democratic Awakening, 114, 199, 222, 239,
    247–248
Democratic transition, 3–4, 6, 10, 224,
    258. *See also* Czechoslovakia; Hungary;
    Poland; Post-Communists; Post-
    totalitarian state
Dresden: characteristics of dissident
    movement in, 8, 91, 93, 95, 113, 132; civic
    movement and, 214; demonstrations in,
    116–126, 135–143, 153, 163, 179–180, 183–
    184, 193, 196, 221; economic decline of,
    40, 42; exit from, 43, 79, 116–119, 160,
    163; negotiations for reforms in, 183,
    185, 188–189, 225, 228; political weak-
    ness of, 44; repression in, 118–121, 126,
    135, 157, 167, 171, 178–180, 183–184, 262–
    263; Round Tables in, 241, 245–247. *See*
    also Dresdeners
Dresdeners, 118, 120

East Berlin: characteristics of, 40, 42, 63,
    75, 245; characteristics of dissident
    movement in, 74, 91–94, 114–116, 126,
    137, 140, 153–154, 193, 199, 202, 213, 218,
    232, 238; exit from, 79, 160, 251; govern-
    ment officials and, 7, 52, 108, 114, 117,
    173, 186, 229; negotiations for reforms
    in, 232, 241; New Forum in, 202, 213–
    219; repression in, 135, 140, 157, 167,
    170–174, 182; unification and, 234
Eastern Europe, 59, 91, 232, 245; com-
    parisons between transitions in GDR
    and, 72, 83, 195, 217, 239, 241; transition
    to democracy, 2, 5–7, 61, 192, 206, 249,
    264. *See also* Czechoslovakia; Hungary;
    Iron Curtain; Poland
East Germany. *See* German Democratic
    Republic

165, 172–173, 180–182, 192, 196–208, 221–225, 229–230, 237, 241–242, 251; economic decline of, 36–37, 40, 42–45, 139; exit from, 79–80, 116, 160–161, 251; labor relations in, 47, 75–76; negotiations for reforms in, 185–189, 227–230; niche society in, 74, 76, 130–131; religion in, 84–88, 91, 127; repression in, 53, 72, 76, 95–96, 99, 117, 122–126, 140, 157, 164, 170–184, 263. *See also* Initiative Group for Life; *Leipziger Volkszeitung*; Leipzig Six; Peace Prayers; St. Nicholas Church

Leipziger Volkszeitung, 45, 102, 122, 176, 205, 228

Leipzig municipal archives, 299

Leipzig Six, 123, 183–186, 228

Lemke, Christiane, 61

Liberal Democrats, 235, 248

Lichbach, Mark, 9, 15

Liebknecht, Karl, 93

Lindenberg, Siegwart, 145

Linz, Juan, 3, 83

Loyalist mobilization, 11, 261–262. *See also* Civic movement; Loyalists; Loyalty; Mobilization; New Forum

Loyalists, 20–22, 24–26, 29–30, 49, 60, 152, 185, 216, 219–220, 257–260. *See also* Civic movement; Exit; Loyalist mobilization; Loyalty; Socialist Unity Party

Loyalty: civic movement and, 195, 204, 206–208, 211, 214–216, 220–223; collective action and, 147, 151–152, 192, 256–263; erosion of Socialist Unity Party, 46–50, 60, 175–178, 187; public expressions of, 72–73, 103, 114, 132; reunification and, 229, 232, 237, 240; statistical evaluation of, 154, 158–161; surveillance and, 70; theory of, 11–33, 256–263. *See also* "Alert loyalists"; Civic movement; Exit; Loyalist mobilization; Socialist Unity Party

Lutheran Church. *See* Union of Evangelical Lutheran Churches

Luxemburg, Rosa, 58, 90, 93, 260

Luxemburg-Liebknecht Day, 93, 96

Macro-level explanation, 5

Magdeburg, 116, 136, 177, 179, 208, 214

Maier, Charles, 34, 71

Marxism-Leninism: declining legitimacy of, 56, 84, 260; ideology and norms, 1, 25, 32–33, 50–58; political parties and, 24, 46, 58; regimes and, 1–3, 8, 16, 23–25, 32, 56; support for, 48–49, 61, 167–168, 238. *See also* Communism

Masur, Kurt, 99, 183–184, 203

Matzke, Cornelia, 85–86

May Day, 93, 132

Melhorn, Ludwig, 87, 94. *See also* Leipzig; Union of Evangelical Lutheran Churches

Meuschel, Sigrid, 191, 198

Meyer, Kurt, 180, 183–184

Michnik, Adam, 249

Micro-mobilization, 77. *See also* Mobilization

Mielke, Erich, 69–70, 111, 115, 170–174, 186, 226, 231

Ministry for State Security. *See* Stasi

Ministry of the Interior: control and, 66, 175, 193; reports of dissident activity from, 116, 121–123, 136, 153, 157, 166, 204, 207, 242, 246. *See also* Socialist Unity Party; Stasi

Mittag, Günter, 39, 52, 186, 226

Mobilization: conditions for, 6, 16, 82, 105–107, 121–141; Eastern bloc and, 2, 264–265; effect of exit on, 143–147, 152–153, 255–262; GDR response to, 165–189; New Forum and, 190–223; niche and, 77; statistical evaluation of, 156–164; success of, 225–230; transition in GDR and, 2–16, 22, 27. *See also* Loyalist mobilization; New Forum; Reformist mobilization; Spontaneous mobilization

Modrow, Hans, 118–121, 183–188, 204, 225–228, 236–245

Monday Peace Prayers, 12, 82, 95, 97–99, 102–106, 123–129, 133–135, 146, 172

Mono-organizational regime, 19, 23, 26, 29, 59, 147, 259. *See also* Exit

Multiparty democracy, 197, 247

National Defense Council, 11, 114

National Front, 236

National People's Army (NVA), 87, 118, 170

Networks: church, 12, 79, 84, 87–88, 92, 218; civil society and, 29, 62; dissident movement and, 87, 113, 156; exit and erosion of, 149–153, 160–161, 215, 218–219, 255–256, 261–262; information and, 91; Leninist societies and, 73; role in New Forum of, 212, 215–219; social opportunities in, 62, 73–76, 78–79. *See also* Niche society

Neubrandenburg, 43, 56, 214

Neues Deutschland, 54, 112, 245

New Forum (Neues Forum): "Awakening 1989" and, 193; breakaway factions of, 248; church involvement in, 84, 119, 128; demonstrations and mobilization and, 114, 119–121, 126–127, 138, 140–141, 190–193, 199–201, 204–205, 221, 232, 256–257, 261–262; GDR opposition to, 185, 188, 193, 195, 226–228, 238; legalization of, 121, 124, 140, 193, 195, 204, 233, 238; manifesto of, 126; platform and goals of, 22, 194–203, 207–208, 239, 246–247, 252–253; sources of support for, 201, 207–213, 221–222; statistical evaluation of, 214–220; weakness of, 198, 205, 210, 223, 240, 247. *See also* Civic movement; Loyalty; Reformist voice

Niche society, 12, 61–62, 73–78, 105, 130–131, 149, 208, 212, 222, 262–264. *See also* Networks

"Noisy exiters," 77, 80

Noncompliance, 87

Nonmarket forces, 17

Nonsocialist world, 34, 67–68, 74, 233

Nonviolence, 95, 104, 120, 123, 126–128, 131, 185, 187, 189, 207

North, Douglass, 59

North Korea, 254–255, 265–266

Oberschall, Anthony, 6, 264

Olson, Mancur, 10, 20–21, 63, 145

Opp, Karl-Dieter, 28, 124–125, 135, 139, 163, 178

Oral histories, 47, 125, 130, 163

Ostpolitik, 64, 67, 244

Parliament, 169, 199, 224, 236, 284, 290, 296, 299, 302. *See also* Politburo; Socialist Unity Party

Party Control Commissions (PKK), 33, 176. *See also* Socialist Unity Party; Stasi

Party of Democratic Socialism (PDS), 238–239, 249

Peace Prayers, 82, 95, 97–106, 123, 125–129, 133–135, 141, 146, 172. *See also* Leipzig; St. Nicholas Church

Perestroika, 38, 45, 51–53, 55, 57, 169, 181, 183, 229, 238. *See also* Exit: economic decline and; Dresden: economic decline of; Leipzig: economic decline of

Plauen, 116–118, 126, 138, 160, 163, 178, 208

Poland, 234–235; Catholic Church in, 105; dissident movement in, 6, 15, 62, 89, 168, 208, 249; exit to, 109; reforms and transition in, 1, 4, 52, 110–111, 168–169, 226

Politburo: characteristics of, 33, 44, 47, 69, 110, 140; economy and, 37–39; reforms and, 52, 90, 184, 225–226, 229, 233, 236, 240; surveillance and control and, 51–54, 89, 100, 110–111, 167–174, 177, 186–188; weaknesses of, 181, 184. *See also* Socialist Unity Party; Stasi

Pommert, Jochen, 228

Poppe, Gerd, 85, 88–89

Post-Communists, 4, 210, 238–239, 244, 249, 265

Post-totalitarian state, 83

Prag, Jochen, 181–182, 209, 229

Process tracing, 275

Propositions (evaluation of exit-voice dynamics), 19–29, 153, 192, 255–260

Protestant Church, 83–84, 93, 100

Pro-unification, 14, 202, 205, 250

Przeworski, Adam, 1, 3, 5–6, 61, 276

"Radio Glasnost," 91, 98

Radio Moscow, 54

Ramet, Sabrina, 61

Rank-and-file party members, 45, 54–55, 117, 176–179, 181, 186–187, 191, 195, 216, 225–226. *See also* Socialist Unity Party

Rebel's Dilemma, 9–10, 12, 15. *See also* Collective action theory

Reformed Church, 128

Reformist mobilization, 13, 152, 215, 218. *See also* Mobilization

Reformist voice, 4, 13, 21–22, 29, 58, 60, 90, 170, 186, 190–192, 211–212, 215, 219, 228–234, 237–240, 244, 249, 253, 256–259. *See also* Voice

Refugees, 17, 63, 65, 108–109, 112, 266

Reich, Jens, 198, 208, 239

Reinhold, Otto, 222

Richter, Reinhard, 88, 128

Romania, 2, 169, 179

Rostock, 43, 86, 213–214

Round Tables, 236–237, 239–240–244, 248, 252, 283

Rucht, Dieter, 247

Samizdat press, 218–219, 273, 274

Saxon State Archives, 299, 302

Saxony: characteristics of, 40–44, 83; characteristics of dissident movement in, 113, 117, 135–137, 186–189, 202–203, 207–208, 245–247; Church and, 95, 99, 104, 127; declining loyalty of party officials in, 132, 136, 164, 168, 184, 228, 260; exit from, 43, 101, 116–117, 158, 163; negotiations for reforms in, 188–189, 228, 260; repression in, 163–164, 171, 186

Schabowski, Günter, 33, 52, 89, 110, 232–233

Schelling, Thomas, 82

Schult, Reinhard, 198

Schumann, Horst, 45

Schwabe, Uwe, 94

Schwerin, 43, 214

Scientific Atheism, 83

Sellout, 197–198, 234, 237, 239

Shevardnadze, Eduard, 169

Shürer, Wolfgang, 36

Sievers, Jürgen, 128

Šik, Ota, 24, 50, 58

"Silent exit," 80. *See also* Exit

Slovakia, 209

Social Democrats (SPD), 113, 207–208, 239, 244, 248–249

Socialism: Europe and fall of, 2–5; exit from, 63, 73–75, 250; failure of, 59–62, 260; opposition in GDR to, 39, 45, 49, 57, 116, 181, 203, 228, 242, 247, 253, 263; social bases of support for, 206–211, 217, 220–222, 257; Soviet Union and, 90, 115, 249; support in GDR for, 46, 50–51, 68–71, 114, 140, 224. *See also* Church role in socialism; Communism; Marxism-Leninism

Socialist Unity Party (SED): civic movement loyalty to, 198, 202–208, 215–216, 238, 258; declining loyalty of members of, 49, 52–54, 58–60, 119, 177, 183, 227, 232; dissident movement and, 97, 114, 116, 118, 127, 195, 232, 235; economic and social policy of, 37–38, 50, 70, 193–194; expulsions and ransoming from, 48, 66–67, 76, 79; Party Congress and, 36, 42, 51; reforms and, 121, 224, 230, 236–243; social bases of support for, 44–48, 52, 157, 216; social control and, 93, 112, 140, 168–170; structure of, 33; USSR and, 52. *See also* Central Committee; Council of Ministers; Ministry of the Interior; National Defense Council; Parliament; Party Control Commissions; Stasi

Steven Pfaff is an associate professor in the Department of Sociology at the University of Washington.

Library of Congress Cataloging-in-Publication Data
Pfaff, Steven
Exit-voice dynamics and the collapse of East Germany :
the crisis of Leninism and the revolution of 1989 / Steven Pfaff.
p. cm.
Includes bibliographical references and index.
ISBN 0-8223-3752-5 (cloth : alk. paper)
ISBN 0-8223-3765-7 (pbk. : alk. paper)
1. Communism—Germany (East)—History. 2. Opposition (Political science)—Germany—East—History. 3. Germany (East)—Politics and government—1989–1990.
I. Title.
HX280.5.A6P43 2006
943'.10879—dc22   2006001660